RACE, SCIENCE
AND SOCIETY

RACE, SCIENCE AND SOCIETY

L. C. Dunn, N. P. Dubinin, Claude Lévi-Strauss
Michel Leiris, Otto Klineberg, André Béteille
E. U. Essien-Udom, Go Gien Tjwan
John Rex and Max Gluckman

Edited and with an introduction by Leo Kuper

⊔⌋ Paris   The Unesco Press

New York   Columbia University Press

First published as *The Race Question in Modern Science*
© Unesco 1956

Revised as *Race, Science and Society* © Unesco 1975

Library of Congress Cataloging in Publication Data
United Nations Educational, Scientific and Cultural
  Organization
  Race, science, and society.
  1. Race—Addresses, essays, lectures. 2. Race problem—
Addresses, essays, lectures. 3. Race discrimination—
Addresses, essays, lectures. I. Kuper, Leo, ed. II. Title.
HT1521. U54 1974   301.45'1'042   74–11278
ISBN 0–231–03908–5
ISBN 0–231–03910–7 (pbk.)

Printed in Great Britain

Contents

6 CONTENTS

Part III CHANGING PERSPECTIVES

ANDRE BETEILLE is Reader in Sociology at the University of Delhi and author of *Caste, Class and Power* and *Castes: Old and New* (*Essays in Social Structure and Social Stratification*).

N. P. DUBININ is Director of the Institute of Genetics at the USSR Academy of Science. He is the author of numerous books on genetics, was awarded the Darwin Medal in 1959 and the Lenin Prize in 1966.

L. C. DUNN is Emeritus Professor of Zoology at Columbia University. He held the chair in zoology at Columbia from 1928 to 1962 and was a research associate at University College, London, from 1961 to 1962. Among his books are *Principles of Genetics* (with Sinott), *Heredity, Race and Society* (with Dobzhansky) and *A Short History of Genetics*.

E. U. ESSIEN-UDOM is head of the Department of Political Science at the University of Ibadan in Nigeria. He is well known for his work on tribalism in Africa and is author of *Black Nationalism: The Rise of the Black Muslims*.

GO GIEN TJWAN is Senior Lecturer at the Institute for Modern Asian History of the University of Amsterdam. From 1952 to 1965 he was Deputy Director of the Indonesian National News Agency. Among his books are *The Assimilation Problem of the Chinese in Indonesia* and *Nationalism, Revolution and Evolution in South-East Asia*.

MAX GLUCKMAN was, until his recent death, Research Professor of Social Anthropology in the University of Manchester. He was Director of the Rhodesia Livingstone Institute from 1941 to 1947 and University Lecturer at Oxford from 1947 to 1949. Among his many books are *Rituals of Rebellion in South-East Africa, Order and Rebellion in Tribal Africa and The Allocation of Responsibility*.

OTTO KLINEBERG is Professor of Psychology at the University of Paris. He was Professor of Social Psychology at Columbia from 1949 to 1961 and held the chair in social psychology there from 1961 to 1962. He was Head of the Division of Applied Sciences at UNESCO from 1953 to 1955.

LEO KUPER is Professor of Sociology at University of California,

Los Angeles. He was formerly Dean of the Faculty of Social Sciences at the University of Natal and is author of, inter alia, *Living in Towns, Passive Resistance in South Africa* and *Durban: A Study in Racial Ecology*.

MICHEL LEIRIS is Senior Research Fellow at the Centre national de la recherche scientifique in Paris. Poet, essayist and ethnologist, his many books include *Afrique Noire* and *La Création Plastique* (with Jacqueline Delange).

CLAUDE LEVI-STRAUSS is Director of the Ecole pratique des hautes études and holds the chair in anthropology at the College de France. Among his most famous books are *Anthropologie Structurale, Le Totemeisme aujourd'hui, La Pensée Sauvage* and *Tristes Topiques*.

JOHN REX is Professor of Sociology at the University of Warwick. From 1964 to 1970 he was Professor of Social Theory and Institutions at the University of Durham and from 1969 to 1971 Chairman of the British Sociological Association. His books include *Race Relations in Sociological Theory* and *Race, Colonialism and the City*.

Foreword

In 1956, Unesco published *The Race Question in Modern Science* representing the status of research on the 'race question' in 1956. Science and history are not, however, static, and between 1956 and 1975 there have been new scientific research and new perspectives. In 1964 and in 1967 Unesco sponsored two international conferences on Race. These meetings discussed the implications of findings in population genetics and in the social sciences as these affected the race 'problem'. They followed similar meetings, held in 1950 and 1951, before the first edition of this book was published. In the appendix to this volume we have printed the four statements on Race issued by Unesco: 1950, 1951, 1964, and 1967. A careful reading of these will indicate the changing emphases over the period of approximately twenty years.

This new volume, entitled *Race, Science and Society* was prepared as part of Unesco's contribution to the International Year to combat racism and racial discrimination. The chapters by Claude Lévi-Strauss and Michel Leiris appeared in the earlier volume in identical form, those by L. C. Dunn and Otto Klineberg, from the same source, have been updated by the authors. The chapters 'Race and Contemporary Genetics', by N. P. Dubinin, 'Tribalism and Racism', by E. U. Essien-Udom, and 'Racialism and the Urban Crisis', by John Rex appear here for the first time while those by André Béteille: 'Race, Caste and Ethnic Identity', Go Gien Tjwan: 'The Changing Trade Position of the Chinese in South-East Asia', and Max Gluckman: 'New Dimensions of Change, Conflict and Settlement' originally appeared as articles in the *International Social Science Journal*.

This volume is introduced by Leo Kuper. This introduction places the articles in a broader historical perspective.

As in the case of the 1956 volume, no attempt has been made to reconcile differing points of view. The chapters speak for themselves. The opinions expressed in this volume form part of the continuing debate on Race, Racism and Racial Discrimination. As such they are the opinions of the writers, and while Unesco has sponsored this discussion, the points of view expressed are not necessarily those of the Secretariat.

Introduction

by LEO KUPER*

Director, African Studies Centre, University of California, Los Angeles

The papers and statements included in this volume span a generation of publications by Unesco in the continuing campaign against racism and racial discrimination. They are directed specifically at the level of information and ideas, but they must be seen in the broader context of United Nations action to combat racism.

The papers may be grouped conveniently under three headings. The first I would describe as the Defence Against Racism. This comprises the opening five papers—the two on biological factors by Dunn and Dubinin, two on history and culture by Lévi-Strauss and Leiris, and the fifth by Klineberg on psychology and race.

The second section consists of four case studies, which examine a variety of social situations and seek to clarify the distinction between racial structures and ethnic, caste and tribal structures, and to form the basis for a comparative sociology of race relations. They include the contributions by Béteille on 'Race, Caste and Ethnic Identity', by Essien-Udom on 'Tribalism and Racism', by Rex on 'Racialism and the Urban Crisis', and by Tjwan on 'The Changing Trade Position of the Chinese in South-East Asia'.

The final paper by Gluckman on 'New Dimensions of Change, Conflict and Settlement', offers a very general perspective and may serve somewhat as a conclusion. It returns to the biological theme as this begins to emerge in the work of students of animal behaviour, but it is more generally concerned with the relations between inequality in technological development and social conflict.

* I would like to thank Michael Banton, Sammy Smooha, Pierre van den Berghe and Marion Glean O'Callaghan for their comments on an earlier draft of this paper.

I
DEFENCE AGAINST RACISM

The phrase I have used, 'defence against racism', implies that the issues are those raised by the advocates of racism, and that the argument takes the form appreciably of rebuttal. The arena of confrontation is essentially defined by racists.

Now one of the more interesting contemporary developments in the field of race relations concerns the right to define. Supporters of the Black Power movement in the USA argue that the person who defines the issues, thereby assumes the initiative, driving the opponent into a defensive position; power consists in originating definitions, and in making them socially effective.

At the time Unesco began its work against racial prejudice and discrimination, it was inevitably concerned with the justifications advanced in support of racial discrimination. It was obliged to respond to the extreme racist ideologies developed by the Nazis, and widely accepted in many circles throughout the world. This new stimulus to racist ideas already well established in the spread of colonialism, presented an immediate and urgent challenge.

Van den Berghe, quoted in the paper by Essien-Udom, defines racism, from a social perspective, as 'any set of beliefs that organic, genetically transmitted differences (whether real or imagined) between human groups are intrinsically associated with the presence or the absence of certain socially relevant abilities or characteristics, hence that such differences are a legitimate basis of invidious distinctions between groups socially defined as races'. Three conditions, that is to say, must be simultaneously present to constitute racism, namely the use of physical criteria, the belief that cultural, moral or intellectual differences correspond to the physical differences, and social actions (of a discriminatory nature) based on those beliefs (Essien-Udom, p. 236).[1] The papers in the first section deal with the physical criteria and the beliefs associated with them, but not with the structures of racial discrimination.

For the biologist, race is essentially an anatomical and physiological concept. The number of races is not objectively given, as appears clearly from Dubinin's paper: it is quite arbitrary, varying with the biological criteria selected as the basis for classification. Given the anatomical and physiological character of this concept of race, it is somewhat surprising to find Dubinin placing the Jews in a category of those claiming racial superiority, a category which includes their Nazi executioners. Yet the only evidence he offers for the assertion that Jews regarded themselves as belonging to a superior *race* is the statement that Jews believed they were the chosen *people* of God on the basis of what was recounted in the Bible (p. 70).

Dunn in 'Race and Biology' presents a flexible, dynamic conception of racial differentiation. He stresses the radical change in perspectives resulting from the rise of the science of genetics. The old views of fixed and absolute biological differences are shown to be without scientific foundation. The human species shares a pool of genes and may be defined as a community of genes. The vast majority of genes are the same for all human beings; only a relatively small proportion differentiates the races.[2] And even then, the differentiation is not rigid. Races, as groups, differ in the frequency with which certain inherited features appear among them, that is to say, there is continuity and overlapping in the distribution of traits. Moreover races are themselves changeable, which is to say that ' "race" is not fixed or static category but a *dynamic* one' (p. 41).

Dubinin in his analysis of 'Race and Contemporary Genetics' deals mainly with the genetics of blood groups. He presents a conception, similar to that of Dunn, of the human species as a single whole, racial difference relating to minor features, and being negligibly small in comparison with the common genetic endowment that is the biological basis of every human being. Far from there being fixed and absolute biological differences between the races, dynamic genetic interaction is taking place between all populations. In consequence, individual variability within racial groups may be very high, so that what applies to the group may not be applicable to all its representatives.

Dubinin emphasises the emergence of consciousness in the evolutionary process. He argues that this consciousness, which is characteristic only of man, distinguishing him from other forms of life, renders all people basically equal. 'It is for this reason that we can say, not emotionally or subjectively, but scientifically, that all are born equal' (p. 69). (The reference here is presumably to equality at the biological, evolutionary level.) It is the evolutionary emergence of consciousness which makes possible rational social communities. By virtue of the social inheritance of accumulated knowledge and skills, man has achieved an enhanced capacity for adapting to his environment. Social evolution has become more important than biological evolution. 'At the last stage of anthropogenesis, race peculiarities became mainly inadaptive traits' (p. 81).

Dunn makes this last point more cautiously. He distinguishes two evolutionary processes: the process of genetic adaptation, 'the assembly of varied combinations of genes formed under the influence of natural selection and other natural forces' (p. 66), and the process of cultural development and adaptation. The acquisition and transmission of culture is now the most important mode of adaptation. 'Race is not a stage in this process, and its biological function is now a secondary one' (p. 66).

Neither contributor is concerned to rebut some of the more primitive forms of racist ideology, which seek to arrange the races in a hierarchy on the basis of cast of feature or hair form or shape of head,[3] or on the basis of the assumed order of evolutionary emergence. Tobias, in an interesting talk addressed to a South African audience, comments that if the human line split off from the ape line well over one million, and possibly ten million years ago, and if the modern races of man developed only 25 or 50 thousand years ago, it is palpably meaningless to compare living races of man with living apes in order to arrange them in some sort of hierarchical order.[4] Klineberg, in the present volume, shows the absurdity of a rank order based on the time sequence in the evolutionary emergence of races, since the same conclusions may be derived from diametrically opposed events. Thus if a racial group evolved earlier, then it is more primitive, but if it evolved later, it is inferior because it has had less time in which to develop (p. 174).

The more pervasive racial prejudices are those expressed in ideologies of cultural and intellectual inferiority. These prejudices were directed especially against African societies, but they were also experienced quite generally by peoples subjected to Western colonial regimes. The remaining papers in Section I are concerned with the rebuttal of these prejudicial beliefs.

Two preliminary questions arise. What is the significance to be attached to ideas concerning the qualities of the different races? Are they the cause of racial prejudice? Leiris (p. 138) takes the opposite view, that the source of racial prejudice must be found elsewhere than in the pseudo-scientific ideas, which are less its cause than its expression. But even though he ascribes a secondary significance to these ideas, he considers it necessary to combat them, since they still continue to deceive many often well-meaning people.

The second question concerns the nature of the defence. The racist beliefs give a negative definition of the qualities of other races. However, the defence, as Lévi-Strauss points out (p. 95), cannot take the form of countenancing this conception of race by showing that the denigrated races have in fact made a distinctive contribution. 'Nothing could be further from our intentions, for such a course of action would simply result in an inversion of the racist doctrine. To attribute special psychological characteristics to the biological races, with a positive definition, is as great a departure from scientific truth as to do so with a negative definition.' He goes on to stress that the distinctive contributions in continents inhabited by peoples of different racial stocks are to be accounted for by geographical, historical and sociological circumstances, not by special aptitudes inherent in the anatomical or physiological make-up of the black, yellow or white man (p. 96).

The first ground of rebuttal is that race, as Tobias (1972: 19–20) comments, is a classification of anatomies used for anatomical purposes with no thought of leaping from anatomy to intelligence, language, religion or level of civilisation. This dissociation between race and culture and race and intelligence, is the basic defence.

The prejudicial beliefs however must be met at a more specific level. There are the problems raised by Lévi-Strauss concerning the diversity of cultures, and the widespread belief among whites that Western culture has demonstrated a superiority, which must be an expression of superior innate racial aptitudes. From the point of view of technical invention, and the associated scientific thought, Western civilisation has proved itself to be more 'cumulative' than other civilisations, by producing an industrial revolution so wide in scope, so comprehensive and so far-reaching in its consequences that the only previous comparison was the neolithic revolution itself (p. 123). But these revolutions do not result from the genius of a given race or culture, but from conditions so generally operative that they are beyond the conscious sphere of man's thought (pp. 123–4).

Leiris deals more generally with the relations between race and culture, inquiring into the relative contribution of each to the shaping of personality and the significance of racial difference for cultural diversity. He argues (pp. 137 and 145) that while there are very real psychological differences between individuals, which may be due, in part, to the individual's biological ancestry, they can in no instance be explained by what is commonly called the individual's race: the widest varieties of character are found in all ethnic groups. In less positive terms, he comments (p. 146) that 'the conclusion to be drawn alike from the anthropological and psychological researches of the last thirty to forty years is that the racial factor is very far from being the dominant element in the formation of personality'. This is consistent with his conclusion (p. 168) that the differences observable between the physiques of the different races afford no clue to the cast of mind and type of behaviour characterising the members of each of the human varieties.

As to race and culture, Leiris makes the distinction in terms of mode of transmission, that the former is transmitted by heredity, the latter by tradition. In the same way that there are no pure races, there are no pure cultures, they are all a product of the co-operation between different peoples. 'Not only do all the indications point to there being no culture all of whose elements are due to a single race, but it is also apparent that no given race necessarily practices a single culture' (p. 160). Moreover the culture of a society can change profoundly without transformation of the racial composition of its members.

In contrast to culture, which is so very general and abstract and difficult to evaluate, the concept of intelligence seemed to provide a means for the scientific exploration of the relationship between race and non-biological characteristics. Here was an instrument for the measurement of innate aptitudes, carefully devised, tested and standardised, yielding quantitative results capable of manipulation by the most refined statistical techniques. Yet it is clear that the intelligence tests are culturally loaded, and that it is impossible in cross-cultural comparison to estimate the extent to which they measure innate capacity. In the paper on 'Race and Psychology', Klineberg examines the factors which affect performance in intelligence tests, he reviews the results of tests administered to different racial groups, with brief comment on the contemporary controversy aroused by the research of Arthur Jensen, and concludes (pp. 195–6) 'that innate racial differences in intelligence have not been demonstrated; that the obtained differences in test results are best explained in terms of the social and educational environment; that as the environmental opportunities of different racial or ethnic groups become more alike, the observed differences in test results also tend to disappear.' Moreover, even those who argue that the difference in averages between groups is due to genetic factors, all admit the existence of overlapping, so that 'any lines of demarcation between groups of people . . . based on alleged genetic differences in average performance do violence to the facts of individual capacities and potentialities' (p. 206).

I have suggested that these opening papers are conceived as a defence against racism. There are, to be sure, passing comments and sections which present a different perspective. Leiris, for example, traces the origins of racism to the period of colonial expansion when it became necessary to justify violence and oppression by the doctrine of racial inferiority. Dubinin sees racial prejudice somewhat similarly as a function of colonialism and imperialism. But the overall perspective is defensive. The papers are however informed by a general spirit of humanism, and there emerges from them a positive affirmation of a common humanity— expressed in the intermingling of peoples, a common biological inheritance, the interpenetration of cultures, the fecundity and enrichment resulting from contact and collaboration between different peoples, and the role of diversity in stimulating the great revolutions in civilisation.

II
SOCIAL STRUCTURE AND RACISM

Section II may be thought of as concerned with the different types of system in which racist ideas are embodied. In any systematic presentation, one would like to have the extremes represented—on the one hand, of rigid barriers and great discontinuities, and on the other, of continuity, mobility and intermingling. The extreme of rigid discrimination in the contemporary world is exemplified by South Africa, which has elaborated a totalitarian system of racism with the most meticulous concern for all the detailed potentialities of racial discrimination. This is clearly the model Essien-Udom has before him in his discussion of racism. Unfortunately, no comparable case study is included of a more fluid situation of race relations, such as might be found in some of the Caribbean or Latin American societies.

The opening papers are rather conceptual in emphasis. Béteille deals with the concepts of race, caste and ethnic identity. He comments on the use of the term caste by schools of American social scientists to describe race relations in the Deep South of the USA, and the distinction drawn by Kingsley Davis between racial caste systems and non-racial caste systems, such as the Hindu. Indeed, in my view, one of the remarkable features of the literature on race relations is the tendency to view race through the lens of other concepts, more particularly those of caste and class, but to some extent also, of ethnic group.

In the case of class, there seems to be a good rationale for this usage, which draws on a general theory of society and of the role of economic forces in group conflict. Thus the whole theoretical framework of Marxism is brought to bear on the analysis of race relations. In the case of the caste concept, there is no general theory of society derived from the analysis of caste structures and caste formation which might provide a context for the study of race relations. Instead, certain formal aspects, of rigid boundaries between groups and of endogamy, are abstracted to give rise to the concept of the racial or colour caste.

The stimulus to define race relations in the American South as caste, may have been the desire to indict, as dramatically as possible, the injustices of racial discrimination. For the American writers who used the term, the caste system must have seemed the very antithesis of democratic values. It is difficult, however, to see what has been gained by this process for the understanding of systems of racial oppression, though to be sure, the caste concept directs attention to a range of problems, such as the significance of ideas about pollution, the extent of consent, the role of religious values and of functional differentiation. The stimulus for the analysis of race relations in class terms derives appreciably from a commitment to Marxist theoretical perspectives. These perspectives are indispensable, but I think that it has been misleading to view racial conflict as an expression of the class struggle. Since the class theoretical perspectives are not discussed in this volume, the reader may wish to refer to the admirable analysis, from a Marxist perspective, of *Class, Caste and Race* by Oliver Cromwell Cox.

The term ethnic group has also been used to include race. This may derive in part, as in Béteille's discussion, from a desire to find a broad comparative concept, which would encompass physical differences, as well as cultural differences based on language, religion or region. For some theorists, the ethnic concept has seemed a good terminological substitute for race, avoiding the confusions of a much abused concept. Perhaps some such motive also contributes to the choice of class and caste concepts for the analysis of race relations. Or to phrase this point differently, one might argue that, since race is essentially an anatomical concept, with no intrinsic relevance for social structure, the forces which make for social differentiation and discrimination between the races must be sought elsewhere than in racial difference.

Béteille's paper examines the relevance of racial difference for social structure from a variety of viewpoints. He inquires first into the extent to which systems of stratification based on caste as in India, and on colour as in the southern United States, can be regarded as analogous, and he draws out the similarities and differences. He surveys the confusing and conflicting evidence on the relationship between race and caste in Indian society and concludes that certain broad differences in appearance do exist between castes at opposite ends of the hierarchy in many parts of the country. He emphasises that there exist in the society beliefs and stereotypes linking racial difference to caste, and that these beliefs are in themselves socially significant. The general perspective he presents, however, is of a complex mosaic of social distinctions, in which racial difference is not a basic aspect of social structure, and in which the very great variety of physical types has prevented a polarisation of the population along racial lines.

Essien-Udom's paper on 'Racism and Tribalism' introduces a related set of conceptual and theoretical problems. Adopting van den Berghe's definition of racism, he characterises, in broad outline, societies in which racism has become a guiding principle of social organisation and group relations, a situation totally in contrast with the Indian caste society of Béteille's analysis. The perspective he presents is that of Third World sociology. He attacks racism directly as an ideology of European origin, which spread during the process of colonisation in Asia, Africa, America and the Caribbean, and which seeks to justify racial domination. It is, of course, this common experience of racism, and the continuing inequality in power and wealth between the white and darker peoples of the world, which provide the basis for movements of Third World solidarity.

The concept of tribalism, and its relation to racism, is highly controversial. Tribalism is a term much used, and much abused, in the discussion of African societies. Many outside observers see in tribalism the source of destructive internal divisions, threatening the integrity of the newly independent African states, and they equate it to some extent with racism in its potential for genocidal conflict.

For Africans concerned with the unification of diverse peoples in the new nation states and the establishment of harmonious conditions for economic development, this is a most disturbing conception. It may seem to be inspired by the same colonial perspectives which are regarded as the source of many of the internal divisions. Be this as it may, some African governments have found it necessary to legislate against organisations based on tribal affiliation. As to the comparison with racism, this is likely to seem somewhat ludicrous to those who have been subjected to racist regimes.

To develop his conception of tribalism and its relationship to racism, Essien-Udom is first obliged to free the word 'tribe' from the ambiguities of the most varied usage, and to purge it of pejorative connotations. He defines it essentially as an ethnic group. Tribalism, in its application to African societies, refers to 'the sentiments of allegiance generally felt by Africans, especially in Black Africa, towards an ethnic group to which they belong and, in contemporary terms, generally to a "way of life" or to a culture and heritage common to them' (p. 245). This feeling of allegiance, and the very general crises of identity in African societies as a result of social change and the incorporation of various tribal entities in single nation states, create a situation easily exploited by individuals or groups of individuals. In West Africa, he writes, these sentiments are exploited principally, though not exclusively, by the elite groups in the society, in their struggle for political power and economic gains (pp. 248–9).

Essien-Udom has no difficulty in establishing that tribalism is a very different phenomenon from racism or 'casteism' or communalism. He is sceptical of a comparative approach in which 'grand theories' of stratification or class domination or pluralism are applied to such varied phenomena. 'A comparison between tribalism, on the one hand, and casteism and racism, on the other hand, is likely to be most superficial' (p. 251). I cannot defend Essien-Udom's rejection of, or scepticism about, comparative analysis in this context. He agrees that tribalism is a form of 'particularism', and that it bears a close resemblance to other forms of particularism. Is not this the basis for comparative analysis? What are the processes by which these units are mobilised for struggle? How do they polarise? What is the significance of religious differences, or of inequality in the control of resources, or in access to positions of power? What is the role played by elites or other strata? Surely, there is a wealth of problems for comparative analysis at the level of process, even though the phenomena differ in their forms and origins.

The paper by Rex on 'Racialism and the Urban Crisis' bridges the colonial and metropolitan worlds in a detailed case study of coloured workers in Britain. It is a particular instance of the 'confrontation between workers from colonial economic contexts and the free and organised working class of the metropolitan countries'. The colonial experience as it affects both the coloniser and the colonised is carried over into the urban metropolitan situation. Intrinsic to the social structure of the metropole are underprivileged situations and roles: it is appreciably into these underprivileged sectors that the coloured immigrant workers are received—into replacement employment, and into replacement housing, and housing in the 'twilight zone'.

Tjwan's paper on 'The Changing Trade Position of the Chinese in South-East Asia' deals with the 12 or 13 million 'ethnic Chinese' living among the peoples in the area of the Southern Seas, with its total population of roughly 230 million. Only a general impression can be derived from this brief discussion ranging over a variety of societies and long periods of time. Moreover it is not very clear that the relationship between the Chinese and the members of their different host societies is correctly described in terms of race relations or racial tension. Tjwan refers to the diversity of physical types among the Chinese, but does not deal with the question of their physical distinctiveness from the members of their host societies, nor with the much more important question of the extent to which they are perceived, and socially distinguished, as being of different racial stock. In the circumstances it seems best to view the 'ethnic Chinese' as 'sharing a common way of life distinct from the indigenous cultures of the host nations' and exercising 'an important economic role' (p. 301), though even this description must be qualified by Tjwan's references to processes of assimilation into the host societies.

Tjwan's study suggests comparisons with racially distinctive minorities, appreciably engaged in trade, such as Indians in East Africa and South Africa. His conclusion that the large scale anti-Chinese disturbances since 1900 resulted from fierce competition between capitalist groups with a similar orientation can be examined in the light of evidence from these societies in Africa. It is of some interest that the Chinese should be viewed as traders, when so many of them followed other occupations, as for example, 'the numerous Chinese coolies working in the tin mines and on the plantations, building roads and loading ships' (p. 310) in the Federation of Malaya. This is a process by which the trading functions of the collectivity are ascribed to its members. Indians in East and South Africa are subject to this same process of prejudicial stereotyping.

Though the case studies in this section are by no means comprehensive, they do range over a wide variety of situations and problems.

III
CHANGING PERSPECTIVES

Among changes in perspective on racism over the period of a generation covered by these papers, I would select first, the movement from defence to attack, second, a greater theoretical emphasis on the structures of power within which racist ideas are expressed, in place of the former preoccupation with prejudice and discrimination, and finally, increasing concern with the international context and implications of race relations.

Though at the end of the Second World War, defensive attitudes were perhaps to be expected, given the ascendancy of racist ideas in the period between the two world wars, the situation has now changed profoundly, as a result of decolonisation, participation of former colonised peoples in the United Nations and its international agencies, and more effective channels and powers for the attack on racism. The attendant change in perspective is very clearly expressed in the 1967 'Statement on Race and Racial Prejudice', prepared by a meeting of experts under Unesco auspices. Opening with the declaration that 'all men are born free and equal both in dignity and rights', and with a review of the findings on race, the experts then mount an attack on what they describe as 'the scourge of racism'. They feel that earlier approaches are inadequate. 'In order to undermine racism it is not sufficient that biologists should expose its fallacies. It is also necessary that psychologists and sociologists should demonstrate its causes.' In seeking these causes, they emphasise that the social structure is always an important factor. 'However, within the same social structure, there may be great individual variation in racialistic behaviour, associated with the personality of the individuals and their personal circumstances.' They conclude with comments on the social causes of race prejudice and suggestions for combating racism.

The mood of the statement is one of 'passionate involvement in the issues', as Banton describes it in a critically constructive paper included in the Unesco publication 'Four Statements on the Race Question' (1969). For some scholars this does present a problem, undermining the authority of the statement. Personally I think there *is* a need for this passionate involvement, for angry denunciation, for attack rather than defence on issues as they are defined in racist thought. The basic conflict of values can only be engaged in at the level of values, and of personal and social commitment. This does not however dispense with the continuing, and indeed growing, need for the most careful scholarship in the field of race relations. The experience of racial domination has entered deeply into western scholarship, shaping many of its perspectives. As these are re-examined, new fields of inquiry open up in what may prove to be a penetrating critique of aspects of Western thought. But quite apart from this critical re-examination of accepted scholarship, there is a continuing challenge posed by the reappearance of old issues in new forms.

Gluckman, in discussing this challenge, gives the example of ethology. He describes it as a fruitful line of research, which has contributed to the understanding of the behaviour of animals and birds in their relationship with their own fellows, and with other species, in an ecological environment. But he argues that it is dangerous to use these findings as modes of interpreting human behaviour. They are liable to lead to the conclusion that such present social arrangements as subordination and segregation are part of our biological endowment, and to distract attention from the social, cultural and historical factors involved. He is however very careful to avoid the suggestion that there is any racist intention in drawing analogies between animal and human social life. His argument is rather that 'periodically, in new forms we are confronted with scientific theories that give a new dimension to existing forms of discrimination and/or hostility between groups of varying ethnic stock, or between the sexes, and that justify anew existing forms of segregation' (pp. 324–5).

Whatever our views on the social purpose of certain inquiries, such as the continued investigation into the relations between race and intelligence, I think it important to protect the academic freedom of those engaged in these forms of research. It seems to me however that there is a corresponding obligation on their part to rebut any misuse of their research findings for the propagation of racial prejudice and discrimination.[5]

The defence against racism in the form of a rebuttal of its justifications was certainly encouraged by the dominant theoretical emphasis on prejudice and discrimination. Since prejudice was in the minds of men, so the argument might run, and since prejudice was a major source of discrimination, the struggle against racial discrimination could be waged appreciably at the level of a battle of minds. But this conception assigned too great a significance both to prejudice and its justifications. It underestimated the extent to which discrimination might be built into the institutions of a society, and function as a stimulus to prejudice. It did not take sufficiently into account the relationship between racial prejudice and the interests it serves in wealth, power and privilege, nor the versatility in its justifications, which may in fact be quite peripheral. Moreover, since it was concerned essentially with the ideas of those who practised discrimination, it was preoccupied with the sentiments of dominant strata, and not with the consciousness of the subordinates.

The change in perspective to greater emphasis on the structure of power within which racism is expressed, and on the interests served by racist ideas, has stimulated the comparative analysis of race relations. The attempt to define what is specific to racial domination and conflict has in turn extended comparative analysis to other structures of domination, such as between ethnic units of the same race, or between religious groups as in Northern Ireland. What is the significance of the political structure relative to the economic structure? Are there common elements, characteristic of systems of group domination, whether based on race, ethnicity or religion, as suggested in the theory of plural societies? Are there common processes of conflict and polarisation, or of integration?

If race prejudice among members of a dominant race is closely related to the structure of power, then it is reasonable to anticipate profound changes in attitude with changes in the distribution of power. Gluckman (p. 323) writes that 'all of us who have lived in African territories when they were dominated by White colonial powers, and after they gained independence, know how quickly the attitudes of, and the relationships between, both Whites and Africans altered.' But very little research has been carried out on changes in attitude following independence, and their study in a variety of contexts would add greatly to our understanding of the functions of prejudice.

Among the many social forces contributing to these changes in perspective, the movements of Black Power or Black Consciousness have been influential. They seek to determine the field of confrontation, to impose their own definitions and to render them effective in action. They are not concerned with the consciousness of ruling strata, at any rate in theory, but with their own consciousness, the consciousness of subordinate racial groups. And it is on this consciousness that they rely in the attack on racial domination. The movements thus have the radicalism of militant challenge and confrontation and this has been heightened in some circles, by an infusion of Marxist-Leninist thought. Race relations policies directed to the prejudices of ruling strata, are, by contrast, relatively conservative.

The major force shaping the new perspectives on race relations has been the change in international relations, and in conceptions of international obligation. Issues of race relations internal to a society have become international issues. The relationship between the rich and the poor nations takes on an aspect of discriminatory race relations. Gluckman argues 'that technological development for the so-called underprivileged nations and the underprivileged sections within nations is essential if those people are to be able to step into such brotherhood as modern mankind shares. That is the only way of achieving any hope that we can end many of the bases of racial or other group differentiation which produce, ever anew, theories of group superiority, in intelligence or civic virtue' (p. 330). I do not know what potentialities for technological development are present in different parts of the world, nor the contribution technological development might make to the cure of what Gluckman describes as 'old-style conflicts', but the argument is in line with Third World perspectives on race relations—the need for greater equality between nations.

References

1. In following Essien-Udom's statement of the conditions which constitute racism, I have inserted the phrase 'of a discriminatory nature'

to define the general nature of the social actions which contribute to racism.

2. Tobias (1972: 23) writes that: 'It has been estimated that 90–95 per cent of genes are common to all men: . . . Only 5–10 per cent of all our genes are concerned with the little superficial frill of variation which makes for the differences among races.'

3. See the example of this type of ideology, quoted by Essien-Udom on pp. 236–7 and the comments by Leiris on pp. 144–5.

4. *Op. cit.*, p. 25.

5. See paragraph 19 of the 1967 'Statement on Race and Racial Prejudice'.

Bibliography

Cox, O. C., *Caste, Class and Race* (New York: Doubleday, 1948).

Tobias, Philip V., 'The Meaning of Race' in P. Baxter and B. Sansom, (eds), *Race and Social Difference* (Harmondsworth: Penguin Books, 1972), pp. 19–43.

Part I

DEFENCE AGAINST RACISM

Race and Biology[*]

by L. C. DUNN

Member of the National Academy of Sciences, Washington D.C.

INTRODUCTION

Our era has often been called 'The Century of Science'. As we look back from our vantage point of 1960, we can see that few or none of the important questions of science have remained in the condition in which they were in 1900. In every field of science there have been fundamental changes in point of view, and this is a mark of progress, since science is in a sense a continuous adaptation to new knowledge.

In some cases the change in point of view is so great as to be 'revolutionary'. Future generations will probably so regard the changes in biology and its applications brought about by the establishment of the laws of heredity. It was the first half of the twentieth century that witnessed the rise of the science of genetics, responsible for a radical change in the way in which race and race differences in man are to be regarded.

The judgement of biology in this case is clear and unequivocal. The modern view of race, founded upon the known facts and theories of heredity, leaves the old views of fixed and absolute biological differences among the races of man, and the hierarchy of superior and inferior races founded upon this old view, without scientific justification. Biologists now agree that all men everywhere belong to a single species, *Homo sapiens*. As is the case with other species, all men share their essential hereditary characters in common, having received them from common ancestors. Other hereditary characters vary from person to person, and where marriages occur chiefly within local populations, isolated from other populations by geographic and similar barriers, some of these characters tend to become more concentrated in some groups than

[*] Revised version of the work first published in *The Race Question in Modern Science* (Paris: Unesco, 1951).

in other more distant ones. If these separations are long-continued in terms of hundreds or thousands of generations, such populations tend to differ from each other in the relative commonness or rarity of hereditary characteristics. Races arising in this way are thus seen to differ rather in degree than in kind. This change in biological outlook has tended to restore that view of the unity of man which we find in ancient religions and mythologies, and which was lost in the period of geographical, cultural and political isolation from which we are now emerging.

The way in which this radical change in view about race came about is intimately connected with the discovery of the mechanism of biological heredity. Biological heredity is what is transmitted over the living bridge of egg and sperm, which is the sole biological connection between the generations. It is necessary to specify it as *biological*, since all humans are strongly influenced by *cultural* inheritance as well. This is what is transmitted outside the body, such as language, custom, education and so on.

Although the internal hidden stream of biological heredity passes continuously from parent to offspring only by means of the single reproductive cell, its effects or manifestations in the individual depend upon the conditions under which he lives. It is obvious that we cannot inherit characteristics as such, for physical traits such as height or skin colour and mental ones such as mathematical ability cannot be present as such in the minute single cell from which each human being takes his origin. What is transmitted by biological heredity is a set of specific potentialities to respond in particular ways to the environment. A person who has 'inherited' musical talent only exhibits this under certain conditions. The same is true for physical characteristics, but in less obvious ways, since the response may occur very early in development, as in the case of eye colour, hair form, and similar traits. Biological heredity thus consists in the passage from parents to child of a set of abilities to respond to a range of possible environments by developing a particular set of characteristics. A human being, like any other living thing, is always a product of both his heredity and his environment.

What is the physical means by which this transmission of heredity occurs? Before 1900 it was thought of as the passage of something from the parents which, like a fluid substance, could mingle and blend in the offspring. The contribution of each parent, popularly referred to as 'blood', was assumed to lose its own individuality in the blend which occurred in the child, and this blending process repeated itself in the children's children and in later descendants. Each person was supposed to have inherited half of his nature from each parent, hence one quarter from each grandparent and so on in decreasing fractions from remoter ancestors. If the parents differed in race or type the children were 'half-bloods', the grandchildren 'quarter-bloods', etc.

Although this blending or blood theory had some support from observation (for example, the descendants of parents differing in skin colour or in height are often of intermediate colour or size), it was based on an assumption which has been shown to be erroneous. This assumption was that the herditary material was infinitely divisible and miscible like a solution. As early as 1865, Mendel, the founder of genetics, had shown that heredity consists in the transmission of discrete elementary particles, now known as genes. Genes are stable living units, perhaps the smallest units in which living matter can perpetuate itself; their peculiarity is precisely that they do not blend or lose their individuality in whatever combinations they take part.

In 1865, Mendel, whose experimental research gave rise to the modern science of genetics, had shown that the old theory was wrong. His results, confirmed by all subsequent studies of inheritance in all forms of life including man, proved clearly that what is transmitted by heredity from parent to offspring is a system of particulate living elements, now known as genes. Each cell in each living body contains in its nucleus hundreds or thousands of these tiny particles.

These living elements form the basis of all life and living activity. Each gene produces a copy of itself at each act of cell division or replication upon which the growth and functioning of the body depends. Each cell in each living body contains in its nucleus duplicate copies of each of the thousands of different genes which the individual received from its parents. When the reproductive cells—eggs or sperm—are formed in a human individual, each one contains one copy of each of the kinds of genes which were present in the person who produced the egg or sperm. Genes are extremely small bodies, beyond the reach of the light microscope. Nevertheless research of the last two decades has clearly shown that they consist of a substance, DNA (desoxyribose nucleic acid) of which the chemical structure and manner of replication is now known. What permitted Mendel to discover them is the fact that each gene may occur in two (or more) alternative forms, known as alleles, and that these alternative forms may have different effects on the processes of growth and development of the individual. Thus if certain marriages between normally pigmented persons regularly produce two kinds of children —one normally pigmented, the other without dark pigment and with pink eyes (albinos) it can be shown that each parent transmitted two different forms (alleles) of a gene. We may call one form *A*, the other *a* and describe each parent, with reference to this one gene, as *Aa*. Mendel showed that such a parent always produces eggs or sperms of two, and only two kinds, again with reference only to this one gene. If half of the eggs transmit *A*, and half *a*, and half of the sperm transmit *A*, and half *a*, then if any sperm may fertilise any egg at random, the possible combinations would be:

Egg		Sperm		Child
A	×	*A*	=	*AA*
A	×	*a*	=	*Aa*
a	×	*A*	=	*aA*
a	×	*a*	=	*aa*

The possible outcomes occur in the proportions:

	Egg	Sperm	Child
	1/4 *AA*	1/2 *Aa*	1/4 *aa*
or	25% *AA*	50% *Aa*	25% *aa*
or	0·25 *AA*	0·5 *Aa*	0·25 *aa*

These are merely different ways of expresssing the same proportion.

Now in fact repeated observation has shown that these are the proportions found among the offspring of such marriages. However, persons with two and with one *A* allele look alike, *AA* and *Aa* having normal pigment, while *aa* is albino. We say that the first two differ in genotype (gene constitution) but the third, the albino, differs from them in both genotype and in appearance. The latter distinction we refer to as the *phenotype* of the person, with respect to the difference in pigmentation. Where one of the two alleles determines the phenotype when received from only one parent, as is the case with persons of genotype *Aa*, Mendel referred to it as *dominant*, while when two like-alleles, one from each parent, are required to produce the phenotype (as in albinism) it is called *recessive*. This is not a constant rule since with many other genes, the effects of both affect the phenotype, *Bb* for example may be different in appearance from both *BB* and *bb*.

What is a universal rule, as proved in thousands of cases in animals, plants and man, is that heredity is transmitted by genes which do not blend or affect each other in any of the combinations through which they pass in the course of transmission from generation to generation. It is this which gives Mendel's rule of disjunction of alternative alleles, or *segregation* (as it is usually called) its great importance.

This 'gene theory' is recognised by biologists as providing the most reasonable basis for explaining the facts of hereditary resemblances and differences. Although all of its implications for other scientific problems such as those of evolution and of individual development, and its practical uses in agriculture, medicine, and industry have not been completely worked out, it is already apparent that the gene theory is one of those basic ideas, like the atomic theory, which must underlie our attempts to understand the material phenomena of life.

It is not strange, therefore, that views about race differences in man should have been so much affected by the gene theory. Under the old blending or blood theory we should expect the descendants of parents showing hereditary differences to become more and more alike. We should thus expect pure races to arise and to become uniform, even though they had originated from a cross of two unlike races. Blending should obviously lead to the disappearance of variability, of differences between related individuals.

If, on the other hand, the biological characters are perpetuated through the transmission of genes which do not blend, then we should expect hereditary variability, once it has arisen, to persist indefinitely, The chief law which Mendel discovered tells us that the variety of genes which the parents received are shuffled and dealt out anew to each child, each gene remaining intact and unchanged, but entering into new combinations in the children. If, as in man, the number of kinds of genes is very high, then the number of different combinations, occurring at random, will be so great that no two people are likely to receive the same assortment.

For example, for each form of gene such as *A* or *a*, *B* or *b*, there are three possible genotypes, *AA*, *Aa*, *aa* and *BB*, *Bb*, *bb*, and these two sets of genotypes can therefore occur in $3 \times 3 = 3^2$ or 9 different combinations. If ten such kinds of gene differences occur within a population, then $3^{10} = 59049$ different genotypes are possible. But the number of different kinds of gene differences is known to be much greater than 10. Each population, whether family, tribe, or racial group, should thus consist of individuals differing from each other, to a greater or lesser degree, in some of their hereditary characters. Consequently 'pure races' should not exist, in the sense of groups of identical individuals or even of individuals corresponding to some ideal racial type; and races might be expected to differ from each other in relative rather than in absolute ways, since the same elements (genes) might circulate through them because of occasional intermarriage either in the present or the past.

As we look upon the present human inhabitants of the earth, there is little doubt that what we see resembles closely what we should expect if the gene theory is true. All men are clearly alike in all the fundamental physical characters. Members of all groups may intermarry and actually do; this condition has apparently obtained for a long time, since different groups of primitive man were also races of one species. Yet every man is unique and differs in minor ways from every other man. This is in part due to the different environments in which people live and in part to the different combinations of genes which they have inherited.

Although genes are not changed by the company they keep and have been proved not to undergo blending or contamination, they do sometimes change spontaneously by a process known as *mutation*. An old gene which has been passed from parent to offspring for many generations may suddenly reproduce in a new form. An old gene which led to development of dark skin colour may give rise to a new gene which is unable to produce pigment, and colourless skin or albinism results. Instances of this have been known among the white, black and yellow kinds of men, so it seems to occur independently of race, skin colour, or environment. It is certainly not an adaptive change, that is, one that makes the person better fitted to his environment, since albinos, for example, are at a disadvantage, particularly in the tropics. The fact that mutations do not appear as adaptive responses to the environment indicates that the origin of new characters is not so be sought, as it was in the days before the rise of genetics, in the inheritance of acquired characters.

The origin of new genes by mutation is apparently the source of the hereditary variability by which individuals and groups of men are distinguished. How the common store of genes with which our species began was changed and distributed among the different groups of mankind will have to be examined in later chapters. Here it should be emphasised that the revolution in thinking about race which has resulted from twentieth-century studies in biology sprang from two main sources: (1) the proof of the gene theory of heredity and the disproof of the blending or blood theory; (2) the discovery that new genes arise by a random process of mutation, and not as adaptive responses to the environment.

WHAT IS RACE?

The chief purpose of this article is to make clear a modern biological view of race, which will necessarily be based on the evidence now available. This is certainly not complete and is sure to increase through the efforts of anthropologists, geneticists, and others who are actively studying the complex problems of human biology.

But although we do not know all about race, we are in the position in which scientific study often finds itself, of having good evidence that certain views once generally held are definitely wrong. In the zig-zag process of learning, advance is often measured by the retreat from error. We know now why certain views about race uniformity and purity and the fixity of racial differences were wrong; and why social and political views of race inequality were wrong. Since the former were often used as a justification for the latter, we should as reasonable beings like to believe that, if we get rid of our biological misconceptions, we should thereby cure the social and political ills of injustice and exploitation which appeared to be based upon wrong biology. Eventually we may expect this to happen, but we should not forget that the way in which human beings as individuals and as groups have acted with regard to race differences has more often stemmed from feelings and from prejudice than from knowledge. Knowledge eventually overcomes prejudice, but the delay may be long unless active steps are taken to implement the improvements in knowledge.

This is clearly illustrated by the fact that although there has been for some time a considerable measure of agreement amongst biologists about the concept of race in plants, animals and man, the word *race* as used in common speech has no clear or exact

meaning at all, and through frequent misuse has acquired un-
pleasant and distressing connotations. Many people become confused when the direct question is put to them as it is in some official
documents: 'To what race do you belong?' One has to stop and
ask oneself: 'Now why do they want to know that?' The existence
of that question is evidence of past misuse. Sometimes a question
about race is intended to reveal one's national origin, and the
answer to that question might be French or Lebanese or Brazilian
or Japanese. But everyone knows that political entities are made
up of people of many different origins. One has only to think of the
USA, in which persons from every part of the world are 'Americans', to see that race and national origin are quite different ideas.

Everyone in Germany in the Nazi period knew what a question
about race was intended to reveal, for the nation was divided into
two categories, Ayran and non-Aryan. Non-Aryans were persons
with one or more grandparents who had been listed as Jewish.
Aryans were the others, some of whose ancestors might have come
from northern or eastern Asia or other non-Aryan regions. The
intention of such a question was to facilitate a political classification and disfranchisement. What it actually did was to set up two
'races' and to define one by an ancient and outmoded linguistic
term ('Aryan') and the other by the religion of some of one's
forbears.

In some countries the immigration laws and the forms for
sorting out applicants for schools or the professions still retain
such questions.

Answers to them usually serve the purposes of racial discrimination rather than of providing reliable information, since it has
proved extremely difficult to frame questions about individuals in
such a way as to reveal their 'race' Before such questions could
have scientific value we should have to have a list of all of the
'races' of the world about which general agreement had been
reached. Such a list does not exist, because anthropologists have
not reached a general agreement on the exact racial classification
of mankind.

Owing to its bad connotations and the absence of such an objective list, doubts have been expressed whether there is any valid and
useful meaning of the word at all which would justify its retention
in our vocabulary. It has been proposed for example to substitute
for race the term 'ethnic group', meaning a people of one race or
nation. Perhaps with sufficient use and general acceptance this

may one day displace the old and misused word. But race has been found to be a useful category for describing the geographically separated varieties of a species of plants or animals. Although it is difficult to delimit the meaning of race, race-formation has been an important process in the evolution of man and as such it must be defined and understood. Thus it seems better to me to define it and explain how it should be used and thus to free it from false meanings than to evade the essential problem by excluding the word.

Nearly all peoples have the idea of blood-relationship and knowledge of biological kinship, and consequently nearly all languages require a word to express it. 'Race' is one of these words. We know that all men living today are descended from common ancestors and are thus blood relatives. The expression 'the human race' embodies this established fact. Sometimes we call ourselves 'the human family', and this is also sound usage. In many languages 'race' and 'family' are used more or less interchangeably.

The meaning of biological relationship is descent from common ancestors. In terms of genetics it means that related persons are those who have had access, through inheritance, to a common store of genes. The most useful biological definition of a population is that of a pool of genes from which each individual, through the egg and sperm from which he took origin, has received a sample from this common pool.

The genes were common to relatives because the related persons were members of a population within which marriages had occurred. Consequently all descendants had a chance of inheriting their genes from a common source. A population, in a biological sense, is thus a collection of individuals who share, through probability of marriage within the population, a common pool of genes. A biological species contains such a pool of genes. In the sense that all men are thus related, however distantly through intermarriage among their ancestors, the whole human race is one community of genes. It is biologically true that of the many thousands of hereditary units, genes, which any person inherits, the vast majority are the same as those in any other human being. These are the genes to which we owe our humanness. Many of them were derived from our animal ancestors; some of them, and particularly the combination in which they appear, are unique among animals and set us off as a species from all others; the species *Homo sapiens* keeps its peculiar inheritance because it does not exchange genes through crossing with any other species.

But within this great community of man there are smaller communities between which there is little or no intermarriage and this partial biological separation or isolation is accompanied by differences between the groups as regards the frequency with which certain biological characters appear in them. Thus, most of the inhabitants of Africa have dark skins, and since this persists in persons of African descent when they live elsewhere for many generations, as in America, it is biologically inherited. Negroes resemble each other in this trait and differ in it from persons of most other geographical areas. The Europeans, the mongoloid peoples of Asia, the aboriginal inhabitants of Australia are, as groups, recognisably different from each other. The characters by which they differ, as groups, are of the same sort as those by which individuals differ from each other.

Look for example at the kind of eyelid which we think of as Mongolian. It has a fold of fat which obscures the outer portion of each eye and makes the eye appear narrower and more slanted than the eyes of Europeans or Negroes. Mongolians have no monopoly of this kind of eyelid. It appears in other peoples as well and is occasionally found as an individual variation in Europeans, especially in children. Or take the tightly curled hair which we think of as negroid. Hair almost exactly like this has been found in families in Norway and in Holland which are unrelated to each other and to Negroes, at least in historic times. In these two instances, a new gene which arose by mutation is probably responsible. We know that both the eye-fold and the woolly hair form depend upon a particular inheritance in which brothers and sisters of the same family may differ.

This illustrates an important fact. Racial differences, even those of the major 'races' above mentioned, are compounded of many individual inherited differences. This means that races are distinguished from each other, as *groups*, by the relative commonness within them of certain inherited characters. Thus the mongoloid eye-fold is very common in mongoloid peoples, but uncommon in Europeans. Woolly hair is very common in negroid peoples but uncommon in Europeans or Mongolians. It is more accurate to describe the difference in this way than to say of any one trait that it is present in all of one group and completely absent in the other. Most people would have said this of woolly hair—present in all Negroes, absent in all Europeans. But when the first woolly-haired Norwegian child was born, the statement became untrue, and this could happen for any one of the 'racial' traits. We are going to find out later how these *new* traits arise. In respect to any one 'racial' character, such as hair form, the relative commonness could change quite quickly. If it were of any advantage to Norwegians to have woolly hair, either biologically or aesthetically, the trait could spread from the small family which shows it now.

This illustrates another point about racial differences. Separate racial traits may change their frequency, that is to say, the 'race' is changeable, even in respect of heredity characters. Of course this is a slow process when many characters are involved, and races are usually distinguished from each other by many differences. But it is evident that if racial differences are particular collections or aggregates of the traits by which individuals may differ, and if these traits are subject to change by mutation, then 'race' is not a fixed or static category but a *dynamic* one. Biologically, a race is a result of the process by which a population becomes adapted to its environment. The particular array of traits which come to be the most frequent, and hence to characterise the group, are probably those which now or at some past time proved to be successful in a particular environment.

This then is the sense in which the word race may have a valid biological meaning. A race, in short, is a group of related inter-marrying individuals, a population, which differs from other populations in the relative commonness of certain hereditary traits.

It is true that a definition like this leaves a good deal of latitude in deciding how big or how small a race may be, that is, how many people shall be included in it, and also in deciding how many races we shall recognise. These last are matters of convenience rather than of primary importance. What is important is to recognise that races, biologically, differ in relative rather than in absolute ways. The race gets its character from the commonness within it of hereditary characters which are not uniformly present in every member. Its stability depends on the durability of the genes responsible for the hereditary characters, and upon the habit of marrying within the race rather than outside it. When either of these changes, then the race changes. From this it must also be evident that there is in the human species no such thing as a pure race in the sense of one in which all members are alike; it is improbable that there ever has been or ever will be such a race of men.

HEREDITY AND ENVIRONMENT

The character of every human individual and of every human group is the joint product of its heredity and its environment. These influences have also been referred to as *nature*, that which is inherent, inborn, and *nurture*, the sum total of the external factors upon which the maintenance of life depends. There has been a strong tendency among most peoples to attribute the differences amongst themselves, and between their group and others, either to one or the other of these two influences. The influence of soil, climate, nearness to the sea and similar geographic variables are clearly apparent. But it is also evident that all people living under the same conditions are not alike, and that these differences are connected with the particular parents, family, tribe, or race from which they spring. Different people attribute different degrees of importance to environment and to heredity in shaping human individuals and groups such as races. They ask: 'Is heredity or environment the determining factor', tending to divide into two groups, environmentalists and hereditarians.

To the biologist this is a false and meaningless dichotomy. None of the reactions which a human being displays could occur without a particular environment, which can vary only within certain restricted limits; and no one is born except from particular parents. Heredity is what the new life starts with, environment is what makes its continuance possible. Both are essential. What we need to know is how they act together in shaping the traits of individuals or races.

Let us take a careful look at heredity. We called it the living link or bridge between the generations. Actually what goes over that bridge are thousands of tiny particles, packed away in the single cell which each of us received from each of our parents. These particles are called *genes*; they are the physical *beginnings* with which our parents endow each of us at conception. What we inherit are *genes*.

From these beginnings the new individual develops by taking in food, first from the mother's body, later directly from the outside world. The most remarkable part of this process by which a new individual develops is that, whatever he takes in, he converts into his own peculiar kind of substance. Lifeless food is not only made into a human being, it is made into a particular kind of person.

The same food that is converted into a blond, blue-eyed, tall man who cannot distinguish between red and green colours of the rainbow and gets hay fever every August, is in his sister converted into a dark, brown-eyed, short person with good colour vision and no hay fever. This latter kind of difference seems to depend upon certain inside directors which determine how the body shall utilise its food and energy. In the brother and sister some of these directors are different. We have referred before to these internal directors as *genes* and later we shall see how they come to be different in brothers and sisters.

In spite of the fact that under certain conditions the brother and sister differ in complexion, one being light and one dark, under other conditions this may not be so. Let the sister spend a long illness in hospital, away from the sunlight, and let the brother work every day in the bright sun. The skin colour of one will get pale and the other will darken. Apparently the difference we saw first depends both upon genes and upon the sun; in fact we could say that the blond differs from the brunette in requiring more sunlight to reach a similar stage of darkness. They differ in responsiveness, and the internal directors or genes therefore do not settle the differences in an absolute way, but chiefly by deciding how the body will react to something in the environment. In the case of eye-colour the difference between brown and blue is settled chiefly by the genes before birth, and we know of no environmental difference that will change the eye colour, although we might find one by searching for it. On the other hand, the response which the brother expresses by sneezing and having a 'running nose', the symptoms of hay fever, can be avoided by keeping away from particular plants or kinds of food or by medication. Under these conditions we should not know he was different from his sister, who does not show this sensitiveness to the same plant or food. His heredity decides his reaction to a particular part of his environment, and in many cases this reaction can be changed by changing the environment. Many of us are susceptible to certain infectious diseases while others are not. Yet we all become alike when a drug is found which will kill the infection or the parasite.

Examples like this, together with the great body of biological research since 1900, show what heredity is. It is the pattern of genes, derived from the ancestry, which determines the possible kinds of response to the environment. Hereditary similarity is the rule throughout mankind, because that particular pattern of genes has been handed down to us which was found by the harsh test of natural selection to give the most successful response to the environments to which our ancestors were exposed. Hereditary differences, except those newly arisen by mutation and hence not tested by natural selection, are usually concerned with less crucial or critical responses. In every race there are not only some people who are colour-blind, like the brother in the example above, but others who are unable to taste certain substances, that is, are taste-blind; others who are smell-blind, and still others sound-blind, or as we say, tone deaf. These differences between people have been shown to be due to differences in single genes, which decide how much light or taste or sound it will take to register a certain sensation in the brain. The study of such relationships, which is still in its infancy, has led to the following analogy. Heredity determines the nature of the internal trigger which the stimulus from the environment may release to produce a given effect. Some triggers are so constituted as to resist most of the range of pressures which are possible in an ordinary environment; for example, they fail to respond to the stimulus of red or green light and hence result in colour-blindness.

In elucidating the ways in which heredity and environment interact and estimating their relative roles in determining particular traits, nothing is more instructive than comparing a character in the two kinds of human twins. Whenever two babies are born at once, one of two things has happened. Either two eggs which happened to be present, instead of the usual one, were fertilised by two sperms and two different individuals thus got born at once; or else one egg, after fertilisation by one sperm, separated into two parts and each part became one of the pair of twins. The first case is like the birth of ordinary brothers and sisters except for their being born at the same time. The second is like the duplication of a single individual. The difference is important, because ordinary brothers and sisters, coming from different eggs and sperm, may get different genes; while two individuals arising from a single egg and a single sperm, must perforce have the same genes. Any differences in the latter therefore cannot be due to heredity, and we have a measure of the degree to which heredity can control a particular trait; and conversely of the degree to which environment can modify a hereditary trait.

We have all been struck by the extreme similarity between the second kind of twins; they are always of the same sex, have the same kind of blood and the same bodily and facial and even mental features, and they react similarly to diseases and to education. These are the 'one-egg' or identical twins; and since they have the same heredity, any differences we see in them must be due to environment. They do show some differences in mental and emotional responses, and some physical traits such as weight may differ a little, but otherwise they remain extremely similar even when separated at birth and reared in different homes.

Members of the other kind of twin pairs, those arising from two eggs (often known as fraternal twins), are no more alike than ordinary brothers and sisters. They exhibit the usual gene differences to be found in any family, and as often as not are of opposite sex.

The greatest biological interest attaches to comparisons of the conditions of single traits in the members of the two kinds of twin pairs. Occasionally, one member of a twin pair is an albino. In all cases in which such a pair has been proved to have been derived from a single egg, then the other member is also an albino. In cases of fraternal twins the other member may or may not be an albino in about the same proportion as pairs of children from such parents born in separate births. In the classical blood groups (A, B, AB, and O, see Table 1 for details) and in all other blood factors so far studied, the members of all one-egg twin pairs are exactly the same, that is, they show 100 per cent concordance, whereas two-egg twin pairs may show discordance in the blood group. In the case of the AB group only about 25 per cent of the two-egg twin pairs are concordant. This alone would indicate that the blood group of a person is probably determined entirely by the genes which he has inherited, and that differences in environment encountered after birth are powerless to change it. The differences in this respect between two-egg twins and between brothers and sisters are known to be due to the transmission of different genes in different eggs and sperm of the same parents, whereas no such differences could occur within the single egg which gave rise to identical twins. Other traits can be arranged on a quantitative scale according to the relative degrees of concordance which they exhibit in one-egg as compared with two-egg twins, and this scale serves to arrange the traits in the order of their sensitiveness to environmental influence. Physical traits in general show high concordance in one-egg twins; in reaction to mental measurements one-egg twins also show greater resemblance than two-egg twins, though the effects of education are clearly in evidence. In reactions to emotional tests there is less difference in the amount of concordance and apparently a greater effect of environmental influences.

One of the chief lessons learned from studying twins, as well as by other methods, is that each individual inherits many potentialities. Some of these, like our blood-types, are realised in all the environments which a human being encounters. These we call hereditary. Others, such as the resistance which we exhibit to certain diseases, and particular mental and emotional reactions, are realised only in certain environments. Variations in these we call environmental. But variation in all of these characters depends on the same biological principle: what human beings are is determined by the way in which the hereditary nature responds to its environment.

THE ORIGIN OF BIOLOGICAL DIFFERENCES

Since all men do not respond in like ways to a similar environment, there must be differences in heredity between persons and groups similar to those between two-egg twins and brothers and sisters. This indicates that there must be some biological mechanism which preserves the general resemblance between parents and offspring, while permitting at the same time particular differences between related persons. Heredity in common parlance is the name usually applied to the transmission of resemblances, but since a lack of resemblance, a variation, may be transmitted—once it has appeared—with equal fidelity, the mechanism of heredity is best described simply as the transmission of genes.

As indicated under 'What is Race?', if the material particles, the genes, remained always the same, all human beings who are descended through hundreds of thousands of generations from the same ancestors would have remained alike in all hereditary characters. In general of course they have remained alike in the hereditary characters by which we recognise them as human beings, and this means that every one of thousands of genes nearly always makes an exact duplicate of itself each time a new cell, a new egg or sperm, is formed. Thus in general the offspring get descendants of the same genes that the parents had, and hence resemble them.

But once in a while when a gene makes a replica of itself, the copy is not quite exact, and the new gene produces a different effect. The new form then acts as an allele of the old and this is the usual source of the variety of alleles, such as the change from *A* to *a* in the case of albinism. That is what happened when the first person with woolly hair appeared in Norway. Suddenly woolly hair appeared in one child of two straight-haired parents, both from families which had never contained a woolly-haired individual. This child transmitted woolly hair to some of his children, and now a number of Norwegians, all related by descent to the original woolly-haired individual, have this quite un-Norwegian type of hair. This kind of sudden change in a gene is called a *mutation*. Perhaps the first man from whom the Negroes inherited woolly hair got it in this way, by mutation, although the story is probably more complex than that; or perhaps human hair was first woolly and a gene mutated from woolly to straight and thus Indians and Europeans got their straight hair. How it happened in history is not known; nor is it known exactly how mutations occur today, in spite of the extensive biological research on this question during the last thirty years. What is important for an understanding of race differences is the fact that *mutations do happen*. It has been shown that genes can change suddenly from one state to another, in somewhat the same way as a light can be switched from bright to dim and back again.

The effects of such changes may be observed as hereditary variations in the structure or functioning of the several systems of the human body—white spots on head or body, various diseases, skin colour, eye-defects, dwarfism and many other variations have arisen in this way. In fact this is probably the chief or only source of new hereditary variations in man, as it is in animals and plants generally.

In general mutations arise suddenly, appear not to be adaptive responses to environmental conditions, and are generally less useful or desirable than the condition from which they arose. It is known from experiments with animals and plants how to make mutations happen more often. Treatment with X-rays, radium, and certain chemicals will make it more likely that an old gene may change into a new one, usually in a less useful form than the old. The effect seems to be directly on the gene rather than by way of a change in the body of the parent. In this way the origin of new genes by mutation, even when brought about artificially, is quite different from the method by which some of our grandparents thought that new characters arose. It used to be supposed that changes in the body or mind, such as greater muscular development, came about in response to the needs of the body, and could be passed on as such to the children. It is in one way unfortunate that this does not occur, for all of us have to begin to learn where our parents began and not where they left off. On the other hand, we are glad to escape the mutilations and deleterious changes caused by accident or disease in our ancestors. There is no evidence that new hereditary characters arise by direct effects of the environment on the body or in response to need. Such acquired characters are not the source of the inherited differences we see in members of the same family or tribe.

Nor is it possible that inherited effects of past environments can account for the differences between the great racial divisions of man. Many people of course still think that the African is black because of inherited effects of hot sun, but it is much more likely that genes for skin colour, like others, change once in a while by mutation and that persons with genes for darker skin colour have been more successful in Africa than persons with fairer skin.

We should remember that the present opinion of most biologists on this question does not rest on absolute disproof of the inheritance of acquired characters. Such disproof would obviously be impossible, because many of the alleged instances of this kind happened so long ago that they cannot be studied now, and it is in any case impossible to prove a universal negative. I think biologists believe rather that positive proof has been provided of the origin by random mutation of most of the hereditary differences which have been studied in plants, animals and man. This view rests chiefly on the proof of the gene theory of heredity, for once heredity was shown to occur by means of genes which change by mutation; then the older views about the origin of variations became unnecessary.

The discovery of the gene mechanism, which began with the work of Mendel, and the confirmation of the idea and its extension to all plants, animals and man are matters that underlie the development of the modern biological views about race which are described under 'Heredity and Environment'. Those who are interested in the details of the gene theory will find it described in the books listed in the bibliography.

Another parallel stream of development in biology which had a strong influence on thinking about race was initiated by the great work of Darwin, published in 1859. He showed that the varieties of living organisms had reached their present condition by a process of descent with modification, guided by the principle of natural selection. In his theory, hereditary variations, of unknown origins, provided the raw material from which the environment selected the better fitted or adapted characters and combinations for survival. Once it was shown that variations arose by random mutation, the way to differentiation of races and species as particular collections of genes, fitted to particular environments, was open. Discussion of the details of this theory would take us too far afield, but some applications of it will be found below.

HOW RACES FORM

If all men living today are descended from common ancestors, and there is good evidence that this is the case, how has mankind become divided up into different races? History alone cannot answer this question, since the great groups of man had already become different before written history began. We must find out about it as we find out about other scientific questions, by studying the processes responsible for it.

We can ask ourselves: why should not all men have remained biologically alike? We studied that question in the last section and found that the elements of heredity, the genes, sometimes change by a process called mutation, and this gives rise to a great variety of genes. These, by coming into new combinations during reproduction (the baby has father's nose, mother's hair, and Uncle John's bad eyesight) produce an almost endless array of kinds of people, so that literally no two persons are the same.

Now the process of heredity is such that we should expect this great variety to continue within any population in which genes have assumed different allelic forms by mutation. This is implicit in Mendel's original theory that genes enter into all possible combinations with each other and are not changed by this process. If we find persons of three genotypes such as AA, Aa and aa in certain proportions in a population at one time we should expect, other things being equal, to find them in the same proportions many generations later. The main reason for this is the constancy of gene reproduction. Whenever, in the process of growth and in the production of the sex cells (egg or sperm), one cell gives rise to a new

one, each gene produces a replica of itself for the new cell; that is
A produces a new *A*, *a* another *a*, *B* a new *B* and so on through the
thousands of genes in each cell. They pass on unchanged from
generation to generation except in the rare event that one changes
by mutation to a new form in which case it reproduces in the new
form and augments the variety. The proportions of *A* to *a*, *B* to *b*,
etc., are not expected to change in the population if matings
among all different genotypes occur at random, that is if *AA*
persons are equally likely to marry *AA*, *Aa* or *aa* persons and
similarly for all other genotypes. Then *AA* persons will always
transmit *A* in all sex cells, *Aa* will transmit *A* in one half and *a*
in the other half of the sex cells, and *aa* will transmit *a* in all sex
cells. With persons choosing their marriage partners generally for
reasons unconnected with genotype (which will usually be unknown to the prospective mate) all the genes in the population can
be thought of as constituting one pool out of which two are drawn
at each new birth. If 90 per cent of the alleles of one gene in the
population are *A* and 10 per cent are *a*, then the following combinations will be found:

Eggs		Sperm		Children
0·9 *A*	×	0·9 *A*	=	0·81 *AA*
0·9 *A*	×	0·1 *a*	=	0·09 *Aa*
0·1 *a*	×	0·9 *A*	=	0·09 *Aa*
0·1 *a*	×	0·1 *a*	=	0·01 *aa*

In the population of children the proportion of *A* to *a* is also
9 to 1; it has not changed, and other things being equal, will not
change. This extension of Mendel's rule is known as the Hardy-
Weinberg rule from the English mathematician and the German
physician who independently called attention to it in 1908. It tells
us that in large populations in which mating takes place at random
with respect to genotype, the relative frequencies of the different
alleles of each kind of gene will tend to remain the same, provided
also that mutation does not alter the frequency of one allele more
than the other, that all of the genotypes have equal chances of
marrying and leaving offspring, and that the gene proportions in
the population are not altered by emigration or immigration.

If these conditions hold, a population will not change but will
retain the genetic variety with which it began. In order to find out
how populations become different and diverge from each other to
produce the mosaic of different populations in the world today, we

must ask whether the conditions responsible for constancy actually do hold. The most important clue comes from the observation that the populations in different parts of the world seem to be fitted for or adapted to the conditions under which they live. Certain hereditary characters such as black skins appear to have been more successful in Africa, others more successful elsewhere. Studies of animal and plant populations have shown that the proportion of a population having those combinations of characters which are advantageous in certain places, as for example in a desert, tend to increase there generation after generation until they constitute the bulk of the population. They gradually supplant the other combinations, although the latter may survive better in the forest or in the mountains. The chief means by which such changes occur is by differential reproduction, certain genotypes leaving more offspring than others. This is the process which Darwin called natural selection. It tends to produce local races and eventually species which are fitted or adapted for life in that locality. This means that all genotypes do not have equal chances of leaving offspring in all environments.

A specific example of the effect of natural selection on human populations is the recent discovery that normal persons who transmit a gene for sickle cell anaemia (which is usually fatal in children who receive such a gene from both parents) have more children than persons without such a gene. This advantage of the carriers of this gene occurs only in areas where malicious (falciparum) malaria has been prevalent. In such areas as in the low coastal regions of British Honduras or in low areas in West Africa, natural selection tends to increase in this way the frequency of the gene. This is sufficient to counterbalance the adverse selection against those who get the gene from both parents for these usually die before they can transmit the gene. Consequently this gene is commoner in certain African peoples and their descendants elsewhere than in peoples whose ancestors have not been exposed to malaria. This produces great regional differences in the frequency of this gene. It is largely a peculiarity of Africans, whose ancestors it may have enabled to survive in malarial regions. Other traits common in Africans such as dark skins and certain of the blood group genes (cf. 'A Biologist's View of Race' below) may also have been favoured by natural selection in certain environments.

Natural selection, favouring some genes in certain places and others in other environments has probably been the most potent factor in causing changes in gene frequency and thus in producing racial differences.

A second factor is sometimes involved in shaping the particular collection of genes which becomes a biological race. It may happen that the frequency of a gene may increase or decrease in a locality, not because it confers some advantage or the reverse, but simply because of accidental or chance fluctuations, which are much more serious in a small population than in a large one. The extinction or spread of family names which occur in small communities may be due simply to a run of luck in a family in the proportion of sons and daughters. In societies in which the name is transmitted through males only, a family with many sons would have its name spread in a small community, while one with no sons would have its name disappear, so that in neighbouring villages a name would be common in one and absent in the other. In large cities such fluctuation would not be noticeable, but small populations may diverge from each other by such accidents. Differences among races in the proportions of persons with different blood group genes may have come about in this way. Such accidents must have been of great importance in earlier stages of human history when the human reproductive communities must have been very small. This risk which new variants or combinations run in small populations has been called random drift.

Finally, after these factors have acted, it is obvious that migration and mixing of different groups may lead to changes in old races or the formation of new ones. This can be seen going on today. New races are forming in the Hawaiian Islands, for example, by the mingling of Chinese and European immigrants with the native people; and in the United States and in South Africa by intermarriage among the descendants of marriages between Negroes and Europeans.

Since biologically races are populations differing in the relative frequencies of some of their genes, the four factors noted above as those which upset the equilibrium and change the frequencies of genes are the chief biological processes responsible for race formation. They are: (1) mutation or change in the elements of heredity, the genes; (2) selection, being differential rates of reproduction, fertility or survival of the possessors of different genes; (3) drift, or the accidents of gene sampling in small populations; (4) differential migration and mixing of populations.

None of these processes would result in hereditary differences among groups of people unless something interfered with the complete freedom of intermarriage among all persons which has been referred to as random mating, for otherwise all would be members of the same biological or reproductive group. Thus we must add a fifth factor of a different kind. This is isolation, geographical or social. Once the other factors are present, isolation is the great race-maker. If the whole population of the world constituted one marriage circle, in which any individual had an equal chance of marrying any other, then the great variety of people which is kept up by mutation and combination of genes would be distributed more or less evenly over the world. Obviously neither condition actually obtains.

The variety of the world's population is distributed in clusters. For example, most of the dark peoples are in one cluster in Africa, although another group occurs in Melanesia, most people with yellow skins are in north-east Asia, most light-skinned people in Europe or countries settled by Europeans, and so on.

Between these separated groups there is relatively little inter-marriage. Choice of marriage partners is limited to those who live near, speak the same language, profess the same religion, and belong to the same class or caste.

These divisions of the world's populations did not always exist as at present. Once there was no human being in the American continents, nor in the islands of the South Seas, nor in Australia. There may even have been a time when the human race was actually one marriage community, because even today all races have many of their genes in common, as though they had all obtained them from a common source.

If it were not for the geographical and cultural barriers which separate people today, we could think of all of the genes in the human race as constituting one great pool.

But the world's population is obviously divided up into many different gene pools *within* which combinations occur more or less at random, but *between* which genes are less frequently exchanged because of the rarity of marriage between different groups. These different gene pools or marriage circles are likely to differ in the genes they contain, that is, different mutations may occur in different separated populations; selection may change the propor-tions of genes in different populations; the changes may occur by accident or by different rates of migration or intermixture. But however the original difference between two populations may have arisen, the difference will persist only if something makes inter-marriage between them infrequent, and this is why isolation is so potent an influence in forming different groups of people. Isolation is often partial; it is anything which tends to cut down exchange of genes between groups. We all know the ways in which our choice of marriage partners is limited. They are not only geographical, but religious, social, economic, linguistic, that is to say, the isolating factors are largely cultural. Thus a common biological community tends to be broken up by non-biological factors into sub-communities, which may then tend to become biologically different.

Races form because of the operation of biological processes. These are determined by the nature of heredity, which provides for a variety of stable hereditary elements, genes, transmitted according to regular laws or principles; and by the nature of the environment, which is broken up into a variety of partially isolated habitats. Particular genes or groups of genes are more successful in (i.e., adapted to) certain environments, others in other environments. These views have been tested experimentally with a variety of plant and animal populations. They have only begun to be tested by observations on human populations, but the basic conceptions derived from experimental biology appear to be generally applicable to all bi-sexual animals including man.

A BIOLOGIST'S VIEW OF RACE

The groups that become partially separated and different go by many names; races, hordes, tribes. All of them have this in common, that they differ from other groups by maintaining a different proportion of the same kinds of hereditary elements—genes.

This is nowhere more clearly shown than in the distribution of the genes which determine certain properties of the blood. There are four kinds of people, called A, B, AB, and O. These four kinds of persons differ in the substances they contain in their red blood cells.

It is well known that the red colour of human blood is due to red particles, which float in the transparent straw-coloured fluid which forms the liquid part of the blood. As soon as blood is taken from the body and allowed to stand, it tends to congeal in a red mass which is called a clot. If the clot is allowed to stand for an hour or so, it contracts and a pale transparent yellowish fluid oozes out. This is called blood serum.

Blood has always played an important part in beliefs, not only about relationship but about the qualities of different persons. It turns out that some of these qualities of blood are quite specific. For example, it is possible to transfer blood from a strong healthy person to one who is ill or has lost a great deal of blood, but only if the transfer (transfusion) is made in specified ways. The rules governing blood transfusion were discovered sixty years ago, when it was shown that the presence or absence of certain substances in the red blood cells are responsible for the success or failure of blood transfusion. These substances in the red cells are called A and B substances, or A and B antigens.

In the serum are other substances which react with the antigens in the blood cells. These are called antibodies. For example, if serum is taken from a person in the A group, it will cause clumping of the cells of a B group person when these are placed in it. Consequently we say that the B persons have anti-A substances or antibodies in their blood. Therefore if cells from an A person are transferred into the circulation of a B person, the cells of the A person will form clots which clog up some of the small blood vessels and this is likely to cause the death of the person who was to have benefited by blood transfusion. When all these combinations of cells and serum are carefully studied it is found that persons can give and receive blood according to the diagram below:

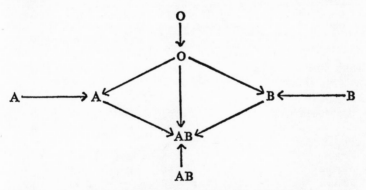

The blood group of each person is determined by his genes. The alleles of this blood group gene are called A, B, and O. Every person can be easily placed in one of the four groups, O, A, B, or AB (Table 1), and we find that the genes responsible for these

Table 1

Person of blood group	Has this substance in his red blood cells	Has these antibodies in his blood serum	Has these alleles
A	A	anti-B	AA or AO
B	B	anti-A	BB or BO
AB	A and B	none	AB
O	none	anti-A and anti-B	OO

groups are present throughout the world, although the proportions of these different genes differ somewhat from place to place and from race to race.

These different groups of people have the same kinds of antigens in the blood, and the variety in the antigens is due to variation in the gene, which probably arose by mutation.

Related people who probably got their genes from the same source have similar proportions of the A and B alleles. This produces the great cluster of blood group O in the American Indians, in whom B is rare or absent, while A is generally also uncommon. There is a group of Indians in Peru in which all persons tested were found to be of group O. Their nearest neighbours are a tribe with

Table 2. The proportions of persons belonging to each of the four blood groups in different populations (%)

	O	A	B	AB
North American Indian (Chippewa)	87·6	12·4	0	0
South American Indian (Matto Grosso)	100·0	0	0	0
Australian:				
Aborigines West	48·1	51·9	0	0
East	58·6	37·8	3·6	0
Europeans:				
English	47·9	42·4	8·3	1·4
Swedes	37·9	46·1	9·5	6·5
Greeks	42·0	39·6	14·2	3·7
Russians	31·9	34·4	24·9	8·8
Asiatic:				
Japanese	30·1	38·4	21·9	9·7
Chinese	34·2	30·8	27·7	7·3

90 per cent group O. Probably A and B were lost from the first tribe, either by accident when its ancestors migrated to a new home, or by some selective factor operating in the new environment.

Notice too the rise in the proportion of blood group B as we go east across Europe from England to Russia (Moscow).

There are some interesting situations in groups known to have split up by migration within historic time. The Icelanders are descended from Vikings from Scandinavia and 'Westmen' from Ireland who settled on the island in the ninth century A.D. Although the majority are supposed to have come from Scandinavia, and Iceland was politically united to Denmark until 1944, the blood types of the Icelanders are much closer to those of the Irish than of the Danes.

Table 3. Percentage of population in each blood group

	O	A	B	AB
Icelanders	55·7	32·1	9·6	2·6
Irish	55·2	31·1	12·1	1·7
Danes	40·7	45·3	10·5	3·5

The Basques, living near the Spanish-French frontier, are unlike both their Spanish and French neighbours, who resemble each other more closely than either resembles the Basques.

Table 4

	O	A	B	AB
Basques	57·2	41·7	1·1	0
French	39·8	42·3	11·8	6·1
Spanish	41·5	46·5	9·2	2·2

As a final example, two groups of people living near each other in Hungary are very unlike each other in blood group distribution. One group is composed of gypsies with a large proportion of blood group B like some peoples of western India, whence the gypsies migrated long ago. The other is composed of 'natives', long settled in Hungary with less than half the proportion of group B. Similar evidence exists for other groups who live near each other. The reason, of course, is found in the rarity of intermarriage between the different groups. This shows that a common environment does not by itself cause convergence, and that there are barriers other than geographical ones which cause peoples to remain distinct. Of course this would happen only if the genes retained their integrity and were passed on uninfluenced by the combinations in which they had taken part.

All these facts could be illustrated just as well by other human genes which can be classified objectively and accurately. The so-called M and N blood types, the varieties of the recently discovered Rh blood gene, genes for taste-blindness, colour-blindness, and others all appear in their several varieties in nearly all human populations but in *different characteristic proportions*. It is important to emphasise that it is varieties or alleles of the *same* genes that are found in all races.

What has caused the separated populations of the world to diverge in this way in the proportions of different forms of the same genes is not known, but we may suspect that natural selection, favouring different alleles in different environments has been an important factor. It is now known, for example, that in European populations persons who get ulcers of the intestine are much more likely to be of blood group O, than A or B or AB; those with a cancer of the stomach are more likely to be of blood group A than of O, or B. There may be other diseases to which persons of blood group B are more susceptible in certain environments. Research on connections between blood group genes and disease and other agencies which may act selectively is proceeding in many countries and may be expected to elucidate the part that natural selection plays in changing the frequencies of such genes.

Grouping by blood type has certain obvious advantages over measuring or photographing in attempting to study the nature and origin of group differences. Blood typing immediately reveals the genetic constitution of the person tested, so that the distribution of these genes in a population is known from the blood group distribution. Description of a population by the genes found in it prevents the loss of the individual in the group because in general there is no 'average' blood type. There are only characteristic proportions in which the same elements are mixed.

These differences in proportions are racial differences, that is, they indicate partial separation of the population in which the different proportions are maintained. The differences may be just as great between populations living in the same city as between populations living half a world away from each other. In Table 5 are shown the blood group varieties in two caste communities in Bombay, as determined by two Indian investigators.

Table 5

	O	A	B	AB
Indians (Bombay C.K.P.)[1]	34·5	28·5	28·5	8·5
Indians (Bombay K.B.)[2]	51·0	24	20	5·0

[1] Members of the caste community Chandraseniya Kayasth Prabhu
[2] Members of the caste community Koknasth Brahman

The blood types of these groups are quite different, and differences like this were also found in six other gene-determined characters. They are in fact at least as different in these traits as American whites and American Negroes, who are separated by the low frequency of intermarriage. These Indian communities are separated by customs which cause marriages to be contracted only between members of certain specified sections within the caste.

These conditions permit the maintenance of gene differences between the groups. No one hesitates to call such differences 'racial' as between Europeans and Negroes, everyone being aware that the ancestors of the Negroes now living in other parts of the world came from Africa a few hundred years ago where they had been practically isolated from the populations of other continents. But there would be a good deal of hesitation in referring to the two Indian caste communities as belonging to different races; the members of these two caste communities have lived together in peace and mutual respect for 2,000 years or more. This is good evidence that biological racial differences are not themselves the cause of race friction or prejudice. Probably the members of these castes do not recognise the biological differences which the scientists found, and after getting on well together for so long their behaviour will probably not be influenced by this new knowledge.

The important thing is not to have an easy and certain answer for every question about racial classification, but rather to understand, from such instances, the nature of racial differences. Once these are seen to consist of collections of individual hereditary elements which do not blend even within the same population, then we can see in a different light the external differences from which we had earlier formed ideas about the fixity of 'racial types'. When we look around us from this second point of view, we find a good many facts which fit together into a consistent picture.

In the first place, no very radical changes in classification of the great branches of mankind are suggested when they are compared by the gene method.

Geographical isolation aided by natural selection has undoubtedly been the great race-maker, and this is clearly reflected in the differences in the frequencies of several genes as between European, African, Asiatic, American Indian and Australian racial stocks. Even these great branches are not discontinuously different, having most of their genes in common. European and Asiatic 'intergrade' in eastern Russia and Siberia, Australian and Asiatic in the southern Pacific, and the other Pacific peoples show resemblances with, and no sharp differences from, Asiatics and Americans. Even the Australians and Europeans, separated so widely (except for the recent migration of Europeans) show clear evidence of common origin.

A racial classification of mankind based on the gene frequency method was that of Boyd (1950) who recognised five major races as follows: (1) European or Caucasoid, (2) African or Negroid, (3) Asiatic or Mongoloid, (4) American Indian, (5) Australoid. These can be characterised as groups by the relative frequencies of some eight genes, most of them concerned with blood antigens. It is obvious that they represent groups isolated geographically. The American Indians separated from their Asiatic ancestors only some 10,000 to 15,000 years ago, so they retain many mongoloid traits but still can be distinguished as a group. In addition to these, transitional groups are recognised, such as the peoples in the Pacific Islands, and in North Africa, and a hypothetical race not now in existence except as a small relic population, the Basques of Spain and France.

On the other hand, another study also published in 1950 by three American anthropologists, Coon, Garn and Birdsell, recognised 30 races, based largely on the classical criteria of physical type. Some of the 30 such as Neo-Hawaiian, American coloured and South African coloured are interesting as examples of races in the making. The authors thereby recognise that race is not something fixed and unchangeable, but a stage in the process by which human populations adapt themselves to special conditions. All of the 30 races above can be grouped into the same five categories recognised by Boyd and by anthropologists generally, since they are clearly based on geographical isolation.

It cannot be said at present that one classification is more correct than the other. The classification is in part a convenience and thus may be somewhat arbitrary, and should be determined by the purpose for which it is to be used. But it must be also a 'natural' classification and express the evolutionary processes which have brought about the racial diversification of mankind.

The classification into a few large races is perhaps the one best justified. Races which have lived in one place for long ages seem to be fitted to live in just such a region. Biologists say they are 'adapted' to the physical conditions, just as those plants which are best able to get along with infrequent rainfall or in extreme cold have survived in desert or mountain conditions.

There is not sufficient scientific information to support conclusive statements about the adaptive value of most of the physical traits in which races differ. Skin pigment has been most discussed. The depth of black or brown skin colour depends, in part, on several genes. These may control the production of the dark pigment, melanin, and its absorption or reflection of the ultraviolet rays of sunlight, which influence the production of vitamin D in the body. As is known, too little vitamin D exposes children to the risk of rickets, too much to overhardening of bones and other tissues. Tropical populations may have required protection against too much absorption of ultraviolet; those in northern latitudes against lack of sun and vitamin D in winter. This might be reversed in the summer in the north when tanning would increase absorption and vitamin D production. Consequently lighter-skinned descendants of equatorial populations may have been able more easily to adapt to northern conditions as in Europe. Racial differences in body form—such as more linear or slender in equatorial regions, more compact in cold regions, have also been suggested as having an adaptive significance, that is, having resulted from differential reproduction of different genotypes in the population (natural selection).

However, clearer evidence of the influence of natural selection in producing differences in gene frequencies follows the pattern outlined for sickle-cell anemia and other abnormal haemoglobins. Hereditary resistance to specific local infectious disease must be a very important adaptive quality but the relations of this to physical characters which differentiate races have not been worked out.

In man, ability to succeed in a great variety of environments is connected with the most important way in which he differs from lower animals, that is, his ability to learn and to profit by experience and especially to live in organised societies and to develop culture. The religious, moral and ethical traditions which all societies develop in some form, language which permits oral and written communication between generations and between different societies, the evolution of political and economic institutions and of literature, art, science, technology and industry—all of these reflect the peculiar mental adaptability and plasticity of man. All civilisations increase the selective advantage of genes for mental capacity and educability and these are found in all races.

No race is uniform with respect to mental traits any more than with respect to physical traits, or blood group or other genes. It is in fact this variety which permitted each race to adapt itself to a variety of environments. In the past, as today, persons must have been found to accomplish successfully all the varied tasks which are required in every human society. We may suspect that when the genes influencing the normal operations of the brain and nervous system are subjected to as extensive study as has been devoted to properties of the blood, a great variety of genotypes will be revealed. If there are, as reliably estimated, millions of different combinations of genes as expressed in the blood, not less should be expected in respect to genes influencing behaviour and mental capacity and special abilities. It would be surprising if these were to be distributed uniformly in all environments in which natural selection has probably fitted different groups to cope with different conditions. We know relatively little now about the distribution of such genes; they are much more difficult to identify and to study objectively than genes which can be classified by physical or chemical means. Perhaps such methods must be used before the knowledge we need can be obtained.

But much past experience should make us prepared to find that the biological capacities to absorb new cultural acquisitions are very widely distributed, however many local differences in the proportions of genes are found.

Peoples of ancient cultural traditions have been able quickly to adapt, as whole societies, to new technical and industrial methods; this has happened in Europe and in Asia and is now happening in Africa. Some of the peoples included in the Soviet State have in two generations changed from a hunting and gathering or a nomadic and pastoral way of life to operating an industrial economy based on machines.

In the light of the recent rapid development of similar technologies in all parts of the world the question may well be asked
whether this growing uniformity in productive methods, with the
greater ease of communication and consequent increase in the
movements and migrations of peoples, and especially in the speed
of urbanisation, will tend to make all people alike. The best answer
to this question comes from recalling the reasons for the existence
of the enormous biological variety in all human populations. These
reasons trace to the orgination of gene differences by random mutation and the maintenance of these differences by the integrity of
individual genes and the tendency to maintenance of variety as
expressed in the Hardy-Weinberg rule. Other factors operating
through migrations and changes in mating patterns will be discussed below under 'Race Separation and Race Fusion'.

RACE SEPARATION AND RACE FUSION

Two processes are clearly in evidence in our human species. One
of these is race formation, by which distinctive collections of genes
are gathered together; the other is race fusion, by which these
collections are disposed. The essential condition for race divergence
is always separation, partial or complete isolation, which reduces
the frequency of marriage between two groups. We can call the
group within which marriages are contracted the *marriage circle*.
We can think of the population of the world as living within
marriage circles of differing sizes. These circles overlap and permit
some intermarriage between circles but less than within a circle.

Now anything which affects the size of the circle, that is, the
number of people within the marriage circle, and the degree of
separation between circles, will affect the distribution of genes.
Every marriage circle is a potential race. I have already pointed out
that members of two different caste communities in the city of
Bombay are as unlike in the frequency of certain genes as are
members of African and European marriage circles. Even if we did
not know of the customs preventing marriage between members of
these different castes, we should have to infer that they existed.
Some of these caste communities are very large (several million)
and others quite small (20,000 to 30,000).

The population of a large and geographically diversified area
like that of Europe must perforce become broken up into smaller

marriage circles. One such was based on caste, the royal families who married within their own circle. More circles were based on geographic isolation, for much of the population lived in villages and marriages were usually contracted between members of the same or nearby villages. If long continued this would lead to some biological divergence and the development of local peculiarities. City people too were partly isolated into different marriage circles, the barriers often being religious or social or linguistic. But such divergences never proceeded very far, for the history of Europe, in numbers of human generations, is a short one, and peoples in other parts of the world, although they could recognise Europeans, could seldom distinguish the different varieties. Whether one recognises few or many races in Europe is a matter of taste about which anthropologists do not agree.

The important fact for us in the present connection is that the marriage circles tended to change as economic, social, and political conditions changed. The movements from country to city which the development of industry greatly accelerated, resulted in a very great enlargement of the marriage circles. Now boys met girls from different parts of the country and wherever other barriers were absent the expected took place. The incipient peculiarities of separated communities were merged in the larger group. The development of cheap transportation had an important effect, especially as between different countries. Most important for Europe, connection with America became very close, and in the American cities members of different European marriage circles met and became members of the same circle. Moreover, the social and economic class barriers tended to get lower as political democracy spread.

These considerations show only that the conditions tending to change gene distribution may be responsive to external factors of many kinds. They do not explain why one group should spread and another contract. Sometimes this is due to pure luck, just as whether we are exposed to a fatal disease may be a matter of chance. Sometimes factors which are only secondarily biological will be decisive, such as customs of early or late marriage, decreed for religious or economic reasons, which determine the rate of natural increase of the group. Sometimes the conjunction of great military or religious leaders will cause one group to expand or migrate at a fortunate time while another disappears for no apparent biological reason.

These are cultural changes, and yet they have greatly affected the distribution of genes. The net effect of industrialisation in Europe and the Americas has been to increase the size of marriage circles, and thereby to reverse the tendency to isolation by which races tended to diverge. Genes in the European world now have a much greater mobility and will tend to spread themselves more evenly. One effect is to make it less likely that members of this large community will marry relatives and thus bring to expression those hidden recessives, many of them deleterious, which nearly everyone conceals. In this sense enlargement of the marriage circle is beneficial.

Such effects are of course not peculiar to Europe. They accompany urbanisation wherever it occurs and the history of the world is replete with other movements of peoples and minglings of races. We often hear it said that intermarriage between races has had biological consequences. There is no good or extensive evidence of this and much to be said on the other side. It is true that the immediate offspring of mixed marriages often have a hard time, falling between two racial communities without belonging to either of them. But the effects in such cases are usually of a social and economic and psychological nature rather than biological. That populations with new biological combinations of traits may arise in this way may be seen in the American Negroes, in the Cape Coloured of South Africa, in some of the populations of Central and South America and the Caribbean in which genes from European, American Indian and sometimes from African ancestors are mingled. Race fusions of this sort have been going on ever since bands of people acquired the means of mobility and migration. Its effects are reflected in the variety found within all human races. Whether the mixture was remote or recent, the result is that all human beings are hybrids or mongrels containing genes from a wide variety of different ancestors.

At times the mingling of races may tend to break up adaptive combinations of genes assembled under the influence of natural selection over long generations of living in one set of environments. This becomes of less importance as man learns to control his environments. He now begins to adapt his environment to his needs rather than the reverse which is the only way open to other creatures. Today he gets rid of malaria by inventing and using DDT to destroy the mosquitoes which transmit it and consequently need not depend upon the slow process by which natural selection builds up inherited resistance to the disease.

One result of recent studies of plant and animal populations suggests a possible biological reason why the genotypes of most human individuals contain unlike alleles in most of their genes. Such hybrids (heterozygotes is the technical phrase) frequently have greater vigour and biological efficiency. The great success of hybrid corn is due to this, and in many animal populations natural selection appears to favour unlike combinations of alleles in preference to the pure or homozygous state. Perhaps man too may owe his position as the most successful and adaptable of animals to his mixed genetic nature.

However this may be, it is in any case clear that the evolutionary processes by which man adapted himself to the varied environments of this planet did not include the formation of pure or uniform races since these do not exist anywhere. Rather the process by which he was able to colonise all the habitable parts of the world was first by the assembly of varied combinations of genes formed under the influence of natural selection and other natural forces. These differed in proportions as different natural conditions required. Race is a stage in this process, always as a flexible means rather than as a fixed or determined final stage. Second, he developed culture and a great variety of techniques by which he bent his physical environments to his human needs and purposes. Cultural acquisitions are transmitted by language and written records, a form of inheritance separate from and independent of biological heredity. This second mode of adaptation is now the most important one by which he conquers new environments such as Antarctica yesterday, and outer space tomorrow. Race is not a stage in this process and its biological function is now a secondary one.

The persistence of race prejudice where it exists is a cultural acquisition which as we have seen finds no justification in biology. It serves no biological function in a world which is now progressing beyond the need of race formation as a means of adaptation. The conditions of modern life, deplorable as they are for the many peoples over whom hangs the threat of insecurity and war are nevertheless those which will tend further to reduce the importance of the conditions which formed biological race differences. This does not mean that biological race differences will disappear; the effects of thousands of generations of human evolution will not be more quickly altered. But they may now be viewed in proper perspective and based on knowledge rather than prejudice. The knowledge of the operation of heredity which we now have should lead also to better understanding of the nature of the biological diversity of individuals which lies at the basis of group diversity. The emphasis on the uniqueness of individuals which this new knowledge promotes should thus improve relations within as well as between human groups.

Men are social beings and religious beings as well as biological ones, and they must depend upon their immediate fellows however close they may be drawn to others in the world community. Attachments to place, to neighbours, to members of the same community of thought and spirit have values which all men need and this is true in spite of all the abuses perpetrated in the name of communities based on race. These need not be given up when the tolerance and sympathy with which we regard members of our own group are extended to all others.

Bibliography

Boyd, W. C., *Genetics and the Races of Man* (Boston, Mass.: Little, Brown & Co., 1950).

Coon, C. S., Jarn, S. M., Birdsell, J. B., *Races—a Study of the Problems of Race Formation in Man* (Springfield, Ill.: C. C. Thomas, 1950).

Dahlberg, G., *Race, Reason and Rubbish* (London and New York: Columbia University Press, 1946).

Dobzhansky, T., *Evolution, Genetics and Man* (New York and London: J. Wiley & Sons, 1955).

Dunn, L. C., *Heredity and Evolution in Human Populations* (Cambridge, Mass.: Harvard University Press, 1959).

Dunn, L. C., Dobzhansky, T., *Heredity, Race and Society* (New York: Mentor Books, 1959).

Huxley, J. S., Haddon, A. C., *We Europeans* (London and New York: Harper, 1936).

Lawler, S. D., Lawler, L. J., *Human Blood Groups and Inheritance* (2nd ed.) (London: Heinemann, 1957).

Penrose, L. S., *Outline of Human Genetics* (London and New York: J. Wiley & Sons, 1959).

Race and Contemporary Genetics

by N. P. DUBININ

Professor, Institute of General Genetics, The Praesidium of the Academy of Sciences of the USSR, Moscow

Man's emergence on the earth is unique in the evolution of life. In the organic world evolution is continuous, but occasionally there are turning-points which throw up qualitatively new traits, and organisms advance another step in their evolution. Of several such revolutionary changes, two rank highest. The first was the appearance of life as such, i.e. a self-organised and self-reproductive open system which made the emergence of life from the inorganic world possible. The second was the emergence of consciousness, the ability to think, and hence, the appearance of a rational human being. Mankind derives from the animal kingdom and is represented by a single species *sapiens* of the monotypical genus *homo* of the family Hominidae which, with the family Pongidae (primates) constitutes a super-family Hominoidae. Since they belong to the same species, all people on the earth are to a large extent biologically similar. All carry genetic information deposited in the DNA molecules which constitute the biological basis of man. In all, the amount of DNA and the number of genes are equal. The normal set of chromosomes in every person is 46 (23 pairs). Unlike many animal subspecies, different human populations do not show any taxonomical variations in chromosomal structure. Possessing a genetic mechanism which should in principle be treated as a part of the universal machinery for transmitting genetic information, mankind, unlike any other animal species, forms a rational social community. Its social progress is the result of sociological processes, and does not depend on a selective mechanism operated by the existence of a variety of races.

It is safe to say that, since mankind came into existence as *Homo sapiens* (a process which took 40,000 years) man has not undergone any appreciable evolutionary changes in terms of genetics.

Skeletons from various groups within the species *Homo sapiens* show no essential changes that reflect any further evolutionary progress over tens of millennia.

The consciousness referred to above, characteristic only of man, makes an unbridgeable gap between him and animals, plants and micro-organisms, distinguishes him from all the other forms of life, and renders all people basically equal irrespective of their race. It is for this reason that we can say, not emotionally or subjectively, but scientifically, that all are born equal. The differences between populations are cultural, accounted for by the vagaries of history and environmental variations.

THEORIES OF THE ALLEGED INEQUALITY OF HUMAN RACES HAVE NO SCIENTIFIC BASIS

The term 'race' is one of the main concepts in zoology and botany, implying, as it does, the existence of natural sub-groups of organisms within a species. These sub-groups differ geographically, ecologically or physiologically. The resemblance which the individuals within the sub-groups bear to each other distinguishes them from members of other sub-groups. The difference between races and species is that races can inter-breed, yielding fertile progeny, but species cannot. Different races can have access to a common gene pool. Hence a race may be absorbed by the species and lose its separate identity. On the other hand, by a process of divergent evolution, a race can give rise to a new species.

It has long been known that various human populations exist, differing in their morphology, pigmentation and in other traits. But only with advances in modern population genetics did it become clear that the factors which cause the differences between human populations are different from those that apply to animal populations. In animals, the changes are mainly brought about by mutations and natural selection, both being forms of adaptive evolution. Historical and social factors and population mixture operate in the case of man; mutation pressure and natural selection are secondary.

Misunderstanding of the qualitative evolutionary peculiarities in man led to misconceptions about race. The problem goes back to the dawn of civilisation. It existed in ancient India and China. It is found in the Bible, according to which the three sons of Noah, Shem, Ham (who was cursed by his father) and Japhet gave rise respectively to the Semitic, the dark-skinned, and the other peoples. In Greek mythology, Phaeton, son of Helios (the Sun) is responsible for the origin of the differences between black and white. Unable to control the chariot of the Sun, he drove it too close to the earth, burning and darkening the skin of the people living in the areas in question. Most of the Greek philosophers attributed the population differences to climate. In 1684, Bernier suggested that mankind consists of four groups: Europeans, people of the Far East, Blacks and Lapps. In 1737, Leibnitz followed the Greek tradition, attributing race differences to the effects of climate. Although Linnaeus (1707–1778) thought that mankind is a single species, he recognised four sub-species: *Homo sapiens Europaeus*, *Home sapiens Asiaticus*, *Homo sapiens Afer*, and *Homo sapiens Americanus*. In 1775, his contemporary, Blumenbach, made a division of mankind into five races: Caucasian (white), Mongolian (yellow), Ethiopian (black), American (red) and Malayan (brown).

Regarding themselves as belonging to a specific race, certain peoples acquired a belief in their superiority over others, e.g. the Jews believed themselves the chosen people of God, on the basis of what was recounted in the Bible.

In the sixteenth and seventeenth centuries, Europeans grabbed vast tracts in the newly-discovered lands in America, Australia and in the Pacific and Indian Oceans. Racial superiority provided the ideological foundation for colonialism in the eighteenth and nineteenth centuries, and was used to justify violence and repression. The illusion of superiority was maintained, first, by the institution of slavery and, afterwards, by ensuring the socio-economic inferiority of the Negro.

In Europe, an Aryan cult was derived from Sanskrit legends about the blond conquerors of darker-skinned inhabitants of India and Persia. Europeans of Indo-European or 'Nordic' stock were held to be descendants of these conquerors. In the four volumes of his 'Essay on the Inequality of Human Races' (1853–1855), Gobineau explained how Aryans are a biological master race, amongst whom the long-headed, light-skinned German race ranks highest. He believed that the mixture of the superior with inferior races was responsible for the disappearance of the great ancient cultures.

Lapouge (1864–1936) explained social phenomena by biological racial differences (anthroposociology). At the International Congress of Eugenics in 1921, he advocated eugenic methods to replace Africans, Asians and 'inferior' whites by whites of the 'superior' race. Chamberlain (1895–1927) and Galton (1822–1911), the founder of eugenics, held that the Nordics constituted a superior human race.

In the 1870s Lombroso suggested that criminality is a biological phenomenon. In 1939, Hooton, in his book 'American Criminal', tried to prove that criminal behaviour is genetically conditioned.

The cult of Aryanism led to the atrocities of genocide. Its ideologist, Rosenberg, wrote in 1934 of the 'hidden mystery of blood' and the new 'science of race'.

Lenz, another leading theoretician, discussed 'race hygiene'. Thus the errors and biased theories have been many. Recent genetic studies permit a more scientific approach.

Considering man as a social being, it becomes easier to understand why people from various populations and races differ. The differences prove to be minor and outward only, all mankind having a common biological make-up and the same intellectual potentialities.

MODERN GENETIC APPROACH

The present world population is 3,600 million. All the earth's inhabitants resemble each other in appearance and inner structure, and in major and minor features. However, they are grouped in 'races', each generally having a common place of origin. Each race can be described by its characteristic physical features: colour of skin, hair and iris; kind and degree of development of hair on face (beard, moustache) and body; form of upper eyelid, nose and lips; length of body (stature), form of head and face. These features are not studied in genetic terms, and are usually treated on a quantitative or descriptive basis. They vary tremendously within, and between, peoples, possibly because of the extensive blending of human populations (as Kant suggested as far back as the eighteenth century). This does not prove that 'pure' races ever inhabited the earth. Nowadays, race-blending is an accelerated process, and new mixed populations are being formed e.g. in tropical America (Indian, white, negro), Hawaii (Polynesian, white,

Mongolian), United States (negro and white). One result has been a good deal of confused and subjective thinking among anthropologists in regard to the origin and classification of human races.

Investigators must devise strictly objective methods for studying changing human populations, as well as their past developments. Here the findings of immuno-genetics have been of vital importance. Studies of the genetics of blood groups reveal a number of remarkable features: (1) antigens of blood groups are strictly determined by specific genes and, throughout life, are practically uninfluenced by environmental variations; (2) the co-dominance of antigen alleles allows the full genotype for both homozygotes and heterozygotes to be unmistakably determined; (3) frequencies of different alleles of blood groups vary for different human populations.

Blood groups ABO were discovered by Landsteiner in 1900, and investigators have meanwhile shown the genetics of these groups (alleles A, B, O) and their geographical distribution (cf. studies published by B. K. Boyd (1950, 1953), A. S. Mourant (1954–1958), T. G. Dobzhansky (1962) et al.).

Table 1 (Boyd) shows the distribution of blood groups O, A, B, AB, and concentrations of each of the three alleles O, A, B, in the populations of the world.

Most human populations were found to include all four blood groups, though the distribution may greatly vary, e.g. American Indians living in Central and South America are exceptional in being almost uniformly O; Australian aborigines and North American Indians have O and A but respectively not B or AB; Indian populations in Central and South America show different frequencies of genes A and B—they fall to zero in some places (Table 2).

Serological studies indicate that antigen A may be divided into antigens A_1 and A_2. This extended the possibilities of population analysis. Blackfeet Indians proved to have A_1. In the Caucasus, the frequency of A_1 is 84%, among negroes, 55%. Allele A_2 was not found in Eastern Asia, Oceania, or among American Indians, although it occurs in Europe, Africa and the Middle East. The A_2/A_1 proportion in Africa is higher than in Europe, and intermediate in the Middle East.

The frequency of gene B is high in Central India (27·8%) and Siberia (27·7%). Gene B frequency regularly diminishes (down to 0) as one moves from these high points towards Western Europe and Central and South America. Candela (1942) accordingly maintained that gene B came into Europe via the Mongol conquerors from Central Asia between the fifth and the fifteenth centuries.

In 1927, Landsteiner and Levine discovered two more human antigens, and designated them M and N. Subsequent studies in allele geographical distribution showed their concentrations to be less subject to variations than alleles of the ABO blood groups.

Appreciable variations for M groups are typical of American Indians and Australian aborigines. In the former, M and NM dominate, and are scarce in the latter (especially M). The highest gene frequency for N (91%) and the lowest for M (0·9%) were found among the Papuans of New Guinea. The opposite was observed among American Indians. The value of antigen MN studies was enhanced when, in 1947, a pair of antigens S and s was discovered, localised in the same chromosome, very close to the gene for MN. Some populations exhibit clear-cut differences for allele S and s concentration, e.g. antigen S occurs in the New Guinea population but not among Australian aborigines. The alleles Hu, He, Miᵃ, Vw, belong to this system. Alleles M_1M_2, N_2, Mq, were also discovered.

In 1940, Landsteiner and Wiener discovered the rhesus-antigens (Rh) system, which involves approximately a dozen alleles. A. E. Mourant (1954) brought together the literature on the incidence of eight of these alleles in different human populations.

The most remarkable finding is that the dominant allele reaches its highest frequency in all populations native to Africa south of the Sahara. The rhesus-negative gene attains its highest frequency (53·1%) among the Basques in the Pyrenees in northern Spain; it is common, though less frequent in neighbouring European peoples, and rare or absent elsewhere. It is therefore assumed to have originated in northern Spain.

Some other blood group systems employed for population investigations are: Lutheran (Luᵃ, Luᵇ), Kell (K,k), Duffi (Fyᵃ, Fyᵇ) and Kidd (Jkᵃ, Jkᵇ, Jkᶜ).

The Kell (K) and Lutheran (Luᵃ) genes have 5% frequencies in most European populations. K is even less frequent in Africa (except among the Bushmen), China, Malaya, and among most American Indians. Luᵃ seems to be absent in India and Australia. The Fyᵃ and Jkᵃ genes are very imperfectly known. The frequency of Fyᵃ is about 40% in Europe, except among the Lapps; it is higher in Asia (up to 90%), lower in Africa (6–8%). The Fy^a and Fy^b alleles are apparently absent among negroes. Allele Fy^a attains a high frequency in American Indians. Allele Jk^a makes up about 50% of the gene pool in England and among white Americans, but about 78% in negroes and 100% in a tribe in Borneo.

From the allele investigations some very important inferences can be drawn. The evidence suggests that human populations are typically Mendelian, i.e. pan-mixing. For example, American negroes possessing 30% genes of the whites, exhibited the following genotype percentage distribution for alleles M and N: 28·42MM + 49·64MN + 21·94 NN. The expected distribution was: 29·16 + 49·89 + 21·86.

The antigen investigations reveal that human heredity carries evidence of both past isolation and of mixture. The present intensive mixture is clearly tending to fuse all human races into a single, but greatly variable, population.

Population diversity can be expressed quantitatively in terms of varied allele concentrations. The distribution of antigens in human populations indicates that they are radically different from animal races and sub-species. In particular, human population variations may derive from genetic drift and population mixtures that are historical and social in origin. Under such circumstances, natural selection plays a secondary role. Each human population is a diversified manifestation of what constitutes a single whole. The differences between them relate to minor features, and are negligibly small compared to the common genetic endowment that is the biological basis of every man on earth who belongs to *Homo sapiens*.

CLASSIFICATION OF HUMAN POPULATIONS

Considering that mankind is a species consisting of Mendelian populations engaged in gene exchanges, race typology presents quite a problem. Dynamic genetic interaction is taking place between all populations. Hence the difficulty of subdividing, into races, the whole diversity of mankind. However, several classifications have been proposed, in which the genetics of blood antigens are combined with other anthropological features, e.g. Boyd (1953), 5 races; Garn (1961), 9; Coon, Garn and Birdsell (1950), 32; Dobzhansky (1962), 34 (see below).

Boyd

1. European (Caucasoid): high frequencies of Ph cde and CDe, moderate frequencies of the other blood-group genes; M usually slightly above 50% and N below 50%.
2. African (negroid): very high frequency of Ph cDe, moderate frequencies of the other blood-group genes.
3. Asian (Mongoloid): high frequency of B, few, if any, cde.
4. American Indian: mostly homozygous O, but sometimes high frequencies of A; absence of B, few, if any, cde, high M.
5. Australoid—moderate to high A, few or no B or cde, high N.

Garn

1. Amerindian: the pre-Columbian populations of the Americas.
2. Polynesian: islands of the Eastern Pacific, from New Zealand to Hawaii and Easter Island.
3. Micronesian: islands of the Western Pacific, from Guam to Marshall and Gilbert Islands.
4. Melanesian-Papuan islands of the Western Pacific, from New Guinea to New Caledonia and Fiji.
5. Australian: Australian aboriginal populations.
6. Asian: from Indonesia and South-East Asia to Tibet, China, Japan, Mongolia, plus the native tribes of Siberia.
7. Indian: populations of the sub-continent of India.
8. European: populations of Europe, the Middle East, and Africa north of the Sahara.
9. African populations of Africa south of the Sahara.

Coon, Garn, Birdsell and Dobzhansky

1. North-West European: Scandinavia, Northern Germany, Northern France, United Kingdom, Ireland.
2. North-East European: Poland, European part of the Soviet Union, most of the present population of Siberia.
3. Alpine: from Central France, South Germany, Switzerland, Northern Italy eastward to the shores of the Black Sea.
4. Mediterranean: peoples on both sides of the Mediterranean, from Tangiers to the Dardanelles, Arabia, Turkey, Iran.
5. Hindu: India, Pakistan.
6. Turkic: Turkestan, Western China.

7. Tibetan: Tibet.
8. North Chinese: Northern and Central China and Manchuria.
9. Classic Mongoloid: Siberia, Mongolia, Korea, Japan.
10. Eskimo: Arctic America.
11. South-East Asian: South China to Thailand, Burma, Malaya and Indonesia.
12. Ainu: aboriginal population of Northern Japan.
13. Lapp: Arctic Scandinavia and Finland.
14. North American Indian: indigenous populations of Canada and the United States.
15. Central American Indian: from South-Western United States, through Central America, to Bolivia.
16. South American Indian: primarily the agricultural peoples of Peru, Bolivia, and Chile.
17. Fuegian: non-agricultural inhabitants of Southern South America.
18. East African: East Africa, Ethiopia, part of Sudan.
19. Sudanese: most of Sudan.
20. Forest Negro: West Africa and much of the Congo.
21. Bantu: South Africa and part of East Africa.
22. Bushman and Hottentot: the aboriginal inhabitants of South Africa.
23. African Pygmy: a small-statured population living in the rain forests of Equatorial Africa.
24. Dravidian: aboriginal populations of Southern India and Ceylon.
25. Negrito: small-statured and frizzly-haired populations scattered from the Philippines to the Andamans, Malaya and New Guinea.
26. Melanesian Papuan: New Guinea to Fiji.
27. Murrayian: aboriginal population of South Eastern Australia.
28. Carpentarian: aboriginal population of Northern and Central Australia.
29. Micronesian: islands of the Western Pacific.
30. Polynesian: islands of the Central and Eastern Pacific.
31. Neo-Hawaiian: an emerging population of Hawaii.
32. Ladino: an emerging population of Central and South America.
33. North American Coloured: negro population of North America.
34. South African Coloured: the analogous population of South Africa.

Boyd's classification is mainly derived from the data on blood group genes; it has not, however, utilised the genetic approach to the actual concept of a human race. The race classification proposed by Coon, Garn, Birdsell and Dobzhansky shows a considerable improvement in this respect, as they did not deal with abstract typological races that never really existed. Their classification treats human evolution as a process that resulted in dynamic race formation in the past which will surely change again in the future.

Some populations blend, but quite a number are reproductively isolated. In the complex conglomeration of Indian castes, inter-marriages are not permitted. Basques seem to be a relic of an ancient population assimilated by their neighbours. In the 34-race classification, Northern Chinese (8) are classic Mongoloids (9), while South Eastern Asians (11) represent a thousand million people who divide up into a number of related Mendelian populations.

The Neanderthalians appear to date from before *Homo sapiens*. They inhabited the continental Old World, were adapted to the tough and varied conditions of the ice age. By the beginning of Upper Palaeolithic, a Cro-Magnon physical type had evolved (Howells, 1964).

The polycentric origin of the major human races from separate Neanderthal races is one suggestion that has been put forward. Weidenreich (1947) holds that modern man originated from four centres or regions, as Europeans, Mongols, Negroes and Australians.

Roginsky (1949) tried to prove the monocentric origin of *Homo sapiens*. He considers that contemporary human races are much closer to each other in bodily structure than Weidenreich's theory would allow, and that the basic event in the appearance of man was the transformation of the Moustier tribes into clans having a highly developed social sense; in the struggle for life, the individual had discovered the advantages of social organisation and shared labour. (Roginsky, 1936–1938; Semenov, 1960–1966; Nesturkh, 1970). Natural selection continued to operate in the adaptive evolution of animals, but lost its primary significance in reaction to human beings, on whom anthropological and social factors were now operating. As man made social progress, his biological level was influenced by the fact that he was conscious of himself and that he had become capable of co-operating with others.

At this point his biological evaluation came to a halt. This, according to Mayr (1968), was because of the exceptional adapta-bility of man, who can live in very varied environments, and because he no longer had any need to develop isolating mecha-nisms (hence the increasing inner integrity of the genetic system of the species as a whole). And, with the ability to think, man became capable of new forms of social relationships, and new ways of satisfying his wants. The development of culture and science (in-accessible to animals) created a completely new social background and led to progress at a fantastic speed.

Assuming that the human race originated in one place, it nevertheless seems that, some dozens of millennia ago, two major subdivisions took place (Roginsky, 1949, 1965; Alēkseev, 1969). According to Roginsky, the Asian or Mongoloid race originated in Asia, north and east of the Himalayas and, 25–30 millennia ago, entered America via the Bering Straits and the Aleutian Islands. From the second, South-Western, subdivision, the Europeoid and Negro-Australoid races derive. Subsequent developments in isola-tion or mixtures through migration were responsible for the thirty or more racial subdivisions which now exist.

REASONS FOR THE DIVERSITY OF RACES AND POPULATIONS

Mutations are the primary source of hereditary variabilities in every population. In pre-social man the effect of most mutations is eliminated by natural selection; this results in adaptive evolution and the survival of a normal, adapted phenotype. On the other hand, human societies display a tremendous range of variations. The reason is that man-made environments cause mutations which are not controlled by natural selection, and this leads to such phenomena as the diversity of blood groups, eye colour, external ear structure, shape of nose, the peculiarities of hair structure, the ability to distinguish the taste of phenylthiocarba-mide, and so on, i.e. a diversity of biochemical, morphological, physiological and other characteristics which do not interfere with the ordinary course of a man's life.

Besides this extensive polymorphism that tends to make every individual unique in genetic terms, there are harmful mutations which disturb physical or mental faculties, and are referred to as the genetic load. The original reference to the genetic load was made in Moscow in studies on wild-type Drosophila (Dubinin et al., 1934) which showed that, although normal in appearance, some viable and adapted variants carried three to four lethal genes and several other genes which reduce viability in heterozygotes; hence part of the progeny of each generation is bound to die, and a part will be born with hereditary defects, i.e. those in which lethal and semi-lethal genes have become homozygous.

Genetic load is characteristic of many animal and plant populations, and occurs in Mendelian populations as a sequel of natural mutagenesis. On an average, 4% of children have hereditary malformations and diseases. The appearance in the environment of as effective a mutagen as an increased radiation background may contribute markedly to the genetic load.

Yet, if environments remain as they are, natural mutagenesis will not by itself disturb human genetic structures in the foreseeable future. Let us take an illustration. The frequency of the gene of albinism is 0·01 in a number of populations. When it becomes homozygous, people are born red-eyed, and without pigmentation. This allele concentration means that albinos are born at a frequency of one person in 10,000. The approximate frequency of natural mutations for this gene is known to be one per 100,000 gametes. Duplication of the allele concentration as a result of mutation pressure will thus occur after 1,000 generations, i.e. 25,000 years (the human reproductive generation being reckoned as 25 years). In other words, if the number of albinos originally created when the allele becomes homozygous is one per 10,000 people, after 25,000 years it will become four. This refers to alleles unaffected by natural selection. Obviously, if bearers have deleterious genes and produce fewer progeny than the normal, the effect of the mutation process will be even slower.

Let us consider a more radical change than just doubling the concentration of a particular allele, e.g. the infusion of a mutant allele into the whole population. This would take far more time. Let us try to imagine that, because of mutation pressure, all people could become albinos. The mutation pressure would have to rise from the original allele concentration of 0·01% to 100%, 'saturating' the whole population. This should take at least 100 times as long as the duplication of allele concentration, i.e. 2·5 million years. In fact, it would be markedly slower: in the course of time not only would there be mutations from the norm to albinos, but also back mutations that would slow down the relative growth rate of the mutant allele concentration.

Thus, though mutations are a vast source of biological variability, they cannot be regarded as having changed the genetic structure of populations since the advent of *Homo sapiens*. It should also be noted that a mutation process is usually uniform for the whole species. Distinctions between populations were initially brought out by gene drift and the isolation of populations. Wright (1930) and Dubinin (1931) established that the isolation of populations caused certain changes in their genetic structure through a mechanism called genetic drift (genetic-automatic processes). The basic principle is that the hereditary transmission of alleles in any limited population involves stochastic processes. Hence, every new generation shows random deviations in allele concentrations which can bring about random but radical changes in the genetic structure of the population. The smaller the population, the greater the effect of genetic-automatic processes, which are crucial in the case of genes controlling neutral characteristics. Human polymorphism is essentially different from that of wild forms because more often than not it has no adaptive meaning.

Dubinin and Romashov (1932) suggested that the genetic characteristics of a population are mainly derived from those of a small band of migrants who came to an unoccupied territory and so founded the population in question.

Birdsell (1957) made estimates of the probable rates of expansion of the original population of Australia from the first invaders who arrived perhaps some 32,000 years ago. The continent was most likely populated by small bands who entered from the north, the first numbering about twenty-five persons. It took some 22 centuries for their descendants to spread throughout the continent, during which time, some tribes increased, others became extinct but affected the common genotype which survived.

In the Palaeolithic Age, mankind probably consisted of small populations, endogamous tribes subject to random genetic drift. The typical pattern of the genetic response of human populations to isolation can still be seen today—stochastic processes of random differentiation brought about through certain mutations (cf. evidence collected by Rychkov (1968) from population samples in the Pamir mountains, the Crimea and Siberia).

Populations grew, migrated as their numbers increased, and intermixed with other populations. Gradually, mankind came to occupy the whole dry land area. The reasons were historical and social and hence different from what applies in the case of such developments among animal subspecies (cf. Roginsky, 1965, 1790).

Differences between human groups stand out only when the groups are large. Variations are transgressive and the individual variability inside groups may be very high. Hence, what applies to the group may not be applicable to all its representatives.

Natural selection played an important part in the formation of primitive human populations, directly, and through social organisation which, allied with a more productive use of labour, helped to eliminate man's direct dependence on his surroundings (cf. Nesturh, 1970). By the late Palaeolithic Age, Cro-Magnons and other populations had a well-developed social system. At the last stage of anthropogenesis, race peculiarities became mainly inadaptive traits.

This last issue has been the subject of much discussion and research. One possible line of investigation is by analogy with differentiations among animal subspecies and races known to be adaptive. Mayr (1942), Rensch (1959) and Ray (1960) maintained a parallelism theory. The possibility of human characteristics depending upon geographic factors was first suggested by Allen in 1906.

The main evidence disclosed by animal studies comes from Allen and Bergmann. Animal races which inhabit the warmer parts of the species range tend to be smaller in body size than races living in colder parts, where the surface area of the body also tends to be less, relative to total body volume. This can be regarded as a matter of adaptation in order to ensure the conservation of heat. If the animal's body is increased, the surface grows as the square, and its bulk as the cube, of its dimensions. Newman (1953), Roberts (1953) and Baker (1958) held that the stature : weight ratio tends to be lower in animals living in cold climates. The application to man of the Bergmann–Allen rules was criticised by Scholander (1950, 1955) on the grounds that clothing, housing and other facilities of civilisation create a 'private' climate, so that diversified outside temperatures can scarcely be held to influence selection—there is a danger here of mistaking non-inheritable deviations for results of selection. In a large sample of white American soldiers, Newman and Munro (1955) found that northerners were appreciably heavier on the average than southerners. Too little time has passed since the colonisation of America to justify suggesting that selection among the northern population is responsible, and the reasons must obviously be socio-economic. It is possible, that, among early hominoids, human body size may have been affective by the Allen–Bergmann adaptive principles, but many consider that, because of cultural and social changes (diet, clothing, housing) they no longer apply to human evolution.

Much research has been devoted to physiological adaptation. Baker (1956) examined groups of negro and white soldiers and found marked differences in their physiological tolerance in wet heat. Bridges (1950), Scholander et al. (1958) failed in attempts to sleep naked on the ground between fires at temperatures close to freezing point (which Australian aborigines can do easily). The astonishing adaptedness of Eskimos to the cold climate is well known. How far does the explanation lie in racial genetic diversity? In experiments with volunteer Norwegian students, Scholander et al. (1958–B) found astounding adaptedness to cold. The students lived for six weeks in the mountains without warm clothing or bed covers. At first they could not sleep, but eventually became able to do so by maintaining higher skin temperatures. Barnicot (1959) surmised that among the Eskimos higher metabolic rates and the efficient blood circulation in body extremities may be due to long-term adaptations.

The applicability to man of Gloger's (1833) rule of the dependence of skin colour on habitat temperature has been extensively discussed in the literature. Skin colour is the most conspicuous of race differences. Schwidetzky (1952), Reche and Lehmann (1959) assumed that skins become dark to adapt to strong sunshine, while they remain light-coloured in cool climates. American Indians and Eskimos, however, fail to conform to the rule.

Despite the parallelism in skin colour revealed by temperature maps (Fleure, 1945; Biasutti, 1959) and statistically significant correlations (Walter, 1958), the question is still open. Sun tan in light-skinned people is acquired by mechanisms different from those which give a naturally dark pigmentation. Protection against skin cancers seems to be one important advantage of the latter, although it can hardly be a factor in natural selection. Cancers induced in man by sunlight are of low malignancy, and mostly occur late in life (Blum, 1959, 1961). Cowles (1959) supposes that a dark skin may provide protection against predators rather than against sunburn. But then, people living in tropical grasslands tend to be more dark-skinned.

The available evidence does not afford proof that any particular racial trait is a matter of genetic adaptation. The human genetic background differs qualitatively from that of animals. The effect of natural selection on some mutations in human populations is beyond doubt, and has been thoroughly investigated in people suffering from hereditary diseases. Positive selection has also been observed, e.g. in the condition known as sickle-cell disease. Normal haemoglobin is homozygous for gene Si^A. Sickle-cell disease, producing severe, lethal anaemia, is caused by homozygosity for gene Si^S. In the case of heterozygotes Si^A/Si^S, superficially normal red blood cells contain some abnormal haemoglobin. The incidence of gene Si^S is high in Africa (about 40% of some tribes have this gene in the heterozygotes). American negroes have 7–13% of these heterozygotes. Allison (1956, 1961, 1963, 1964) has shown that the incidence of gene Si^S is high because heterozygous carriers of it are more resistant to malaria.

Similar to sickle-cell disease is another blood disease, thalassaemia. Here the homozygotes (Si Si) also die of anaemia. This gene is found most frequently in the Mediterranean area (especially in Italy and Greece), and in Siberia. In Italy there about 5% heterozygotes, up to 10% in some areas, with a stable survival rate of the gene.

GROWTH OF HUMAN RACE AND EFFECTS ON HEREDITY

At any one time, the human race is a product of its changing numbers and population mixtures. The two essential features in modern times are growth and mixture.

During the next thirty years the world's population will double, i.e. by the year 2000 it should reach 6,000–7,000 million. By mid-1969 it was estimated at 3,552 million (Peoples' Republic of China 740 million; India 537 million; USSR 240 million; United States 203 million). According to United Nations estimates, the average annual increment is 50 million (cf. June 1968 to June 1969, 69 million). It is estimated that it once took 70,000 years to double the world's population. At the growth rate in 1850, it would have taken 200 years, while today it takes 30 years. The population remained small for a long time, but by 1830 it had risen to 1,000 million. It doubled in a century, reaching 2,000 million by 1930. The third 1,000 million was added in 30 years (1930–1960);

according to United Nations estimates, the fourth will be added in 15 years and, by the year 2000, the figure will be 7,000 million.

This growth is bound to affect the whole genetic composition of mankind. And, presumably, higher physical and intellectual standards will be made possible by higher living standards and the genetic divergence of individuals.

Population mixtures have been taking place for 10,000–15,000 years. The accelerating present trend towards pooling heredity in one vast population started when Columbus discovered America in 1492. Four races can be said to have originated within the last few centuries. North American Coloured (33) are a mixture of Forest Negro (20), Bantu (21), North-West European (1), Alpine (3), Mediterranean (4) and probably some others. South African Coloured (34) are a mixture of (21), (22), (1) and (3). Ladino (32) are a mixture of (15), (16), (4), (20) and (21). Neo-Hawaiian (31) are a mixture of (30), (1), (9), (4), (8) and (11). Mixed populations have thus been formed in America, Africa, Asia and Australia.

Of Mexico's 36 million people, some 60% descend from marriages between Indians and Europeans. Of Colombia's 15 million population, some 40% are hybrid, complex mixtures of negro, European, Indian and others. Contacts at land frontiers between races gave rise to intermediate, hybrid populations, e.g. the Ural group derived from Europeoid and Mongoloid stock.

European races show a marked trend towards fusion. And, in America, Glass and Lee (1966) investigated negro mixtures with whites. Brought to the New World by force three and a half centuries ago, the negro genotype now carries 30% genes of the white. At this rate, after 75 generations (i.e. 2,000 years), negro and white gene pools will coalesce in a single population. This will occur even if prejudices against inter-marriages continue—if they disappear, the process will be sharply accelerated.

On the whole, it is safe to say that half mankind is a product of race mixtures. People from mixed races are physically normal and have normal children. Their intelligence level is maintained and may often be outstanding.

The blending of human populations poses a number of problems, however. According to Houser's estimate (1960), the world population will amount to 6,267 million people by the year 2000, distributed as follows (in millions): Africa 517; North America 312; Central and South America 529; Asia 3,870; Europe (including all the Soviet Union) 947; Australasia 29. These populations thus vary greatly in size, and mixtures may not produce varieties as desirable as they do now. What kind of man will emerge from random blends of the gene pools of the living races considering that a total population fusion could occur within 2,000–3,000 years?

MAN'S SOCIAL INHERITANCE

Man must be regarded as a social being whose development has been different from that of animals because of social relationships, culture and science, and his concept of good and evil. It is because of this social inheritance that, as a species, *Homo sapiens* is unique. This evolutionary advantage explains man's development rather than genetic evolution, which is relatively slow, and it also lies at the origin of his enhanced capacity for adapting to his environment. Lenin wrote of man's unparalleled capacity for exploring, by creative thinking, the endless variety of the controversial phenomena of his existence, and hence, his inexhaustible capacity for self-development.

In other words, to make progress, *Homo sapiens* had no further need of genetic evolution.

History corroborates. Since the Middle Ages, for example, no genetic changes followed from the development of culture and science. Current scientific and technological advances (the breakthrough in space, penetration of the molecular mechanisms of the gene, discovery of atomic energy) will have produced astounding changes by the beginning of the twenty-first century, but no genetic changes are to be expected.

Progress, accordingly, derives rather from the development of man's productive capacity and the further uses to which he can put his achievements. Through education and social organisation generally, every generation can pass on what it has learned to the next. In man, social evolution has become more important than biological evolution, and has allowed fantastically rapid development.

Individual traits are conditioned both by the genotype inherited from parents and by social and physical surroundings. The latter are especially important in childhood and adolescence. If subjected to different social environments, even identical twins who are genetically similar will have different personalities, though remaining remarkably alike in appearance (Gottesman, 1968). In conditions of poverty people have little opportunity to develop their mental faculties or indulge in refined emotions. Such conditions can continue to influence generations of people. Genealogical research indicates that criminal tendencies, prostitution, alcoholism, and so on, can continue from generation to generation.

Research provides no evidence of the existence of genes which might explain the persistence of these social characteristics. On the other hand, the recurrence of certain environmental conditions over a number of generations can breed specific types of social behaviour. The inheritance is social, not genetic.

Science, religion, culture, standards of good and evil and various forms of behaviour in human society are passed on—by nurture, not by nature.

All people are not born the same in genetic terms nor, of course, are they equally capable of learning. None of us can eliminate the genetic inheritance received from our parents. Each possesses a unique genetic organisation and reacts in his own way to social and physical influences. The genetic programme is stored in the DNA molecules and passed from generation to generation through the germ cells. Identical twins from two halves of a fertilised cocyte are genetically identical and, as a rule, display remarkable physical alikeness. This is genetic inheritance. The evidence suggests that most genetic information will be preserved in an endless number of succeeding generations.

The social inheritance of accumulated knowledge and skills is steadily growing, and there is no logical limit to the progress—social, scientific, cultural, moral—of which man is potentially capable. The biological level he has already reached is fully adequate in this regard. A new man can be created by social transformations.

And we must not forget the genetic diversity of people. Biological singularities combined with the social inheritance explain the individuality of each man. This is a matter of vital moral and ethical importance.

Biological and social standardisation would destroy something essential in man. Consciousness of the inevitability of dying, for example, could be considered as a standardising factor, but it is at the same time the source of his ability to reason and so, to progress.

Social inheritance has a direct bearing on the racial problem. Stable genetic information passes from generation to generation through the germ cells, but social change occurs in every generation. Were it not for education and other ways in which knowledge is acquired and transmitted, we might still be at the level of our most primitive ancestors. Rational man's potentialities for cultural development are inexhaustible. Differences in cultural level between different populations and races are social rather than biological. Every man, regardless of his race, has the ability to think; given a favourable environment there is no reason why he should not be able to reach the summit.

CONCLUSIONS

Objective research indicates that, in biological terms, all human races are at the same level. No appreciable racial diversity has been found for the large and highly developed brain, with many convolutions and fissures on the surface of its hemispheres, which all possess. All have hands, the product and implement of labour, legs with a foot structure adapted for standing and locomotion, and other human biological features that are common to all races without exception.

Within a particular race there are enormous possibilities for individual and biological diversity. Races reflect a parallel diversity inside the species as a whole. Experience has shown that in any race people respond flexibly to social and environmental change; above all, the history of this century suggests that individuals, populations and races make rapid progress as soon as they obtain favourable social conditions.

Human races belong to a single, unique species, *Homo sapiens*. Recent genetic knowledge suggests that all people have the ability to reason, that they are born equal, and that there is no hierarchy of superior and inferior races. Racial variations do not affect man as a social animal; in proclaiming the contrary, racialism perverts genetic data. Racialist theories are pseudo-scientific, with no basis in biological fact. Racial prejudices will disappear when colonialism and imperialism also disappear. Most colonial people have by now won independence and become members of the United Nations; the experience of the Soviet Union and other socialistic countries implies that, regardless of their national and racial differences, all peoples can successfully develop.

The four statements on the race question issued by Unesco in 1950, 1951, 1964 and 1967 convincingly uphold the thesis that all people are born free and equal in dignity and rights, expose the erroneous nature of racialist doctrines, and show that attempts to justify racial discrimination on biological grounds are basically pseudo-scientific.

Human genetics has incontrovertibly shown that races and populations are specific manifestations of the single whole which is mankind. Further research can lead to biological improvement and prepare for the day when all races and populations will constitute a single human population.

Before that can happen, each nation must first be ensured the conditions in which it can make cultural progress and prosper; and this in turn presupposes a raising of the world's capacity to produce, and radical changes in the whole of human society.

Table 1. Frequencies of blood groups O, A, B and AB in samples of typical populations

Population	Place	Number tested	Phenotypes %				Gene frequencies		
			O	A	B	AB	O	A	B
American Indians (Utes)	Montana	138	97·4	2·6	0·0	0·0	0·987	0·013	0·000
American Indians (Blackfeet)	Montana	115	23·5	76·5	0·0	0·0	0·485	0·515	0·000
American Indians (Navajo)	North Mexico	359	77·7	22·5	0·0	0·0	0·875	0·125	0·000
Caucasians	Montana	291	42·3	44·7	10·3	2·7	0·650	0·257	0·053
Polynesians	Hawaii	413	36·5	60·8	2·2	0·5	0·604	0·382	0·018
Australian Aborigines	South Australia	54	42·6	57·4	0·0	0·0	0·654	0·346	0·000
Basques	San Sebastian	91	57·2	41·7	1·1	0·0	0·756	0·239	0·008
Eskimo	Cape Farewell	484	41·1	53·8	3·5	1·4	0·642	0·333	0·027
Buriats	Siberia	1320	32·4	20·2	39·2	8·2	0·570	0·156	0·277
Chinese	Peking	1000	30·7	25·1	34·2	10·0	0·554	0·193	0·250
Pygmies	Belgian Congo	132	30·6	30·3	29·1	10·1	0·554	0·227	0·219
Asiatic Indians	South-western India	400	29·2	26·8	34·0	10·0	0·540	0·208	0·254
Asiatic Indians	Bengal	160	32·5	20·0	39·4	8·1	0·571	0·154	0·278
Siamese	Bangkok	213	37·1	17·8	35·2	9·9	0·595	0·148	0·257
Japanese	Tokyo	29,799	30·1	38·4	21·9	9·7	0·549	0·279	0·172
English	London	422	47·9	42·4	8·3	1·4	0·692	0·250	0·050
Germans	Berlin	39,174	36·5	42·5	14·5	6·5	0·604	0·285	0·110

Table 2. Frequencies of blood groups O, A, B and AB in Indian populations of Central and South America

Population	Place	Number tested	Phenotypes % O	A	B	AB	Gene frequencies O	A	B
Indians	Mexico and Guatemala	1089	95·35	3·44	0·9	0·09	0·9746	0·0190	0·0064
Maya	Honduras	194	64·95	18·04	13·40	3·61	0·7971	0·1143	0·0886
Lenka	Honduras	152	90·79	6·58	2·63	0·00	0·9553	0·0335	0·0132
Kekchi	British Honduras	162	95·06	3·09	1·23	0·62	0·9659	0·0117	0·0124
Guyami	Panama	240	100·00	0·00	0·00	0·00	1·0000	0·0000	0·0000
San-Blas	Panama	388	100·00	0·00	0·00	0·00	1·0000	0·0000	0·0000
Miskito	Nicaragua	150	90·00	8·67	1·33	0·00	0·9490	0·0443	0·0067
Sumu	Nicaragua	103	100·00	0·00	0·00	0·00	1·0000	1·0000	0·0000
Indians	Ecuador	9167	95·37	3·35	1·05	0·23	0·977	0·015	0·007
Xipibo	Peru	142	93·30	0·00	0·07	0·00	0·977	0·000	0·003
Aguaruna	Peru	151	100·00	0·00	0·00	0·00	1·0000	0·0000	0·0000
Tikuma	Peru	122	100·00	0·00	0·00	0·00	1·0000	0·0000	0·0000

Table 3 Blood group frequencies in Indian populations of Central and South America and some other populations

Population	Place	Number tested	Phenotypes %			Gene frequencies	
Quiche	Guatemala	203	55·17	36·46	8·37	0·7340	0·2659
Xicaque	Honduras	194	43·29	44·32	12·37	0·6546	0·3454
Lenka	Honduras	152	57·90	36·84	5·27	0·7632	0·2368
Kekchi	British Honduras	162	44·45	46·29	9·26	0·6759	0·3241
Guyami	Panama	240	48·33	42·92	8·75	0·6979	0·3021
San-Blas	Panama	388	50·77	42·01	7·22	0·7178	0·2822
Miskito	Nicaragua	150	58·00	38·00	4·00	0·7700	0·2300
Sumu	Nicaragua	103	80·58	18·43	0·99	0·8981	0·1019
Quechua	Ecuador	372	62·90	32·53	4·57	0·792	0·208
Xipibo	Peru	142	47·89	44·37	7·74	0·701	0·299
Aguarana	Peru	151	40·40	45·70	13·90	0·632	0·368
Tikuna	Peru	122	67·21	27·87	4·92	0·811	0·189
Blackfeet	Montana	95	54·7	40·0	5·3	0·74	0·23
Navajo	New Mexico	361	84·5	14·4	1·1	0·917	0·083
Aborigines	Australia	372	02·4	30·4	67·2	0·176	0·824
Papuans	New Guinea	355	01·1	15·5	83·4	0·088	0·911

Table 4. Percentage frequencies in various populations of eight forms of the Rh blood-group gene

Population	CDE	CDe	CdE	Cde	Genes cDE	cdE	cDe	cde
					Europe			
English	0·1	43·1	0	0·7	13·6	0·8	2·8	38·8
Danes	0·1	42·2	0	1·3	15·1	0·7	1·8	38·8
Germans	0·4	43·9	0	0·6	13·7	1·0	2·6	37·8
Italians	0·4	47·6	0·3	0·7	10·8	0·7	1·6	38·0
Spaniards	0·1	43·2	0	1·9	12·0	0	3·7	38·0
Basques	0	37·6	0	1·5	7·1	0·2	0·5	53·1
					Africa			
Egyptians	0	49·5	0	0	9·0	0	17·3	24·3
Hutu	0	8·3	0	1·6	5·7	0	62·9	21·6
Kikuyu	0	7·3	0	1·4	9·9	1·4	58·5	20·4
Shona (S. Rhodesia)	0	6·9	0	0	6·4	0	62·7	23·9
Bantu (S. Africa)	0	4·7	0	5·8	8·5	0	59·6	21·4
Bushmen	0	9·0	0	0	2·0	0	89·0	0
					Asia			
Yemenite Jews	0·5	56·1	0	1·0	7·9	0	6·4	28·2
East Pakistan	1·6	63·3	0	6·5	7·6	0	3·9	17·1
South Chinese	0·5	75·9	0	0	19·5	0	4·1	0
Japanese	0·4	60·2	0	0	30·8	3·3	0	5·3
					Australasia			
Australian aborigines	2·1	56·4	0	12·9	20·1	0	8·5	0
Papuans	1·6	94·4	0	0	2·0	0	2·0	0
Javanese	1·2	84·0	0	0	8·3	0	6·5	0
Marshallese	0	95·1	0	0	4·4	0	0·5	0
					America			
Eskimos (Greenland)	3·4	72·5	0	0	22·0	0	2·1	0
Chippewa	2·0	33·7	0	0	53·0	3·2	0	8·0
Blood	4·1	47·8	0	0	34·8	3·4	0	9·9
Navajo	1·3	43·1	0	0	27·7	0	28·0	0

Bibliography

Alēkseev, V. P., *Ot žlvotnyh-k čeloveku* (Moscow: Sov. Rossija, 1969). 'O pervičnoj differenciacii čelovečestva na rasy, Pervičnye očagi rascobrazovanija', *Sov. ětnografija*, No. 1 (1969), pp. 12–24.

Alēkseev, 'Deklaracija o rase i rasovyh predrassudkah' (Unesco, Paris, 26 September 1967), *Voprosy antropologii*, No. 30 (1968), p. 160.

Allen, J. A., 'The influence of physical conditions in the genesis of species', *Annual Report Smithsonian Institute for 1905* (Washington, 1906), pp. 374–402.

Allison, A. C., 'The sickle-cell and haemoglobin C genes in some African populations', *Annals Human Genetics*, Vol. 21, No. 1 (1956), pp. 67–83.

Allison, A. C., 'Genetic factors in resistance to malaria', *Annals New York Academy of Science*, Vol. 91, No. 3, (1961), pp. 710–29.

Allison, A. C., 'Inherited factors in blood conferring resistance to protozoa', in *Immunity to Protozoa* (Oxford: Blackwell Scientific, 1963), pp. 109–22.

Allison, A. C., 'Polymorphism and natural selection in human populations', *Cold Spring Harbor Symposium Quantative Biology*, Vol. 29 (1964), pp. 137–49.

Baker, P. T., 'The biological adaptation of man to hot deserts', *American Naturalist*, Vol. 92, No. 867 (1958), pp. 337–57.

Barnicot, N. A., 'Climatic factors in the evolution of human populations', *Cold Spring Harbor Symposium Quantitative Biology*, Vol. 24 (1959), pp. 115–29.

Biasutti, R., *Le razze e i popoli della terra* (3rd ed.) (t.l. Torino, 1959).

Birdsell, J. B., 'Some population problems involving Pleistocene man,' *Cold Spring Harbor Symposium Quantitative Biology*, Vol. 22 (1957), pp. 47–69.

Blum, H. F., *Carcinogenesis by Ultraviolet Light* (Princeton, N.J.: Princeton University Press, 1959).

Blum, H. F., 'Does the melanin pigment of human skin have adaptive value?' *Quarterly Review Biology*, Vol. 36, No. 1 (1961), pp. 50–63.

Boyd, W. C., *Genetics and the Races of Man* (Boston: Little, Brown and Co., 1950), pp. 210–51 (Blood Groups).

Boyd, W. C., 'The contributions of genetics to anthropology'. in A. Kroeber (ed.), *Anthropology Today* (Chicago: University of Chicago Press 1953), pp. 488–506.

Bridges, E. L., *The Uttermost Part of the Earth* (N.Y.: Dutton, 1950).

Coon, C. S., Garn, S. M., Birdsell, J. B., *Races: A Study of the Problems of Race Formation in Man* (Springfield, Illinois: Thomas, 1950).

Cowles, R. B., 'Some ecological factors bearing on the origin and evolution of pigment in the human skin', *American Naturalist*, Vol. 93, No. 872 (1959), pp. 283–93.

Dobzhansky, Th., *Mankind Evolving* (New Haven-London: Yale University Press, 1962).

Dubinin, N. P., 'Genetiko-avtomaticeskie processy i ih značenie dlja mehanizma organiceskoj ėvoljucii', *Žurnal ėksperim, biol.*, Vol 7, No. 5–6 (1931), pp. 468–79.

Dubinin, N. P. and Romasov, D. D., 'Genetičeskoe stroenie vida i ego ėvoljucija', *Biol. žurnal*, Vol. 1, No. 5–6 (1932), pp. 52–95.

Dubinin, N. P., 'Eksperimental'nyj analiz ěkogenotipov Drosophila melanogaster', *Bibl. žurnal*, Vol. 3, No. 1 (1934), pp. 166–206 and 207–16 (parts I and II).

Fleure, H., 'The distribution of types of skin colour', *Geographical Review*, Vol. 35 (1945).

Garn, S., *Human races* (Springfield, Illinois: Thomas, 1961).

Glass B., 'The effect of changes in the physical environment on genetic change', in J. D. Roslansky (ed.) *Genetics and the Future of Man* (Amsterdam: North-Holland Publ. Co., 1966), pp. 23–47.

Gloger, C., *Das Abhändern de Vögel durch Einfluss des Klimas, Nach zoologischen, zunächst von den europäischen, Landvögeln entnommenen Beonachtungen dargestellt, mit den entsprechenden Erfahrungen bei den europäischen Säugetieren verglichen und durch Tahtsachen aus dem Gebiete der Physiologie, der Physik und der physischen Geographie erläutert* (Breslau, 1833).

Gottesman, I. I., 'A sampler of human behavioral genetics' in Th. Dobzhansky, N. K. Hecht, W. C. Steere (eds.), *Evolutionary biology*, Vol. 2 (1968), pp. 276–320.

Hauser, P. M., 'Demographic dimensions of world politics', *Science*, Vol. 131, No. 3414 (1960), pp. 1641–7.

Landsteiner, K., 'Zur Kenntnis der antifermentativen, lytischen und agglutinierenden Wirkungen des Blutserums und der Lymphe', *Cbl. Bakteriol.*, Abt.1, Originale, Vol. 27 (1900), pp. 357–62.

Landsteiner, K., 'Ueber Agglutinationserscheinungen normalen menschlichen Blutes', *Wien. Klin. Wochenschr.*, Vol. 14, No. 146 (1901), pp. 1132–4.

Landsteiner, K., Levine, P., 'Further observations on individual differences of human blood', *Proceedings of the Society of Experimental Biology and Medicine*, Vol. 24, No. 9 (1927), pp. 941–2.

Landstener, K., Wiener, A. S., 'An agglutinable factor in human blood recognized by immune sera for Rhesus blood', *Proceedings of the Society of Experimental Biology and Medicine*, Vol. 43, No. 1 (1940), p. 223.

Lenz, F., *Menschliche Auslese und Rassenhygiene* (Eugenik) (3, Aufl.) (München, 1931), p. 415.

Mayr, E., *Systematics and the Origin of Species* (N.Y.: Columbia University Press, 1942).

Mourant, A. E., *The Distribution of the Human Blood Groups* (Oxford: Blackwell Scientific, 1954).

Mourant, A. E., Kopeć, A. C., Domaniewska-Sobczak, K., *The ABO Blood Groups: Comprehensive Tables and Maps of World Distribution* (Oxford: Blackwell Scientific, 1958).

Nesturh, M. F., *Čelověčeskie* (3rd ed.) (Moscow: Prosvescenie, 1965).

Nesturh, M. F., *Proishoždenie čeloveka* (2nd ed). (Moscow, Nauka, 1970).

Newman, M. T., 'The application of ecological rules to the racial anthropology of the aboriginal New World', *American Anthropologist*, Vol. 55 (1953), pp. 311–27.

Newman, R. W., Munro, E. H., 'The relation of climate and body size in US males', *American Journal of Physical Anthropology*, New Series, Vol. 13, No. 1 (1955), pp. 1–17.

Ray, C., 'The application of Bergmann's and Allen's rules to the poikilotherms', *Journal of Morphology*, Vol. 106 (1960), pp. 85–108.

Reche, O., Lehmann, W., 'Die Genetik der Rassenbildung beim Menschen', in G. Heberer (ed.) *Die Evolution der Organismen* (2nd Aufl.) (Stuttgart: Fischer, 1959), pp. 1143–91.

Rensch, B., *Homo sapiens. Vom Tier zum Halbgott* (Göttingen: Vandenhoeck and Ruprecht, 1959).

Roberts, D. F., 'Body weight, race, and climate', *American Journal of Physical Anthropology*, New Series, Vol. 11, No. 4 (1953), pp. 533–58.

Roginskij, J. J. 'K voprosu o periodizacii processa čelovečeskoj ěvoljucii', *Antropol. žurnal*, No. 4 (1936), pp. 346–51.

Roginskij, J. J. 'Problema proishoždenija mongol'skogo rasovogo tipa', *Antropol. žurnal*, No. 2 (1937).

Roginskij, J. J. 'Problema proishoždenija Homo Sapiens', *Uspehi sovremen. biol.*, Vol. 9, No. 1 (1938), pp. 115–36.

Roginskij, J. J., *Teorii monocentrizma i policentrizma v probleme proishoždenija čeloveka i ego ras* (Moscow: Ed. MGU, 1949).

Rosenberg, A., 'Der Kampf um die Weltanschauung', *Völk. Beob.*, No. 23 (1934), p. 11.

Ryčkov, J. G., *Reakcija populjacij na izoljaciju. Problemy ěvoljucii*, Vol. 1 (Novosibirsk: Nauka, 1968), pp. 212–36.

Scholander, P. F., Walters, V., Hock, R., Irving, L., 'Body insulation of some arctic and tropical mammals and birds', *Biolical Bulletin*, Vol. 99, No. 2 (1950), pp. 225–36.

Scholander, P. F., Hock, R., Walters, V., Johnson, F., Irving, L., 'Heat regulation in some arctic and tropical mammals and birds', *Biolical Bulletin*, Vol. 99, No. 2 (1950a), 237–58.

Scholander, P. F., Hock, R., Walters, V., Irving, L., 'Adaptation to cold in arctic and tropical mammals and birds in relation to body temperature, insulation, and basal metabolic rate', *Biolical Bulletin*, Vol. 99, No. 2 (1950b), pp. 259–71.

Scholander, P. F., 'Evolution of climatic adaptations in homeotherms', *Evolution*, Vol. 9, No. 1 (1955), pp. 15–26.

Scholander, P. F., Hammel, H. T., Hart, J. S., Le Messurier, D. H., Steen, J., 'Cold adaptation in Australian aborigenes', *Journal of Applied Physiology*, Vol. 13 (1958), pp. 211–18.

Scholander, P. F., Hammel, H. T., Andersen, K. L., Løning, Y., 'Metabolic acclimation to cold in man', *Journal of Applied Physiology*, Vol. 12, No. 1 (1958), pp. 1–8.

Schwidetcky, I., 'Selektionstheorie und Rassenbildung beim Menschen', *Experientia*, Vol. 8, No. 3 (1952), pp. 85–98.

Semenov, J. I., 'V. I. Lenine o kategorii "obščestverno-ėkonomičeskij uklad" ', *Učenye zapiski Krasnojarskogo pedinstituta*, Vol. 18 (1960).

Semenov, J. I., 'V. I. Lenine o tvorceskom haraktere čelovečeskogo poznanija', *Učenye zapiski Krasnojarskogo pedinstituta*, Vol. 18 (1960).

Semenov, J. I., 'O Meste "Klassičeskih neandertal 'sev v čelovečeskoj ėvoljucii" ', *Vestnik Akad. nauk SSSR*, No. 3 (1960).

Semenov, J. I., *Vozniknovenie čelovečeskogo obščestva* (Krasnojarsk, 1962).

Semenov, J. I., *Social Life of Early Man* (New York, 1961).

Semenov, J. I., 'Učenie Morgana, Marksism i sovremennaja ėtnografija', *Sov. ėtnografija*, No. 4 (1964), pp. 170–85.

Semenov, J. I., 'Vozniknovenie obščestvennyh otnoščenij', V sbor, *U istokov čelovečestva* (Moscow, 1964).

Semenov, J. I., *Gruppovoj brak, ego priroda mesto v ėvoljucii semejno-bracnyh otnšenij* (Moscow, Nauka, 1964).

Semenov, J. I., 'Problema social'no-ėkonomičeskogo stroja Drevnego Vostoka', *Narody Azii i Afriki*, No. 4 (1965), pp. 69–89.

Semenov, J. I., *Kak vozniklo čelovečestvo* (Moscow, Nauka, 1966).

Stern, C., *Principles of Human Genetics* (2nd ed.) (San Francisco-London, 1960).

Walter, H., 'Der Zusammenhang von Hautfarbenverteilung und Intensität der ultravioletten Strahlung', *Homo*, Vol. 9, No. 1 (1958), pp. 1–13.

Race and History[*]

by CLAUDE LÉVI-STRAUSS

Professor, Laboratoire d'anthropologie sociale du Collège de France et de l'Ecole pratique des hautes études, Paris

RACE AND CULTURE

It may seem somewhat surprising, in a series of booklets intended to combat racial prejudice, to speak of the contributions made by various races of men to world civilisation. It would be a waste of time to devote so much talent and effort to demonstrating that, in the present state of scientific knowledge, there is no justification for asserting that any one race is intellectually superior or inferior to another, if we were, in the end, indirectly to countenance the concept of race by seeming to show that the great ethnic groups constituting human kind as a whole have, as such, made their own peculiar contributions to the common heritage.

Nothing could be further from our intentions, for such a course of action would simply result in an inversion of the racist doctrine. To attribute special psychological characteristics to the biological races, with a positive definition, is as great a departure from scientific truth as to do so with a negative definition. It must not be forgotten that Gobineau, whose work was the progenitor of racist theories, regarded 'the inequality of the human races' as qualitative, not quantitative; in his view, the great primary races of early man—the white, the yellow and the black—differed in their special aptitudes rather than in their absolute value. Degeneration resulted from miscegenation, rather than from the relative position of individual races in a common scale of values; it was therefore the fate in store for all mankind, since all mankind, irrespective of race, was bound to exhibit an increasing intermixture of blood. The original sin of anthropology, however, consists in its confusion of the idea of race, in the purely biological sense (assuming that there is any factual basis for the idea, even in this

[*] First published in *The Race Question in Modern Science* (Paris: Unesco, 1952).

limited field—which is disputed by modern genetics), with the sociological and psychological productions of human civilisations. Once he had made this mistake, Gobineau was inevitably committed to the path leading from an honest intellectual error to the unintentional justification of all forms of discrimination and exploitation.

When, therefore, in this paper, we speak of the contributions of different races of men to civilisation, we do not mean that the cultural contributions of Asia or Europe, Africa or America are in any way distinctive because these continents are, generally speaking, inhabited by peoples of different racial stocks. If their contributions are distinctive—and there can be little doubt that they are—the fact is to be accounted for by geographical, historical and sociological circumstances, not by special aptitudes inherent in the anatomical or physiological make-up of the black, yellow or white man. It seemed to us, however, that the very effort made in this series of booklets to prove this negative side of the argument, involved a risk of pushing into the background another very important aspect of the life of man—the fact that the development of human life is not everywhere the same but rather takes form in an extraordinary diversity of societies and civilisations. This intellectual, aesthetic and sociological diversity is in no way the outcome of the biological differences, in certain observable features, between different groups of men; it is simply a parallel phenomenon in a different sphere. But, at the same time, we must note two important respects in which there is a sharp distinction. First, the order of magnitude is different. There are many more human cultures than human races, since the first are to be counted in thousands and the second in single units; two cultures developed by men of the same race may differ as much as, or more than, two cultures associated with groups of entirely different racial origin. Second, in contrast to the diversity of races, where interest is confined to their historical origin or their distribution over the face of the world, the diversity of cultures gives rise to many problems; it may be wondered whether it is an advantage or a disadvantage for human kind, and there are many subsidiary questions to be considered under this general head.

Last and most important, the nature of the diversity must be investigated even at the risk of allowing the racial prejudices whose biological foundation has so lately been destroyed to develop again on new grounds. It would be useless to argue the man in the street out of attaching an intellectual or moral significance to the fact of having a black or white skin, straight or frizzy hair, unless we had an answer to another question which, as experience proves he will immediately ask: if there are no innate racial aptitudes, how can we explain the fact that the white man's civilisation has made the tremendous advances with which we are all familiar while the civilisations of the coloured peoples have lagged behind, some of them having come only half way along the road, and others being still thousands or tens of thousands of years behind the times? We cannot therefore claim to have formulated a convincing denial of the inequality of the human *races*, so long as we fail to consider the problem of the inequality—or diversity—of human *cultures*, which is in fact—however unjustifiably—closely associated with it in the public mind.

THE DIVERSITY OF CULTURES

If we are to understand how, and to what extent, the various human cultures differ from one another, and whether these differences conflict or cancel one another out or, on the contrary, are all instrumental in forming a harmonious whole, the first thing to do is to draw up a list of them. But here we immediately run into difficulties, for we are forced to recognise that human cultures do not all differ from one another in the same way or on the same level. First, we have societies co-existing in space, some close together and some far apart but, on the whole, contemporary with one another. Second, we have social systems that have followed one another in time, of which we can have no knowledge by direct experience. Anyone can become an ethnographer and go out to share the life of a particular society which interests him. But not even the historian or archeologist can have any personal contact with a vanished civilisation; all his knowledge must be gleaned from the writings or the monuments which it or other societies have left behind. Nor must we forget that those contemporary societies which have no knowledge of writing, like those which we call 'savage' or 'primitive', were preceded by other forms of society of which we can learn nothing, even indirectly. If we are honest in drawing up our list, we shall have, in such cases, to leave blank spaces, which will probably be far more numerous than the spaces in which we feel we can make some entry. The first thing to be noted is therefore that, in fact in the present, as well as in fact and in the very nature of things in the past, the diversity of human cultures is much greater and richer than we can ever hope to appreciate to the full.

But however humble we may be in our approach, and however well we may appreciate our limitations in this respect, there are other problems to be considered. What are we to understand by 'different' cultures? Some cultures appear to qualify for this description, but, if they are derived from a common stock, they cannot differ in the same way as two societies which have had no contacts with one another at any stage of their development. For instance, the ancient Inca Empire in Peru and the Kingdom of Dahomey in Africa are more absolutely different than are, let us say, England and the United States today, although these two societies also are to be regarded as distinct. Conversely, societies which have been in very close contact since a recent date give the impression of representing a single civilisation, whereas in fact they have reached the present stage by different paths, which we are not entitled to ignore. Forces working in contrary directions operate simultaneously in human societies, some being conducive to the preservation and even the accentuation of particularism, while others tend to promote convergence and affinity. Striking instances are to be found in the study of language for, while languages whose origin is the same tend to develop differences from one another—e.g. Russian, French and English—languages of different origin which are spoken in adjacent territories developed common characteristics: Russian, for example, has developed differences from other Slavic languages in certain respects and grown closer, at least in certain phonetic features, to the Finno–Ugrian and Turkish languages spoken in its immediate geographic neighbourhood.

A study of such facts—and we could easily find similar instances in other aspects of civilisation, such as social institutions, art and religion—leads us to ask whether, in the inter-relations of human societies, there may not be an *optimum* degree of diversity, which they cannot surpass but which they can also not fall short of without incurring risks. This optimum would vary according to the number of societies, their numerical strength, their geographical distance from one another, and the means of communication (material and intellectual) at their disposal. The problem of diversity does not, in fact, arise solely with regard to the inter-relations of cultures; the same problem is found within each individual society with regard to the inter-relations of the constituent groups: the various castes, classes, professions or religious denominations develop certain differences, which each of them considers to be extremely important. It may be wondered whether this internal differentiation does not tend to increase when the society becomes larger and otherwise more homogeneous; this may perhaps have been what happened in ancient India, where the caste system developed as a sequel to the establishment of the Aryan hegemony.

It is thus clear that the concept of the diversity of human cultures cannot be static. It is not the diversity of a collection of lifeless samples or the diversity to be found in the arid pages of a catalogue. Men have doubtless developed differentiated cultures as a result of geographical distance, the special features of their environment, or their ignorance of the rest of mankind; but this would be strictly and absolutely true only if every culture or society had been born and had developed without the slightest contact with any others. Such a case never occurs however, except possibly in such exceptional instances as that of the Tasmanians (and, even then, only for a limited period). Human societies are never alone; when they appear to be most divided, the division is always between groups or clusters of societies. It would not, for instance, be an unwarranted presumption that the civilisations of North and South America were cut off from almost all contacts with the rest of the world for a period lasting from 10,000 to 25,000 years. But the great section of mankind thus isolated consisted of a multitude of societies, great and small, having very close contacts with one another. Moreover, side by side with the differences due to isolation, there are others equally important which are due to proximity, bred of the desire to assert independence and individuality. Many customs have come into being, not because of an intrinsic need for them or of a favourable chance, but solely because of a group's desire not to be left behind by a neighbouring group which was laying down specific rules in matters in which the first group had not yet thought of prescribing laws. We should not, therefore, be tempted to a piece-meal study of the diversity of human cultures, for that diversity depends less on the isolation of the various groups than on the relations between them.

THE ETHNOCENTRIC ATTITUDE

Yet it would seem that the diversity of cultures has seldom been recognised by men for what it is—a natural phenomenon resulting from the direct or indirect contacts between societies; men have tended rather to regard diversity as something abnormal or outrageous; advances in our knowledge of these matters served less to destroy this illusion and replace it by a more accurate picture than to make us accept it or accommodate ourselves to it.

The attitude of longest standing which no doubt has a firm psychological foundation, as it tends to reappear in each one of us when we are caught unawares, is to reject out of hand the cultural institutions—ethical, religious, social or aesthetic which are furthest removed from those with which we identify ourselves. 'Barbarous habits', 'not what we do', 'ought not to be allowed', etc. are all crude reactions indicative of the same instinctive antipathy, the same repugnance for ways of life, thought or belief to which we are unaccustomed. The ancient world thus lumped together everything not covered by Greek (and later the Greco-Roman) culture under the heading of 'barbarian': Western civilisation later used the term 'savage' in the same sense. Underlying both these epithets is the same sort of attitude. The word 'barbarian' is probably connected etymologically with the inarticulate confusion of birdsong, in contra-distinction to the significant sounds of human speech, while 'savage'—'of the woods'—also conjures up a brutish way of life as opposed to human civilisation. In both cases, there is a refusal even to admit the fact of cultural diversity; instead, anything which does not conform to the standard of the society in which the individual lives is denied the name of culture and relegated to the realm of nature.

There is no need to dwell on this naïve attitude, which is nevertheless deeply rooted in most men, since this article—and all those in the same series—in fact refutes it. It will be enough, in this context, to note that a rather interesting paradox lies behind it. This attitude of mind, which excludes 'savages' (or any people one may choose to regard as savages) from human kind, is precisely the attitude most strikingly characteristic of those same savages. We know, in fact, that the concept of humanity as covering all forms of the human species, irrespective of race or civilisation, came into being very late in history and is by no means widespread.

Even where it seems strongest, there is no certainty—as recent history proves—that it is safe from the dangers of misunderstanding or retrogression. So far as great sections of the human species have been concerned, however, and for tens of thousands of years, there seems to have been no hint of any such idea. Humanity is confined to the borders of the tribe, the linguistic group or even, in some instances, to the village, so that many so-called primitive peoples describe themselves as 'the men' (or sometimes—though hardly more discreetly—as 'the good', 'the excellent', 'the well-achieved'), thus implying that the other tribes, groups or villages have no part in the human virtues or even in human nature, but that their members are, at best, 'bad', 'wicked', 'ground-monkeys', or 'lousy eggs'. They often go further and rob the outsider of even this modicum of actuality, by referring to him as a 'ghost' or an 'apparition'. In this way, curious situations arise in which two parties at issue present a tragic reflection of one another's attitude. In the Greater Antilles, a few years after the discovery of America, while the Spaniards were sending out Commissions of investigation to discover whether or not the natives had a soul, the latter spent their time drowning white prisoners in order to ascertain, by long observation, whether or not their bodies would decompose.

This strange and tragic anecdote is a good illustration of the paradox inherent in cultural relativism (which we shall find again elsewhere in other forms); the more we claim to discriminate between cultures and customs as good and bad, the more completely do we identify ourselves with those we would condemn. By refusing to consider as human those who seem to us to be the most 'savage' or 'barbarous' of their representatives, we merely adopt one of their own characteristic attitudes. The barbarian is, first and foremost, the man who believes in barbarism.

Admittedly the great philosophic and religious systems which humanity has evolved—Buddhism, Christianity or Islam, the Stoic, Kantian or Marxist doctrines—have constantly condemned this aberration. But the simple statement that all men are naturally equal and should be bound together in brotherhood, irrespective of race or culture, is not very satisfactory to the intellect, for it overlooks a factual diversity which we cannot help but see; and we are not entitled, either in theory or in practice, to behave as if there were no such diversity, simply because we say that it does not affect the essence of the question. The preamble to Unesco's second

Statement on the race problem very rightly observes that the thing which convinces the man in the street that there are separate races is 'the immediate evidence of his senses when he sees an African, a European, an Asiatic and an American Indian together'.

Likewise, the strength and the weakness of the great declarations of human rights has always been that, in proclaiming an ideal, they too often forget that man grows to man's estate surrounded, not by humanity in the abstract, but by a traditional culture, where even the most revolutionary changes leave whole sectors quite unaltered. Such declarations can themselves be accounted for by the situation existing at a particular moment in time and in particular space. Faced with the two temptations of condemning things which are offensive to him emotionally or of denying differences which are beyond his intellectual grasp, modern man has launched out on countless lines of philosophical and sociological speculation in a vain attempt to achieve a compromise between these two contradictory poles, and to account for the diversity of cultures while seeking, at the same time, to eradicate what still shocks and offends him in that diversity.

But however much these lines of speculation may differ, and however strange some of them may be, they all, in point of fact, come back to a single formula, which might probably best be described by the expression *false evolutionism*. In what does this consist? It is really an attempt to wipe out the diversity of cultures while pretending to accord it full recognition. If the various conditions in which human societies are found, both in the past and in far distant lands, are treated as *phases* or *stages* in a single line of development, starting from the same point and leading to the same end, it seems clear that the diversity is merely apparent. Humanity is claimed to be one and the same everywhere, but this unity and identity can be achieved only gradually; the variety of cultures we find in the world illustrates the several stages in a process which conceals the ultimate reality or delays our recognition of it.

This may seem an over-simplification in view of the enormous achievements of Darwinism. But Darwinism is in no way implicated here, for the doctrine of biological evolution, and the pseudo-evolutionism we have in mind, are two very different things. The first was developed as a great working hypothesis, based on observations in which there was very little need for interpretation. The various types in the genealogy of the horse, for instance, can be arranged in an evolutive series for two reasons: firstly, a horse can only be sired by a horse; and secondly, skeletons varying gradually from the most recent to the most ancient forms are found at different levels in the earth, representing earlier and earlier periods of history as we dig deeper. It is thus highly probable that *Hipparion* was the real ancestor of *Equus caballus*. The same reasoning is probably applicable to the human species and the different races constituting it. When, however, we turn from biology to culture, things become far more complicated. We may find material objects in the soil, and note that the form or manufacture of a certain type of object varies progressively according to the depth of the geological strata. But an axe does not give birth to an axe in the physical sense that an animal gives birth to an animal. Therefore, to say that an axe has developed out of another axe is to speak metaphorically and with a rough approximation to truth, but without the scientific exactitude which a similar expression has in biological parlance. What is true of material objects whose physical presence in the earth can be related to determinable periods, is even more true of institutions, beliefs and customs, whose past history is generally a closed book to us. The idea of biological evolution is a hypothesis with one of the highest coefficients of probability to be found in any of the natural sciences, whilst the concept of social or cultural evolution offers at best a tempting, but suspiciously convenient method of presenting facts.

Incidentally, this difference, which is too often overlooked, between true and false evolutionism can be explained by the dates of their development. The doctrine of biological evolution admittedly gave sociological evolutionism a decided fillip but the latter actually preceded the former. Without going back to the views which Pascal took over from antiquity, and looking upon humanity as a living being passing through the successive stages of childhood, adolescence and maturity, we may see in the eighteenth century the elaboration of all the basic images which were later to be bandied about—Vico's 'spirals', and his 'three ages' foreshadowing Comte's 'three states', and Condorcet's 'stairway'. Spencer and Tylor, the two founders of social evolutionism, worked out and published their doctrine before the appearance of the *Origin of Species*, or without having read that work. Prior in date to the scientific theory of biological evolution, social evolutionism is thus too often merely a pseudo-scientific mask for an old philosophical problem, which there is no certainty of our ever solving by observation and inductive reasoning.

ARCHAIC AND PRIMITIVE CULTURES

We have already suggested that, from its own point of view, each society may divide cultures into three categories; contemporary cultures found in another part of the world; cultures which have developed in approximately the same area as the society in question, but at an earlier period; and finally, those earlier in time and occupying a different area in space.

We have seen that our knowledge of these three groups cannot be equally exact. In the last case, when we are concerned with cultures which have left behind no written records or buildings, and which employed very primitive techniques (as is true for one half of the inhabited world and for 90–99 per cent, varying according to region, of the time since the dawn of civilisation), it may be said that we can really know nothing of them, and that our best efforts at understanding them can be no more than suppositions.

On the other hand, there is a great temptation to try to arrange cultures in the first category in an order representing a succession in time. It is, after all, natural that contemporary societies with no knowledge of electricity and the steam engine should call to mind the corresponding phase in the development of Western civilisation. It is natural to compare native tribes, ignorant of writing and metallurgy but depicting figures on walls of rock and manufacturing stone implements, with the primitive forms of that same civilisation, which, as the traces left behind in the caves of France and Spain bear witness, looked similar. It is in such matters that false evolutionism has mainly been given free rein. But the almost irresistible temptation to indulge in such comparisons whenever opporunity offers (is not the Western traveller wont to see the 'Middle Ages' in the East, 'the days of Louis XIV' in pre-1914 Peking, and 'Stone Age' among the Aborigines in Australia or New Guinea?), is extraordinarily dangerous. We can know only certain aspects of a vanished civilisation; and the older the civilisation, the fewer are those aspects since we can only have knowledge of things which have survived the assaults of time. There is therefore a tendency to take the part for the whole and to conclude that, since *certain* aspects of two civilisations (one contemporary and the other lost in the past) show similarities, there must be resemblances in *all* aspects. Not only is this reasoning logically indefensible but, in many cases, it is actually refuted by the facts.

Until a relatively recent date, the Tasmanians and Patagonians used chipped stone implements, and certain Australian and American tribes still make such tools. But studying these teaches us very little about the use of similar tools in the palaeolithic period. How were the famous 'hand-axes' used? And yet their purpose must have been so specific that their form and manufacture remained rigidly standardised for one or two hundred thousand years over an area stretching from England to South Africa and from France to China. What was the use of the extraordinary flat, triangular Levalloisian pieces? Hundreds of them are found in deposits and yet we have no hypothesis to explain them. What were the so-called *Bâtons de commandement*, made of reindeer antler? What technical methods were used in the Tardenoisian cultures, which have left behind them an incredible number of tiny fragments of chipped stone, in an infinite variety of geometrical shapes, but very few tools adapted to the size of the human hand? All these questions indicate that there may well be one resemblance between palaeolithic societies and certain contemporary native societies; both alike have used chipped-stone tools. But, even in the technological sphere, it is difficult to go further than that; the employment of the material, the types of instruments and therefore the purpose for which they were used, were quite different, and one group can teach us very little about the other in this respect. How then can we gain any idea of the language, social institutions or religious beliefs of the peoples concerned?

According to one of the commonest explanations derived from the theory of cultural evolution, the rock paintings left behind by the middle palaeolithic societies were used for purposes of magic ritual in connection with hunting. The line of reasoning is as follows: primitive peoples of the present day practise hunting rites, which often seem to us to serve no practical purpose; the many prehistoric paintings on rock walls deep in caves appear to us to serve no practical purpose; the artists who executed them were hunters; they were therefore used in hunting rites. We have only to set out his implicit argument to see how entirely inconsequent it is. It is, incidentally, most current among non-specialists, for ethnographers, who have had actual dealings with the primitive peoples whom the pseudo-scientist is so cheerfully prepared to serve up for whatever purpose happens to concern him at the moment, with little regard for the true nature of human cultures, agree that there is nothing in the facts observed to justify any sort of hypothesis about these paintings. While we are on the subject of cave paintings, we must point out that, except for the cave paintings found in South Africa (which some hold to be the work of native peoples in recent times), primitive art is as far removed from Magdalenian and Aurignacian art as from contemporary European art, for it is marked by a very high degree of stylisation, sometimes leading to complete distortion, while prehistoric art displays a striking realism. We might be tempted to regard this characteristic as the origin of European art; but even that would be untrue, since, in the same area, palaeolithic art was succeeded by other forms of a different character; the identity of geographical position does not alter the fact different peoples have followed one another on the same stretch of earth, knowing nothing or caring nothing for the work of their predecessors, and each bringing in conflicting beliefs, techniques and styles of their own.

The state which the civilisations of America had reached before Columbus' discovery is reminiscent of the neolithic period in Europe. But this comparison does not stand up to closer examination either; in Europe, agriculture and the domestication of animals moved forward in step, whereas in America, while agriculture was exceptionally highly developed, the use of domestic animals was almost entirely unknown or, at all events, extremely restricted. In America, stone tools were still used in a type of agriculture which, in Europe, is associated with the beginnings of metallurgy.

There is no need to quote further instances, for there is another and much more fundamental difficulty in the way of any effort, after discovering the richness and individuality of human cultures, to treat all as the counterparts of a more or less remote period in Western civilisation: broadly speaking (and for the time being leaving aside America, to which we shall return later), all human societies have behind them a past of approximately equal length. If we were to treat certain societies as 'stages' in the development of certain others, we should be forced to admit that, while something was happening in the latter, nothing—or very little—was going on in the former. In fact, we are inclined to talk of 'peoples with no history' (sometimes implying that they are the happiest). This ellipsis means that their history is and will always be unknown to us, not that they actually have no history. For tens and even hundreds of millenaries, men there loved, hated, suffered, invented and fought as others did. In actual fact, there are no peoples still in their childhood; all are adult, even those who have not kept a diary of their childhood and adolescence.

We might, of course, say that human societies have made a varying use of their past time and that some have even wasted it; that some were dashing on while others were loitering along the road. This would suggest a distinction between two types of history: a progressive, acquisitive type, in which discoveries and inventions are accumulated to build up great civilisations; and another type, possibly equally active and calling for the utilisation of as much talent, but lacking the gift of synthesis which is the hallmark of the first. All innovations, instead of being added to previous innovations tending in the same direction, would be absorbed into a sort of undulating tide which, once in motion, could never be canalised in a permanent direction.

This conception seems to us to be far more flexible and capable of differentiation than the over-simplified views we have dealt with in the preceding paragraphs. We may well give it a place in our tentative interpretation of the diversity of cultures without doing injustice to any of them. But before we reach that stage there are several other questions to be considered.

THE IDEA OF PROGRESS

We must first consider the cultures in the second category we defined above: the historical predecessors of the 'observer's' culture. The situation here is far more complicated than in the cases we have considered earlier. For in this case the hypothesis of evolution, which appears so tenuous and doubtful as a means of classifying contemporary societies occupying different areas in space, seems hard to refute, and would indeed appear to be directly borne out by the facts. We know, from the concordant evidence of archaeology, prehistoric study and palaeontology, that the area now known as Europe was first inhabited by various species of the genus *Homo*, who used rough chipped flint implements; that these first cultures were succeeded by others in which stone was first more skilfully fashioned by chipping, and later ground and polished, while the working of bone and ivory was also perfected; that pottery, weaving, agriculture and stock rearing then came in, associated with a developing use of metals, the stages of which can also be distinguished. These successive forms therefore appear to represent evolution and progress; some are superior and others inferior. But, if all this is true, it is surely inevitable that the distinctions thus made must affect our attitude towards contemporary forms of culture exhibiting similar variations. The conclusions we reached above are thus in danger of being compromised by this new line of reasoning.

The progress which humanity has made since its earliest days is so clear and so striking that an attempt to question it could be no more than an exercise of rhetoric. And yet, it is not as easy as it seems to arrange mankind's achievements in a regular and continuous series. About 50 years ago, scholars had a delightfully simple scheme to represent man's advance: the old stone age, the new stone age, the copper, bronze and iron ages. But in this, everything was over-simplified. We now suspect that stone was sometimes worked simultaneously by the chipping and polishing methods; when the latter replaced the former, it did not simply represent a natural technical advance from the previous stage, but also an attempt to copy, in stone, the metal arms and tools possessed by other civilisations, more 'advanced' but actually contemporary with their imitators. On the other hand, potterymaking, which used to be regarded as a distinctive feature of the so-called 'polished stone age', was associated with the chipping process of fashioning stone in certain parts of northern Europe.

To go no further than the period when chipped-stone implements were manufactured, known as the palaeolithic age, it was thought only a few years ago that the variants of this method—characteristic of the 'core-tool', 'flake-tool' and 'blade-tool' industries—represented a historical progression in three stages, known respectively as lower palaeolithic, middle palaeolithic and upper palaeolithic. It is now recognised that these variants were all found together, representing not stages in a single advance, but aspects or, to use the technical term, 'facies' of a technique which may not have been static but whose changes and variations were extremely complex. In fact, the Levallois culture which we have already mentioned, and which reached its peak between the 250th and 70th millenary B.C., attained to a perfection in the art of chipping stone which was scarcely equalled until the end of the neolithic period, 245,000 to 65,000 years later, and which we would find it extremely difficult to copy today.

Everything we have said about the development of cultures is also true of races, although (as the orders of magnitude are different) it is impossible to correlate the two processes. In Europe, Neanderthal Man was not anterior to the oldest known forms of *Homo sapiens*; the latter were his contemporaries and maybe even his predecessors. And it is possible that the most diverse types of *Hominidae* may have been contemporary even though they did not occupy the same parts of the world—'pygmies' living in South Africa, 'giants' in China and Indonesia, etc.

Once more, the object of our argument is not to deny the fact of human progress but to suggest that we might be more cautious in our conception of it. As our prehistoric and archaeological knowledge grows, we tend to make increasing use of a spatial scheme of distribution instead of a time scale scheme. The implications are, that 'progress' (if this term may still be used to describe something very different from its first connotation) is neither continuous nor inevitable; its course consists in a series of leaps and bounds, or, as the biologists would say, mutations. These leaps and bounds are not always in the same direction; the general trend may change too, rather like the progress of the knight in chess, who always has several moves open to him but never in the same direction. Advancing humanity can hardly be likened to a person climbing stairs and, with each movement, adding a new step to all those he has already mounted; a more accurate metaphor would be that of a gambler who has staked his money on several dice and, at each throw, sees them scatter over the cloth, giving a different score each time. What he wins on one, he is always liable to lose on another, and it is only occasionally that history is 'cumulative', that is to say, that the scores add up to a lucky combination.

The case of the Americas proves convincingly that 'cumulative' history is not the prerogative of any one civilisation or any one period. Man first came to that enormous continent, no doubt in small nomadic groups crossing the Bering Straits during the final stages of the ice age, at some date which cannot have been much earlier than the 20th millenary B.C. In twenty or twenty-five thousand years, these men produced one of the most amazing examples of 'cumulative' history the world has ever seen: exploring the whole range of the resources of their new natural environment, cultivating a wide variety of plants (besides domesticating certain species of animals) for food, medicines and poisons, and—as nowhere else—using poisonous substances as a staple article of diet (e.g. manioc) or as stimulants or anaesthetics; collecting various

poisons or drugs for use on the animal species particularly susceptible to each of them; and finally developing certain industries,
such as weaving, ceramics and the working of precious metals, to the
highest pitch of perfection. To appreciate this tremendous achievement, we need only assess the contribution which America has
made to the civilisations of the Old World, starting with the potato,
rubber, tobacco and coca (the basis of modern anaesthetics),
representing four pillars of Western culture, though admittedly on very different grounds; followed by maize and ground-
nuts, which were to revolutionise the economy of Africa before
perhaps coming into general use as an article of diet in Europe;
coca, vanilla, the tomato, the pineapple, pepper, several species of
beans, cottons and gourds. Finally, the zero on the use of which
arithmetic and, indirectly, modern mathematics are founded, was
known and employed by the Maya at least 500 years before it was
discovered by the Indian scholars, from whom Europe received it
via the Arabs. Possibly for that reason, the Maya calendar, at the
same period of history, was more accurate than that of the Old
World. Much has already been written on the question whether the
political system of the Inca was socialistic or totalitarian, but, at
all events, the ideas underlying it were close to some of those most
characteristic of the modern world, and the system was several
centuries ahead of similar developments in Europe. The recent
revival of interest in curare would serve to remind us, if a reminder
were needed, that the scientific knowledge of the American Indians
concerning many vegetable substances not used elsewhere in the
world may even now have much to teach the rest of the globe.

'STATIONARY' AND 'CUMULATIVE' HISTORY

The foregoing discussion of the American case would suggest that
we ought to consider the difference between 'stationary history'
and 'cumulative history' rather more carefully. Have we not, perhaps, acknowledged the 'cumulative' character of American history simply because we recognise America as the source of a
number of contributions we have taken from it, or which are
similar to those we ourselves have made? What would be the
observer's attitude towards a civilisation which had concentrated
on developing values of its own, none of which was likely to affect
his civilisation? Would he not be inclined to describe that civilisa-

tion as 'stationary'? In other words, does the distinction between the two types of history depend on the intrinsic nature of the cultures to which the terms are applied, or does it not rather result from the ethnocentric point of view which we always adopt in assessing the value of a different culture? We should thus regard as 'cumulative' any culture developing in a direction similar to our own, that is to say, whose development would appear to us to be significant. Other cultures, on the contrary, would seem to us to be 'stationary', not necessarily because they are so in fact, but because the line of their development has no meaning for us, and cannot be measured in terms of the criteria we employ.

That this is indeed so is apparent from even a brief consideration of the cases in which we apply the same distinction, not in relation to societies other than our own, but within our own society. The distinction is made more often than we might think. People of advanced years generally consider that history during their old age is stationary, in contrast to the cumulative history they saw being made when they were young. A period in which they are no longer actively concerned, when they have no part to play, has no real meaning for them; nothing happens, or what does happen seems to them to be unproductive of good; while their grandchildren throw themselves into the life of that same period with all the passionate enthusiasm which their elders have forgotten. The opponents of political system are disinclined to admit that the system can evolve; they condemn it as a whole, and would excise it from history as a horrible interval when life is at a standstill only to begin again when the interval is over. The supporters of the régime hold quite a different view, especially, we may note, when they take an intimate part, in a high position, in the running of the machine. The quality of the history of a culture or a cultural progression or, to use a more accurate term, its *eventfulness*, thus depends not on its intrinsic qualities but on our situation with regard to it and on the number and variety of our interests involved.

The contrast between progressive and stagnant cultures would thus appear to result, in the first place, from a difference of focus. To a viewer gazing through a microscope focused on a certain distance from the objective, bodies placed even a few hundredths of a millimetre nearer or further away will appear blurred and 'woolly', or may even be invisible; he sees through them. Another comparison may be made to disclose the same illusion. It is the

illustration used to explain the rudiments of the theory of relativity. In order to show that the dimensions and the speed of dis-
placement of a body are not absolute values but depend on the
position of the observer, it is pointed out that, to a traveller sitting
at the window of a train, the speed and length of other trains vary
according to whether they are moving in the same or the contrary
direction. Any member of a civilisation is as closely associated
with it as this hypothetical traveller is with his train for, from birth
onwards, a thousand conscious and unconscious influences in our
environment instil into us a complex system of criteria, consisting
in value judgements, motivations and centres of interest, and including the conscious reflection upon the historical development
of our civilisation which our education imposes and without which
our civilisation would be inconceivable or would seem contrary to
actual behaviour. Wherever we go, we are bound to carry this
system of criteria with us, and external cultural phenomena can be
observed only through the distorting glass it interposes, even when
it does not prevent us from seeing anything at all.

To a very large extent, the distinction between 'moving cultures'
and 'static cultures' is to be explained by a difference of position
similar to that which makes our traveller think that a train,
actually moving, is either travelling forward or stationary. There
is, it is true, a difference, whose importance will be fully apparent
when we reach the stage—already foreshadowed—of seeking to
formulate a general theory of relativity in a sense different from
that of Einstein, i.e. applicable both to the physical and to the social
sciences: the process seems to be identical in both cases, but the
other way round. To the observer of the physical world (as the
example of the traveller shows) systems developing in the same
direction as his own appear to be motionless, while those which
seem to move swiftest are moving in different directions. The reverse is true of cultures, since they appear to us to be in more active
development when moving in the same direction as our own, and
stationary when they are following another line. In the social
sciences, however, speed has only a metaphorical value. If the
comparison is to hold, we must substitute for this factor *information* or *meaning*. We know, of course, that it is possible to accumulate far more information about a train moving parallel to our own
at approximately the same speed (by looking at the faces of the
travellers, counting them, etc.) than about a train which we are
passing or which is passing us at a high speed, or which is gone in

a flash because it is travelling in a different direction. In the extreme case, it passes so quickly that we have only a confused impression of it, from which even the indications of speed are lacking; it is reduced to a momentary obscuration of the field of vision; it is no longer a train; it no longer has any *meaning*. There would thus seem to be some relationship between the physical concept of *apparent movement* and another concept involving alike physics, psychology and sociology—the concept of the *amount of information* capable of passing from one individual to another or from one group to another, which will be determined by the relative diversity of their respective cultures.

Whenever we are inclined to describe a human culture as stagnant or stationary, we should therefore ask ourselves whether its apparent immobility may not result from our ignorance of its true interests, whether conscious or unconscious, and whether, as its criteria are different from our own, the culture in question may not suffer from the same illusion with respect to us. In other words, we may well seem to one another to be quite uninteresting, simply because we are dissimilar.

For the last two or three centuries, the whole trend of Western civilisation has been to equip man with increasingly powerful mechanical resources. If this criterion is accepted, the quantity of energy available for each member of the population will be taken as indicating the relative level of development in human societies. Western civilisation, as represented in North America, will take first place, followed by the European societies, with a mass of Asiatic and African societies, rapidly becoming indistinguishable from one another, bringing up the rear. But these hundreds, or even thousands of societies which are commonly called 'underdeveloped' and 'primitive', and which merge into an undifferentiated mass when regarded from the point of view we have just described (and which is hardly appropriate in relation to them, since they have had no such line of development or, if they have, it has occupied a place of very secondary importance) are by no means identical. From other points of view, they are diametrically opposed to one another; the classification of societies will therefore differ according to the point of view adopted.

If the criterion chosen had been the degree of ability to overcome even the most inhospitable geographical conditions, there can be scarcely any doubt that the Eskimos, on the one hand, and the Bedouins, on the other, would carry off the palm. India has been more successful than any other civilisation in elaborating a philosophical and religious system, and China, a way of life capable of minimising the psychological consequences of over-population. As long as thirteen centuries ago, Islam formulated a theory that all aspects of human life—technological, economic, social and spiritual—are closely inter-related—a theory that has only recently been rediscovered in the West in certain aspects of Marxist thought and in the development of modern ethnology. We are familiar with the pre-eminent position in the intellectual life of the Middle Ages which the Arabs owed to this prophetic vision. The West, for all its mastery of machines, exhibits evidence of only the most elementary understanding of the use and potential resources of that super-machine, the human body. In this sphere, on the contrary, as on the related question of the connection between the physical and the mental, the East and the Far East are several thousand years ahead; they have produced the great theoretical and practical *summae* represented by Yoga in India, the Chinese 'breath-techniques', or the visceral control of the ancient Maoris. The cultivation of plants without soil, which has recently attracted public attention, was practised for centuries by certain Polynesian peoples, who might also have taught the world the art of navigation, and who amazed it, in the eighteenth century, by their revelation of a freer and more generous type of social and ethical organisation than had previously been dreamt of.

In all matters touching on the organisation of the family and the achievement of harmonious relations between the family group and the social group, the Australian aborigines, though backward in the economic sphere, are so far ahead of the rest of mankind that, to understand the careful and deliberate systems of rules they have elaborated, we have to use all the refinements of modern mathematics. It was they in fact who discovered that the ties of marriage represent the very warp and woof of society, while other social institutions are simply embroideries on that background; for, even in modern societies, where the importance of the family tends to be limited, family ties still count for much: their ramifications are less extensive but, at the point where one tie ceases to hold, others, involving other families, immediately come into play. The family connections due to inter-marriage may result in the formation of broad links between a few groups, or of narrow links between a great number of groups; whether they are broad or narrow, however, it is those links which maintain the whole social structure and to which it owes its flexibility. The Australians, with an admirable grasp of the facts, have converted this machinery into terms of theory, and listed the main methods by which it may be produced, with the advantages and drawbacks attaching to each. They have gone further than empirical observation to discover the mathematical laws governing the systems, so that it is no exaggeration to say that they are not merely the founders of general sociology as a whole, but are the real innovators of measurement in the social sciences.

The wealth and boldness of aesthetic imagination found in the Melanesians, and their talent for embodying in social life the most obscure products of the mind's subconscious activity, mark one of the highest peaks to which men have attained in these two directions. The African contribution is more complex, but also less obvious, for we have only recently suspected what an important part the continent had played as the cultural melting pot of the Old World—the place where countless influences came together and mingled to branch out anew or to lie dormant but, in every case, taking a new turn. The Egyptian civilisation, whose importance to mankind is common knowledge, can be understood only when it is viewed as the co-product of Asia and Africa: and the great political systems of ancient Africa, its legal organisation, its philosophical doctrines which for so long remained unknown to Western students, its plastic arts and music, systematically exploring all the opportunities opened up by each of these modes of expression, are all signs of an extraordinarily fertile past. There is, incidentally, direct evidence of this great past in the perfection of the ancient African methods of working bronze and ivory, which were far superior to any employed in the West at the same period. We have already referred to the American contribution and there is no need to revert to it now.

Moreover, it is unwise to concentrate attention too much upon these isolated contributions, for they might give us the doubly false impression that world civilisation is a sort of motley. Too much publicity has been given to the various peoples who were first with any discovery: the Phoenicians with the use of the alphabet; the Chinese with paper, gunpowder and the compass; the Indians with glass and steel. These things in themselves are less important than the way in which each culture puts them together, adopts them or rejects them. And the originality of each culture consists rather in its individual way of solving problems, and in the perspective in which it views the general values which must be approximately the same for all mankind, since all men, without exception, possess a language, techniques, a form of art, some sort of scientific knowledge, religious beliefs, and some form of social, economic and political organisation. The relations are never quite the same, however, in every culture, and modern ethnology is concentrating increasingly on discovering the underlying reasons for the choices made, rather than on listing mere external features.

THE PLACE OF WESTERN CIVILISATION

It may perhaps be objected that such arguments are theoretical. As a matter of abstract logic, it may be said, it is possible that no culture is capable of a true judgement of any other, since no culture can lay aside its own limitations, and its appreciation is therefore inevitably relative. But look around you; mark what has been happening in the world for the past 100 years, and all your speculations will come to nought. Far from 'keeping themselves to themselves', all civilisations, one after the other, recognise the superiority of one of their number—Western civilisation. Are we not witnesses to the fact that the whole world is gradually adopting its technological methods, its way of life, its amusements and even its costume? Just as Diogenes demonstrated movement by walking, it is the course followed by all human cultures, from the countless thousands of Asia to the lost tribes in the remote fastnesses of the Brazilian or African jungles which proves, by the unanimous acceptance of a single form of human civilisation, such as history has never witnessed before, that that civilisation is superior to any other; the complaint which the 'underdeveloped' countries advance against the others at international meetings is not that they are being westernised, but that there is too much delay in giving them the means to westernise themselves.

This is the most difficult point in our argument; indeed it would be of no use to attempt to defend the individuality of human cultures against those cultures themselves. Moreover, it is extremely difficult for an ethnologist to assess at its true value such a phenomenon as the universal acceptance of Western civilisation. There are several reasons for this fact. In the first place, there has probably never before in history been a world civilisation or, if any parallel does exist, it must be sought in remote prehistoric times, about which we know practically nothing. Secondly, there is very considerable doubt about the permanence of this phenomenon. It is a fact that for the past 150 years there has been a tendency for Western civilisation to spread throughout the world, either in its entirety or by the development of certain of its key features, such as industrialisation; and that, where other cultures are seeking to preserve some part of their traditional heritage, the attempt is usually confined to the superstructure of society, that is to say, to the least enduring aspects of a culture, which it may be expected will be swept away by the far more radical changes which are taking place. The process is still going on, however, and we cannot yet know what the result will be. Will it end in the complete westernisation of our planet, with Russian or American variations? Will syncretic forms come into being, as seems possible so far as the Islamic world, India and China, are concerned? Or is the tide already on the turn and will it now ebb back, before the imminent collapse of the Western world, brought to ruin, like the prehistoric monsters, by a physical expansion out of proportion to the structure on which their working depends? We must take all these possibilities into account in attempting to assess the process going on under our eyes, whose agents, instruments or victims we are, whether we know it or not.

In the first place, we may note that acceptance of the Western way of life, or certain aspects of it, is by no means as spontaneous as Westerners would like to believe. It is less the result of free choice than of the absence of any alternative. Western civilisation has stationed its soldiers, trading posts, plantations and missionaries throughout the world; directly or indirectly it has intervened in the lives of the coloured peoples; it has caused a revolutionary upheaval in their traditional way of life, either by imposing its own customs, or by creating such conditions as to cause the collapse of the existing native patterns without putting anything else in their place. The subjugated and disorganised peoples have therefore had no choice but to accept the substitute solutions offered them or, if they were not prepared to do that, to seek to imitate Western ways sufficiently to be able to fight them on their own ground. When the balance of power is not so unequal, societies do not so easily surrender: their *Weltanschauung* tends rather to be similar to that of the poor tribe in eastern Brazil, whose members adopted the ethnographer, Curt Nimuendaju, as one of themselves and who, whenever he returned to them after a visit to civilisation, would weep for pity to think of the sufferings he must have endured so far away from the only place—their village—where, in their opinion, life was worth living.

Nevertheless, this reservation merely shifts the question to another point. If Western culture's claim to superiority is not founded upon free acceptance, must it not be founded upon its greater vitality and energy, which have enabled it to compel acceptance? Here we are down to bedrock. For this inequality of force is not to be accounted for by the subjective attitude of the community as a whole, as was the acceptance we were discussing above. It is an objective fact, and can only be explained by objective causes.

This is not the place to embark on a study of the philosophy of civilisation; volumes might be devoted to a discussion of the nature of the values professed by Western civilisation. We shall deal only with the most obvious of those values, those that are least open to question. They would seem to be two: in the first place, to borrow Dr Leslie White's phrase, Western civilisation seeks continually to increase the *per capita* supply of energy; second, it seeks to protect and prolong human life. To put the matter in a nutshell, the second aspect may be regarded as a derivative of the first, since the absolute quantity of energy available increases in proportion to the length and health of the individual life. For the sake of avoiding argument, we may also admit at once that compensatory phenomena, acting, as it were, as a brake, may go with these developments, such as the great slaughters of world warfare and the inequalities in the consumption of available energy between individuals and classes.

Once this is admitted, it is immediately apparent that, while Western civilisation may indeed have devoted itself to these forms of development, to the exclusion of all others—wherein perhaps its weakness lies—it is certainly not the only civilisation which has done so. All human societies, from the earliest times, have acted in the same way: and very early and primitive societies, which we should be inclined to compare with the 'barbarian' peoples of today, made the most decisive advances in this respect. At present, their achievements still constitute the bulk of what we call civilisation. We are still dependent upon the tremendous discoveries which marked the phase we describe, without the slightest exaggeration, as the neolithic revolution: agriculture, stock-rearing, pottery, weaving. In the last eight or ten thousand years, all we have done is to improve all these 'arts of civilisation'.

Admittedly, some people exhibit an unfortunate tendency to regard only the more recent discoveries as brought about by human effort, intelligence and imagination, while the discoveries humanity made in the 'barbarian' period are regarded as due to chance, so that, upon the whole, humanity can claim little credit for them. This error seems to us so common and so serious, and is so likely to prevent a proper appreciation of the relations between cultures, that we think it essential to clear it up once and for all.

CHANCE AND CIVILISATION

Treatises on ethnology, including some of the best, tell us that man owes his knowledge of fire to the accident of lightning or of a bush fire; that the discovery of a wild animal accidentally roasted in such circumstances revealed to him the possibility of cooking his food; and that the invention of pottery was the result of someone's leaving a lump of clay near a fire. The conclusion seems to be that man began his career in a sort of technological golden age, when inventions could, as it were, be picked off the trees as easily as fruit or flowers. Only modern man would seem to find it necessary to strain and toil; only to modern man would genius seem to grant a flash of insight.

This naïve attitude is the result of a complete failure to appreciate the complexity and diversity of operations involved in even the most elementary technical processes. To make a useful stone implement, it is not enough to keep on striking a piece of flint until it splits; this became quite apparent when people first tried to reproduce the main types of prehistoric tools. That attempt—in conjunction with observation of the same methods still in use among certain native peoples—taught us that the processes involved are extremely complicated, necessitating, in some cases, the prior manufacture of veritable 'chipping tools'; hammers with a counterweight to control the impact and direction of the blow; shock-absorbers to prevent the vibration from shattering the flake. A considerable body of knowledge about the local origin of the materials employed, the processes of extracting them, their resistance and structure, is also necessary; so is a certain muscular skill and 'knack', acquired by training; in short, the manufacture of such tools calls for a 'lithurgy' matching, *mutatis mutandis*, the various main divisions of metallurgy.

Similarly, while a natural conflagration might on occasion broil or roast a carcass, it is very hard to imagine (except in the case of volcanic eruptions, which are restricted to a relatively small number of areas in the world) that it could suggest boiling or steaming food. The latter methods of cooking, however, are no less universally employed than the others. There is, therefore, no reason for ruling out invention, which must certainly have been necessary for the development of the latter methods, when trying to explain the origin of the former.

Pottery is a very good instance, for it is commonly believed that nothing could be simpler than to hollow out a lump of clay and harden it in the fire. We can only suggest trying it. In the first place, it is essential to find clays suitable for baking; but while many natural conditions are necessary for this purpose, none of them is sufficient in itself, for no clay would, after baking, produce a receptacle suitable for use unless it were mixed with some inert body chosen for its special properties. Elaborate modelling techniques are necessary to make possible the achievement of keeping in shape for some time a plastic body which will not 'hold' in the natural state, and simultaneously to mould it; lastly, it is necessary to discover the particular type of fuel, the sort of furnace, the degree of heat, and the duration of the baking process which will make the clay hard and impermeable and avoid the manifold dangers of cracking, crumbling and distortion. Many other instances might be quoted.

There are far too many complicated operations involved for chance to account for all. Each one by itself means nothing, and only deliberate imaginative combination, based on research and experiment, can make success possible. Chance admittedly has an influence, but, by itself, produces no result. For about 2,500 years, the Western world knew of the existence of electricity—which was no doubt discovered by accident—but that discovery bore no fruit until Ampère and Faraday and others set deliberately to work on the hypotheses they had formulated. Chance played no more important a part in the invention of the bow, the boomerang or the blowpipe, in the development of agriculture or stock-rearing, than in the discovery of penicillin, into which, of course, we know it entered to some extent. We must therefore distinguish carefully between the transmission of a technique from one generation to another, which is always relatively easy, as it is brought about by daily observation and training, and the invention and improvement of new techniques by each individual generation. The latter always necessitate the same power of imagination and the same tireless efforts on the part of certain individuals, whatever may be the particular technique in question. The societies we describe as 'primitive' have as many Pasteurs and Palissys as the others.

We shall shortly come back to chance and probability, but in a different position and a different role; we shall not advance them as a simple explanation for the appearance of full-blown inventions, but as an aid to the interpretation of a phenomenon found in another connection—the fact that, in spite of our having every reason to suppose that the quantity of imagination, inventive power and creative energy has been more or less constant throughout the history of mankind, the combination has resulted in important cultural mutations only at certain periods and in certain places. Purely personal factors are not enough to account for this result: a sufficient number of individuals must first be psychologically predisposed in a given direction, to ensure the inventor's immediate appeal to the public; this condition itself depends upon the combination of a considerable number of other historical, economic and sociological factors. We should thus be led, in order to explain the differences in the progress of civilisations, to invoke so many complex and unrelated causes that we could have no hope of understanding them, either for practical reasons, or even for theoretical reasons, such as the inevitable disturbances provoked by the very use of mass observation methods. In order to untangle such a skein of countless filaments, it would in fact be necessary to submit the society in question (and the surrounding world) to a comprehensive ethnographical study covering every moment of its life. Even apart from the enormous scope of the undertaking, we know that ethnographers working on an infinitely smaller scale often find their opportunities for observation limited by the subtle changes introduced by their very presence in the human group they are studying. We also know that, in modern societies, one of the most efficient methods of sounding reactions—public opinion polls—tend to modify opinion at the same time, since they introduce among the population a factor which was previously absent— awareness of their own opinions.

This justifies the introduction into the social sciences of the concept of probability, which has long since been recognised in certain branches of physics, e.g. thermodynamics. We shall return to this question: for the time being we may content ourselves with a reminder that the complexity of modern discoveries is not the result of the more common occurrence or better supply of genius among our contemporaries. Rather the reverse, since we have seen that, through the centuries, the progress of each generation depends merely on its adding a constant contribution to the capital inherited from earlier generations. Nine-tenths of our present wealth is due to our predecessors—even more if the date when the main discoveries made their appearance is assessed in relation to the approximate date of the dawn of civilisation. We then find that agriculture was developed during a recent phase, representing 2 per cent of that period of time; metallurgy would represent 0·7 per cent, the alphabet 0·35 per cent, Galileo's physics 0·035 per cent and Darwin's theories 0·009 per cent.* The whole of the scientific and industrial revolution of the West would therefore fall within a period equivalent to approximately one-half of one-thousandth of the life span of humanity to date. Some caution therefore seems advisable in asserting that this revolution is destined to change the whole meaning of human history.

It is nevertheless true—and this we think finally sums up our problem—that, from the point of view of technical inventions (and the scientific thought which makes such inventions possible), Western civilisation has proved itself to be more 'cumulative' than other civilisations. Starting with the same initial stock of neolithic culture, it successfully introduced a number of improvements (alphabetic script, arithmetic and geometry), some of which, incidentally, it rapidly forgot; but, after a period of stagnation, lasting roughly for 2,000 or 2,500 years (from the first millenary B.C. until approximately the eighteenth century A.D.), it suddenly produced an industrial revolution so wide in scope, so comprehensive and so far-reaching in its consequences that the only previous comparison was the neolithic revolution itself.

Twice in its history, at an interval of approximately 10,000 years, then, humanity has accumulated a great number of inventions tending in the same direction; enough such inventions, exhibiting a sufficient degree of continuity have come close enough together in time for technical co-ordination to take place at a high level; this co-ordination has brought about important changes in man's relations with nature, which, in their turn, have made others possible. This process, which has so far occurred twice, and only

* Leslie A. White, *The Science of Culture* (New York, 1949), p. 356.

twice, in the history of humanity, may be illustrated by the simile of a chain reaction brought about by catalytic agents. What can account for it?

First of all, we must not overlook the fact that other revolutions with the same cumulative features may have occurred elsewhere and at other times, but in different spheres of human activity. We have explained above why our own industrial revolution and the neolithic revolution (which preceded it in time but concerned similar matters) are the only groups of events which we can appreciate as revolutions, because they are measurable by our criteria. All the other changes which have certainly come about are only partially perceptible to us, or are seriously distorted in our eyes. They cannot have any meaning for modern Western man (or, at all events, not their full meaning); they may even be invisible to him.

Second, the case of the neolithic revolution (the only one which modern Western man can visualise clearly enough) should suggest a certain moderation of the claims he may be tempted to make concerning the pre-eminence of any given race, region or country. The industrial revolution began in Western Europe, moving on to the United States of America and then to Japan; since 1917 it has been gathering momentum in the Soviet Union, and in the near future, no doubt, we shall see it in progress elsewhere; now here, now there, within a space of 50 years, it flares up or dies down. What then of the claims to be first in the field, on which we pride ourselves so much, when we have to take into account thousands upon thousands of years?

The neolithic revolution broke out simultaneously, to within 1,000 or 2,000 years, around the Aegean, in Egypt, the Near East, the Valley of the Indus, and China; and since radio-active carbon has been used for determining archaeological ages, we are beginning to suspect that the neolithic age in America is older than we used to think and cannot have begun much later than in the Old World. It is probable that three or four small valleys might claim to have led in the race by a few centuries. What can we know of that today? On the other hand, we are certain that the question of who was first matters not at all, for the very reason that the simultaneity of the same technological upheavals (closely followed by social upheavals) over such enormous stretches of territory, so remote from one another, is a clear indication that they resulted not from the genius of a given race or culture but from conditions so generally operative that they are beyond the conscious sphere of man's thought. We can therefore be sure that, if the industrial revolution had not begun in North-Western Europe, it would have come about at some other time in a different part of the world. And if, as seems probable, it is to extend to cover the whole of the inhabited globe, every culture will introduce into it so many contributions of its own that future historians, thousands of years hence, will quite rightly think it pointless to discuss the question of which culture can claim to have led the rest by 100 or 200 years.

If this is admitted, we need to introduce a new qualification, if not of the truth, at least of the precision of our distinction between stationary history and cumulative history. Not only is this distinction relative to our own interests, as we have already shown, but it can never be entirely clear cut. So far as technical inventions are concerned, it is quite certain that no period and no culture is absolutely stationary. All peoples have a grasp of techniques, which are sufficiently elaborate to enable them to control their environment and adapt, improve or abandon these techniques as they proceed. If it were not so, they would have disappeared long since. There is thus never a clear dividing line between 'cumulative' and 'non-cumulative' history; all history is cumulative and the difference is simply of degree. We know, for instance, that the ancient Chinese and the Eskimos had developed the mechanical arts to a very high pitch; they very nearly reached the point at which the 'chain reaction' would set in and carry them from one type of civilisation to another. Everyone knows the story of gunpowder; from the technical point of view, the Chinese had solved all the problems involved in its use save that of securing a large-scale effect. The ancient Mexicans were not ignorant of the wheel, as is often alleged; they were perfectly familiar with it in the manufacture of toy animals on wheels for children to play with; they merely needed to take one more step forward to have the use of the cart.

In these circumstances, the problem of the relatively small number (for each individual system of criteria) of 'more cumulative' cultures, as compared with the 'less cumulative' cultures, comes down to a problem familiar in connection with the theory of probabilities. It is the problem of determining the relative probability of a complex combination, as compared with other similar but less complex combinations. In roulette, for instance, a series of two consecutive numbers (such as 7 and 8, 12 and 13, 30 and 31) is quite frequent; a series of three is rarer, and a series of four very much more so. And it is only once in a very large number of spins that a series of six, seven or eight numbers may occur in their natural order. If our attention is concentrated exclusively on the long series (if, for instance, we are betting on series of five consecutive numbers), the shorter series will obviously mean no more to us than a non-consecutive series. But this is to overlook the fact that they differ from the series in which we are interested only by a fraction and that, when viewed from another angle, they may display a similar degree of regularity. We may carry our comparison further. Any player who transferred all his winnings to longer and longer series of numbers might grow discouraged, after thousands and millions of tries, at the fact that no series of nine consecutive numbers ever turned up, and might come to the conclusion that he would have been better advised to stop earlier. Yet there is no reason why another player, following the same system but with a different type of series (such as a certain alternation between red and black or between odd and even) might not find significant combinations where the first player would see nothing but confusion. Mankind is not developing along a single line. And if, in one sphere, it appears to be stationary or even retrograde, that does not mean that, from another point of view, important changes may not be taking place in it.

The great eighteenth-century Scottish philosopher, Hume, set out one day to clear up the mistaken problem which has puzzled many people, why not all women, but only a small minority, are pretty. He had no difficulty in showing that the question means nothing at all. If all women were at least as pretty as the most beautiful woman of our acquaintance, we should think they were all ordinary and should reserve the adjective for the small minority who surpassed the average. Similarly, when we are interested in a certain type of progress, we restrict the term 'progressive' to those cultures which are in the van in that type of development, and pay little attention to the others. Progress thus never represents anything more than the maximum progress in a given direction, predetermined by the interests of the observer.

COLLABORATION BETWEEN CULTURES

Lastly, there is one more point of view from which we must consider our problem. A gambler such as we have discussed in the preceding paragraphs, who placed his bets only upon the longest series (however arranged), would almost certainly be ruined. But this would not be so if there were a coalition of gamblers betting on the same series at several different tables, with an agreement that they would pool the numbers which each of them might require to proceed with his series. For if I, for instance, have already got 21 and 22 myself, and need 23 to go on, there is obviously more chance of its turning up if 10 tables, instead of only one, are in play.

The situation of the various cultures which have achieved the most cumulative forms of history is very similar. Such history has never been produced by isolated cultures but by cultures which, voluntarily or involuntarily, have combined their play and, by a wide variety of means (migration, borrowing, trade and warfare), have formed such *coalitions* as we have visualised in our example. This brings out very clearly the absurdity of claiming that one culture is superior to another. For, if a culture were left to its own resources, it could never hope to be 'superior'; like the single gambler, it would never manage to achieve more than short series of a few units, and the prospect of a long series turning up in its history (though not theoretically impossible) would be so slight that all hope of it would depend on the ability to continue the game for a time infinitely longer than the whole period of human history to date. But, as we said above, no single culture stands alone; it is always part of a coalition including other cultures, and, for that reason, is able to build up cumulative series. The probability of a long series appearing naturally depends on the scope, duration and variation allowed for in the organisation of the coalition.

Two consequences follow.

In the course of this study, we have several times raised the question why mankind remained stationary for nine-tenths or even more of its history; the earliest civilisations date back from 200,000 to 500,000 years, while living conditions have been transformed only in the last 10,000 years. If we are correct in our analysis, the reason was not that palaeolithic man was less intelligent or less gifted than his neolithic successor, but simply that, in human history, the combination took a time to come about; it might have occurred much earlier or much later. There is no more significance in this than there is in the number of spins a gambler has to wait before a given combination is produced; it might happen at the first spin, the thousandth, the millionth or never. But, throughout that time of waiting, humanity, like the gambler, goes on betting. Not always of its own free will, and not always appreciating exactly what it is doing, it 'sets up business' in culture, embarks on 'operation civilisation', achieving varying measures of success in each of its undertakings. In some cases, it very nearly succeeds, in others, it endangers its earlier gains. The great simplifications which are permissible because of our ignorance of most aspects of prehistoric societies help to illustrate more closely this hesitant progress, with its manifold ramifications. There can be no more striking examples of regression than the descent from the peak of Levallois culture to the mediocrity of the Mousterian civilisation, or from the splendour of the Aurignacian and Solutrean cultures to the rudeness of the Magdalenean, and to the extreme contrasts we find in the various aspects of mesolithic culture.

What is true in time is equally true in space, although it must be expressed in a different way. A culture's chance of uniting the complex body of inventions of all sorts which we describe as a civilisation depends on the number and diversity of the other cultures with which it is working out, generally involuntarily, a common strategy. Number and diversity: a comparison of the Old World with the New on the eve of the latter's discovery provides a good illustration of the need for these two factors.

Europe at the beginning of the Renaissance was the meeting-place and melting-pot of the most diverse influences: the Greek, Roman, Germanic and Anglo-Saxon traditions combined with the influences of Arabia and China. Pre-Columbian America enjoyed no fewer cultural contacts, quantitatively speaking, as the various American cultures maintained relations with one another and the two Americas together represent a whole hemisphere. But, while the cultures which were cross-fertilising each other in Europe had resulted from differentiation dating back several tens of thousands of years, those on the more recently occupied American continent had had less time to develop divergencies; the picture they offered was relatively homogeneous. Thus, although it would not be true to say that the cultural standard of Mexico or Peru was inferior to that of Europe at the time of the discovery (we have in fact seen that, in some respects, it was superior), the various aspects of culture were possibly less well organised in relation to each other. Side by side with amazing achievements, we find strange deficiencies in the pre-Columbian civilisations; there are, so to speak, gaps in them. They also afford evidence of the coexistence—not so contradictory as it may seem—of relatively advanced forms of culture with others which were abortive. Their organisation, less flexible and diversified, probably explains their collapse before a handful of conquerors. And the underlying reason for this may be sought in the fact that the partners to the American cultural 'coalition' were less dissimilar from one another than their counterparts in the Old World.

No society is therefore essentially and intrinsically cumulative. Cumulative history is not the prerogative of certain races or certain cultures, marking them off from the rest. It is the result of their *conduct* rather than their *nature*. It represents a certain 'way of life' of cultures which depends on their capacity to 'go-along-together'. In this sense, it may be said that cumulative history is the type of history characteristic of grouped societies—social super-organisms —while stationary history (supposing it to exist) would be the distinguishing feature of an inferior form of social life, the isolated society.

The one real calamity, the one fatal flaw which can afflict a group of men and prevent them from fulfilment is to be alone.

We can thus see how clumsy and intellectually unsatisfactory the generally accepted efforts to defend the contributions of various human races and cultures to civilisation often are. We list features, we sift questions of origin, we allot first places. However well-intentioned they may be, these efforts serve no purpose, for, in three respects, they miss their aim. In the first place, there can never be any certainty about a particular culture's credit for an invention or discovery. For 100 years, it was firmly believed that maize had been produced by the American Indians, by crossing wild grasses; this explanation is still accepted for the time being, but there is increasing doubt about it, for it may well be, after all, that maize was introduced into America (we cannot tell when or how) from South-East Asia.

In the second place, all cultural contributions can be divided into two groups. On the one hand, we have isolated acquisitions or features, whose importance is evident but which are also somewhat limited. It is a fact that tobacco came from America; but after all, and despite the best efforts of international institutions, we cannot feel overwhelmed with gratitude to the American Indians every time we smoke a cigarette. Tobacco is a delightful adjunct to the art of living, as other adjuncts are useful (such as rubber);

we are indebted to these things for pleasures and conveniences we should not otherwise enjoy, but if we were deprived of them, our civilisation would not rock on its foundations and, had there been any pressing need, we could have found them for ourselves or substituted something else for them.

At the other end of the scale (with a whole series of intermediates, of course), there are systematised contributions, representing the peculiar form in which each society has chosen to express and satisfy the generality of human aspirations. There is no denying the originality and particularity of these patterns, but, as they all represent the exclusive choice of a single group, it is difficult to see how one civilisation can hope to benefit from the way of life of another, unless it is prepared to renounce its own individuality. Attempted compromises are, in fact, likely to produce only two results: either the disorganisation and collapse of the pattern of one of the groups; or a new combination, which then, however, represents the emergence of a third pattern, and cannot be assimilated to either of the others. The question with which we are concerned, indeed, is not to discover whether or not a society can derive benefit from the way of life of its neighbours, but whether, and if so to what extent, it can succeed in understanding or even in knowing them. We have already seen that there can be no definite reply to this question.

Finally, wherever a contribution is made, there must be a recipient. But, while there are in fact real cultures which can be localised in time and space, and which may be said to have 'contributed' and to be continuing their contributions, what can this 'world civilisation' be, which is supposed to be the recipient of all these contributions? It is not another civilisation distinct from all the others, and yet real in the same sense that they are. When we speak of world civilisation, we have in mind no single period, no single group of men: we are employing an abstract conception, to which we attribute a moral or logical significance—moral, if we are thinking of an aim to be pursued by existing societies; logical, if we are using the one term to cover the common features which analysis may reveal in the different cultures. In both cases, we must not shut our eyes to the fact that the concept of world civilisation is very sketchy and imperfect, and that its intellectual and emotional content is tenuous. To attempt to assess cultural contributions with all the weight of countless centuries behind them, rich with the thoughts and sorrows, hopes and toil of the men and women who brought them into being, by reference to the sole yard-stick of a world civilisation which is still a hollow shell, would be greatly to impoverish them, draining away their life-blood and leaving nothing but the bare bones behind.

We have sought, on the contrary, to show that the true contribution of a culture consists, not in the list of inventions which it has personally produced, but in its difference from others. The sense of gratitude and respect which each single member of a given culture can and should feel towards all others can only be based on the conviction that the other cultures differ from his own in countless ways, even if the ultimate essence of these differences eludes him or if, in spite of his best efforts, he can reach no more than an imperfect understanding of them.

Second, we have taken the notion of world civilisation as a sort of limiting concept or as an epitome of a highly complex process. If our arguments are valid, there is not, and can never be, a world civilisation in the absolute sense in which that term is often used, since civilisation implies, and indeed consists in, the co-existence of cultures exhibiting the maximum possible diversities. A world civilisation could, in fact, represent no more than a world-wide coalition of cultures, each of which would preserve its own originality.

THE COUNTER-CURRENTS OF PROGRESS

We thus surely find ourselves faced with a curious paradox.

Taking the terms in the sense in which we have been using them above, we have seen that all cultural progress depends on a coalition of cultures. The essence of such a coalition is the pooling (conscious or unconscious, voluntary or involuntary, deliberate or accidental, on their own initiative or under compulsion) of the wins which each culture has scored in the course of its historical development. Lastly, we have recognised, that, the greater the diversity between the cultures concerned, the more fruitful such a coalition will be. If this is admitted, we seem to have two conditions which are mutually contradictory. For the inevitable consequence of the practice of *playing as a syndicate*, which is the source of all progress, is, sooner or later, to make the character of each player's resources *uniform*. If, therefore, one of the first requisites is diversity, it must be recognised that the chances of winning become progressively less as the game goes on.

There are, it would seem, two possibilities of remedying this inevitable development. The first would be for each player deliberately to introduce *differences* in his own game; this is possible, because each society (the 'player' in our hypothetical illustration) consists of a coalition of denominational, professional and economic groups, and because the society's stake is the sum total of the stakes of all these constituent groups. Social inequalities are the most striking instance of this solution. The great revolutions we have chosen to illustrate our argument—the neolithic and the industrial—were accompanied not only by the introduction of diversity into the body of society, as Spencer perceived, but by the introduction of differences in status between the several groups, particularly from the economic point of view. It was noted a long time ago that the discoveries of the neolithic age rapidly brought about social differentiation, as the great cities of ancient times grew up in the East, and states, castes and classes appeared on the scene. The same applies to the industrial revolution, which was conditioned by the emergence of a proletariat and is leading on to new and more elaborate forms of exploiting human labour. Hitherto, the tendency has been to treat these social changes as the consequence of the technical changes, the relation of the latter to the former being that of cause and effect. If we are right in our interpretation, this causality (and the succession in time which it implies) must be rejected—as, incidentally, is the general trend in modern science—in favour of a functional correlation between the two phenomena. We may note in passing that recognition of the fact that the historical concomitant of technical progress has been the development of the exploitation of man by man may somewhat temper the pride we are so apt to take in the first of these developments.

The second remedy is very largely modelled on the first: it is to bring into the coalition, whether they will or no, new partners from outside, whose 'stakes' are very different from those of the parties to the original coalition. This solution has also been tried and, while the first may roughly be identified with capitalism, the second may well be illustrated by the history of imperialism and colonialism. The colonial expansion of the nineteenth century gave industrial Europe a fresh impetus (which admittedly benefited other parts of the world as well) whereas, but for the introduction of the colonial peoples, the momentum might have been lost much sooner.

It will be apparent that, in both cases, the remedy consists in broadening the coalition, either by increasing internal diversity or by admitting new partners; in fact, the problem is always to increase the number of players or, in other words, to restore the complexity and diversity of the original situation. It is also apparent, however, that these remedies can only temporarily retard the process. Exploitation is possible only within a coalition; there is contact and interchange between the major and the minor parties. They, in turn, in spite of the apparently unilateral relationship between them, are bound, consciously or unconsciously, to pool their stakes and, as time goes by, the differences between them will tend to diminish. This process is illustrated by the social improvements that are being brought about and the gradual attainment of independence by the colonial peoples; although we have still far to go in both these directions, we must know that the trend of developments is inevitable. It may be that the emergence of antagonistic political and social systems should, in fact, be regarded as a third solution; conceivably, by a constant shifting of the grounds of diversity, it may be possible to maintain indefinitely, in varying forms which will constantly take men unawares, that state of disequilibrium which is necessary of the biological and cultural survival of mankind.

However this may be, it is difficult to conceive as other than contradictory a process which may be summed up as follows: if men are to progress, they must collaborate; and, in the course of their collaboration, the differences in their contributions will gradually be evened out, although collaboration was originally necessary and advantageous simply because of those differences.

Even if there is no solution, however, it is the sacred duty of mankind to bear these two contradictory facts in mind, and never to lose sight of the one through an exclusive concern with the other; man must, no doubt, guard against the blind particularism which would restrict the dignity of humankind to a single race, culture or society; but he must never forget, on the other hand, that no section of humanity has succeeded in finding universally applicable formulas, and that it is impossible to imagine mankind pursuing a single way of life for, in such a case, mankind would be ossified.

From this point of view our international institutions have a tremendous task before them and bear a very heavy responsibility. Both task and responsibility are more complex than is thought. For our international institutions have a double part to play; they have first, to wind up the past and, second, to issue a summons to fresh activity: In the first place, they have to assist mankind to get rid, with as little discomfort and danger as possible, of those diversities now serving no useful purpose, the abortive remnants of forms of collaboration whose putrefying vestiges represent a constant risk of infection to the body of international society. They will have to cut them out, resorting to amputation where necessary, and foster the development of other forms of adaptation.

At the same time, they must never for a moment lose sight of the fact that, if these new forms are to have the same functional value as the earlier forms, they cannot be merely copied or modelled on the same pattern; if they were, they would gradually lose their efficacy, until in the end they would be of no use at all. International institutions must be aware, on the contrary, that mankind is rich in unexpected resources, each of which, on first appearance, will always amaze men; that progress is not a comfortable 'bettering of what we have', in which we might look for an indolent repose, but is a succession of adventures, partings of the way, and constant shocks. Humanity is forever involved in two conflicting currents, the one tending towards unification, and the other towards the maintenance or restoration of diversity. As a result of the position of each period or culture in the system, as a result of the way it is facing each thinks that only one of these two currents represents an advance, while the other appears to be the negation of the first. But we should be purblind if we said, as we might be tempted to do, that humanity is constantly unmaking what it makes. For in different spheres and at different levels, both currents are in truth two aspects of the same process.

The need to preserve the diversity of cultures in a world which is threatened by monotony and uniformity has surely not escaped out international institutions. They must also be aware that it is not enough to nurture local traditions and to save the past for a short period longer. It is diversity itself which must be saved, not the outward and visible form in which each period has clothed that diversity, and which can never be preserved beyond the period which gave it birth. We must therefore hearken for the stirrings of new life, foster latent potentialities, and encourage every natural inclination for collaboration which the future history of the world may hold; we must also be prepared to view without surprise, repugnance or revolt whatever may strike us as strange in the many new forms of social expression. Tolerance is not a contemplative attitude, dispensing indulgence to what has been or what is still in being. It is a dynamic attitude, consisting in the anticipation, understanding and promotion of what is struggling into being. We can see the diversity of human cultures behind us, around us, and before us. The only demand that we can justly make (entailing corresponding duties for every individual) is that all the forms this diversity may take may be so many contributions to the fullness of all the others.

Bibliography

Auger, P., *L'homme microscopique* (Paris, 1952).
Boas, F., *The Mind of Primitive Man* (New York, 1931).
Dilthey, W., *Gesammelte Schriften* (Leipzig, 1914–31).
Dixon, R. B., *The Building of Cultures* (New York, London, 1928).
De Gobineau, A., *Essai sur l'inégalité des races humaines* (2nd ed.) (Paris, 1884).
Hawkes, C. F. C., *Prehistoric Foundations of Europe* (London, 1939).
Herskovits, M. J., *Man and his Works* (New York, 1948).
Kroeber, A. L., *Anthropology* (New ed.) (New York, 1948).
Leroi-Gourhan, A., *L'homme et la matière* (Paris, 1943).
Linton, R., *The Study of Man* (New York, 1936).
Moraze, Ch., *Essai sur la civilisation d'occident*, Vol. 1 (Paris, 1949).
Pirenne, J., *Les grands courants de l'histoire universelle*, Vol. 1 (Paris, 1947).
Pittard, E., *Les races et l'histoire* (Paris, 1922).
Spengler, O., *The Decline of the West* (New York, 1927–28).
Toynbee, A. J., *A Study of History* (London, 1934).
White, L. A., *The Science of Culture* (New York, 1949).

Race and Culture*

by MICHEL LEIRIS

Chargé de recherches at the Centre National de la Recherche Scientifique and Staff Member of the Musée de l'Homme, Paris

> The nature of men is identical; what divides them is their customs.
>
> CONFUCIUS, 551–478 B.C.

After causing innumerable casualties, World War II ended with the defeat of Nazi Germany and her allies. The National Socialists had gained power on the strength of their racist ideology, and more particularly of their anti-Semitism, and it was in the name of that ideology that they went to war to 'unite all Germans in a greater Germany' and force recognition of German superiority on the whole world. Thus the fall of Adolf Hitler lent colour to the assumption that racism was dead. However, such a view both assumes the non-existence of forms of racism other than the Hitlerite, admittedly the most extreme and virulent of them, and overlooks the strong conviction of most white people—even those who do not on that account consider themselves racists—of their congenital superiority.

Admittedly, the white man has something to be proud of in his great inventions and discoveries, his technical equipment and his political power. It is, questionable, however, whether these achievements have yet brought a greater sum of happiness to mankind as a whole. For instance, it can hardly be claimed that the pygmy hunter of the Congo forests lives a life less well adjusted than a European or American factory worker. Nor should we forget that, though science has brought us undeniable progress in such fields as sanitation, for instance, it has also enabled us to perfect the means of destruction to such a point that for some decades past, armed conflicts have been truly cataclysmic in their effects. Be that as it

* First published in *The Race Question in Modern Science* (Paris: Unesco, and London: Sidgwick and Jackson, 1956).

may, and despite his consciousness that the civilisation he regards as the only one worthy of the name is increasingly threatened with overthrow from within and without, the Western white man still claims the right of passage at the great cross roads to which his means of communication have reduced the world. A lack of historical perspective prevents his realising not merely how recent is his privileged position, but how transitory it may prove, and he regards it as a sign that he is predestined to create the values which men of other races and other cultures are at best merely capable of receiving from him. Though he will readily admit that a number of inventions have come to him from the Chinese (to whom he is willing to concede a modicum of 'brains' and wisdom), and that such things as jazz have been given to him by the Negro (whom he nevertheless persists in regarding as an overgrown child), he is persuaded that his culture is of his own exclusive making and that only he can claim to have received—by right of blood and character—a 'civilising mission'.

In an article published in *the Unesco Courier*, July 1950, Dr Alfred Metraux (an ethnographer whose work has covered perhaps more of the world than that of any other) wrote:

'Racism is one of the most disturbing phenomena of the great revolution of the modern world. At the very time when industrial civilisation is penetrating to all points of the globe and is uprooting men of every colour from their age-old traditions, a doctrine, speciously scientific in appearance, is invoked in order to rob these men of their full share in the advantage of the civilisation forced upon them.

'There exists in the structure of Western civilisation a fatal contradiction. On the one hand, it wishes and insists that certain cultural values, to which it attributes the highest virtues, be assimilated by other people. But, conversely, it will not admit that two-thirds of humanity is capable of attaining this standard which it has set up. Ironically, the worst sufferers from racial dogma are usually the people whose intellect most forcibly demonstrates its falseness.'

By an irony as strange, the more capable the so-called inferior races prove themselves of attaining emancipation, the more emphatic grows the assertion of racial dogma, stiffened by the coloured races' acquisition of a minimum of political rights or by their emergence as competitors. And the crowning paradox is that, to provide a rational justification for their blind prejudice, appeal is made to our age's gods—science and scientific objectivity.

It is true, as the writer of the article points out, that there has been no lack of anthropologists to condemn the arbitrary basis adopted for the classification of the human species into different groups and to maintain the proposition that a pure race is an impossibility. Moreover, it may today be taken as proved that 'race' is a purely biological concept, from which—at least in the present stage of our knowledge—it is impossible to draw any valid conclusion whatever as to the disposition or mental capacity of a particular individual. Nevertheless, racism, overt or covert, continues to be a baneful influence, and the majority of people still regard the human species as falling into distinct ethnic groups, each with its own mentality transmissible by heredity. It is accepted by them as basic truth that, despite the faults which must be recognised in the white race and the innate virtues they are prepared to concede to other races, the highest type of humanity is, if not the whole, at least the best, of the white race.

The error vitiating this apparent scientific justification of race prejudice lies in the failure to distinguish between *natural* and *cultural* traits, i.e. innate characteristics traceable to a man's ethnic origin, and those deriving from background and upbringing. All too often we fail, ignorantly or wilfully, to distinguish this social heritage from the *racial* heritage in the shape of physical peculiarities (for instance, pigmentation and other less striking characteristics). While there are undoubtedly very real psychological differences between individuals, which may be due in part to the subjects' individual biological ancestry (though our knowledge of the subject is still very vague), they can in no instance be explained by what is commonly called the individual's 'race', i.e. the ethnic group of which he is a member by descent. Similarly, while history has seen the development of distinctive civilisations and there are differences of varying degrees between contemporary human societies, the explanation must not be sought in the racial evolution of mankind (brought about by such factors as changes in the combination or structure of the genes—the elements determining heredity—by hybridisation and natural selection) which has produced variations from what was probably an ancestral stock common to all humanity. The differences in question are cultural variations and cannot be explained either in terms of biological background or even of the influence of geographical setting, impossible though it is to overlook the importance of this last factor as at least one element in the situation with which a society must cope.

Although the source of race prejudice must be sought elsewhere than in the pseudo-scientific ideas which are less its cause than its expression and although these ideas are of merely secondary importance as a means of justifying and commending prejudices, they still continue to deceive many often well-meaning people, and it is thus important to combat them.

The object of the present paper, then, is to set forth what is generally acknowledged regarding the respective influence of race and culture. We have to show that, apart from his personal experience, a given individual is principally indebted for his psychological conditioning to the culture in which he was brought up, the latter being itself the product of history. We have to convince the world that, far from being the more explicit expression of something instinctive, race prejudice is a prejudice in the truest and worst sense—i.e. a preconceived opinion—cultural in origin and barely three centuries old, which has grown up and taken the form we know today for economic and political reasons.

SCOPE AND CONCEPT OF 'RACE'

The concept of race might at first sight be thought to be very simple and obvious: for instance an American office worker in Wall Street, a Vietnamese carpenter building a junk, or a peasant of the Guinea Coast are men of three quite distinct races—white, yellow and black—whose ways of life are widely different, whose languages are not the same and who in all probability follow different religions. We accept without question that each of these three men represents a distinct variant of the human species, in the light of their differences not only in physique but in dress, occupation and (in all probability) in mentality, thinking, behaviour and, briefly, all that goes to make up personality. As our most immediate impression of a person is of his bodily appearance we are quick to assume a necessary connection between external physical appearance and manner of life and thought: we feel that in the nature of things, the white employee will pass his spare time in reading, the yellow man in gambling and the black in singing and dancing. We tend to see race as the primary factor from which all the rest follows, and the reflection that today there are large numbers of men of the yellow and black races pursuing the same occupations and living under the same conditions as whites only makes us feel that there is something freakish or at best artificial about it, as though the real man had been given a kind of veneer making him less 'natural'.

We perceive clear-cut differences between the three major groups into which most scientists are agreed in dividing the human species, Caucasians (or whites), Mongols and Negroes. However, the question grows more complex the moment we consider the fact of interbreeding between these groups. An individual with one white and one black parent is what is called a 'mulatto'. But should the mulatto be classified as white or black? A white man, even if not an avowed racist, will in all probability regard the mulatto as a 'coloured man' and will tend to include him among the blacks, but this classification is glaringly arbitrary, since from the anthropological point of view, the heredity of the mulatto is at least as much white as black. We therefore have to realise that, while there are men who can be classified as white, black or yellow, there are others whose mixed ancestry prevents their due classification.

Race Differs from Culture, Language and Religion

In the case of the major racial groups, classification is relatively simple though there are doubtful cases (for instance, are Polynesians, Caucasians or Mongoloids?). There are peoples who indisputably belong to one of the three branches; no one could cavil at the statement that an Englishman belongs to the white race, a Baoulé to the black or a Chinese to the yellow. It is when we attempt to make subdivisions within the three main divisions that we begin to see how equivocal is the commonly held idea of race.

To say that an Englishman is a member of the white race, obviously admits of no argument and is indeed the merest common sense. It is, however, absurd to talk about an English 'race' or even to regard the English as being of the 'Nordic' race. In point of fact, history teaches that, like all the people of Europe, the English people has become what it is through successive contributions by different peoples. England is a Celtic country, partially colonised by successive waves of Saxons, Danes and Normans from France, with some addition of Roman stock from the age of

Julius Caesar onwards. Moreover, while an Englishman can be identified by his way of dressing, or even by his behaviour, it is impossible to tell that he is an Englishman merely from his physical appearance. Among the English, as among other Europeans, there are both fair people and dark, tall men and short, and (to follow a very common anthropological criterion) dolichocephalics (or long-headed people) and brachycephalics (or people with broad heads). It may be claimed that an Englishman can readily be identified from certain external characteristics which give him a 'look' of his own: restraint in gesture (unlike the conventional gesticulating southerner), gait and facial expression all expressing what is usually included under the rather vague term of 'phlegm'. However, anyone who made this claim would be likely to be found at fault in many instances, for by no means all the English have these characteristics, and even if they are the characteristics of the 'typical Englishman', the fact would still remain that these outward characteristics are not 'physique' in the true sense: bodily attitudes and motions and expressions of the face all come under the heading of behaviour; and being habits determined by the subject's social background, are cultural, not 'natural'. Moreover, though loosely describable as 'traits', they typify not a whole nation, but a particular social group within it and thus cannot be included among the distinctive marks of race.

Accordingly any confusion between 'race' and 'nation' must be avoided and there are sound reasons against the misuse of the terms, even in speech.

At first sight it might seem to make little difference to use the term 'Latin race' instead of the correct 'Latin civilisation'. There never was a Latin race, i.e. (in Professor H. E. Vallois' definition) a *natural group of men displaying a particular set of common hereditary physical characteristics*', but there was a people of Latin speech and its civilisation spread over the greater part of western Europe and even parts of Africa and the East, to include a wide variety of peoples. Thus 'Latinity' was not confined to Italy nor even to Mediterranean Europe and today its traces can be found in countries (e.g. England and western Germany) whose peoples do not regard themselves as being a part of the Latin world of today. Here the kinship with Latin civilisation is as undeniable as the proportion of Latin blood is obviously minute.

There has been similar—and notoriously disastrous—muddled thinking about the 'Aryan' race. There never was an Aryan race and all we are entitled to infer is the existence in the second millennium before our era of a group of peoples inhabiting the steppes of Turkistan and Central Russia with a common 'Indo-European' language and culture, who overran or influenced a very wide area so that their tongue is the ancestor of many others including Sanskrit, ancient Greek, Latin and the majority of the languages spoken in Europe today. Quite obviously, the use of a common language does not mean that all individuals speaking it are of the same race, since the fact that one person speaks Chinese while another speaks English or Arabic or Russian is determined, not by biological heredity, but by what each has been taught.

A similar confusion, which unhappily appears far from being resolved today, concerns the Jews, who are also deemed to be a race whereas the only valid criteria for determining membership of the group are confessional (adherence to the Jewish faith) or at most, cultural, i.e. the survival of certain modes of behaviour not directly religious in origin, but common to Jews of different countries, as a result of the long segregation imposed by Christianity and still continuing to some extent. Originally the Hebrews were Semitic-language pastoralists like the Arabs of today, but at an early stage in their history, there was intermixture between them and other peoples of the Near East, including the Hittites, whose language was of the Indo-European group, as well as such major episodes as the sojourn in Egypt, terminated by the Exodus (second millennium, B.C.), the Babylonian captivity (sixth century B.C.), the Hellenisation of Alexander's day (fourth century B.C.), and conquest by Rome. Thus even before the Diaspora (dispersion) throughout the Roman Empire following the destruction of Jerusalem by Titus (A.D. 70), there was intensive interbreeding. In antiquity the Jewish people appears to have been made up of nearly the same racial elements as the Greeks of the Islands and Asia Minor. Today Jews are so little recognisable anthropologically—despite the existence of a so-called Jewish 'type', which itself differs as between the Ashkenazim or Northern and the Sephardim or Southern Jews—that the Nazis themselves were forced to use special badges to distinguish them and to adopt a religious criterion to determine who were Jews: those persons were considered as of Jewish race whose ancestry included a prescribed number of practising Jews. Such inconsistencies are typical of doctrines like racism, which have no hesitation in doing violence to the facts of science and even to common sense as their political needs require.

What is a Race?

We have seen then that a national community is not a race and that race cannot be defined in terms of common culture, language or religion. Further, emigration by the white and yellow races and the slave trade in the case of the black, have made it impossible to draw clear lines of geographical demarcation between the three major racial groups. This means that we must approach the question of race from the standpoint of physical anthropology—the only one from which such a concept (essentially biological since it relates to heredity) can have any validity—and then go on to consider whether the fact of an individual's belonging to a particular race has psychological implications which might tend to differentiate him from the cultural point of view.

As we have seen, the concept of 'races' is in essence that the species *Homo sapiens* can be sub-divided into groups equivalent to botanical 'varieties' in terms of certain transmissible physical characteristics. Even from this angle the question is of some delicacy because no single characteristic can be selected as the criterion for the definition of a race (for instance, there are dark-skinned Hindus, but they are differentiated from Negroes in too many other particulars for it to be possible to place both in the same category). Moreover, each of the characteristics in question admits of a considerable degree of variation from the norm—so much so that, far from accurately reflecting the facts, any division into categories must be arbitrary. In practice, a race—or sub-race—may be defined as a group whose members' physical characteristics conform, on average, to those arbitrarily selected as differentials, and there will be overlapping between peoples: for instance, the lighter skinned individuals, in peoples classified as of the black race, will on occasion be no more—or even less—pigmented than the darkest skinned individuals in populations classified as white. Thus, instead of arriving at a table of races displaying clear-cut divisions, all that can be isolated are groups of individuals who may be regarded as typical of their races because they present all the characteristics accepted as distinguishing these races, but who have congeners lacking some of those characteristics or displaying them in a less marked form. Should we then conclude that these typical individuals are representative of the pure or almost pure stock of the race in question, whereas the remainder are mere mongrels?

Nothing entitles us to make such a statement. The Mendelian

law of heredity shows the biological heritage of the individual as consisting of a long series of characteristics contributed by both parents which (to borrow the image used by Ruth Benedict) 'have to be conceived not as ink and water mingling but as a pile of beads sorted out anew for every individual'. Novel arrangements of these elements occur so constantly in new individuals that a multitude of different combinations is produced in no more than a few generations. Thus the 'typical specimen' in no sense reflects the former and 'purer' state of the race, but is merely a statistical concept expressing the frequency of certain distinctive combinations.

Hence, from the genetic point of view, it would appear impossible to regard the world population of today as other than more or less a hodgepodge, since the widest variety of types occurs from the prehistory epoch downwards and the indications are that folk migrations and considerable intermingling took place very early in the evolution of mankind. For instance, as far as Europe is concerned, in the lower palaeolithic period we already find distinct species.

Then a number of races succeed each other: in the middle palaeolithic epoch we have the Neanderthal Man (who may be either a very primitive variety of the species *Homo sapiens* or a separate species); in the upper palaeolithic age we first find representatives of *Homo sapiens* of today; the Cro-Magnon stock (of whom the Canary Islanders, descended from the ancient Guanches, may well be a modern remnant) and the quite distinct Chancelade and Grimaldi races (of a type reminiscent of the Negroid races of today). In the mesolithic period we find a mixture of races in existence from which there emerged in the neolithic period the Nordic, the Mediterranean and the Alpine types, who, up to our day, have constituted the essential anthropological elements in the population of Europe.

In the case of small societies, relatively stable and isolated (e.g. an Eskimo community living in an almost closed 'hunting' economy) the representatives of the various clans making up the community have approximately the same heredity. Here, it is possible to talk of racial purity, but not in the case of larger groups where crossings between families and the introduction of heterogeneous elements have occurred on an extensive scale. Applied to large groups with an eventful past and distributed over wide areas, the word 'race' means merely that it is possible to go beyond the

differences between nations or tribes and identify groups characterised by the occurrence of physical features which are, to some
extent temporary, since for demographic reasons alone, the groups
concerned are in constant evolution and the historic process of
contacts and blending continues.

What does the Individual Man owe to his Race?

It may be taken, then, that from the point of view of physical
anthropology, the species *Homo sapiens* consists of a number of
races or groups differentiated by the frequency of particular physical traits which—be it remembered—represent only a mere fraction
of a biological heritage otherwise common to all human beings.
Although it follows that the similarities between men are much
greater than the differences, we are inclined to regard as fundamental differences which are really no more than variations on the
same theme, for, just as we are likely to notice much more difference between the faces of our immediate neighbours than between
those of persons strange to us, so a quite false impression of great
physical differences between the various races of men is reinforced by the fact of such differences between our own kind being
more striking than those between varieties of other species.

The temptation to postulate psychological differences from
such differences in external aspect is the stronger in that the men
of different races in practice often have different cultures. There is
not merely a physical but a mental difference between a magistrate
in one of our great cities and a notable of the Congo. However, the
mental difference between them is not a necessary corollary of the
physical, but a consequence merely of their belonging to two
different cultures. Even so it is not so great as to preclude the
finding of certain resemblances between the two men arising from
their roughly analogous positions in their respective societies, just
as a Norman and a Mandigo peasant, both living off their own
holdings, are likely to present some points of resemblance additional to those common to all men.

The assumption has often been made that what white men
imagine to be the primitive features in the physique of coloured
peoples are indicative of mental inferiority. Even the premise is
vitiated by its naïvety, as the thinner-lipped, and hairier white man
more closely resembles the anthropoid in these respects than does
the Negro. As to mental inferiority, neither anthropological re-

search on such subjects as the weight and structure of the brain in the different races nor psychologists' attempts at direct evaluation of relative intellectual capacity have produced any proof of it.

It has indeed been found that on average the Negro brain weighs a little less than the European, but the difference (considerably less than can be found between the brains of individual members of one race) is so minute that no conclusions can be drawn from it, while the fact that the brains of a number of great men have been found, after death, to be below average size shows that a greater weight of brain does not necessarily mean greater intelligence.

As regards psychological tests, in proportion as we have learned better how to make allowance for the influence of the physical and social environment (the influence of the state of health, social setting upbringing, standard of education, etc.) the results have pointed increasingly to a fundamental equivalence in the intellectual attributes of all human groups. In the present condition of science it is not possible to say of a particular race that it is more (or less) 'intelligent' than another. While it can undoubtedly be shown that a member of a poor and isolated group—or of a lower social class—is handicapped vis-à-vis the members of a group living under better economic conditions (e.g. better nourished, living under healthier conditions and with more incentives), this proves nothing as to the aptitudes which the less privileged individual might display in a more favourable setting. Similarly, in assuming the superiority of so-called 'primitives' over the 'civilised' as regards sensory perception—a superiority regarded as a kind of counterweight to their assumed inferiority intellectually—we are jumping to conclusions and failing to give proper weight to the former's training in observation: a member, say of a community living mainly by hunting and food-gathering, acquires notable superiority over the civilised man in the interpretation of visual, auditory and olfactory impressions, skill in finding his way, etc. . . . and here again, the operative factor is cultural rather than racial.

Lastly, research into character has not been able to show that it is dependent on race: the widest varieties of character are found in all ethnic groups, and there is no reason whatever for assuming greater uniformity under this head in any particular group. For instance, to assume a tendency to irresponsibility in the Negro and to contemplation in the average oriental is to draw a false conclusion from incomplete data: probably white people would be less inclined to picture the Negro as irresponsible if these ideas of him were not based on individuals deprived by slavery or colonisation of their natural background and forced by their masters to tasks to which they can bring no interest. Quite apart from its possibly debasing effect on its victims, such a life leaves them with little choice save between revolt and a resigned or smiling fatalism, which may indeed mask the spirit of rebellion. Similarly, even without the example of Japan's emergence as a full-fledged imperialist power after centuries of almost uninterrupted peace abroad and concentration mainly on questions of etiquette and aesthetic values, we should be less inclined to regard the yellow man as naturally contemplative if, from the beginning, we had gained our impression of China, not from her philosophers and the inventions for which we are indebted to her, but from the realistic literature which, like the licentious novel *Kin P'ing Mei*, first published in 1610, shows us a type of Chinese more inclined to riotous gallantry than to art and mysticism.

Accordingly, the conclusion to be drawn alike from the anthropological and the psychological researches of the last thirty to forty years is that the racial factor is very far from being the dominant element in the formation of personality. This should be no cause for astonishment if we remember that psychological traits cannot be transmitted direct as part of the heredity (for instance, there is no gene governing mind-wandering or power of concentration) which in this sphere comes into play only so far as it affects the organs through which the psychological mechanisms operate, such as the nervous system and the endocrine glands. These, though of real importance in the determination of the affective make-up of normal individuals, obviously exercise a more limited influence on the intellectual and moral qualities compared with that of differences of environment. Under this head the major factors are the character and intellectual level of the parents (owing to the growing child's intimate contact with them), both social and academic training, religious teaching and training in self-mastery, source of livelihood and place in society, in other words elements in no respect traceable to the individual's biological heredity and still less to his race, but largely determined by the setting in which he grows up, the society of which he is a part and the culture to which he belongs.

MAN AND HIS CULTURES

It is a long-standing and widespread Western habit of mind to regard the converse of 'civilisation' as 'savagery' (the state of life of the 'savage', in Latin *silvaticus*, the man of the woods), urban life being taken, rightly or wrongly, as a symbol of refinement in contrast to the supposedly cruder life of forest or bush, and to divide the human race into two categories in terms of these two opposing ways of life. It is accepted as true that parts of the world are inhabited by peoples classifiable on the above basis as savages and held to have risen comparatively little above the level of the beasts, while in other regions there are highly evolved or sophisticated 'civilised' peoples essentially differentiated from the first category as being *par excellence* the trustees and apostles of culture.

The colonial expansion which began with the maritime discoveries of the late fifteenth century introduced the Western stock even into the regions furthest from Europe in space and most unlike in climate, and temporarily at least, Western suzerainty was imposed there and Western culture imported. One consequence was the prevalence in the West until recently, of the view—naïvely egocentric notwithstanding their grounds for pride in their impressive technological progress—that civilisation and culture were synonymous with the Western varieties, if only, in the latter case, the culture of the most privileged classes in the West. The exotic peoples with whom the Western nations made contact either as subject races in their colonies or in their search for products unobtainable in Europe, or new markets for their goods or incidentally to their dispositions for the safeguarding of their earlier conquests, were regarded either as untamed 'savages' ruled by their instincts, or, in the case of peoples deemed inferior but anyhow semi-civilised, as 'barbarians', the contemptuous name given by Ancient Greece to foreigners. The position today is that the majority of Occidentals, whether they regard the way of life of the so called 'uncultured' peoples as approximately that of the beasts or as 'primitive' in the sense of Paradisiac, believe that there are 'wild men' in the world-beings without civilisation representing a phase in the history of humanity analogous to that of childhood in the life of the individual.

Either their noteworthy architectural remains or their close contacts with the classical world (Greece and Rome) fairly early enabled certain major Oriental cultures—or successive series of cultures—to secure acceptance by the West, and Egypt, Phoenicia and Palestine in the Near East, Assyria, Chaldea and Persia, in the Middle East were all sufficiently well known for swift acknowledgement of their title to be described as civilisations worthy of the name. Similarly, India, China, Japan and the great states of pre-Columbian America were not long in receiving their due and no one today would dispute their right to a place of high honour at the very least in any general history of humanity. However, it took the West much longer to realise that peoples little advanced technologically and with no written language as we understand it—like the majority of the black races of Africa, the Melanesians and Polynesians, the modern Indians of North and South America and the Eskimos—nevertheless have their own 'civilisation', i.e. a culture which, even among the humblest of them, at some moment showed itself possessed of some power of expansion (even if that power is now lost or the culture is shrinking) and which is broadly common to a number of societies over a reasonably extensive geographical area.

The knowledge of anthropology (now a systematic discipline) possessed by Western science of the middle twentieth century warrants the assertion that there is no extant group of human beings today which can be described as being 'in the natural state'. For confirmation we need look no further than the elementary fact that nowhere in the world is there a people who leave the human body in an absolutely natural state, without clothing, adornment or some modification (tattooing, scarification or other forms of mutilation), as though—whatever the diversity of the forms taken by what the West calls modesty—the human body in its pristine state could not be tolerated. The truth is that 'natural man' is a figment of the mind and the note which distinguishes Man from the animal world is essentially that he has a culture, whereas the beasts have not, for lack of the capacity for abstract thought, needed for the development of systems of conventional symbols such as language, or the retention for future use of the tools made for a specific task. While it may not be an adequate definition of man to say that he is a *social animal* (since a very wide variety of other species are gregarious), he is sufficiently differentiated if described as *possessing culture*, since he is unique among living creatures in employing such artificial aids as speech and tools in his dealings with his fellows and his environment.

What is Culture?

Among human beings as among all other mammals, the general behaviour of the individual is determined partly by instinct (an item of his biological heritage), partly by his personal experience and partly by what he learns from other members of his species. In Man, however, with his unique powers of symbolising, experience becomes more readily transmissible and in some sort 'storable', since all the acquisitions of a generation can be conveyed to the next through language, and can thus develop into a 'culture', a social legacy distinct from the biological legacy and from the acquisitions of the individual and definable in the terms adopted by Ralph Linton as 'a configuration of learned behaviour and results of behaviour whose component elements are shared and transmitted by the members of a particular society'.

Whereas race is strictly a question of heredity, culture is essentially one of *tradition* in the broadest sense, which includes the formal training of the young in a body of knowledge or a creed, the inheriting of customs or attitudes from previous generations, the borrowing of techniques or fashions from other countries, the spread of opinions through propaganda or conversation, the adoption—or 'selling'—of new products or devices, or even the circulation of legends or jests by word of mouth. In other words, tradition in this sense covers provinces clearly unconnected with biological heredity and all alike consisting in the transmission, by word of mouth, image or mere example, of characteristics which, taken together, differentiate a milieu, society or group of societies throughout a period of reasonable length and thus constitute its culture.

As culture, then, comprehends all that is inherited or transmitted through society, it follows that its individual elements are proportionately diverse. They include not only beliefs, knowledge, sentiments and literature (and illiterate peoples often have an immensely rich oral literature), but the language or other systems of symbols which are their vehicles. Other elements are the rules of kinship, methods of education, forms of government and all the fashions followed in social relations. Gestures, bodily attitudes and even facial expressions are also included, since they are in large measure acquired by the community through education or imitation; and so, among the material elements, are fashions in housing and clothing and ranges of tools, manufactures and artistic production, all of which are to some extent traditional. Far from being restricted to or identical with what is commonly implied in describing a person as 'cultured' or otherwise (i.e. having a greater or lesser sum of knowledge of a greater or lesser variety of the principal branches of arts, letters and science in their Western forms), that is, the ornamental culture which is mainly an outcrop of the vaster mass which conditions it and of which it is only a partial expression, culture in the true sense should be regarded as comprising the whole more or less coherent structure of concepts, sentiments, mechanisms, institutions and objects which explicitly or implicitly condition the conduct of members of a group.

In this context, a group's future is as truly the product of its culture as its culture is of its past, for its culture both epitomises its past experience (what has been retained of the responses of its members in earlier generations to the situations and problems which confronted them) and also—and as a consequence—provides each new generation with a starting point (a system of rules and models of behaviour, values, concepts, techniques, instruments, etc.) round which it will plan its way of life and on which the individual will draw to some extent, and which he will apply in his own way and according to his own means in the specific situation confronting him. Thus it is something which can never be regarded as fixed for ever, but is constantly undergoing changes, sometimes small enough or slow enough to be almost imperceptible or to remain long unnoticed, sometimes of such scope or speed as to appear revolutionary.

Culture and Personality

From the psychological point of view, the culture of a given society is the sum of the ways of thought, reactions and habits of behaviour acquired by its members through teaching or imitation and more or less common to them all.

Quite apart from individual variations (which by definition cannot be regarded as 'cultural', as they do not pertain to the community), there is no question of all the facets of a given society's culture being displayed in all the members of that society. While some of its elements can be described as general, there are others which the mere division of labour (found in all contemporary societies, if only in the form of the allocation of trades and social functions between the two sexes and the various age groups) makes the preserve of certain recognised categories of individuals, others again peculiar to a particular family or set and yet others (opinions, tastes, choice of specific commodities or furniture) which are merely common to a number of individuals between whom there is otherwise nothing particular in common. This uneven occurrence of the individual items making up a culture is a consequence, direct or indirect, of the economic structure of a particular society and (in the case of societies where even a slightly more advanced division of labour prevails) of its subdivision into castes or classes.

While culture may vary between groups, sub-groups and to a certain extent families, and while it is more or less rigid and contains elements of varying compulsive force, it is at the same time a paramount factor in the shaping of individual personality.

Since personality consists in the sum of the outward behaviour and psychological attitudes distinguishing the individual—he being unique, whatever the general type under which he is classifiable—it is affected by a number of factors: biological heredity, which affects the physical organs, and also transmits a range of the comportments which are instinctive or more accurately 'non-acquired'; the experience of the individual in his private life, at his work, and as a member of society—in other words, his life-story over the period (which may be lengthy) from birth until his character may be regarded as set; and his cultural background, whence he derives a proportion of his acquired behaviour by means of his social heritage.

Though biological heredity influences the personality of the individual (to the extent to which his bodily characteristics and more particularly his nervous and glandular make-up are inherited), this is true of the family, rather than of the racial ancestry. Even where individual pedigrees are concerned, we lack the requisite knowledge of the biological make-up of all ancestors, so that in any case our knowledge of what an individual may owe to his heredity is scanty. Furthermore, it can be demonstrated that all normal men, whatever their race, have the same general equipment of non-acquired behaviour (research into child behaviour brings out clearly the similarity of initial responses and shows that the explanation of subsequent variations in behaviour can be explained by differences in individual make-up or by early training); thus, it is not in the so-called 'instinct' that the differences between individuals reside. It must also be borne in mind that the true category of unlearned behaviour is confined to the basic reflexes, and the common tendency to extend it is an error, much behaviour so classified being in fact the result of habits acquired, though never explicitly taught, at so early an age as to give the impression of something inborn.

While undoubtedly there are idiosyncrasies, in addition to those distinguishing individuals, which may be broadly regarded as differentiating the members of a particular society from the rest of the world, it is under the head of acquired behaviour that they will be found; they are thus, by definition, cultural.

To judge of the importance of his culture as a factor in the formation of the individual's personality, we need only remember that it is not merely in the form of the heritage handed down to him through education that his group's culture affects him: it conditions his whole experience. He is born into the world in a particular physical environment (what one might call the bio-geographical habitat) and in a particular social setting. Even the first is not a 'natural' but to some extent a 'cultural' environment, for the habitat of a settled population (agriculturalists or city dwellers) is invariably of its own making to a greater or lesser degree, and, even in the case of nomadic groups, the physical environment will include artificial elements in the shape of tents, etc.; in addition, the impact on the individual of both the natural and the artificial elements in his environment is not direct but is modified by the culture (knowledge, belief and activities) of the group. The influence of the social environment is twofold: direct through the examples available to the newcomer in the behaviour of older members of his society and through the group's speech, in which the whole of its past experience is crystallised and which may therefore be likened to a concise encyclopedia; and indirect, through the influence of the culture concerned on the personalities and the conduct towards the child of the individuals (e.g. parents) playing a prominent part in the subject's life, from early child-hood—a crucial phase which will condition all later development.

In general, the individual is so thoroughly conditioned by his culture that even in the satisfaction of his most elementary needs—those which may be classified as biological because they are shared by man with the other mammals, e.g. feeding, protection and reproduction—he only breaks free of the bonds of custom in the most exceptional circumstances: a normal Western man will only eat dog if threatened with starvation, while many peoples would be utterly nauseated by foods which are a delight to us. Similarly, a man's choice of dress will be appropriate to his station (or to the rank for which he wishes to pass) and often custom, or fashion, will override practical considerations. Lastly, there is no society in which sexual life is absolutely free and, while the details may vary from culture to culture, there are rules everywhere against inter- course within prohibted degrees locally regarded as incestuous and hence criminal. It should also be noted that the individual is at least partially influenced by his culture even where he may seem furthest from the discipline of society: for instance, dreams are not, as was long believed, mere phantasies, but expressions of interests and conflicts which vary according to culture in terms of images drawn directly or indirectly from the cultural environment. Thus culture affects the life of the individual at every level and its in- fluence is as apparent in the way in which a man satisfies his physical needs as in his ethics or his intellectual life.

The inference to be drawn from all this is that while obviously there are variations in the psychological heritage of individuals the fact of a man's belonging to a particular ethnic group affords no basis for deducing what are likely to be his aptitudes. On the other hand, the cultural environment is a factor of primary importance not merely because it determines what the individual learns and how he learns it, but because it is in the strict sense the 'environ- ment' within which and in terms of which he reacts. For instance, it is a safe assumption that, if an African baby were adopted at birth by whites and brought up as their own child, there would be no marked psychological differences imputable to his origin be- tween him and his foster parents' natural children of the same sex; he would express himself in the same idiom with the same accent; he would have the same equipment of ideas, feelings and habits and would differ from his brothers and sisters by adoption only to the extent to which the members of any group fall short of uniformity, however great and numerous the analogies between them. It should, of course, be realised that this example is purely hypo- thetical as, even in an adoptive family free of race prejudice in any form, such a child would in fact be in a different position from the rest. For the experiment to be valid, one would have to be able to eliminate the probable influence on the subject (of unforeseeable effect and importance) of his being regarded as different from others, if not by his immediate circle, at least by other members of

the same society. The point however is that the special differentiating factor which might become operative would be not *race* but
race prejudice, which, even without positive discrimination, puts
its victims in a position differing in kind from that of persons
whom no preconceived idea can cause to be regarded as not 'like
everyone else'.

How Cultures Live

Being identified with a way of life peculiar to a specified human
society in a specified epoch, a culture, however slow its evolution,
can never be entirely static. Insofar at least as it exists as an
organised system, recognisable despite its variations, it is the
apanage of a group which is constantly changing through the mere
processes of death and birth. Its radius (i.e. 'membership') may
increase or decrease, but at every stage in its history, it consists
exclusively of elements socially transmissible (by inheritance or
borrowing) and hence—though there are bound to be modifications
or even major alterations, with the rejection of former elements
and the addition of new—the culture itself is able to continue
through all the transformations of the fluid group it represents, and
share its hazards or disasters, assimilate new elements and export
certain of its own, more or less replace the culture of a different
group (through conquest or otherwise) or conversely be absorbed
by another culture (leaving few, or no, visible traces behind it).
Clearly, then, a culture is essentially a provisional and infinitely
flexible system. Almost everywhere in the world we find the old
comparing the way of life of the young unfavourably with 'the
good old days', and that in itself amounts to an explicit or implicit
admission that customs have changed and that the culture of their
society has evolved further. The change may be brought about in
either of two ways, by invention or discovery within the society, or
by borrowing (spontaneous or under constraint) from outside.

Even when they result from an invention (a new application of
existing knowledge of any kind) or a discovery (the appearance of
new knowledge, scientific or otherwise), innovations in a culture
are never entirely original in that they never 'start from scratch':
for instance, the invention of the loom not merely implied prior
knowledge of certain laws and of other simpler mechanisms, but
also the response to a need arising at a particular moment in the
evolution of modern industry. Similarly, the discovery of America

would have been impossible without the compass, while Christopher Columbus would never even have thought of sailing westwards if the march of events had not made a maritime trade route to the Indies a felt need. In the aesthetic sphere, the work of Phidias could never have come about without Polycletes, nor Andalusian folk music of today have developed without Arab music; and, as a last example, in the sphere of government, it was on Athenian life and aspirations already existing that Solon drew to endow his fellow citizens with a new Constitution, which in fact was no more than a codification of the existing social complex. Thus no invention, discovery or innovation can be ascribed exclusively to one individual. Inventors, or pioneers on other lines, are, indeed, found in all civilisations. However, an invention is not the result of a single flash of genius, but the last stage in a gradual advance, as the following sequence exemplifies: in 1663, the Marquess of Worcester devised a 'steam fountain' on his estate near London, based on principles suggested about 50 years earlier by a Frenchman, Salomon de Caus. Later came the invention of the pressure boiler by another Frenchman, Denis Papin, leading in turn to that of the reciprocating engine by James Watt and the final step was George Stephenson's construction of the 'Rocket' locomotive in 1814. Neither inventions nor discoveries are ever more than modifications, variable in their degree and their repercussions, which are the latest of a long series of earlier inventions and discoveries in a culture which is itself the work of a community and the product of indigenous innovations or borrowings from abroad by earlier generations. This is as true of innovations in religion, philosophy, art or ethics as of those in the various branches of science and technology. The work of great founders of religions (e.g. Buddha, Jesus or Mohammed) has never amounted to more than the more or less drastic reform of an existing religion or the combination of elements from a number of sources to construct a new creed. Again, it is traditional problems to which a culture's philosophers or moralists devote their time. The statement of the problems and the solutions propounded vary with the age, and divergent opinions on them may obtain concurrently, but nevertheless, the chain of tradition remains unbroken: each thinker takes up the question at the point where it was left by some predecessor.

It is not otherwise with works of literature or plastic art: however revolutionary it may seem, such work always has its antecedents, as with the cubists claiming aesthetic descent from the impressionist, Paul Cézanne, and finding in African Negro sculpture, not lessons only, but a precedent to justify their own experiments. Lastly, even in social relations in the strict sense, non-conformists of every variety—and there are such in all peoples and all circles—normally claim a precedent for their views and, if they make innovations, confine themselves to developing further or more consciously what has elsewhere remained more or less rudimentary. Thus a culture is clearly the work neither of a 'culture hero' (as in so many mythologies) nor of a few great geniuses, inventors or lawgivers; it is the fruit of co-operation. From a certain point of view, the earliest representatives of the human species might of all men be most legitimately described as 'creators'; but even here we have to bear in mind that they had behind them not a void but the example of other species.

Generally speaking, Western man of our own day is dazzled by the inventions and discoveries which can be credited to his culture and is almost ready to think that he has a monopoly in this field. To make this assumption would be to forget firstly that discoveries such as Einstein's theory of relativity, or nuclear fission are the crown of a long process of evolution leading up to them and secondly that innumerable inventions, today out of date and their makers forgotten, showed in their age and place a degree of genius at least equal to that of the most famous of our own scientists. For instance, the primitive inhabitants of Australia made boomerangs which could return to the point from which they were thrown, with neither laboratories nor scientific research services to help them with the complex ballistic problems involved. Similarly the ancestors of the Polynesians of today, moving onward from island to island without compasses and with outrigger canoes as their only vessels, accomplished feats in no wise inferior to those of Christopher Columbus and the great Portuguese navigators.

Fecundity of Contacts

Although no culture is absolutely static, it is indisputable that a high density of population furnishes more favourable conditions for new developments in the culture of the group concerned, as the multiplicity of contacts between individuals brings greater intensity to the intellectual life of each. Furthermore, in such numerous and

thickly settled groups, a more extensive division of labour becomes possible—as noted years ago by Emile Durkheim, founder
of the French Sociological School—and the increase in specialisation results not merely in technological progress, but in the subdivision of the group into separate social classes between which
tensions or conflicts of interests or self-esteem are bound to arise,
this in its turn involving sooner or later a modification of the
established cultural forms. In societies of this degree of complexity,
the individual is on average confronted with a wider variety of
situations which he must tackle along new lines and thus modify
the traditional responses in the light of his numerous experiences.

Similarly the less isolated a people is, the more windows it has
on the outer world and the more its opportunities for contact with
other peoples, the more likelihood of its culture growing richer
alike by direct borrowings and as a result of its members' diversified experience and increased need to meet new situations. Even
war is a means of contact between peoples though far from the
most desirable type, as all too often, only fragments of a culture, if
anything, survive the trials of military conquest or oppression. A
good example of cultural stagnation brought about by isolation is
that of the Tasmanians who, being cut off from the rest of humanity by their island's geographical position, were still technologically at the middle palaeolithic stage when the English settled
there at the beginning of last century. In fact, the ending of their
isolation was far from advantageous to the Tasmanians, for today
they are totally extinct, having perished piecemeal in their contact
warfare against the colonists; hence the conclusion to be drawn is
that, while in principle, contact, even through war, aids cultural
evolution, it is essential, if such contact is to be fruitful, that it
occurs between peoples whose technological levels are not too
different (to avoid the mere extermination of one of them or its
reduction to a state of near-servitude resulting in its traditional
culture's extinction). It is also essential that armaments should not
have achieved—as is unhappily the case with the great nations of
the modern world—such a degree of effectiveness that both sides,
even if they escape utter destruction, emerge from the conflict
ruined.

We have seen, then, that the means, external or internal, where-
by a culture is transformed include contact between individuals
and between peoples, borrowings, the making of new combinations
from existing elements and the discovery of new relationships or

facts. So great is the part played by borrowings that we may say the same of cultures as of races, that they are never 'pure' and that there is none of them which, in its present state, is not the result of co-operation between different peoples. The civilisation of which the Western world is so proud has been built of a myriad contributions, of which many are non-European in origin. The alphabet first reached the Phoenicians from the Semitic communities bordering the Sinai Peninsula, travelled from them to the Greeks and Romans and then spread through the western-most parts of Europe. Our numerals and algebra come to us from the Arabs whose philosophers and scientists incidentally played an important part in the various renaissances of medieval Europe. The earliest astronomers were Chaldeans; steel was invented in India or Turkistan; coffee comes from Ethiopia; tea, porcelain, gunpowder, silk, rice and the compass were given us by the Chinese who also were acquainted with printing centuries before Gutenberg, and early discovered how to make paper. Maize, tobacco, the potato, quinine, coca, vanilla and cacao we owe to the American Indians. The explanation of the 'miracle of Greece' is really that Greece was a crossroads, where vast numbers of different peoples and cultures met. Lastly, we should recollect that the wall paintings and engravings of the Aurignacian and Magdalenian ages (the most ancient works of art known in Europe, of which it may be said with truth that their beauty has never been exceeded) were the work of men of the Grimaldi type, probably not unlike the Negro races of today; that, in another aesthetic sphere, the jazz which plays so important a part in our leisure, was evolved by the descendants of Negroes taken to the United States as slaves, to whom that country also owes the oral literature on which the famous Uncle Remus stories are based.

Race History and Cultural Differences

However numerous the exchanges between different cultures in the courses of history, and despite the fact that none of these cultures can be regarded as 'pure-bred', the fact is that differences do exist and it is possible to identify specific culture areas and periods: for instance, there was a Germanic culture described by Tacitus and of interest to him precisely because of its differences from Latin culture. In our own day, the task of the anthropologist is to study cultures diverging considerably from what with certain variants is the common culture of the Western nations. This must suggest the question whether there is a causal relationship between race and culture and whether each of the various ethnic groups has on balance a predisposition to develop certain cultural forms. However, such a notion cannot survive a scrutiny of the facts and it can be taken as established today that hereditary physical differences are negligible as causes of the differences in culture observable between the peoples. What should rather be taken into consideration is the history of those peoples.

The first point which stands out is that a given culture is not the creation of a particular race, but normally of several. Let us take as an example what we call 'Egyptian civilisation', i.e. the cultural *continuum* found in Egypt between the neolithic age (when wheat and the same type of barley as today were already being cultivated in the Fayum area) and the third century of our own era, when Christianity spread over the country; the excavation of tombs has shown that from the polished stone age onwards the population of Egypt was Hamitic, while an entirely different strain is found in addition from the beginning of the dynastic epoch. At various times the country was invaded by the Hyksos (nomads from Asia who arrived in the second millennium B.C. and introduced the horse and the war chariot), by the Libyans, by the Peoples of the Sea (who may have included the Achaeans), the Assyrians, and the Persians (whose sway ended only with Egypt's annexation by Alexander in 332 B.C. and entry into the Greek orbit, in which she remained until the defeat of Antony and Cleopatra in 31 B.C.); while after a period of relative isolation there was sustained intercourse with the neighbouring countries of the Near East. The vicissitudes of Egypt's history appear to have had little effect on the physical type, which was stabilised at an early epoch, and although they altered her culture, she remained throughout the home of a civilisation based economically on an oasis (in this case, the Nile Valley fertilised by the annual floods). Alexandria, capital of the Ptolemies, as a cosmopolitan city at the cross-roads of Asia, Africa and Europe, enjoyed a period of great brilliance during the hellenistic age. In Europe too, there is proof of the successive rise and decline of a number of races in the course of prehistory, while from the neolithic age onwards, the flow of trade points to true 'cultural relations' between different peoples. It is notable that in Equatorial Africa even the pygmies, who are exclusively hunters and food-gatherers, live in a kind of economic symbiosis with the settled Negroes who are their neighbours, and exchange game for agricultural products; this relationship is not without other cultural consequences and today the languages of the various groups of pygmies are those of the groups of Negro agriculturalists with whom they are thus linked.

Not only do all the indications point to there being no culture all of whose elements are due to a single race, but it is also apparent that no given race necessarily practises a single culture. In our own time, social transformations of considerable extent have taken place with no corresponding alteration in racial type of which the revolution engendered in Japan by the Emperor Mutsuhito (1866–1912) is the perfect example. To take another instance, the Manchus, who were a semi-civilised Tungus tribe when they conquered China in the middle of the seventeenth century, provided a dynasty which reigned gloriously over a country passing through one of the most brilliant periods of its civilisation; and later China first overthrew the Manchu dynasty in 1912 in favour of a Republic and is now in the process of socialisation. Again, when the expansion of Asia began after the death of Mohammed in A.D. 632, some Arab groups founded great states and built cities where the arts and sciences flourished, whereas other groups which had stayed in Arabia, remained simple pastoralists driving their flocks from grazing to grazing. Even before the total disruption of its ways of life first by the razzias of Muslim slavers, next by the seaborne traffic in human beings run by Europeans, and finally by European conquest, Negro Africa suffered the handicap of relative isolation. Nevertheless, its history tells us of such empires as the Ghana Kingdom in West Africa, roughly coeval with our own Middle Ages, which aroused the admiration of Arab travellers; and today, though many Negro tribes appear never to have achieved a political organisation on a broader basis than the village, we find, as in Nigeria, great cities founded long before the European occupation. How then is it possible to claim that each physical type connotes a certain type of culture, especially if we look beyond the Negroes of Africa itself to those others, to the number of some 35 millions, who today form part of the population of the Americas and the West Indies? Though the descendants of Africans whose culture was utterly overset by the scourge of slavery, which robbed them of their freedom and their country, these people have nevertheless succeeded in adapting themselves to a cultural setting very different from that in which their ancestors were bred, and have since contrived (despite the prejudice of which they are the victims) to play a major role in many sectors in building and spreading the civilisation of which Occidentals had believed themselves to be the exclusive representatives; in literature alone, a Negro, Aimé Césaire, of Martinique is among the major contemporary French poets, and another Negro, Richard Wright of Mississippi, may be accounted among the most talented of American novelists.

From the history of Europe as well, we can learn how much the customs of peoples can change without major alteration of their racial composition, and hence how fluid is 'national character'. Who would suspect that the peaceable farmers of modern Scandinavia were the descendants of the dreaded Vikings, whose long ships raided so much of Europe in the ninth century? Or would a Frenchman of 1950 recognise as his fellow-countrymen the contemporaries of Charles Martel, who conquered the Arabs at Poitiers if he had not learned it in the schools? It is also worth remembering that when Julius Caesar first landed in Great Britain in 52 B.C., the Britons struck the invaders as so barbarous that Cicero, writing to his friend Atticus, advised him against buying any of them as slaves because 'they are so utterly stupid and incapable of learning'. Nor should we forget that, after the fall of the Roman Empire, the inhabitants of Europe took many centuries to establish solidly organised and militarily formidable states; throughout the whole of the Middle Ages—conventionally taken as ending in 1453 with Mohammed II's capture of Constantinople —Europe had to defend itself alike against Mongol peoples such as the Huns (who nearly reached the Atlantic), the Avars, the Magyars (who finally settled in Hungary) and the Turks (to whom part of south-east Europe was subject for many centuries) and against the Arabs (who, after conquering North Africa, were settled for some time in Spain and the islands of the Mediterranean). At that epoch it would have been difficult to foresee that Europeans would one day found empires.

Analogous examples of variability in the aptitudes of a given nation are afforded by the history of the fine arts: the music, painting and sculpture or architecture of some country will pass through a brilliant period and then for some centuries at least nothing further of any note will be produced. Can it seriously be claimed that such fluctuations in artistic talent are due to changes in the distribution of the genes?

It is thus fruitless to seek in the biology of race an explanation of the difference observable between the cultural achievements of the various peoples. However, seeking to find the explanation, say, in the nature of the habitat is nearly as misleading and, just as North American Indians, despite a high degree of racial uniformity, display wide differences in culture (for instance the warrior Apaches of the south-west and the much more peaceable Pueblos who are racially identical), so a given climate does not imply a particular type of dwelling and costume (in the Sudan we find great variety in the types of house and heavily robed peoples living cheek by jowl with others almost naked). The life of a social group is of course conditioned by its biogeographical setting, agriculture is as out of the question in the Arctic zone as are cattle and horse breeding in the extensive areas of Africa infested by the tsetse fly; it is also indisputable that, as a general rule, a temperate climate is more favourable to human settlement and demographic development than one of extremes either way. However, varying techniques can secure very different results from similar biogeographical conditions: thus, as Pierre Gourou has pointed out, the practice of cultivating rice in flooded fields in tropical Asia has for ages past permitted a high density of population precluded in almost all other tropical areas, where land is cleared by fire and cultivated dry, by the poverty and instability of the soil. The explanation of the cultural diversity of the various peoples is accordingly more likely to be found in their past history than in their present geographical situation; the factors likely to be of preponderant importance are the knowledge acquired in the different areas they traversed during the wanderings (often long and complex) preceding their final settlement in the areas where we find them today, the degree of isolation in which they have lived or, conversely, their contacts with other peoples and the opportunities they have had of borrowing from other cultures—all of them explicitly classifiable as historical.

Franz Boas has written:

'The history of mankind proves that advances of culture depend upon the opportunities presented to a social group to learn from the experience of their neighbours. The discoveries of the group spread to others and, the more varied the contacts, the greater are the opportunities to learn. The tribes of simplest culture are on the whole those that have been isolated for very long periods and hence could not profit from the cultural achievements of their neighbours.'

The peoples of Europe—whose overseas expansion, be it remembered, is of very recent date, today restricted by the evolution of the very peoples they formerly surpassed in technique—owed their cultural lead to the opportunities they have long had of frequent contacts among themselves and with contrasting groups. The Romans, who may be regarded as the founders of the first major state to exist in Europe, borrowed from Asia in the construction of their Empire, and their only enduring successor, the Byzantine Empire, owed more of its administrative organisation to Persia than to Rome. Conversely, the relative isolation of Africans for so many ages should be an added reason for admiring their success, despite these adverse conditions, in founding, before the fifteenth century, such a state as Benin (a prosperous kingdom which produced masterpieces in bronze and ivory in an age when Europe cannot have supplied the Negro artists with models), or making sixteenth-century Timbuctoo, the capital of the Songoi Empire, one of the principal intellectual centres of the Muslim world. Not merely for Africa's sake, but for that of the rest of the world, it is regrettable that the rapid expansion of the European nations, at a period when the material equipment available to them was out of all proportion to those in the hands of other people, should have nipped in the bud a score of cultures whose full potentialities we shall never know.

Can a Hierarchy of Cultures be Established?

Fundamentally, the cultures of the peoples reflect their past history and vary with their experiences. In peoples, as in individuals, the acquired qualities count for far more than the innate: their differing experience involves a corresponding difference in their acquired knowledge so that the world of today is populated by human groups of widely differing cultures, each having certain dominant preoccupations which may be regarded as representing (in Professor M. J. Herskovits' words) the 'focus of its culture'.

Main interest and scales of values may differ entirely between any two societies. The Hindus have gone deeply into the techniques of control of the self and meditation, but until recent days had devoted little attention to the material techniques on which their American and European contemporaries concentrated, and the latter in their turn show little inclination to metaphysical speculation and still less to the practice of philosophy. In Thibet the monastic life has always been preferred to the military interests which unhappily loom so large in our lives today. Among the Hamitic Negroes of East Africa, stock-raising is held in such esteem that their cattle are capital rather than food and we find a people like the Banyoro divided into two castes of which the higher concerns itself with stock-raising and the lower with agriculture; but conversely many societies of black agriculturalists in West Africa leave the care of their cattle to Fulani whom they despise. The existence of such degrees of cultural specialisation should counsel caution in making value judgements of a culture; there is no culture which will not be found defective in certain respects and highly advanced in others, or which, on examination, will not prove more complex than the apparent simplicity of its structure had suggested. Although they used no draught animals and had not invented the wheel or discovered iron, the pre-Columbian Indian races have nevertheless left us impressive monuments which testify to the existence of a highly developed social organisation and are among the finest works of man, while one such nation, the Mayas, arrived at the concept of zero independently of the Arabs. Again, no one will seek to dispute that the Chinese created a great civilisation, but for long ages they neither consumed their cattle's milk nor used the dung in agriculture. The Polynesians, though technologically only at the polished stone stage, developed a very rich mythology, while Negroes who had been thought to be, at best, suitable only as servile labour for the plantations of the New World, have made extensive contributions to the arts; incidentally, it was in Africa that the two varieties of millet, which have since spread throughout Asia, were first cultivated. Even the Australian aborigines, whose technology is rudimentary in the extreme, have marriage rules based on theories of consanguinity of the utmost subtlety. Lastly, our own civilisation, despite its high technological development, is defective in many respects, as is proved by such facts as the high number of maladjusted persons found in the West, not to mention the social problems which the Western countries have still not solved nor the wars on which they periodically embark.

The truth is that all cultures have their successes and failures, their faults and virtues. Even language, the instrument and channel of thought, cannot serve as a yardstick to measure their relative worth; extremely rich grammatical forms are found in the speech of peoples without a written language and regarded as uncivilised. It would be equally vain to judge a culture by the criterion of our own ethical standards, for—apart from the fact that our ethics are too often no more than theoretical—many non-European societies are in certain respects more humane than our own. As the great African expert, Maurice Delafosse, points out: 'In African Negro society there are neither widows nor orphans, both alike being an automatic responsibility either of their families or of the husband's heir'; again, there are cultures in Siberia and elsewhere in which individuals whom we should shun as abnormal are regarded as inspired by the Gods and as such have their special place in social life. Men whose culture differs from our own are neither more nor less moral than ourselves; each society has its own moral standards, by which it divides its own members into good and evil, and one can certainly not form a judgement on the morality of a culture (or a race) on the strength of the behaviour, sometimes culpable from our point of view, of a proportion of its members living under the special conditions created by their status as a subject people or abrupt transplantation to another country as soldiers or labourers usually living under conditions of hardship. Lastly the argument of some anthropologists that, certain peoples are inferior on the grounds that they have produced no 'great men' is untenable. Apart from the desirability of an initial definition of what is meant by a 'great man' (a conqueror with innumerable victims to his credit; a great scientist, artist, philosopher or poet; the founder of a religion or a great saint), it is clear that, as the essential condition for classification as a 'great man' is the eventual widespread recognition of such 'greatness', it is impossible by definition for an isolated society to have produced what we call a 'great man'. It must however be emphasised that even in regions which were long isolated—in Africa and Polynesia for instance—we find strong personalities such as the Mandingue emperor, Gongo Moussa (to whom is ascribed the introduction in the fourteenth century of the type of architecture still characteristic of the mosques and larger houses of the western Sudan), the Zulu conqueror Chaka, the Liberian prophet Harris (who preached a syncretic Christianity on the Ivory Coast in 1913 and 1914), Finau, King of Tonga, or Kamehameha, King of Hawaii (a contemporary of Cook). These and a score of others may well have been prevented merely by their too isolated and demographically restricted cultural environment from achieving recognition by a sufficient number of people to qualify—on quantitative as opposed to qualitative grounds—as 'great men' comparable in stature to our own Alexander, Plutarch, Luther or the Roi Soleil. Moreover, it is undeniable that even a relatively elementary technology implies a considerable background of knowledge and skill and that the development of a culture, however rudimentary, at all adapted to its environment, would be inconceivable if the community in question had never produced a mind above the average.

Our notions of culture being themselves integral elements in a culture (that of the society to which we belong), it is impossible for us to adopt the impartial point of view from which alone a valid hierarchy of cultures could be established. Judgements in this matter are necessarily relative and dependent on the point of view, and an African, Indian or Polynesian would be as fully justified in passing a severe judgement on the ignorance of most of us in matters of genealogy as we should on his ignorance of the laws of electricity or Archimedes' principle. What we are entitled to assert, however, as a positive fact is that there are cultures which at a particular point in history come into possession of technical resources sufficiently developed for the balance of power to operate in their favour and that such cultures tend to supplant other civilisations with inferior technical equipment with which they enter into contact. Today, Western civilisation is in that position and—whatever the political difficulties and antagonisms of the nations representative of it—it is spreading over the world, if only in the form of its industrial product. The power of expansion conferred by technology and science might finally achieve recognition as the decisive criterion according to which each culture could be described as more or less 'great'; but it should be understood that 'greatness' must not be interpreted solely in what might be described as a *volumetric* sense and that it is moreover on strictly *pragmatic* grounds (i.e. in terms of the effectiveness of its recipes) that the value of a science can be assessed and that it can be regarded as living or dead and distinguished from a merely 'magical' technique. If the experimental method—in whose use the Western and Westernised nations of today excel—is an undoubted advance on *a priori* and empirical methods, it is essentially so because its results (unlike those of the other methods named) can serve as a starting point for new developments capable in their turn of practical application. Incidentally, it must be obvious that, since science as a whole is the product of a vast amount of experiment and development, to which all races have contributed for many thousands of years, it can in no respect be regarded by white men as their exclusive preserve and as indicating in themselves some congenital aptitude.

Subject to these explicit reservations, it is right to emphasise the capital importance of technology (i.e. the means of acting on the natural environment), not merely in the day to day life of societies but in their evolution. The chief milestones in the history of mankind are advances in technology which in turn have the widest repercussions in all other sectors of culture. The process begins with tool-making and the use of fire at the very beginnings of prehistory and even before the emergence of *Homo sapiens*; next comes the domestication of plants and animals for food, which raises the potential density of population and is the direct cause of the settlement of human groups in villages (a notable transformation of the natural environment), followed in turn by increasing division of labour and the emergence of crafts. At each stage the direct increase in economic resources leaves a sufficient margin for considerable development in other sectors. The latest such milestone is the development of power resources which marks the beginning of the modern age.

The earliest civilisations of any size, being based on agriculture, were restricted to areas made fertile by great rivers (the Nile, the Euphrates, the Tigris, the Indus, the Ganges, and the Blue and Yellow Rivers). They were followed by trading civilisations lying on inland seas or seas with frequent land masses (the Phoenicians and Greeks in the Mediterranean, and the Malays in the China Seas), which were later displaced by civilisations based on large-scale industry whose vital centres were the coal deposits in Europe, North America and Asia, and trading on a world-wide basis. Now that we have entered the atomic age, no one knows where—wars permitting—the principal centres of production will arise in the world nor whether the setting for the great civilisations of the future may not be regions today regarded as backward, whose inhabitants' only crime is that they belong to cultures less well equipped than our own with means of modifying their natural environment but possibly better balanced from the point of view of social relations.

THERE IS NO INBORN RACIAL AVERSION

The differences observable between the physiques of the different races (and we must remember that the only features so far used by anthropologists as practical criteria or differentiation are purely superficial, such as colour of skin, colour and form of eyes and hair, shape of the skull, nose and lips, stature, etc.) afford no clue to the cast of mind and type of behaviour characterising the members of each of the human varieties: outside the field of pure biology, the word 'race' is utterly meaningless. Independently of their political division into nationalities, men can undoubtedly be classified in groups characterised by a certain community of behaviour, but only in terms of their several 'cultures', in other words from the standpoint of the history of their respective civilisations; the groups thus delimited are quite distinct from the categories which can be determined in terms of physical similarity, while their relative worth can be determined in the light of pragmatic considerations only, and such judgements lack all absolute validity since they are necessarily conditioned by our own culture. In any case, the scale of values thus arrived at might well be relevant for a specific period only, since cultures, even more than races, are fluid, and peoples are capable of very rapid cultural evolution after centuries of near-stagnation. In the light of this, it may be asked what is the origin of the prejudice behind the attempt to classify certain human groups as inferior on the ground that their racial composition is an irremediable handicap.

The first point which emerges from any examination of the data of ethnography and history is that race prejudice is not universal and is of recent origin. Many of the societies investigated by anthropologists do indeed display group pride, but while the group regards itself as privileged compared with other groups, it makes no 'racist' claims and, for instance, is not above entering into temporary alliances with other groups or providing itself with women from them. Much more than 'blood', the unifying elements are common interests and a variety of activities conducted in association. In the majority of cases such groups are not in fact 'races'—if very isolated, they may at most be homogeneous offshoots of a race—but are merely societies whose antagonism to other societies, whether traditional or arising from specific questions of interest, is not biological but purely cultural. The peoples whom the Greeks described as 'barbarians' were not regarded by them as racially inferior but as not having attained the same level of civilisation as themselves; Alexander himself married two Persian princesses and 10,000 of his soldiers married Hindus. The main interest her subject peoples had for Rome was as a source of tribute and, since she did not pursue the same ends of systematic exploitation of the earth and its population as more recent imperialisms, she had no reason to practise racial discrimination against them. The Christian faith preached the brotherhood of man and, while all too often it fell short of its own principle in practice, it never evolved a racist ideology. The Crusades were launched against the 'infidels', the Inquisition persecuted heretics and Jews, and Catholics and Protestants exterminated each other, but in every case the motives alleged were religious and not racial. The picture only begins to change with the opening of the period of colonial expansion by the European peoples, when it becomes necessary to excuse violence and oppression by decreeing the inferiority of those enslaved or robbed of their own land and denying the title of men to the cheated peoples. (Differences in customs and the physical stigma of colour made the task an easy one.)

That the origins of race prejudice are economic and social becomes perfectly clear, if we bear in mind that the first great apostle of racism, Count de Gobineau, said himself that he wrote his two notorious 'Essays' to combat liberalism: the better to defend the threatened interest of the aristocratic caste of Europe, against the rising tide of democracy, he postulated their descent from a socalled superior race which he labelled 'Aryan', and for which he postulated a civilising mission. We find the same motive yet again in the attempt by anthropologists such as Broca and Vacher de Lapouge of France and the German Ammon to demonstrate by anthropometry that class distinctions reflect differences in race (and hence are part of the natural order). However, the amazing intermingling of human groups which has taken place in Europe as in the rest of the world since prehistoric times, and the unceasing movements of population occurring in the countries of modern Europe are enough to demonstrate the fatuity of the attempt. Later, racism took on the virulent quality we know so well and, more particularly in Germany, appeared in nationalist guise, though still remaining in essence an ideology designed to introduce or perpetuate a system of caste economically and politically favourable to a minority, e.g. by cementing a nation's unity by the idea of itself as a master race, by inculcating in colonial populations the feeling that they are irremediably inferior to the colonisers, by preventing part of the population within a country from rising in the social scale, by eliminating competition in employment or by neutralising popular discontent by supplying the people with a scapegoat which is also a profitable source of loot. There is bitter irony in the fact that racism developed parallel with the growth of democracy, which made an appeal to the new-born prestige of science necessary for the calming of consciences uneasy over flagrant violation of the rights of a section of mankind or refusal to recognise those rights.

Racial prejudice is not innate. As Ashley Montagu has noted: 'In America, where white and black populations frequently live side by side, it is an indisputable fact that white children do not learn to consider themselves superior to Negro children until they are told that they are so.' When a tendency to racism (in the form either of voluntary endogamy or the more or less aggressive assertion of one's own 'race's' virtue) is found in an 'outcast' group, it should be regarded as no more than the normal reaction of the 'insulted and injured' against the ostracism or persecution of which they are the victims and not as indicating the universality of racial prejudice. Whatever the role of the aggressive instinct in human psychology, there is no tendency for men to commit hostile acts against others because they are of a different breed and, if such acts are all too often committed, the reason is not hostility of biological origin; just as there has never, to the writer's knowledge, been an instance of a dog fight in which spaniels combined against bulldogs.

There are no races of masters as opposed to races of slaves: slavery is not coeval with mankind and only appeared in societies whose technology was sufficiently developed to make slave-owning profitable.

From the sexual point of view, there appears no evidence of any repulsion between race and race, and indeed all the facts so far collected demonstrate that there has been continual cross-breeding between races since the most ancient times. Nor is there the slightest evidence of such cross-breeding having given bad results since a civilisation as brilliant as that of Greece arose in a human environment in which miscegenation appears to have been rampant.

Race prejudice is no more hereditary than it is spontaneous: it is in the strictest sense a 'prejudice', that is, a cultural value judgement with no objective basis. Far from being in the order of things or innate in human nature, it is one of the myths whose origin is much more propaganda by special interests than the tradition of centuries. Since there is an essential connection between it and the antagonisms arising out of the economic structure of modern societies, its disappearance, like that of other prejudices which are less the causes than the symptoms of social injustice, will go hand in hand with the transformation of their economic structure by the peoples. Thus the co-operation on an equal footing of all human groups, whatever they be, will open undreamed-of prospects for civilisation.

Bibliography

Benedict, Ruth, *Race: Science and Politics* (New York: The Viking Press, 1945).

Boas, Franz, 'Racial purity', *Asia*, Vol. 40 (1940).

Civilisation. Le mot et l-idée. Survey by Lucien Febvre, E. Tonnelat, Marcel Mauss, Alfredo Niceforo, Louis Weber. Discussion. Fondation 'Pour la Science'. Première semaine internationale de synthèse, Vol. 2 (Paris: Alcan, 1930).

Delafosse, Maurice, *Civilisations négro-africaines* (Paris: Stock, 1925).

Durkheim, Emile, *De la division du travail social* (2nd ed.) (Paris: Alcan, 1902).

Finot, Jean, *Le préjugé des races* (Paris: Alcan, 1906).

Gourou, Pierre, *Les pays tropicaux* (Paris: Presses Universitaires de France, 1948).

Herskovits, M. J., *Man and his Works* (New York: Alfred A. Knopf, 1949).

Huxley, Julian S. and Haddon, A. C., *We Europeans: a Survey of 'Racial' Problems* (New York: Harper and Brothers, 1936).

L'espèce humaine, Edited by Paul Rivet, *Encyclopédie française permanente*, Vol. VII (Paris, 1936).

Lester, Paul et Millot, Jacques, *Les races humaines* (Paris: Armand Colin, 1936).

Lévi-Strauss, Claude, *Les structures élémentaires de la parenté* (Paris: Presses Universitaires de France, 1949).

Linton, Ralph, *The Study of Man* (New York, London: D. Appleton-Century Company, 1936).

Linton, Ralph, *The Cultural Background of Personality* (New York, London: D. Appleton-Century Company, 1945).

Montagu, Ashley, *Man's Most Dangerous Myth: the Fallacy of Race* (New York: Columbia University Press, 1942).

Scientific Aspects of the Race Problem, By H. S. Jennings, Charles A. Berger, Dom Thomas Verner Moore, Aleys Hrdlicka, Robert H. Lowie, Otto Klineberg (Washington D.C.: The Catholic University of America Press, and London: Longmans, 1941).

The science of man in the world crisis, Edited by Ralph Linton (New York: Columbia University Press, 1945).

Vallois, Henri V., *Anthropologie de la population française* (Paris: Didier, Toulouse, 1943).

When peoples meet, Edited by Alain Locke and Bernhard J. Stern (New York, Philadelphia: Hinds, Hayden and Eldredge, 1942).

White, Leslie A., *The Science of Culture* (New York: Farrar, Straus and Co., 1949).

Race and Psychology[*]
The problem of genetic differences
(Revised edition)

by OTTO KLINEBERG

Professor Emeritus of Social Psychology, Columbia University, New York and Directeur d'etudes associé Ecole pratique des hautes etudes, Paris

When the first edition of this chapter was published in 1950, there was good reason to believe that the notion of a genetic or inborn racial hierarchy had practically disappeared from the thinking of social and biological scientists concerned with this issue. The general position could perhaps best be stated in negative terms, namely that there was no acceptable scientific evidence in favour of such a hierarchy and that consequently any political or educational programme based on the alleged innate inferiority of any racial or ethnic group had no scientific validity. Some years earlier (1944) Gunnar Myrdal and his associates in *An American Dilemma* had called for an educational offensive to reduce the gap between this position of the social scientists on the one hand, and that of the general public on the other. In the years that followed it began to appear that at least in the United States a real change in this respect had occurred in the general public. When a representative sample of White Americans were asked the question: 'In general, do you think that Negroes are as intelligent as White people—that is, can they learn things just as well if they are given the same education and training?'—the proportion answering in the affirmative rose from 50% in 1942 to almost 80% in 1964 (Hyman and Sheatsley). It looked as if this particular issue were dead, or at least dying. Myrdal went so far as to say in a Nobel Symposium published in 1970: 'The racial inferiority doctrine has disappeared, which is an undivided advance, since it has no scientific basis' (p. 158).

* Revised version of the work first published in *The Race Question in Modern Science* (Paris: Unesco, 1951).

This 'disappearance' is far from complete, however, and the question of innate psychological differences continues to attract considerable attention, not only in the United States but elsewhere, and not only in the general public but also among scholars. In 1962, Carleton S. Coon presented the theory that human evolution had occurred more rapidly in Europe than in Africa, and that as a consequence modern man emerged in Europe earlier. With some caution, he added that though dead men cannot take intelligence tests, it may be inferred that 'the sub-species which first crossed the evolutionary threshold into the category of *Homo sapiens* have evolved the most . . . and the levels of civilisation attained by some of its populations may be related phenomena' (pp. ix–x). In a comment on this theory, Weyl and Possony (1963) conclude that 'differences in structure, physique and mentality among the racial divisions of mankind can be derived' (p. 280). The context makes it clear that the innate inferiority of the African is indicated by his evolution at a later date.

One is struck by the versatility of those who insist that there must be innate psychological differences between racial groups. In many of the earlier writings on the origin of races, for example, and also in some museums of natural history, one may find an evolutionary genealogical tree, in which whites are presented as having evolved most recently. There the inference is that Africans are more primitive and therefore inferior. In other words, if the African evolved earlier he is more primitive; if later, he is inferior because he has had less time in which to develop. (It should be added that Coon himself in 1964 signed a Unesco statement to the effect that there is no scientific evidence of innate psychological differences between ethnic groups.)

A second example of this versatility is found in the interpretation of certain test results. In 1931, Myrtle McGraw applied the Bühler Babytests to black and white infants in the South and found the latter to be superior. This was interpreted (by others) as proving that even before culture had had the opportunity to exercise its influence, inborn group differences could still be demonstrated. (McGraw herself in a letter to the *American Psychologist* repudiated this interpretation of her results.) More recently, Géber and her associates (Géber and Dean, 1957) used the Gesell tests on infants in Uganda, and found them to be definitely in advance of the norms established in New Haven. Weyl and Possony (1963) comment: 'A superficial conclusion from this might be the mental superiority at birth of negro children. Actually, the reverse is indicated' (p. 226). To these writers, early rapid development signifies an inferior brain, which more quickly reaches its full maturity. Again, if black infants do poorly on tests, they must be inferior; if they do well, this indicates that they will be inferior later.

By far the most striking recent development—striking because of its identification with a reputable psychologist at a great university (University of California at Berkeley) and also because of the intense public reaction with which it was received—is represented by the publication in 1969 of a monograph by A. R. Jensen in the *Harvard Educational Review*. In answer to his own question, 'How far can we boost IQ and scholastic achievement?' Jensen developed the thesis that genetic factors 'may play a part' in intelligence differences between black and white children. Jensen's position will be discussed more fully below; at this point it may simply be noted that the *Harvard Educational Review* devoted three whole issues to the views of Jensen and of his critics, the latter ranging all the way from temperate discussion of his genetic assumptions to vituperative attacks on his 'racist' and reactionary viewpoint. The popular press, throughout the United States and a number of other countries, seized upon Jensen's thesis with enthusiasm, and gave it a truly remarkable amount of publicity. It seems highly probable that opposition to the notion of innate psychological differences between blacks and whites is not very firmly rooted in the popular mind.

Another move in a direction similar to that of Jensen has been made by William Shockley, Nobel Prize-winning physicist at Standford University, also in California, who urged the United States National Academy of Sciences to conduct extensive research into the problem of genetic (including racial) intelligence. Basing his argument in part on the results obtained by blacks and whites on intelligence tests, Shockley insists that the failure to study the nature of the genetic potential of the blacks represents a profound degree of moral irresponsibility. The National Academy of Sciences accepted the proposition that the study of human racial differences is a relevant research topic, but it rejected the recommendation to undertake such research under Academy auspices. Shockley's request and the Academy's reaction to it have also attracted extensive newspaper and magazine coverage.

Jensen's thesis reappears, in less temperate form in the volume by Hans Eysenck, *Race, Intelligence and Education* (London, 1971) without the addition of significant new material.

The issue of racial differences in innate intellectual capacities may not, therefore, be regarded as entirely resolved. In a series of statements issued by experts convened by Unesco, the position taken is that there is no adequate scientific evidence, based either on tests or on other varieties of data, which justifies the conclusion that such differences exist. To take only the most recent of these, dated September 1967, the conclusion is reached that: 'The peoples of the world appear to possess equal biological potentialities for attaining any level of civilisation', and further that: 'Racism falsely claims that there is a scientific basis for arranging groups hierarchically in terms of psychological and cultural characteristics that are immutable and innate'.

In what follows the attempt will be made to present and assess the varieties of evidence related to this thesis, with particular reference to the results obtained through the application of psychological tests.

WHY USE TESTS?

There is an Article in the Universal Declaration of Human Rights which reads as follows:

Everyone is entitled to all the rights and freedoms set forth in this Declaration, without distinction of any kind, such as race, colour, language, religion, political or other opinion, national or social origin, property, birth or other status.

One of the obstacles to the realisation of this part of the Declaration is the belief, widely and stubbornly held, that some races and peoples are inferior, and that they therefore do not have the same 'rights' as others.

As has already been noted, scholars and scientists have in some cases attempted to support the argument in favour of a racial hierarchy. It is a curious, although perhaps understandable fact, however, that those scientists who have expressed themselves in this manner, have usually arrived at the conclusion that their own people are superior to all others. Some of the German scholars, for example, were convinced that the people of northern Europe excelled the rest of mankind in intellectual endowment as well as in character and morality. An Italian anthropologist was equally certain that the peoples of the Mediterranean were responsible for most of the great contributions to our civilisation. For some black scholars, everything good in contemporary civilisation has come out of Africa.

These rival claims are historically interesting, but they do not help us to arrive at the truth concerning the relation of race to psychology. We need a more objective method, a more certain technique; one that is not so dependent on purely subjective judgments as to who has superior intellectual endowment, or what is a greater contribution to civilisation. We need proof that is scientifically sound; evidence that is scientifically acceptable.

Psychologists have developed a method which, with all its faults, appears at first glance to have considerable advantages for this purpose—the psychological test. Instead of having to decide whether a German scientific discovery represents a higher intellectual achievement than an Italian painting, the test permits us to present to a group of Germans and Italians a series of problems to solve, and we can then determine who solves them more quickly and more effectively. If someone else doubts our results he may repeat the study, using the same or other subjects, and the same or other tests. If his results agree with ours, our confidence in them is increased; if not, we must suspend judgement until other investigations help to determine who is right.

This is all that would be necessary to settle the question of superior and inferior races if psychological tests were perfect instruments for the measurement of native or innate differences in ability. It is true that they were accepted as such for a long time, at least by some psychologists and educators, as well as by many laymen. We now know, however, that they are far from perfect. The successful solution of the problems presented by the tests depends on many factors—the previous experience and education of the person tested, his degree of familiarity with the subject matter of the test, his motivation or desire to obtain a good score, his emotional state, his rapport with the experimenter, his knowledge of the language in which the test is administered and also his physical health and well-being, as well as on the native capacity of the person tested. It is only when such factors are 'held constant' that is to say, when they are in essential respects similar for all subjects tested, that we have the right to conclude that those who obtain higher scores on the test are *innately* superior to those whose scores are lower.

This makes it immediately obvious that we must use great

caution in interpreting the results when a psychological test is administered to two different racial or national groups. Living under different conditions, dissimilar in culture, education and point of view, such groups may differ widely in the test results not because they have an unequal heredity but because they have an unequal social environment. The great French psychologist Alfred Binet, who was responsible for developing the first scale of intelligence tests in 1905, was aware of this limitation in the application of his method. He pointed out that his tests could safely be used in order to arrive at inborn differences only if the various individuals or groups tested had had substantially the same opportunities. Many psychologists neglected or forgot Binet's wise counsel, and drew unjustified conclusions from their data.

In view of the many ways in which culture and previous experience may affect test scores, it is not surprising to find that the British psychologist Philip E. Vernon, who has had long experience in research and teaching in this field, concludes: 'There is no such thing as a culture-fair test, and never can be' (1968).

In many cases, however, racial or ethnic differences in test scores continue to be taken seriously, and are still occasionally used to justify far-reaching implications for educational policy. For that reason the attempt will now be made to review and to assess the main conclusions that emerge from the research related to this issue.

FACTORS RELEVANT TO TEST PERFORMANCE

Attitudes Towards the Test

One of the major arguments against the notion of a 'culture-fair' or 'culture-free' test is the fact that groups, and even individuals, vary so greatly in their attitude toward the test. The very act of competing against others in a test situation is itself influenced by the values and attitudes developed in a particular society. Professor S. D. Porteus in *The Psychology of a Primitive People* (1931) tells of an interesting experience in the course of administering psychological tests to a group of Australian aborigines. The tests that he used were made up of a series of mazes, the problem consisting of tracing a pathway through the maze until the exit was successfully reached. Each subject was, of course, expected to perform the task by himself, without any assistance from others. This situation turned out to be a strange one for these Australian natives. They were accustomed to solving their problems together, in groups. 'Not only is every problem in tribal life debated and settled by the council of elders but it is always discussed until a unanimous decision is reached'. The subjects were frequently puzzled by the fact that the examiner would give them no assistance when they experienced some difficulty in solving the problem of the maze. This was particularly true in the case of one group of natives who had recently made the psychologist a 'blood brother' of their own tribe, and they could not understand why he refused to help them. Such an attitude naturally resulted in a great deal of delay, as the subject would pause again and again for approval or assistance from the examiner. It goes without saying that the test scores suffered correspondingly.

A similar indifference to the kind of competition taken for granted in our own society was noted by the present writer in an investigation undertaken among the Yakima, a tribe of American Indians living in the state of Washington on the west coast of the United States. The tests used were a group of performance tests, in which no knowledge of language is necessary, and the task consists of placing pieces of wood of various shape into the appropriate areas of a wooden frame. The scores obtained depend on the speed with which the task is completed and the number of errors made in the process. The subjects are told to put the pieces in their correct places 'as quickly as possible'. These Indian children, however, never hurried. They saw no reason to work quickly. Our culture places a premium on speed, on getting things done in as short a time as possible; the Indian children had not acquired this attitude. They went at their task slowly and deliberately, with none of that scrambling impatience that is so often found among American children. The Indians, as a consequence, took much longer to finish the tests, though they made somewhat fewer errors than the white Americans with whom they were compared.

The writer made an analogous observation among the Dakota (Sioux) Indians in the state of South Dakota. There it is regarded as incorrect to answer a question in the presence of others who do not know the answer: this might be interpreted as showing off, or as bringing shame to others, and is consequently condemned by the whole group. These Indian children also have developed the conviction that it is wrong to reply to a question unless one is absolutely certain of the answer. Psychologists who have given the Binet test to these children have observed that they never guess at the answer: if they are not sure, they keep quiet indefinitely. This, too, reduces their scores to a certain extent, since a guess may succeed, and since credit is given for an answer that is even partly correct.

Another psychologist, Professor S. E. Asch, has noted that the Hopi Indian children of Arizona refuse to compete against one another. One school teacher tried to get them to do so by an ingenious method. She wrote a number of arithmetic problems on the blackboard, lined up the children, each one facing one problem, and instructed them to turn around as soon as they had finished. She observed that as each child completed his problem he looked along the line to see how the others were progressing; only when they were all through did they turn around, together. This attitude would also reduce test scores, particularly in the application of group tests, which are administered to a number of persons at the same time.

As a final example in this context may be noted the experience of the anthropologist Margaret Mead with Samoan children, and reported in her *Coming-of-Age in Samoa*. She was administering the Binet test, which has as one of its items the 'Ball-and-Field' problem. A ball is lost in a circular field, and the task of the subject is to trace a pathway along which he would walk in order to find the ball. These Samoan children, instead of tracing the most efficient pathway, used the occasion to make a pretty design. Their aesthetic interest was evidently stronger than their desire to solve the problem presented to them.

These examples all indicate the possibility that the cultural background of the individual may determine his general approach to the test situation in such a manner as markedly to influence his test score. Even in the case of minority groups within the same society, such as for example American blacks, there is evidence to indicate that their attitude toward the test, their motivation to do their best, may not be similar to what is found in the white children with whom they are compared. They are often suspicious of the test and what it means, and they may lack confidence in their ability to do well.

In a study by Roen (1960), for example, it was demonstrated that there was a high negative correlation between intelligence score and lack of self-confidence in Negroes; in other words, more self-confidence went with better scores. For whites, there was also a negative correlation, but not nearly so striking. The author suggests that Negroes 'as a group, lacking support from pride in significant historical achievement, and developing in an environment of negative experiences, incorporate intellectually defeating personality traits that play a significant role in their ability to score on measures of intelligence' (p. 150). This is only one of many studies which show how the competitive spirit required to obtain good individual scores and to solve problems quickly and effectively may be influenced by personal and social attitudes.

Attitudes Towards the Children Tested

Expectations regarding performance may be important not only for those who are tested, but also for those who do the testing—and teaching. Clark (1963) has presented the view that culturally disadvantaged (one might add also culturally different) children are the unfortunate victims of teachers' educational self-fulfilling prophecies; in other words, if children are expected to do poorly, they will do poorly. This hypothesis was tested experimentally by Rosenthal and Jacobson and published in *Pygmalion in the Classroom* (1968); they gave to teachers the names of children who allegedly had done well on a 'test for intellectual blooming' which indicated that they would show striking gains in intellectual competence during the next eight months of school. Eight months later this experimental group, together with a control group of equal competence whose names had *not* been given to the teachers, were retested on the same intelligence test. The experimental group—those whom the teachers *expected* to do well—gained 4 more points in IQ than did the control group; on a reasoning test, the difference was 7 points. As the authors point out, the difference between the two groups *was in the mind of the teachers*. This finding appears to be of very real importance in the comparisons that have been made, and continue to be made, between ethnic groups.

The Effect of Language

One of the clearest and most obvious ways in which social and educational background may influence test results, is through its effect on language. Most of the psychological tests in general use, including those devised by Binet, are verbal in character. For the successful solution of the problems presented, not only must the subject have an adequate comprehension of the questions asked; not only must he be able to answer intelligibly once the solution has been reached; he must also be able to manipulate words successfully in order to reach a solution. So important is language facility in many of these tests that psychologists can often reach quite an accurate estimate of a subject's mental level merely by knowing the extent of his vocabulary. This fact early led to the conclusion that these intelligence tests were unfair to the foreign-born, or to others (like the American Indians in the United States, for example) who had inadequate knowledge of the language in which the test was administered. Even if they spoke and used that language with relative ease, they were still handicapped if that were not their native language, or if they were bilingual.

This was demonstrated years ago. Welsh children speaking only English obtained better scores on the Binet scale than those who spoke both Welsh and English. In Belgium, the Walloon children who spoke only French, were superior to Flemish children who spoke both French and Flemish. In the United States, children of Italian parentage who still spoke Italian in their homes were inferior to those who spoke only English. In Canada, Ontario Indians who spoke nothing but English were superior to those who were bilingual. This result has been found in the case of other groups as well. It is not to be interpreted to mean that bilingualism causes a definite or permanent intellectual inferiority; it more probably is due to the simple fact that the vocabulary of a young child is so limited that if he learns words in two languages, he will not know so many in either one. With the passage of time, the handicap due to bilingualism will be more than compensated by its undoubted advantages.

The Effect of Poverty

The influence of poverty or of socio-economic class on test performance cannot be kept separate from the issues already raised. Low expectations as to pupil performance may affect the poor white as well as black; differences in language patterns have been demonstrated in the case of the poor in England (by Bernstein, 1960) and in the United States (John, 1963). The fact of poverty and its consequences acquire importance in this context because of the proportionately greater frequency of poverty among minority groups, and particularly among the blacks in the United States.

This consideration alone should impose considerable caution in arguing from the inferior test results obtained by black children (an average IQ of 85 as compared with the 'normal' 100). Research conducted in many countries and by many psychologists indicates beyond a shadow of a doubt that the test performance of poor white children is markedly inferior to that of the well-to-do; the difference between groups at the extremes of the economic range is in the neighbourhood of 20 points in IQ, that is to say, greater than that between American blacks and whites.

To this it is retorted that even when the comparison is between blacks and whites of the same economic level the difference, though smaller, still persists. All that this really means, however, is that poverty, although of great importance, is not the only factor responsible. In a critical review of the research on ethnic differences in the United States, Dreger and Miller (1960), who incidentally do not take sides in the nature–nurture controversy, correctly point out that it is not enough to equate ethnic groups in terms of social class and economic variables; the difference is not solely socio-economic. They add that even those blacks whose economic status is higher than that of most white persons will still in the majority of cases be prevented from living the same kind of life in all respects; many other factors may also be important.

To return to the effect of poverty, psychologists have so far not sufficiently emphasised its role in causing fundamental impairment to mental development as a consequence of malnutrition. In a survey of the relation between nutrition and learning, Eichenwald and Fry (1969) bring together an impressive mass of data in this connection, based partly on animal experimentation and partly on observations of the effects of nutritional deficiencies on human beings in many parts of the world, including Africa and Latin America. They conclude that malnutrition during a critical period of early life may 'permanently and profoundly affect the future intellectual and emotional development of the individual'. The factor of malnutrition appears to be of fundamental importance in assessing the intellectual potentialities of poor, including poor black, people.

The Effect of Previous Learning and Experience

The importance of this factor is implied in what has been said above, since language, attitudes and motives are all influenced by previous experience. There are, however, some additional considerations that deserve attention. In the early days of testing, many psychologists believed that the elimination of the handicap due to language was equivalent to eliminating the influence of culture and experience in general. One psychologist, for example, Professor Florence L. Goodenough of the University of Minnesota, devised a performance test consisting in 'Drawing a Man'; scores were determined not by the aesthetic quality of the drawing, but by the inclusion of the largest possible number of essential aspects, by proper attention to bodily proportions, etc. She regarded this test as 'culture-free' that is, independent of the previous background and experience of the subjects, and therefore capable of measuring native differences in intelligence. In 1926, she conducted a study by means of this test, and reported definite differences in the 'intelligence' of various immigrant groups in the United States, as well as between whites and Negroes. In the years that have passed since then, many investigators have made use of this test, and they have been able to demonstrate that, contrary to the earlier view, the results are indeed affected by many aspects of previous experience. Professor Goodenough herself later recognised this fact, and very honestly and courageously, pointed out her former error. Writing with Dale B. Harris on 'Studies in the Psychology of Children's Drawings' in the *Psychological Bulletin* for September 1950, she expresses the opinion that:

'. . . the search for a culture-free test, whether of intelligence, artistic ability, personal-social characteristics, or any other measurable trait is illusory, and . . . the naive assumption that the mere freedom from verbal requirements renders a test equally suitable for all groups is no longer tenable.'

She goes on to state that her own earlier study reporting differences among the children of immigrants to the United States 'is certainly no exception to the rule' and adds, 'the writer hereby apologises for it'.

   More recent evidence along the same lines comes from a study by Wayne Dennis (1966) who gave the 'Draw a Man' test to samples of children in approximately fifty different cultures. Averages ranged from an IQ of 124 for children in American and English suburbs, in a Japanese fishing village, and among the Hopi Indians. The lowest average, 52, was found in children of a nomadic Bedouin tribe in Syria; this is explained by their limited experience in graphic art. Children of Lebanese Arabs, on the other hand, with considerable exposure to Western culture obtained an average IQ of 94.

Since many tests of intelligence involved ability in handling physical objects, including pictures, the role of previous experience may be of paramount importance. Research in Africa has shown such factors to be very significant. Biesheuvel, who has spent many years testing in Africa, points out that even drawings of highly familiar objects may not be recognised by children who have had little experience with pictorial representation. Other investigators have indicated that the performance on non-language tests may be greatly influenced by the degree of opportunity to play with mechanical toys or other objects which prepare the way for a solution of the problems presented by the tests.

Qualitative Differences in Test Performance

Factors related to cultural background and previous experience may also determine qualitative differences in the nature of test performance. Strauss (1954), for example, found that university students in Ceylon obtained better scores than Americans on verbal tests, but were markedly inferior on non-verbal or performance tests. He suggests that their culture 'has the effect of defining a set of role behaviours that on the one hand tends to depreciate manual and technical ability, and on the other hand tends to emphasise and reward the verbal type of scholarly excellence'.

A number of other investigators have been concerned with qualitative differences in test scores obtained by various ethnic groups. Vernon (1969) for example, found an entirely different pattern of abilities in the case of Jamaican and Eskimo boys, respectively; the former were better in arithmetic and word-learning, the latter in tests dependent on induction and on drawing. Lesser et al. (1965) also found qualitative (as well as quantitative) differences in the abilities of young Chinese, Jewish, Negro and Puerto Rican children in the United States; Iscoe and Pierce Jones (1964) showed that although Negro children were inferior to whites in general test scores, they were superior in measures of what the authors call 'divergent thinking', based on the ability to suggest a number of different uses for familiar objects. Clearly differences in the measured capacity of ethnic groups may be a function of the particular test applied.

If every test is 'culture-bound' that is to say, affected by the whole complex of previous education, training and experience, can the use of tests give us any information at all about racial differences, or similarities, in intelligence? If we cannot disentangle hereditary from environmental influences in the results, has the testing method any relevance at all to our problem? We can of course legitimately say that racial differences in intelligence cannot be demonstrated by means of the tests, for the reasons given; we can at least say: 'Not proven!' Is that all we can say? Or is there some more positive manner in which the tests may be used to answer the questions we are raising?

Let us look at the problem a little differently. It is true that the test scores obtained by two different groups are due to the interaction of hereditary and environmental factors which cannot be disentangled. The inferiority of one of these groups to the other may then be due to an inferior heredity, or to a poorer environment, or both. Suppose now we make the two environments more similar; equalise them as far as possible. If as the environments become more alike, the difference in test scores tends to disappear; if when the environments are to all practical purposes equalised, the difference in test scores disappears completely; we then have a strong argument in favour of the environmental rather than the hereditary explanation of the observed differences. What do the results show?

THE EFFECTS OF CHANGES IN THE ENVIRONMENT

If a test which has been found to be useful in establishing differences among children in Paris or New York is administered to children in Mozambique or New Guinea, we could hardly expect the latter groups to do as well as the former. That should be obvious, though unfortunately it has not always been recognised. The examples given above indicate some, though not all, of the ways in which the different background of these groups would affect the scores obtained. There are, however, a number of countries in which groups of different ethnic or racial origin live side by side, and it would seem at first sight a simple matter to use such groups as a basis for comparison. If in the United States, for example, we find Americans of Scandinavian, Italian, Chinese,

Negro and American Indian origin, all living in an 'American' environment, can we not assume that they all have the same cultural background, the same educational and economic opportunities, so that any differences in test results could with scientific safety be attributed to differences in hereditary capacity?

Unfortunately, this is not the case. The American Indian, for example, usually lives on reservations separate from the surrounding community; he usually goes to different schools; he lives a different life; he speaks English, but frequently not too well; his economic status is on the average inferior. The Negro, although his position in American life has improved markedly in recent years, is still in most cases subject to very definite handicaps; his economic status is also on the average very much below that of the whites; the schools which he attends have certainly been inferior in the past, and to a certain extent are still inferior today; he finds it more difficult to obtain certain types of employment, or to participate fully in American life.

Once that is understood, it should not be surprising to find that American Indians and Negroes, adults as well as children, do on the average obtain test scores inferior to those of whites. But, it must be noted, this is a difference *on the average*. There are many *individual* Negroes who obtain scores higher than those of a great many individual whites. What is more important, there are sometimes whole groups of Negroes who do better on the tests than groups of whites with whom they have been compared.

This important fact first aroused widespread interest at the time of the First World War, when over a million recruits in the American Army, including many Negroes, were given psychological tests. The results showed in the first place that Negroes from the south (where educational and economic handicaps were greater) obtained scores which on the average were definitely inferior to those of Negroes from the north (where such handicaps, though they existed, were much less severe). Even more strikingly, the *Negroes* from some of the *northern* states turned out to be superior to the *whites* from some of the *southern* states! This was true in the case of both types of intelligence tests used, one depending on language, the other a performance or non-language test. It began to appear, at least to some psychologists, as if the colour of the skin were less important in determining success with the tests, than the opportunities given to the individual to acquire the needed abilities.

Further evidence began to accumulate. Two American psychologists, Joseph Peterson and Lyle H. Lanier, became aware of the importance of comparing Negroes and whites not only in situations in which their respective environments were very different, but also in situations where their environments were approximately the same. In a study published in *Mental Measurement Monographs*, 1929, they pointed out that:

A useful check on the reliability of a given race difference obtained in any locality and under any specific set of circumstances is to take what seem to be fairly representative samplings from widely different environments and to compare the various results as checks upon one another with a view to determining just which factors persistently yield differences in favour of one or the other race.

In line with this reasoning, they administered a number of psychological tests to white and Negro boys in several cities, including Nashville (which is in the southern state of Tennessee, and where Negro and white children went to separate schools), and New York (where there is a unified public school system for all children). Results showed that in Nashville there was a marked superiority of the white over the Negro children, whereas in New York there were no significant differences between the two racial groups. Here again we have evidence in favour of the view that, when the environments are similar, the test results appear to be similar as well.

As an indication of the wide differences in test scores, within the same racial group, which accompany differences in the environment, one finds at one extreme a group of Negro children in rural Tennessee obtaining an average IQ of 58, and at the other extreme Negro children in Los Angeles, California, with an average IQ of 105. For the white population as a whole, an IQ of 100 is to be expected; that is by definition the standard or norm with which these results are to be compared. In the inferior environment of rural Tennessee, the Negro score goes far below this standard; in the more favourable environment of a big city like Los Angeles, the Negro score reaches and even exceeds by a small amount the 'normal' IQ. This is an important result and its implications for so-called racial differences in innate capacity appear to be obvious.

There is, however, another possible explanation of these results which must be considered. The Negroes living in New York, Los Angeles, and other places not in the south of the United States, have for the most part come from the south. That is to say, either they themselves or their families formerly lived in one of the southern states, where there has always been the greatest concentration of Negroes, and to which the African slaves were usually brought; for one reason or another they left their homes and migrated northwards. It has frequently been suggested that in any such migration there would be a tendency for people with greater energy and initiative, with greater potentiality for adaptation to a new environment, and therefore presumably with superior intelligence, to leave; whereas those with inferior intelligence remain behind. This is usually referred to as the hypothesis of *selective migration*. In terms of this hypothesis, Negroes in the north would obtain better scores on intelligence tests, not because they had profited from the opportunities presented by a superior environment, but because they were naturally brighter to start with. They proved it, so the argument runs, by migrating. If selective migration really operates in this way, then the superiority of Negroes in New York over those in Tennessee would prove nothing about the effect of environment.

The argument in favour of selective migration is not very convincing. Why should superior people migrate? Is it not as reasonable to assume that those who are successful, who have position and status in their own community, who have acquired property, who are leaders, would be more likely to stay where they are? Is it not likely that those who have failed, who have not succeeded in establishing any roots, who cannot find a job, would be most eager to search for greener pastures? Since one can defend with equal logic either side of the argument, it becomes important to obtain objective and definite facts regarding the nature of migration in relation to intelligence.

This was attempted in a series of investigations carried out in 1934 and 1935. The first question studied was: Why do people migrate? A series of personal interviews, either with the migrants themselves or with their families, indicated that a number of factors were responsible. Some of the migrants left for the north in the hope of improving their economic position or obtaining a better education; these were possibly the more intelligent ones. Others, however, migrated because they could not find jobs in the south, or because they were in trouble with the law and were about to be arrested, or because they were invited north by a friend or relative who was already established there; in none of these cases is there any indication that migration was determined by superior intelligence. Apparently migration occurs for a variety of reasons, and no one factor—such as intelligence—can be regarded as exclusively responsible.

A second approach to this problem was more direct. Those who migrated had previously gone to school in the south; they had been in competition, therefore, with others who had not migrated. If the theory of selective migration is sound, then the migrants should reveal in their school marks a definite superiority over the remainder of the population. A careful search through the school records in several southern cities, and a detailed statistical comparison of the school marks obtained by the migrants and non-migrants, respectively, showed no differences between the two groups. Some of the migrants were superior, others inferior, still others about average. Thus, there was no evidence that those who migrated were 'selected' for their superior intellectual ability. Some sort of 'selection' undoubtedly does occur, since not everyone migrates, but it is a 'selection' in which many different factors enter. It may be added that studies of migration of whites from rural communities in the United States to large cities, and of a similar type of migration in Germany, showed the same results. Selective migration cannot be used as a principle of explanation. In the context of our present discussion, that means that the superior results obtained by Negro children in Los Angeles or New York are not to be explained by the exodus of the best genes in southern Negroes, but by the better environmental opportunities provided by the northern cities.

This last conclusion is strengthened by the results of a third approach which was made to this problem. In New York City there are many Negro children who have come from the south; some have arrived only recently, others have lived there for several years. If the environment of New York, which is certainly superior to that from which they have come, exerts a favourable influence on the test scores, such an influence should increase with the number of years the children have lived in New York. This is exactly what the investigation showed. Several different tests were applied to a large number of Negro school children, both boys and girls, and it was found that there was a close relationship between test scores and length of residence in New York. There were many exceptions, of course; this result did not hold for every individual, but the general trend was clear and undeniable. In general, those who had lived there the longest obtained on the average the best scores; those who had arrived only recently from the south, the poorest scores. This result has been obtained also in the case of two other cities, Washington and Philadelphia, where similar investigations were conducted. The conclusion is justified that, as the environments of two different racial groups become more and more alike, the differences in test scores are reduced and tend to disappear. There is no indication that a racial factor enters into these results; on the contrary, the evidence points clearly *away* from an explanation in terms of inherited racial differences in intellectual capacity.

Corroboration of this result is found in a study in the United Kingdom by Vernon (1968) who reported that immigrant pupils from India, Pakistan and the West Indies who attended London primary schools for less than two years had an average IQ of 76, whereas for those with six years or more it was 91. He states that 'there is no reason to think that the earlier arrivals were of better quality than the more recent ones, hence this 15 point difference probably represents a genuine improvement among the longer residents'. In other words, not selective migration but an improved environment is considered responsible for the higher scores of the older residents.

Another ethnic group which has been studied in considerable detail, and with a large variety of tests, is the American Indian. In general, their test scores are the lowest of all groups examined in the United States; their average IQ is in the neighbourhood of 81, instead of the 'normal' 100. This result is not at all surprising, in the light of the 'cultural' factors discussed above. Not only do most American Indians occupy an inferior economic position in comparison with the rest of the American population; in addition, their whole background and previous experience are so different from those of white Americans that it can hardly be expected that they should do equally well on tests that have been designed for use with the latter. Their relative unfamiliarity with the English language frequently constitutes an additional handicap. In one study conducted among the Indians of Ontario, Canada, it was demonstrated that they obtained considerably better results when examined by means of non-language or performance tests than when the usual language tests were used. This result has been duplicated in the case of other American Indian groups as well.

On the more positive side, the late Professor T. R. Garth of the

University of Denver, Colorado, tried to discover what would happen if American Indian children were given the opportunity to live in a social environment similar to that of other American children. He therefore made a study of Indian children who had been placed in white foster homes, cared for by white foster parents. His results are reported in the *Psychological Bulletin*, 1935. These Indian foster children obtained an average IQ of 102, which is a striking improvement on the usual American Indian average of 81. This result would show conclusively that when the social environments of the two ethnic groups are similar the test scores are similar also, were it not for the possibility that those Indian children who had been taken into white homes were unusually bright. It may very well be that when white families take Indian children into their homes they attempt to choose as far as possible children of superior intelligence. This is the problem of 'selection' once more, referring in this context not to migration, but to choice of children who will receive exceptional educational opportunities.

Unfortunately we do not know in this case exactly what factors entered into the selection of these Indian children. Professor Garth did his best to eliminate the possibility of explaining the superiority of these foster children on an hereditary basis by testing also the siblings (brothers and sisters) of these children. The siblings had not been taken into white homes; they remained on the 'reservation' in the customary Indian social environment. They obtained a much lower average IQ, namely 87·5. This suggests that it is the environment, and not heredity, which is responsible for the result, since children from the same families reacted so differently under the two sets of environmental conditions. The proof is not complete, however, since even in the same family the inherited capacity of two different children cannot be assumed to be similar in every instance.

More convincing evidence does come, however, from a later study conducted by Professor J. H. Rohrer of the University of Oklahoma, and published in the *Journal of Social Psychology*, in 1942. He administered intelligence tests to the Osage Indians, who are exceptional in that they live under social and economic conditions which are similar to those of the whites with whom they were compared. This is mainly due to the fortunate accident that on the land which was given to them by the American government as a 'reservation' oil was later discovered. As a consequence the economic position of these Indians improved substantially, and they were able to create for themselves and their families living conditions, and a social and educational environment, far superior to those of most American Indian communities. With these facts in mind, it is illuminating to look at their performance on the intelligence tests; on two different tests, one a non-language test, the second depending on language, they obtained average IQs of 104 and 100 respectively. The apparent inferiority of American Indian children disappeared completely; if anything, they were slightly superior to the white children. There can be no doubt in this case that when American Indian children are given educational opportunities comparable to those of whites, their test results improve correspondingly.

This result can definitely *not* be explained by selection. It was *after* the Osage Indians had been given their land that oil was discovered; they did not choose this particular region. They were merely lucky, and their good fortune gave them opportunities denied to others. This is reflected not only in their superior economic status, but also in their greater success in solving the problems presented by the intelligence tests. The conclusion is justified that, given equal opportunities, American Indian children reveal capacities equal to any others.

More recently evidence has accumulated to indicate that training may markedly raise the level of performance. McFie (1961) was able to produce a substantial improvement in the test scores of his African subjects as a result of education which placed emphasis on drawing and construction; there was a significant increase in both speed and accuracy of performance. Lloyd and Pidgeon (1961) also report that in testing school children in Natal, they were able to produce a marked rise in the test scores of African children after two short sessions of coaching. The authors warn against any assumptions about the innate abilities of children from different cultures on the basis of these tests.

A significant review by Hunt (1971) of a number of educational programmes, directed not only to the children of the poor but also to the mothers of such children, has shown how much can be done to improve performance. He writes: 'These findings of substantial gains in the IQs of children of mothers so taught . . . provides a substantial hope of developing a method of preventing the development of incompetence in children of poverty. . . .' Hunt adds that this perspective is applicable to both the black and the white poor.

With these findings in mind, it is difficult to understand why Jensen answers his own question, 'How much can we boost IQ and scholastic achievement?' with the conclusion that the gains are small. Many of his critics have pointed out that gains have indeed been obtained, and that they would be much more substantial if the relevant programmes were maintained over a sufficiently long period, and affected a wider range of the child's experience. A statement by the Council of the Society for the Psychological Study of Social Issues, a division of the American Psychological Association, includes these words:

'One of our most serious objections to Jensen's article is to his vigorous assertion that compensatory education has apparently failed. The major failure in so-called compensatory education has been in the planning, size, and scope of the programme. We maintain that a variety of programmes planned to teach specific skills have been effective and that a few well-designed programmes which teach problem-solving and thinking have also been successful. The results from these programmes strongly suggest that continuous and carefully planned intervention procedures can have a substantially positive influence on the performance of disadvantaged children.'

Jensen has been severely criticised on a number of counts, including the neglect of many of the research findings that throw doubt on his thesis, and the fact that a good deal of his argument is really irrelevant to the subject of race differences. He makes a strong case, for example, in favour of the role of genetic factors in determining variations among individuals and families; most psychologists would agree that heredity does play an important part in connection with such individual variations, without, however, accepting his inference that this implies ethnic differences as well. On this latter point the conclusion is still 'Not proven'. It should also be emphasised that Jensen is not nearly so dogmatic in his assertions as some newspapers reported. His actual words are that it is a 'reasonable hypothesis' that genetic factors 'may play a part' in intelligence differences between black and white children. The many factors that enter into test performance, and that have been reviewed above, indicate, however, that even this relatively temperate position rests on no solid evidence, and that his hypothesis is far from 'reasonable' in the light of the various considerations.

One further important environmental factor emerges from the report prepared by J. S. Coleman and his colleagues for the United States Office of Education, and published under the title *Equality of Educational Opportunity* in 1966. When a pupil from a minority group living in 'a home without much educational strength is put with schoolmates with strong educational backgrounds, his achievement is likely to increase'. The effect is similar when those with 'strong educational backgrounds' are black rather than white, but it is not surprising, in view of the whole history of the United States, that such favourable home backgrounds are found much more frequently in the case of white children. For this reason, one of Coleman's findings is of great significance, namely that 'the average Negro elementary child is in schools where 16% of the students are whites'; the proportion rises in secondary schools, but in 1966 it was still only 24%. In this connection it should be pointed out that the United States Government and the law courts are strongly committed to reducing this disproportion, and are insisting on a much more significant degree of school desegregation, but the actual changes in the schools take place very slowly.

The earlier research, reviewed above, indicated that the average test performance of American Indian children was very low, in fact several IQ points below that of the blacks. In the sample of children included in the Coleman Report, however, the American Indians were roughly midway between whites and blacks. These children at the elementary level attended schools where 60% of their classmates were white, instead of the 16% indicated for black children; at the secondary level the figure rose to 70% as contrasted with 24%. In the light of Coleman's thesis, these differences in the degree of contact with children from stronger educational backgrounds would account for the better performances of this sample of American Indian children, and would also constitute a strong argument in favour of the thesis that success in the tests can definitely be increased under favourable environmental conditions, Jensen to the contrary notwithstanding.

The net result of all the research that has been conducted in this field is to the effect that innate racial differences in intelligence have not been demonstrated; that the obtained differences in test results are best explained in terms of the social and educational environment: that as the environmental opportunities of different racial or ethnic groups become more alike, the observed differences in test results also tend to disappear. The evidence is overwhelmingly against the view that race is a factor which determines level of intelligence. As formulated in the Unesco Statement on Race:

'It is now generally recognised that the intelligence tests do not in themselves enable us to differentiate safely between what is due to innate capacity and what is the result of environmental influences, training and education. Wherever it has been possible to make allowances for differences in environmental opportunities, the tests have shown essential similarity in mental characteristics among human groups.'

SOME RELATED PROBLEMS

In addition to the question as to the relation of race to the average innate intelligence of the different groups, there are several problems which require further discussion. These problems, too, have been approached from many different viewpoints, and with a frequent disregard for the line of demarcation between fact and fiction. They are the concern not only of the psychologist but often also of the biologist, the anthropologist, the sociologist and the historian. In what follows, they will be examined in the light of the contribution which can be made to their solution through the application of psychological techniques. Reference will be made to other aspects only when this is necessary to understand the purpose and the results of the psychological investigations.

PHYSIQUE AND MENTALITY

There is a widespread popular belief that the physical appearance of an individual gives us a substantial amount of information regarding his psychological characteristics. The assumption is often made, for example, that a high forehead indicates superior intelligence, a receding chin means weakness and lack of determination, thick lips denote sensuality, and so on. Books of fiction are particularly rich in such allusions. Perhaps the most famous literary expression of this is to be found in Shakespeare's *Julius Caesar*:

> *Let me have men about me that are fat;*
> *Sleek-headed men and such as sleep o'nights;*
> *Yond' Cassius has a lean and hungry look;*
> *He thinks too much: such men are dangerous.*

Races, after all, consist of groups of men who differ from other groups in their inherited physical characteristics. If these are in some manner related to mentality we would have a basis for believing in inherited psychological differences between races. Some anthropologists have expressed themselves to this effect. Professor A. L. Kroeber of the University of California, for example, wrote in 1934: 'There is . . . no sound reason to expect anything else but that races which differ anatomically: also differ in some degree physiologically and psychologically.' Professor Franz Boas of Columbia University wrote in the first edition of his famous book *The Mind of Primitive Man* in 1911:

'It does not seem probable that the minds of races which show variations in their anatomical structure should act in exactly the same way. Differences of structure must be accompanied by differences of function, physiological as well as psychological; and, as we found clear evidence of differences in structure between the races, so we must anticipate that differences in mental characteristics will be found.'

It is significant that this passage does not appear in the later edition (1938) of this book, and it seems highly probable that Boas changed his mind on this point. In any case, neither Kroeber nor Boas thought that this relation between 'structure' and 'function' indicated that some races were psychologically *superior* to others but merely that they were different. Both these anthropologists, and Boas in particular, were leaders in the attack upon the notion of a racial hierarchy.

Even in the more restricted meaning, however, the view expressed above cannot be regarded as acceptable; the inference from physical to psychological characteristics is very doubtful indeed. There has so far been no scientifically acceptable demonstration of a relationship between anatomical features and traits of personality. To mention one example, an investigation was made into the degree of correspondence or the correlation between the height of the forehead on the one hand, and scores in an intelligence test on the other. The popular view was not substantiated. The students with high foreheads did not turn out to be more intelligent than those whose foreheads were low. A similar result was obtained in the case of many other physical characteristics. There appears to be no difference, either in intelligence or personality, between blondes and brunettes, between people who are tall or short, round-headed or long-headed, who have round or narrow eyes, or thin or thick lips. Even the size of the head appears to have no significant relation to psychological characteristics, except in extreme or abnormal cases. We are safe in concluding that none of the specific anatomical features which have been used in race classification have any meaning as clues to mentality. Research is continuing in this field, but the emphasis is being placed on the total constitution rather than on single physical traits; there is still no certainty, however, as to whether such a constitutional approach will turn out to be a sound one. In any case, it will have little or no relevance to the problem of race, since all racial groups include a number of different constitutional types. We are justified in concluding that the anatomical or structural differences between racial groups are *not* necessarily accompanied by corresponding psychological differences.

There is, however, one aspect of 'physique' which requires an additional comment. Even though the size of the head has no significant relationship with any known measure of intelligence, the popular view to the contrary is still widely held. In connection with race differences, this may lead to the view that the races of men differ in brain size, and particularly in the quantity of grey matter in the cerebral cortex; further, that blacks have smaller brains than whites, and that this accounts for their apparently inferior intellectual performance. Recently (1970) Professor Philip V. Tobias of the University of the Witwatersrand in Johannesburg, South Africa, published a careful review of the research conducted on this topic, and concluded that 'there is no acceptable evidence for such structural differences in the brains of these two racial groups; and certainly nothing which provides a satisfactory anatomical basis for explaining any difference in IQ or in other mental and performance tests, in temperament or in behaviour'. One cannot help being struck by the fact that this paper was presented to an audience in South Africa.

In any case, the relation between brain and behaviour has been shown to be much more complex than was formerly realised. It is a common practice to credit the characteristics of the brain with the major responsibility for the quality of one's intellect. Recent research, although conducted on rats rather than on men, strongly suggests that this is far too simple a formulation. A group of investigators at the University of California at Berkeley, including particularly Krech (1965) and Rosenzweig (1966), separated two identical samples of rats, kept one sample in isolation, and gave to the other as rich and varied an experience as it is possible to give to rats. Later the brains of these two samples were examined, both chemically and microscopically, and a number of differences were noted, the most striking being the greater size and complexity of the brains of those rats which had received the greater stimulation. Although it is always somewhat dangerous to extrapolate from rats to men, the evidence does point to the influence of training and exercise on the development of the brain, leading at least to a partial reversal of the usual formulation; instead of the brain's determining the nature of behaviour, it is behaviour which to some extent determines the nature of the brain.

THE UPPER LIMITS OF ABILITY

Another way of approaching the problem of racial or ethnic differences in intelligence is to look at the superior rather than at the average members of the group. It has been suggested that the contributions of such a group will depend not so much upon the ability of the majority, as upon its outstanding or exceptional individuals, those who are at the upper end of the distribution scale. Ethnic groups have therefore been compared in terms of the frequency of occurrence of 'men of genius'. This is obviously a difficult and complicated task. There is no simple criterion by which we can recognise the man of genius, and history is filled with examples of men who were accepted as such only long after their death, or conversely, of men who were highly regarded at one time and later passed into oblivion. In addition, the creations of genius build upon the achievements of an earlier day; one cannot expect a Beethoven to emerge suddenly without the background of European music which serves as his heritage, or an Einstein to develop a theory of relativity without a knowledge of what his predecessors in physics have discovered. In terms of their own cultural background, there have been undoubtedly inventors, innovators, 'men of genius' in all societies.

To turn once again to the contributions of psychologists to this problem, it becomes immediately apparent that the upper limits of ability, as measured by intelligence tests, are reached by members of many different ethnic groups. One striking example is furnished by the case of an American Negro girl who at the age of nine years obtained an IQ of 200. This is a very remarkable performance. It means that this 9-year old girl did as well on the test as the average 18-year old. There are very few children indeed, out of the many thousands who have been tested all over the world, who have matched this achievement. This particular child was apparently of pure Negro ancestry—there is no record of white admixture on either side of the family. Her background was superior; her mother was formerly a schoolteacher, and her father was a university graduate. The psychologists who described her case in the *Journal of Social Psychology* in 1935, Professors Witty and Jenkins, believe that in her case there was the optimum combination of excellent biological inheritance and a favourable opportunity for development. In any case, it is clear that Negro ancestry is not accompanied by any special limitations on an individual's capacity for achievement. This child was of course exceptional, but there are a great many Negroes to be found at the upper end of the distribution curve. The results of the tests lend no support to the view that Negroes differ from whites in their ability to produce outstanding individuals.

THE EFFECTS OF RACE MIXTURE

The problem of race mixture has important points of contact with the whole problem of the relation between race and psychology. In the minds of most people, the decision as to the relative superiority and inferiority of different racial or ethnic groups would necessarily determine their attitude toward the mixing of races. Those who regard another racial group as inferior usually object to inter-mixture on the ground that this would reduce the quality of their own, presumably superior, race. In that case, acceptance of the position developed here, namely that there is no indication that some races are biologically inferior to others, would presumably eliminate all serious objections to race mixture.

The problem is, however, somewhat more complicated. The attitude toward ethnic mixture is so bound up with emotional and even religious considerations, that it is not an easy matter to look upon it as a purely scientific issue. In addition, even from the scientific point of view, it has sometimes been argued that race mixture is biologically harmful in itself, and that the question of original superiority or inferiority of the racial groups which enter into the mixture is irrelevant. This is the position taken, for example, by the American geneticist C. B. Davenport, who in a series of publications has described what he regards as the unfortunate consequences of race mixture. A hybrid people, in his view, is disharmonious, badly put together. The mixed population may inherit some characteristics from one parent race, others from the other, and the two sets may not combine properly. The arms and legs of the Negro, for example, are long in proportion to his trunk, whereas those of the whites are relatively short. A racial mixture might result in an individual with the long legs of the Negro and the short arms of the white; he would be at a disadvantage, says Davenport, because he would have to stoop more to pick up a thing on the ground! This does not appear to be such a very great disadvantage. Besides, if the hybrid inherited the short legs of the white and the long arms of the Negro, he could pick things off the ground more easily than either the Negro or white parents. Davenport's views have been challenged by other geneticists, who have pointed out that size is not inherited separately for different organs of the body, and whose careful investigations do not show any greater disharmony among hybrids than among either of the parent races.

This is a matter for the biologists to settle; but it is of concern to the psychologist as well, and the hybrid has been studied by means of psychological tests in the hope of throwing some light on the effects of race mixture. Davenport himself, with his colleague Morris Steggerda, applied psychological tests in Jamaica to groups of whites, blacks (pure Negroes), and browns (white-Negro mixtures). The results showed that the blacks were only slightly inferior to the whites, and that both whites and blacks were definitely superior to the browns. This is interpreted as supporting the view that race mixture has harmful consequences, and that the disharmonies which it produces are to be found in the mental as well as the physical sphere.

Other studies do not, however, support this conclusion. They show either that the hybrids are intermediate in score between whites and Negroes, or—when careful anthropometric measurements are used on a population which is relatively homogeneous from the economic and educational viewpoints—that there is no relationship whatsoever between degree of intermixture and test scores. Taking all the results together, they indicate neither a definite superiority nor an inferiority of the hybrids as compared with parent groups. The effects of race mixture are neither good nor bad in themselves; they depend on the quality of the individuals who have entered into the mixture, and on the manner in which the hybrid is accepted or treated by the community as a whole. It is clearly the attitude towards the hybrids, not any special hybrid biology, which determines their place in the community.

The Unesco Statement on Race summarises clearly the conclusions which the available information justifies:

'. . . no convincing evidence has been adduced that race-mixture of itself produces biologically bad effects. Statements that human hybrids frequently show undesirable traits, both physically and mentally, physical disharmonies and mental degeneracies, are not supported by the facts.'

And further: 'There is no evidence that race mixture as such produces bad results from the biological point of view. The social results of race mixture, whether for good or ill, are to be traced to social factors.'

THE PROBLEM OF RATE OF GROWTH

Reference was made above to the interpretation which has been given to the findings by Dr Géber regarding the precocity of black children in Uganda, namely, that their early development pointed to their later inferiority. (This interpretation was definitely not given by Dr Géber herself.) It has even been suggested that this may be related to certain anatomical and physiological differences, which result in an earlier closure of the sutures of the skull in the so-called inferior races. This would mean that the brain no longer has room to grow, and as a consequence further mental development would be impossible.

This whole notion must now be regarded as one of the many myths which have developed in connection with the problem of race. Mental growth is certainly not determined by anything so mechanical as the presence or absence of open sutures in the skull. Cases could be cited almost *ad infinitum* of individuals who continue their mental growth throughout life, without being hampered by the fact that their skulls no longer increase in size. In any case, as far as racial groups are concerned, such anatomical and physiological differences have never been demonstrated; on the contrary, careful studies of Negro and white children show no difference in the average age at which the sutures of the skull finally close.

When intelligence tests are administered to children of different ages, there is some slight indication that the difference in test scores between Negro and white children becomes more marked with increasing age. The evidence is conflicting, however; not all the relevant investigations show this phenomenon. When it does occur, it can be explained by factors that have nothing to do with hereditary differences in rate of mental development. It has already been indicated that many groups of Negroes live in an inferior educational and social environment; a number of investigations have revealed that, as children—white as well as Negro—grow up in such an inferior environment, their *relative* mental level (as compared with other children of the same age) tends very definitely to drop. One such study was conducted among canal-boat children in England. These children went to school only occasionally, and their homes were intellectually at a very low level. It was revealed that the average IQ of the very young children, six years old and younger, was fairly high, in the neighbourhood of 90, but that it declined sharply with age; the oldest group, 12 years of age and over, had an IQ of only 60. Similar results were obtained in the case of American children living in the mountains of Kentucky and Virginia. These were white children, and no one has as yet suggested that this might be due to a racial factor affecting rate of mental growth. What appears to happen is that an inferior environment exerts a cumulative negative influence as the years go by, and this affects both white and Negro children in the same manner. There is no scientific basis for the belief that races differ in this respect.

CULTURAL DIFFERENCES

In what has been said here, there is no implication that all ethnic groups are alike in their behaviour. Of course they are not alike; or rather, they are alike in some respects but not in others. A Chinese and a Frenchman, simply as human beings, will have a great deal in common; they will also differ because one has been brought up in one society, the other in another. They will also differ in their physical appearance, their inherited physical type or 'race', but as has been indicated above the differences in 'race', that is to say, the physical and anotomical differences, appear to have nothing to do with the differences in behaviour.

Why, then, are there differences in behaviour or in 'culture' between such groups, if race plays no part? How did such differences arise? This is not an easy question to answer. The causes may lie deep in history; they may be related to the physical environment, to contacts with surrounding peoples, to the inventions and discoveries of individuals, to the problems which had to be solved, and to the ways hit upon, sometimes by accident, for their solution. In most cases, we simply do not know how or why they arose in the first place. For our purposes, the important thing is that they are there. Far from denying them, we must recognise their existence and understand their nature. In understanding them, however, we must beware of two important errors. The first error is to ascribe them to race. The second is to look upon other cultures as inferior to our own, simply because they are different.

The first of these errors has already been discussed at length. The second is also important, however, and leads to attitudes of condescension and feelings of superiority which are not conducive to good human relations. It is an error which has manifested itself all through history, and to which many different peoples have contributed. Perhaps it has been reflected most frequently in the writings of Western man, but it is by no means exclusive to them. There is an account of a Chinese emperor who wrote to the King of England in 1793, stating: 'We possess all things. I set no value on objects strange or ingenious.' But there is no people which possesses 'all things'. The world is richer for the variety of ways of life which have been developed in different nations. No one nation has a monopoly on what is good and true and valuable in human civilisation.

At this particular moment it may be of value to look once more at the contents of a letter written by an Eskimo who could not understand why men hunt one another like seals and steal from people they have never seen or known. He apostrophises his own country: 'How well it is that you are covered with ice and snow! How well it is that, if in your rocks there is gold and silver, for which others are so greedy, it is covered with so much snow that they cannot get at it. Your unfruitfulness makes us happy and saves us from molestation.' He expresses his surprise that Europeans have not learned better manners from the Eskimo, and—

the crowning touch—proposes to send medicine men as missionaries to teach them the advantages of peace. Yes indeed, we can learn something from the ways of life of others.

People differ, of course, but not because of their race. As John Stuart Mill, the great English philosopher and economist, expressed it: 'Of all the vulgar modes of escaping from the consideration of the effect of social and moral influences upon the human mind, the most vulgar is that of attributing the diversities of conduct and character to inherent natural differences.'

SOME CONCLUDING CONSIDERATIONS

The Relevance of Tests

The discussion of the various environmental factors which enter into test performance may appear to cast doubt on the possibility of applying tests in order to study either individual or group differences. In particular, if the tests are inevitably 'culture-bound', how can they ever be used in the comparison of groups with varying cultural background? It is true that tests do always reflect the norms and preoccupations of the group responsible for their origin. Intelligence has been defined as the ability to solve new problems, but such problems always bear some relation to previous experience; they are not equally 'new' to all those whose abilities are presumably being measured. Within a single culture, however, tests are useful (although far from perfect) predictors of later success. They may also serve as a measure of the extent to which the members of one group may learn to cope with the problems devised by another, as well as the factors responsible for success or failure respectively. The fact that African children who attend school do so much better on the tests than those who do not; that the scores of American Indian children rise when their economy improves; that Jamaican children in London and blacks in New York show gains in performance proportional to their length of sojourn in the new environment—these and other findings argue strongly in favour of an environmental explanation of group differences. The application of tests helps to give to this conclusion the added weight that comes from empirical evidence.

The Overlapping of Test Results

The case was described above of a little black girl who obtained a

Binet IQ of 200—a score reached by only a tiny proportion of all the children in the world who have been tested. This means, as has clearly been indicated, that the range or limits of measured performance is the same, or approximately the same, for American blacks and whites. Whatever the differences in averages may be, there is always overlapping, which in technical terms means that a certain percentage of the 'inferior' group will reach or exceed the average of the 'superior'. Even those who argue that the difference in averages is due to genetic factors all admit the existence of overlapping. Jensen, for example, writes that 'the full range of human talents is represented in all the races of man and in all socioeconomic levels' and that 'it is unjust to allow the mere fact of an individual's racial or social background to affect the treatment accorded to him' (p. 78). These remarks have received only a tiny fraction of the attention given to the rest of his thesis, but their practical implications are far-reaching. Whatever criteria we use, whether we measure, in his terms, 'associative learning ability', 'abstract problem-solving', or anything else, we cannot ignore the fundamental phenomenon of overlapping. Any lines of demarcation between groups of people, therefore, in employment, in education, in opportunities for development, based on alleged genetic differences in average performance do violence to the facts of individual capacities and potentialities.

'Racism in Reverse'

This term has occasionally been used to designate a tendency on the part of certain groups of blacks to draw lines of demarcation between themselves and whites, similar to those which the whites have done with regard to them. This complex phenomenon is relevant in the present context only insofar as it includes the belief on the part of these blacks that they are genetically different in their psychology because they are black. The concepts of *négritude* and African personality are usually presented as having a cultural rather than a racial meaning, but occasionally they have led to the view that African origin is somehow associated with intrinsic, genetically determined psychological characteristics. The thesis that African personality is related to specific traditions and cultural background, and that Afro-American psychology has been greatly influenced by black experience in America and by an emerging Afro–American culture, is entirely reasonable. When, however, as some appear to believe, there is something like African 'soul' which is regarded as inherently associated with a black skin, we are back to a form of racial psychology for which there is no scientific basis.

The Role of Heredity

As has already been indicated, the position here presented should not be interpreted as entirely rejecting the role of heredity. Psychologists and other scientists do not hold the view that heredity plays no part whatsoever in the explanation of psychological differences. *Individuals* and *families* are not equally endowed; some are superior in their inheritance of mental capacity, others inferior. No one can safely deny this fact. There is overwhelming evidence in its support. That is quite a different matter, however, from saying that *races* or *ethnic groups* differ in their psychological inheritance. For that there is no evidence. On the contrary, every racial group contains individuals who are well endowed, others who are inferior, and still others in between. As far as we can judge, the range of capacities and the frequency of occurrence of various levels of inherited ability are about the same in all racial groups.

The scientist knows of no relation between race and psychology.

Note. The term *race* has been used in this paper because Unesco uses it. It is in fact highly ambiguous; physical anthropologists and geneticists vary greatly both in their definition of race, and in their classification of human races. Even if care is taken to use the term in its most acceptable sense, as referring to a group that differs from others in the presence and range of inherited (usually physical) characteristics, a great deal of confusion remains. The research dealing with so-called racial differences in psychology has involved ethnic groups characterised by differences not only in physical characteristics but also in language, religion, national origin, culture in general, or any combination of these factors. It would be preferable, in this context, to refer to the problem of genetic psychological differences between ethnic groups or populations rather than between races.

Part II

SOCIAL STRUCTURE AND RACISM

Race, Caste and Ethnic Identity[*][†]

by ANDRÉ BÉTEILLE

Reader in Sociology, University of Delhi

INDIAN CASTE AND COLOUR CASTE

The attempt to view race and caste within the same framework of understanding could take us in two different directions. In the first place, we might consider to what extent systems of stratification based on caste (as in India) and on colour (as in the Southern United States) can be regarded as analogous in structure; this is a problem in comparative sociology. In the second place, we might ask how far in India caste distinctions correspond to differences in physical or racial type; this problem is of more special interest to students of Indian society and history.[1]

When American social anthropologists, mainly under the influence of Lloyd Warner, began to study the Deep South of the United States in the thirties, they found it useful to speak of a caste system in representing the cleavages between Negroes and whites in rural and urban communities there.[2] Gunnar Myrdal employed similar terms and categories in his classic study of the American Negro made at about the same time.[3] The metaphor of caste has since then been widely used in describing multiracial societies in other parts of the world, notably South Africa.[4]

There are certain obvious parallels between the Indian caste system and the system of stratification based on colour, whether in the US South or in South Africa. In studying the US South both

* I am grateful to my colleagues A. Sharma and S. C. Tiwari of the Department of Anthropology and M. S. A. Rao of the Department of Sociology, University of Delhi for much help in the preparation of this Chapter.

† First published in the *International Social Science Journal*, Vol. 23, No. 4 (1971).

Warner and Myrdal were struck by the rigid distinctions maintained between Negroes and whites which seemed to them to be in marked contrast with the more flexible pattern of relations in a class system. Their purpose in labelling as 'caste' the system of stratification based on colour was not so much to explore its similarity with the Indian system as to emphasise its difference from the class system in America and other Western societies.

It might be useful to explore a little further the similarities between the Indian caste system and what I shall call for short the colour-caste system. In both systems the component units are differentiated from each other by clearly defined boundaries. Differences between castes are reinforced by a measure of homogeneity within the caste.

Caste systems may be described as systems of cumulative inequality. Advantages of status tend to be combined with advantages of wealth and power, and those who are socially underprivileged also tend to be at the bottom of the economic and political scales. There are many exceptions to this in the colour-caste system where poor whites co-exist with well-to-do Negroes,[5] but exceptions of the same kind have existed in Indian society for a long time.[6]

In both systems the component units maintain their social identity through strict rules of endogamy. In a class system individuals tend to marry within their own class but there are no prescribed rules which require them to do so. In the US South marriages between Negroes and whites were strictly forbidden and this is still the case in South Africa. In India the principle of endogamy was in certain areas mitigated by the practice of hypergamy (*anuloma*) by which a man from a higher caste could under prescribed conditions marry a girl from a lower caste. It must be emphasised that traditionally the practice of hypergamy was governed by strict rules which recognised the distinctions between castes as well as their hierarchical order; and, as Mrs Karve has pointed out, it 'is found in certain parts of India among only certain castes and is not a general practice in any region'.[7] Those who define systems of stratification in terms of the rigidity of marriage rules are bound to be struck by the similarity between the Indian and the colour-caste systems.

Closely associated with the rules regulating marriage are certain attitudes towards women characteristic of both types of society. A very high value is placed on the purity of women belonging to the upper strata and they are protected from sexual contamination by men of the lower strata by sanctions of the most stringent kind.[8] On the other hand, there is a strong element of 'sexual exploitation' in the relations between men of the upper strata and women of the lower. Berreman notes that the 'sexual advantage' enjoyed by high caste men in an Indian village studied by him are similar even in their details to those enjoyed by white men in the town studied by Dollard in the US South.[9]

We might at this stage sum up the characteristics of castes by saying that they are hierarchically ranked groups or categories based on hereditary membership which maintain their social identity by strict rules of endogamy. The fact of hereditary membership is of great importance. It fixes the social status of the individual at birth and prevents his movement from one group or category to another. In spite of many exceptions, these factors combine to fit the social divisions in a caste society into an uncommonly rigid mould.

If I began by considering the similarities between the two types of social stratification, this was not to imply that I consider these to be in some sense more fundamental than their differences. Opinion is sharply divided on the significance to be attached to these similarities and differences,[10] and scholars like Dumont[11] and Leach[12] would consider it misleading to describe systems of stratification based on colour as caste. For them, the institution of caste in the true sense of the term is a unique feature of the pan-Indian civilisation.

The differences between the two types of caste system—using the same term for convenience—are obvious enough, but it has not proved easy to sum them up in a formula. Some would draw the distinction by saying that one represents a 'cultural model' and the other a 'biological model'.[13] The caste system in India is certainly a cultural phenomenon, but is it adequate to represent the colour-caste system in the US South (or in South Africa) simply in biological terms? Both Warner[14] and Myrdal[15] had first considered and then rejected the view that the groups they were studying be described as races. A quick look at their argument will throw some light on the complex relations between race, culture and society and help us to probe a little deeper into the subject of our study.

Warner insists that in the stratification system of the Deep South the categories Negro and white are socially and not biologically defined. Persons who are socially defined as Negroes might be biologically classified as white and people who are regarded as Negroes in one society might in another society be viewed as Whites.[16] Myrdal's position is similar. He points out, first, that 'the "Negro race" is defined in America by the white people' and, second, that 'this definition of the Negro race in the United States is at variance with that held in the rest of the American continent.'[17] What is significant is not merely the presence of physical distinctions but also the manner in which they are socially recognised which is essentially conventional. Neither Negroes nor whites in the US South can be regarded as races in the strictly biological sense of the term.

Kingsley Davis sought to characterise the distinction which we are considering as being between 'racial' and 'non-racial' caste systems.

A non-racial caste system, such as the Hindu, is one in which the criterion of caste status is primarily descent symbolised in purely socio-economic terms; while a racial system is one in which the criterion is primarily physiognomic, usually chromatic, with socio-economic differences implied.[18]

We have just seen why it is not wholly satisfactory to describe the caste system in the United States as racial; and it is not entirely clear that the chromatic differences there are more fundamental than the socio-economic ones as Davis would seem to suggest. Nor is it wholly satisfactory in this context to view 'race' and 'descent' in opposition for in both cases we are concerned with the cultural definition of biological processes.

It is true, nonetheless, that *visible* physical differences are much more conspicuous in the colour-caste system than in the Indian. An outsider in the US South will not have much difficulty in deciding in the majority of cases who belongs to which caste merely from appearance. In India he will find it difficult if not impossible to do this beyond a certain point. But this in itself would not establish the absence of more fundamental genetic differences between castes in Indian society. Indeed, their complete absence would be surprising in view of the fact that members of most castes are believed to have practised strict endogamy for countless generations.

Those who emphasise the differences between the Indian and the American systems would base their argument on the uniqueness of Hindu cultural values. In fact, one might distinguish between the 'structural' view of caste which draws attention to broad similarities and the 'cultural' view which regards the caste system in India as unique.[19] There is no doubt that in India caste is embedded in a system of religious values which has no counterpart either in the US South or in South Africa.

Western scholars have been struck by the importance of hierarchy in the Hindu scheme of values.[20] Central to this are the notions of *dharma* and *karma*.[21] These are both complex, philosophical notions and it is difficult to put them in a nutshell. Very briefly, *dharma* implies right conduct in accordance with one's station in life, defined largely by one's caste; *karma* explains—and justifies—one's birth in a particular station in terms of one's actions in a previous life. In other words, more rules and standards of worth would differ from one caste to another. Most Western observers have been struck by the iniquity of the system, but scholars like Leach would point out that it ensured a measure of material and psychological security to all sections of society, particularly to those at the bottom of the hierarchy.[22]

In contrast to the values of traditional India, the American creed has always placed the highest social value on the equality of men. Thus, the moral environment in which rigid social distinctions exist in America is quite different from the moral environment in India. One may say that the American system is disharmonic; inequalities exist in fact although rejected by the normative order. The traditional Indian system was, by contrast, harmonic; rigid social distinctions not only existed but were generally accepted as legitimate. If this argument is correct, then the two types of system would show very different patterns of tension and conflict.

The values of a society are not easy to describe in an objective way. They are often ambiguous and made up of conflicting elements. It is difficult to believe that hierarchical values were accepted in the same way by all strata of Indian society. Most of what we know about traditional Indian values is based on texts written by people who belonged to the top of the hierarchical system. Perhaps we will never know in quite the same detail how the order of caste was perceived by people at the bottom of the hierarchy.

Berreman, who, unlike most students of Indian society, has studied a village community by living with the lower castes, would contend that there are sharp differences of perspective between the lower and the upper strata.[23] Others also have noted the presence of tensions and conflicts between castes which would not be expected if everyone accepted without question the position assigned to him within the hierarchical order.[24] However, most of these tendencies have been recorded within the past twenty years and their emergence in contemporary India would not contradict the assertion that traditionally the Indian caste system approximated to the harmonic type.

Berreman also rejects the view that the American value system can be defined unambiguously in terms of its emphasis on equality.[25] He quotes Spiro's critique of Myrdal to support his argument:

The assumption of egalitarian culture norms is untenable unless one adopts an idealist conception of ideal norms which are irrelevant to human behaviour and aspirations. Actually discrimination against the Negro is not in violation of southern ideal norms; it is in conformity with them.[26]

There is also the question of the colour-caste system in South Africa. Can we say, perhaps, that here we have a normative order which accepts the existing structure of inequality between groups as legitimate?

Differences between the colour-caste system and the Indian system are not confined to the realm of values. There are important differences in the structure and composition of the groups which constitute the two types of system. In the US South there are only two principal castes, Negroes and whites; in South Africa there are four, Africans, whites, coloureds and Asians.[27] In India the caste system comprises a large number of groups whose mutual relations are of an extremely complex nature.

In India it is not at all uncommon for a single village to have as many as twenty or thirty castes.[28] Each linguistic region in the country has between 200 and 300 castes. Many of these are divided into sub-castes which might in turn be further subdivided.[29] If we leave the village and take a larger territorial unit, it becomes impossible even to determine the exact number of castes in it. The distinctions between caste, sub-caste and sub-sub-caste become blurred. The same caste might be called by different names and different castes by the same name.

There is no single rank order for all the castes and sub-castes which applies in every region. Perhaps all that can be said very

firmly for the country as a whole is that Brahmins rank at the top
and Harijans at the bottom. There is a great deal of ambiguity in
the middle region. The different cultivating castes make competing
claims to superior status. The Brahmins (like the Harijans) are
themselves divided into a number of castes and sub-castes whose
mutual ranks are by no means easy to determine.[30] All this is not
to deny that a certain measure of consensus in regard to caste
ranking does exist within the local community.[31] This consensus
was probably stronger in the past than it is today.

It can be argued that structurally there is a basic difference
between a dichotomous system and a system of gradation in which
there are many terms. Once again, the two types of system are
likely to display very different patterns of social conflict. Theories
of social class and of conflict assign a crucial significance to the
dichotomous division of society.[32] Where the contending parties
are two in number, the conflict tends to be intense; where they are
many, a shifting pattern of coalitions reduces the intensity of conflict. The same theory can be extended to caste. Where the community is divided into Negroes and whites, the conflict is likely
to be sharp; where it is divided into twenty or thirty groups, no
particular conflict is likely to absorb the energies of the community
as a whole.

CASTE DISTINCTIONS AND PHYSICAL DIFFERENCES

In this section we shall try to see if any relationship can be established between caste distinctions and physical differences in the
Indian population. It might be said at the outset that if such a
relationship exists it is not likely to be either simple or direct.
Physical differences are not polarised in India but are spread over
a continuum. The population cannot be readily divided into races
or even into clearly recognisable physical types. The caste system
in its turn is a system of great complexity. It is divided and sub-
divided into innumerable groups and a consideration of these
might provide a convenient point of departure.

The word 'caste' is used in India to refer to groups and categories of very different kinds. Two types of distinctions are particularly important. The first is between *varna* and *jati* and the
second is between caste and sub-caste. The difference between
varna and *jati* can be briefly described as the difference between

a model or a conceptual scheme on the one hand and a set of real social groups or categories on the other. There are only four *varnas* which are arranged in a particular order whereas *jatis* are many and their rank order is both more ambiguous and more flexible.[33] *Jatis* should not be viewed as having grown out of divisions and subdivisions within a set of four original *varnas*. Rather, as Mrs Karve has argued, *varna* and *jati* have co-existed as two different but related systems for at least two thousand years.[34]

The distinction between caste and sub-caste is of a different kind. Both are real social divisions, but one is more inclusive than the other. If we take potters or carpenters as examples of castes, we will find that in any given region there are two or three different kinds of potters or of carpenters, differentiated according to technique or provenance or sect or some other less tangible factor. These different divisions we might refer to as sub-castes. They are similar in structure to the more inclusive groupings and are generally endogamous. Scholars like Ghurye would maintain that the different types of potters are sub-castes, being products of segmentation within the potter caste.[35] Mrs Karve, on the other hand, has argued that the different types of potters are often unrelated and that each should be called a caste and the potters as a whole a 'caste cluster'.[36] Her argument is important in this context because she has tried to support it with anthropometric data.[37]

Sometimes there are several levels of differentiation and not just two. Thus, the Tamil Brahmins are of three main kinds: (1) temple priests; (2) domestic priests for the Non-Brahmins; and (3) scholars and landowners. The last are divided into Smartha and Shri Vaishnava. Smartha Brahmins, in their turn, are further subdivided into Vadama, Brihacharanam, Astasahashram and Vattima. The Vadama, finally, are divided into Vadadesha and Chozhadesha Vadama.[38] This kind of differentiation makes it useful to view caste as a segmentary or structural system.[39] For even though each segment is endogamous, the social distance between segments is variable. Thus, the social distance between Vadama and Brihacharanam is smaller than the distance between Vadama and a Shri Vaishnava segment which in turn is smaller than that between any Brahmin segment and any Non-Brahmin segment. This way of viewing the system leads us to ask if there is any relationship between social distance and racial distance.

Most anthropologists who have analysed caste from the biological point of view would concede that some physical differences do

exist between castes. But they are sharply divided on the significance they attach to these differences. On the whole, earlier
scholars emphasised the differences in physical type they observed
between castes. Contemporary scholars are more inclined to stress
the fact that most castes are more or less heterogeneous in their
physical composition and that variations within the caste are
sometimes greater than variations between castes.

It is not enough to know that castes differ from each other in
their biological make up. We would like to know in addition
whether the extent to which they differ in this regard is related to
their social distance. Castes which are socially adjacent might be
quite different in their biological composition while those which
are at opposite ends of the social scale might show very little
difference biologically. To answer this kind of question satis-
factorily we will need a great deal of systematic empirical material.
The evidence that we now have is scanty and does not all point in
the same direction.

The first serious effort to study physical or racial differences
between castes in a systematic way was made towards the end of
the last century by Sir Herbert Risley.[40] Risley not only believed
that such differences existed but argued that they were systematically related to differences of social rank between castes:

If we take a series of castes in Bengal, Bihar, the United Provinces
of Agra and Oudh, or Madras, and arrange them in the order of
the average nasal index so that the caste with the finest nose shall
be at the top, and that with the coarsest at the bottom of the list,
it will be found that this order substantially corresponds with the
accepted order of social precedence.[41]

Risley was also struck by the fact that the upper castes were in
general lighter skinned than the lower and drew attention to a
number of local proverbs in which this distinction was given
recognition.

Risley developed an elaborate theory to explain the social ranking of castes. He argued that the caste system was the outcome of
the encounter between two distinct racial groups, one representing
a light-skinned, narrow-nosed, 'Aryan' type, and the other, a dark-
skinned, broad-nosed, 'non-Aryan' type. The Aryans, according
to the theory, were not only the dominant group but also adopted
the practice of hypergamy. This practice led to the formation of a
series of intermediate groups whose social rank varied directly

with their amount of Aryan blood. Risley sought to support his arguments with anthropometric data. His conclusions were challenged by later scholars who found fault with both his data and his methods.[42]

Ghurye criticised Risley's work but did not reject his argument altogether. He emphasised the importance of regional variations and noted that a caste which ranked very high in one area might closely resemble in its physical features a caste which ranked very low in an adjacent area. He pointed out that in many parts of the country there was no clear relationship of the kind which Risley had sought to demonstrate: 'Outside Hindustan in each of the linguistic areas we find that the physical type of the population is mixed, and does not conform in its gradation to the scale of social precedence of the various castes'.[43]

But Ghurye agreed that in the Hindi speaking area itself there was a close correspondence between the 'physical hierarchy' and the 'social hierarchy'. Here the Brahmins were long headed and narrow nosed, and very low castes like the Chamar and the Pasi were broad headed and broad nosed. On the basis of such evidence, Ghurye was prepared to conclude that here, at least, 'Restrictions on marriage of a fundamentally endogamous nature were thus racial in origin'.[44]

The most comprehensive single investigation so far carried out is the anthropometric study of Bengal made jointly by an anthropologist, D. N. Majumdar and a statistician, C. R. Rao.[45] The data were collected from a defined cultural region, Bengal, comprising both West Bengal and East Pakistan. Sixty-seven groups were investigated, including Muslims, Christians, a few tribal groups and a large number of Hindu castes. These groups were studied with regard to sixteen basic anthropometric characters and a number of indices derived from them. Some serological data were collected in addition. The anthropometric data were analysed by means of rigorous and sophisticated statistical tests.

In spite of many qualifications, Majumdar concluded that there was some clustering of groups according to their social proximity. The tribal and semi-tribal groups tended to be clustered at one end and at the other end were the higher castes such as Brahmin, Baidya and Kayastha.[46] Majumdar pointed out that these data confirmed the observations made by him in two other areas in India, Gujarat and Uttar Pradesh. 'In all the three surveys, it has been found that some correlation exists between the order of social precedence in a state or region, and the ethnic constellations based on anthropometric data.'[47] It must be emphasised, however, that the relationships which emerge from the study by Majumdar and Rao are of a far more complex nature than the one which Risley believed he had established.

Studies made more recently do not all support Majumdar's conclusions. Karve and Malhotra have published the results of a detailed comparison between eight Brahmin 'sub-castes' in Maharashtra, taking anthropometric, somatoscopic and serological data into account.[48] Their data show the existence of significant differences among some of the Brahmin 'sub-castes'. Comparing their findings with those of other scholars, they conclude that there is no necessary relationship between social distance and physical distance. Thus there is no justification for assuming that the distance between the Brahmin 'castes' under investigation is less than the distance between a Brahmin 'caste' and a Non-Brahmin 'caste', for some Brahmins are closer to members of other 'castes' than to each other.[49] It would appear that the more closely we look at the system the less firm we can be about the linkage between caste and race.

The shift from morphological to genetical indicators would seem to confirm the view that the linkage between social and physical distance is tenuous and uncertain. As my last example I shall take a study by Sanghvi and Khanolkar which examines the distribution of seven genetical traits among six endogamous groups in Bombay.[50] Of the six groups, four are Brahmins; one is a high Non-Brahmin caste, Chandraseniya Kayashth Prabhu (CKP), ranking next only to the Brahmins; and the other is a Cultivating caste, Maratha (MK), belonging to the middle level of the hierarchy. As the authors point out, all these groups have been regarded by earlier anthropologists as being of the same physical type.

The results of the analysis show a rather complex pattern of variations. Some of the Brahmin groups are quite close to each other, and one of them is very similar in its genetical composition to the Non-Brahmin Marathas. The Koknasth Brahman (KB) are, on the other hand, quite distinctive in their genetical composition as are also the Chandraseniya Kayasth Prabhu (CKP). Moreover, these two groups are markedly different from each other. 'The magnitude of differences between the groups KB and CKP for each one of the seven genetical characters is more or less similar to that between American whites and American Negroes.'[51] Although the Chandraseniya Kayasth Prabhu are Non-Brahmins, they rank very high and might be regarded as being socially proximate to the Koknasth Brahman.

This leads us to a consideration of the social significance of genotypical as opposed to phenotypical differences. Earlier anthropologists such as Risley sought to establish a relationship between the social rank of a caste and the physical appearance of its members. They were encouraged in their pursuit by beliefs widely held in Indian society about the existence of such a relationship.[52] Upper castes are universally believed to be light skinned and narrow nosed and lower castes to be dark skinned and broad nosed. It would now appear that two socially adjacent castes whose members are very similar in their physical appearance might nevertheless be quite different in their genetical composition.

Genetical differences are likely to acquire social significance only if their existence is widely known or if they are reflected in clear differences in physical type. As I have indicated, certain broad differences in appearance exist between castes at opposite ends of the hierarchy in many parts of the country and equally significant are the beliefs and stereotypes regarding these differences which persist in spite of much evidence to the contrary. Beliefs which are technically wrong or inconsistent sometimes assume crucial significance in social life. As Passin has argued,

The relation of caste to race is not simply a question of whether the groups are in fact racially different, but rather that there seems to be some disposition to attribute racial difference to even the most marginal cues in caste and caste-like situations.[53]

This is particularly true in the Indian context where in some languages the same word is used to denote both caste and race.[54]

What is important in social life is the sense of solidarity which people feel when they belong to the same community and the feeling of distance which separates members who belong to different communities. The sense of community is often based on the feeling that its members have a common origin. This feeling may be vague or it may be consciously formulated in an ideology. It may be strengthened if the community is marked out by distinctive physical features, but this is not a necessary condition for its existence. Sometimes a strong sense of community can exist even in the absence of visible physical indicators. This leads us to a consideration of ethnic groups and identities.

THE CONCEPT OF ETHNICITY

The systematic use of the concept of ethnicity is of relatively recent origin in sociology and social anthropology although the presence of ethnic groups in the United States has been widely discussed for many years.

An ethnic group is a distinct category of the population in a larger society whose culture is usually different from its own. The members of such a group are, or feel themselves, or are thought to be bound together by common ties of race or nationality or culture.[55]

As this description suggests, there is no single criterion by which ethnic groups can be defined.

In the United States the term 'ethnic group' came into use to describe immigrants from the different parts of the world. Examples of these would be the Irish, the Italians and the Poles who settled in the country in successive waves of migration. These groups were not all differentiated by visible physical indicators. Initially there were major differences of language, culture and religion among the groups. As some of these differences began to diminish among second- and third-generation immigrants, it was felt that a culturally homogeneous population would emerge out of the melting pot of American society. But in spite of a high degree of mobility, both horizontal and vertical, and a certain amount of intermarriage between groups, ethnic identities have proved to be remarkably persistent in American society.[56]

The presence of ethnic groups is of course not a unique feature of American society. They exist in all societies where cultural differences are given a particular meaning and are organised in a particular way. Ethnic differentiation has been a conspicuous feature of the so-called plural societies of South and South-East Asia.[57] Sometimes this differentiation is associated with the presence of large groups, such as the Chinese and the Indians in Malaysia, which differ markedly from each other in language, religion and provenance. The coexistence of such disparate groups is likely to generate tensions and conflicts which might, in the extreme case, threaten the integrity of the political framework itself.

Ethnic identities might persist even when ethnic groups are not visibly different or politically organised. In a recent collection of papers Barth and his colleagues have argued persuasively that ethnic identities do not depend for their survival on any particular aggregate of cultural traits. 'It is important to recognise that although ethnic categories take cultural differences into account, we can assume no simple one-to-one relationship between ethnic units and cultural similarities and differences.'[58] Eidheim gives a graphic account of the manner in which an ethnic boundary is maintained between Lapps and Norwegians even in the absence of any readily visible physical or cultural differences between them.[59]

Ethnic groups are generally endogamous and in that sense they tend to be biologically self-perpetuating.[60] Even in the complete absence of diacritical distinctions endogamy could of course serve to keep ethnic boundaries intact. When all marriages do not take place within the group, ethnic boundaries might still be maintained if intermarriage is governed by the rule of hypergamy; the practice of hypergamy acts as an important boundary maintaining mechanism among certain sections of the hill Rajputs in India.[61] Far from dissolving ethnic boundaries altogether, intermarriage might under certain conditons serve to bring these boundaries into sharper relief.

Thus, the concept of ethnic group is somewhat broader in its scope than that of race. Ethnic differences might be based at least partly on race as in the case of Malays, Chinese and Indians in Malaysia or of Negroes, Indians and whites in the Caribbean. They might also exist in a society which is racially more or less homogeneous as in the case of the Pathans in West Pakistan and Afghanistan or of some of the multi-tribal systems in East Africa.

The caste system, in its turn, may be viewed as a particular case of ethnic differentiation, Whether or not 'racial' differences exist between castes, they are often differentiated from each other culturally, in their dress, diet and rituals. Where even these distinctions are feeble or absent, the boundaries between castes are maintained by the rules of endogamy and hypergamy. However, even if we regard caste as a system of ethnic groups, it is a system in which the different groups are all integrated within a hierarchical order. Ethnic groups are not necessarily arranged in a hierarchy and they are not always integrated within a unitary system.

We notice a close similarity between caste in India and ethnic groups in the United States when we examine the part they play in the political process.[62] In the United States ethnic solidarities are widely used for mobilising political support and ethnic rivalries have to be taken into account in formulating electoral strategies.[63] In India caste enters into the political process in a number of ways.[64] Caste associations have not only acted as pressure groups but, in at least one area, have transformed themselves into political parties.[65] Rivalries between parties are sometimes heightened when they base their support on mutually antagonistic castes.[66] However, in both India and the United States the relationship between caste or ethnic identity and the political process is complex and ambiguous. The political process brings out not only the cleavages between such groups but also the possibilities of coalitions among them.

The Harijans provide a particular example of solidarity based on caste or ethnic identity. In the past the barrier of pollution kept them segregated from many areas of social life. These barriers have now been legally abolished but the Harijans retain much of their traditional stigma and continue to be socially and economically underprivileged. But they are now provided with opportunities to organise themselves politically.[67] This has enabled them to gain some advantages but it has also brought them into confrontation with the upper castes whose members are not always in a mood to accept them as equals. The situation of the Harijans in contemporary India—like that of the Negroes in the United States —reveals a paradox. The lessening of cultural distance has in both cases been accompanied not by a decrease but by an increase in tension and conflict.

India has not only a Harijan problem, there is also an Adivasi or tribal problem. Harijans and Adivasis are officially grouped together as the backward classes and their separate identity is given constitutional recognition.[68] The tribal people numbered about 30 million at the 1961 census and they constituted over 6 per cent of the Indian population. They are divided into a large number of separate tribes, differing in race, language and culture. They are concentrated in particular areas in the country which tend to be geographically isolated but there is no policy of keeping them in reservations.

The tribal population of India does not belong to any single racial or physical type. The differences between the 'Veddoid' type common among certain tribes in central and south India and the 'Palaeo-Mongoloid' type found in the north-east hill areas might be greater than the differences between the tribal people and their non-tribal neighbours in any particular area. But Fürer-Haimendorf has rightly pointed out that differences of the latter kind also exist[69] and Majumdar's anthropometric data seem to point in the same direction.[70]

After drawing attention to differences in physical type between the tribal and the non-tribal population, Fürer-Haimendorf says, 'It is all the more remarkable that despite racial differences no less fundamental than those found in countries with acute race problems, there have never been any cases of racial tension in India.'[71] One important factor is the very great variety of physical types which has prevented a polarisation of the population along racial lines. This does not mean that differences do not exist or are not socially recognised. In fact, tribal solidarity is perhaps being given a new lease of life by democratic politics. But the conflict is transferred on to a different plane where the cleavage between tribals and non-tribals becomes one among a number of politically relevant ethnic distinctions.

We have so far considered ethnic differentiation among groups which are hierarchically arranged, for, although the Adivasis are in the strict sense outside the caste system, they are almost everywhere ranked below the caste Hindus. We may now turn to ethnic differentiation between groups which are not hierarchically arranged, such as those based on religion or on language. In some sense these provide the most fundamental cleavages in contemporary Indian society. When one talks about 'national integration' in India one has primarily in mind the problems of holding together the different religious and linguistic communities. While one can distinguish analytically between ethnic identities of different kinds—hierarchical and non-hierarchical—in reality these often tend to become confused.

India has been described as multi-religious nation. The Hindus are in an overwhelming majority, accounting for around 80 per cent of the population; the Muslims constitute a significant minority with a little more than 10 per cent of the population. There are other religious groups which are of significance in particular regions, such as the Sikhs in the Punjab and the Christians in Kerala. But for the country as a whole the cleavage which has greatest significance is the one between Hindus and Muslims. If there is a 'communal' problem in the country its prototype is the one which grows out of the relations between these two communities.[72]

Hindus and Muslims in India do not belong to separate races. In fact, they are both racially very mixed. This is only to be expected since the majority of Indian Muslims are the descendants of converts from Hinduism. Spear argues that there were two main types of conversion: clan or group conversion as a consequence of which castes such as Rajputs, Jats and Gujjars in north India have Hindu as well as Muslim sections; and mass conversions through which low-caste Hindus, particularly in Bengal, embraced Islam.[73] The last point finds confirmation in Majumdar's anthropometric data referred to above; the low-caste Namasudras are closer in their physical appearance to the Muslims than they are to the upper caste Hindus.[74]

Hindus and Muslims have coexisted as communities in different parts of India for a millennium. Religious differences have been associated with a host of other differences in ways of life. These differences have not always been the same, but the fact of difference has remained, heightened at times and subdued at others. Hindus and Muslims might not differ in physical type but religious ideology has provided each community with a basis for consciously organising its identity in opposition to the other. Over the centuries the two communities have borrowed much from each other and during the last few decades they have been exposed to similar forces of change. But this has not erased the boundaries between them. In fact, the pattern of Hindu-Muslim relations in recent Indian history would seem to show that groups might become more conscious of their opposed identities precisely at a time when external differences between them are being reduced.

The population of India is also divided on the basis of language. The divisions of language and religion generally cut across and do not reinforce each other as they do to a large extent in countries like Malaysia and Ceylon. This, in addition to the fact that both linguistic and religious groups are many and not two each, tends to make the conflict between communities diffused rather than polarised.

Over a dozen major languages are spoken in India but there is none which is the mother tongue of a majority of the people. The speakers of the different languages are not randomly distributed throughout the country. Each language has its 'homeland' so that linguistic differences largely coincide with regional differences.

The different states which constitute the Union of India are in effect linguistic units. This means that the ethnic identity provided by language has both a cultural basis and a political organisation.

Differences between linguistic groups can give rise to two kinds of tensions. At one level are the disputes between the different linguistic states over particular issues, for instance the question of boundaries or the distribution of river water.[75] At another level one encounters the problem of linguistic minorities in practically every state; these problems are likely to be particularly acute in large metropolitan cities like Bombay or Calcutta which attract people from all over the country. Ethnic boundaries based on language are in a way crucial; they restrict communication between people in the literal sense of the term.

Differences of language have in reality very little to do with differences of race although in one important case linguistic differences have been represented in a racial idiom. The different languages of India belong to two major families, the Indo-Aryan languages spoken in the north by about three-quarters of the population and the Dravidian languages spoken in the four southern states by about a quarter of the population. People in the southern states have, particularly since independence, sometimes expressed a fear of domination by the north[76] and a separatist political movement developed there although its influence has been confined almost wholly to one state, Tamilnad.[77] One of the arguments advanced by leaders of this movement was that South Indians, being Dravidians, had a separate identity in race, language and culture and should free themselves from the domination of the Aryan North Indians.[78] Tamil separatism has now become subdued and one no longer hears the racial argument very frequently but language barriers are in other respects no less significant than they were before.

CONCLUSIONS

We have moved a long distance from a consideration of racial differences to differences of quite another kind which are at times expressed in a racial idiom. Ethnic identity must not be thought of as something which defines the character of one group in opposition to another for all time. In India the same individual has a number of different identities according to caste, religion and language and any one of these might become more important than the others, depending upon context and situation. It is not enough to know that boundaries exist between groups, one must also examine the situations under which some boundaries are ignored and others become significant. Thus, in one context Tamil-speaking Hindus and Muslims might unite to defend themselves against 'Aryan' domination; in another context Hindus from both north and south India might regard Muslims as aliens among them.

Although ethnic differences have a bearing on social conflict, a knowledge of the former is not enough to predict the pattern of the latter. In order to understand the scale and intensity of conflicts between ethnic groups we have to take a number of factors into account. These are (i) the objective differences between them; (ii) the social awareness of these differences; and (iii) the political organisation of this awareness.

As we have seen, the objective differences themselves are of many kinds. They may be roughly grouped together as physical or cultural. Cultural differences in turn can be based on religion, language or region. There is no direct relationship between the degree of these differences and the extent to which people are aware of them. Differences of colour might exist to the same degree in two societies and yet people might be acutely aware of them in one society and not in the other. Cutural differences are more difficult to measure. And, in any case, there are no satisfactory criteria by which one can compare the awareness of, say, religious differences with that of linguistic differences.

People might be highly conscious of their differences, whether physical or cultural, without their consciousness acquiring a political form. In traditional Indian society there were not only differences between castes, but people were universally aware of these differences. Yet castes were not always organised into mutually antagonistic groups. They began to organise themselves into associations at a time when people were beginning to feel that caste consciousness would fade away. The course of political conflict remains unpredictable. There is no general theory which can enable us to delineate in exact terms the relationship between cultural differences and their organisation into mutually antagonistic groups.

References

1. For an interesting discussion see Anthony de Reuck and Julie Knight (eds), *Caste and Race, Comparative Approaches* (London, 1967).

2. Among the more notable community studies going back to this period are John Dollard, *Caste and Class in a Southern Town* (New Haven, 1937) and Allison Davis, Burleigh B. Gardner and Mary R. Gardner, *Deep South, A Social Anthropological Study of Caste and Class* (Chicago, 1941).

3. Gunnar Myrdal, *An American Dilemma, The Negro Problem in Modern Democracy* (New York, 1944), pp. 667, 688.

4. Pierre L. van den Berghe, *Race and Racism, A Comparative Perspective* (New York, 1967), speaks of whites, Africans, Asians and coloureds as constituting the four 'castes' or 'colour-castes' of South African society.

5. Myrdal, op. cit.

6. André Béteille, *Castes: Old and New, Essays in Social Structure and Social Stratification* (Bombay, 1969), p. 3.

7. Irawati Karve, *Hindu Society, An Interpretation* (Poona, 1961), p. 16.

8. For American examples see the case studies by Dollard and by Davis, Gardner and Gardner cited above; for an Indian case study see E. Kathleen Gough, 'Caste in a Tanjore village', in E. R. Leach (ed.), *Aspects of Caste in South India, Ceylon and North-West Pakistan* (Cambridge, 1960), p. 49.

9. Gerald D. Berreman, *Hindus of the Himalayas* (Berkeley, 1963), pp. 243–5.

10. See de Reuck and Knight (eds), op. cit.

11. Louis Dumont, 'Caste, racism and "stratification": reflections of a social anthropologist', *Contributions to Indian Sociology*, No. 5 (1961), pp. 20–43.

12. E. R. Leach, 'Introduction: What should we mean by caste?' in E. R. Leach (ed.), op. cit.

13. S. J. Tambiah presents this opposition as a 'gross simplification' in a discussion reported in de Reuck and Knight (eds), op. cit. pp. 328–9.

14. W. Lloyd Warner, 'Introduction: Deep South—A Social Anthropological Study of Caste and Class' in Davis, Gardner and Gardner, op. cit. pp. 3–14.

15. Myrdal, op. cit.

16. Warner, op. cit.

17. Myrdal, op. cit., p. 113.

18. Kingsley Davis, 'Intermarriage in caste society', *American Anthropologist*, Vol. 43 (1941), pp. 386–7.

19. Louis Dumont, 'Caste: a phenomenon of social structure or an aspect of Indian culture?' in de Reuck and Knight (eds), op. cit., pp. 28–38.

20. Louis Dumont, *Homo hierarchicus, essai sur le système des castes* (Paris, 1966).

21. Karve, op. cit.

22. Leach, op. cit.

23. Berreman, op. cit.

24. André Béteille, 'The politics of "non-antagonistic" strata' *Contributions to Indian Sociology*, New Series, No. 3 (1969), pp. 17–31. One way in which conflicts between castes were structured in the past was through the opposition between the 'Right-hand' and the 'Left-hand' castes prevalent in many parts of South India; see J. H. Hutton, *Caste in India: Its Nature, Function, and Origins* (Bombay, 1961).

25. Gerald D. Berreman, 'Caste in cross-cultural perspective', in G. Devos and H. Wagatsuma (eds), *Japan's Invisible Race, Caste in Culture and Personality* (Berkeley, 1966), p. 297.

26. Ibid.

27. Van den Berghe, op. cit.

28. For typical village studies see Adrian C. Mayer, *Caste and Kinship in Central India, A Village and its Region* (London, 1960); and André Béteille, *Caste, Class, and Power, Changing Patterns of Stratification in a Tanjore Village* (Berkeley, 1965).

29. Béteille, *Caste, Class, and Power*, op. cit.

30. Ibid.

31. McKim Marriott, 'Caste ranking and food transactions: a matrix analysis' in Milton Singer and Bernard S. Cohn (eds), *Structure and Change in Indian Society* (Chicago, 1969), pp. 133–71.

32. Ralf Dahrendorf, *Class and Class Conflict in an Industrial Society* (London, 1959).

33. M. N. Srinivas, '*Varna* and *Caste*' in M. N. Srinivas, *Caste in Modern India and Other Essays* (Bombay, 1962), pp. 63–9.

34. Karve, op. cit.

35. G. S. Ghurye, *Caste and Race in India* (London, 1932).

36. Karve, op. cit.

37. I. Karve and K. C. Malhotra, 'A biological comparison of eight endogamous groups of the same rank', *Current Anthropology*, Vol. 9 (1968), pp. 109–16.

38. Béteille, *Caste, Class, and Power*, op. cit.

39. Ibid.

40. H. H. Risley, *The People of India* (Calcutta, 1908).

41. Ibid., p. 29.

42. P. C. Mahalanobis, 'A revision of Risley's anthropometric data', *Samkhya*, Vol. I (1933), pp. 76–105; Ghurye, op. cit.

43. Ghurye, op. cit., p. 111.

44. Ibid., p. 107.

45. D. N. Majumdar and C. R. Rao, *Race Elements in Bengal, A Quantitative Study* (Calcutta, 1960).

46. Ibid., p. 102.

47. Ibid., p. 103.

48. Karve and Malhotra, op. cit.

49. Ibid., p. 115.

50. L. D. Sanghvi and V. R. Khanolkar, 'Data relating to seven genetical characters in six endogamous groups in Bombay', *Annals of Eugenics*, Vol. 15 (1950–51), pp. 52–76.

51. Ibid., p. 62.

52. André Béteille, 'Race and descent as social categories in India', *Daedalus*, Vol. 96 (1967), pp. 444–63.

53. In a discussion reported in de Reuck and Knight (eds), op. cit., pp. 110–11.

54. Béteille, 'Race and Descent', op. cit.

55. H. S. Morris, 'Ethnic Groups' in David L. Sills (ed.), *International Encyclopedia of the Social Sciences*, Vol. 5 (1968), p. 167.

56. Nathan Glazer and Daniel Patrick Moynihan, *Beyond the Melting Pot: The Negroes, Puerto Ricans, Jews, Italians, and Irish of New York City* (Cambridge, Mass., 1963).

57. J. S. Furnivall, *Colonial Policy and Practice, A Comparative Study of Burma and Netherlands India* (New York, 1956).

58. Fredrik Barth, 'Introduction' in Fredrik Barth (ed.), *Ethnic Groups and Boundaries, The Social Organization of Culture Difference* (London, 1969), p. 14.

59. Harald Eidheim, 'When ethnic identity is a social stigma' in Barth (ed.), op. cit., pp. 39–57.

60. Barth, op. cit., p. 10.

61. I am indebted for this information to Jonathan P. Parry who has made an intensive study of the hill Rajputs in Kangra district.

62. Lloyd I. Rudolph and Susanne Hoeber Rudolph, *The Modernity of Tradition, Political Development in India* (Chicago, 1967); André Béteille, 'Caste and politics in Tamilnad' in Béteille, *Castes: Old and New*, op. cit.

63. Glazer and Moynihan, op. cit.

64. Rajni Kothari (ed.), *Caste in Indian Politics* (New Delhi, 1970).

65. Lloyd I. Rudolph and Susanne Hoeber Rudolph, 'The political role of India's caste associations', *Pacific Affairs*, Vol. 33 (1960), pp. 5–22.

66. Selig S. Harrison, 'Caste and the Andhra communists', *American Political Science Review*, Vol. 50 (1956).

67. Owen M. Lynch, *The Politics of Untouchability* (New York, 1969).

68. André Béteille, 'The future of the backward classes, the compet-

ing demands of status and power', *Perspectives, Supplement to the Indian Journal of Public Administration*, Vol. 11 (1965), pp. 1–39.

69. Christoph von Fürer-Haimendorf, 'The position of the tribal population in modern India' in Philip Mason (ed.), *India and Ceylon: Unity and Diversity* (London, 1967), pp. 182–222.

70. Majumdar and Rao, op. cit.

71. Fürer-Haimendorf, op. cit., p. 188.

72. See, for instance, the issue of *Seminar*, No. 24 (August 1961) devoted to Communalism.

73. Percival Spear, 'The position of the Muslims, before and after partition' in Mason (ed.), op. cit., pp. 33–4.

74. Majumdar and Rao, op. cit., p. 102.

75. Selig S. Harrison, *India: The Most Dangerous Decade* (Bombay, 1960).

76. See, for instance, the issue of *Seminar*, No. 23 (July 1961), devoted to North and South.

77. Robert L. Hardgrave Jr., *The Dravidian Movement* (Bombay, 1965).

78. Béteille, 'Race and descent as social categories in India', op. cit.

Tribalism and Racism

by E. U. ESSIEN-UDOM

Professor, Department of Political Science, University of Ibadan

INTRODUCTION

In 1903 W. E. B. Du Bois, the eminent Afro-American scholar (later a Ghanaian citizen by naturalisation), in an often-quoted statement, observed: 'The problem of the twentieth century is the problem of the colour-line,—the relation of the darker to the lighter races of men in Asia and Africa, in America and the islands of the sea.'[1] In 1940, Du Bois observed further that because of the social heritage of slavery, discrimination and insult a real sense of kinship had developed between black Americans and Africans and that this heritage of abuse and exploitation based on race and colour 'binds together not simply the children of Africa, but extends through yellow Asia and into the South Seas'.[2] In 1953 Du Bois still maintained that 'the colour line is a great problem of this century', but in retrospect he could 'see more clearly than yesterday that back of the problem of race and colour, lies a greater problem which both obscures and implements it: and that is the fact that so many civilised persons are willing to live in comfort even if the price of this is poverty, ignorance and disease of the majority of their fellowmen . . .'[3]

The problem of race relations remains a thorny issue in the world today, in countries such as the Republic of South Africa, Namibia, Zimbabwe, the United States of America, the United Kingdom, etc. Many world problems are somewhat coloured by the phenomenon of racial differences. Though not openly admitted, race plays some part in the global political strategies of the Great powers. It affects as well the lesser Asian and African powers, whose very survival could well depend on the decisions taken, whether or not to deploy nuclear weapons in war, for example, by the two Super powers, the United States and the Soviet Union. The problem of race relations has echoed and re-echoed in debates of the United Nations since its founding. Race was an important criterion used for determining the countries which were invited to the Asian-African Conference at Bandung, Indonesia in April 1955. In fact, one of the resolutions of the Conference declared that over and above the question of colonialism, 'we are all interested in racial equality . . . the touchstone for those who are here assembled and the people they represent. There has not been, nor is there now any Western colonial regime, although they differ in their systems and methods, that has not inflicted, on a larger or lesser scale, on the population they dominate the doctrine of their racial inferiority.'[4] But racial problems are complicated by the relative economic and political power between the white and darker peoples of the world. It so happens that the rich and powerful nations generally speaking coincide with the white nations, and the poor and weak with the darker nations.

As others have pointed out recognition of racial differences seems to be of ancient origin, and discrimination against dark-skinned people is probably equally as old. But, 'race' with its concomitant 'racism' as it is known today is a phenomenon of modern time.[5] The modern ideas about race and the modern manifestations of 'racism' are of European origin. Their spread in Asia and Africa, in America and the Caribbean derives from superior technology, which made it possible for Europe to establish colonial rule in those parts of the world. European officials, Christian missionaries, merchants and European settlers in those countries have been the principal agents for spreading the modern ideas of race and racialist practices. It can be said that through these agents of colonialism and imperialism European 'racism' also provoked counter-racism among the darker peoples.

What then is 'race' and 'racism'? Here we shall employ the definition offered by Pierre L. van den Berghe, who uses the term to refer to 'a human group that defines itself and/or is defined by other groups as different from other groups by virtue of innate and immutable physical characteristics. These physical characteristics are in turn believed to be intrinsically related to moral, intellectual, and other non-physical attributes or abilities.[6] The crucial factor in this definition is that a racial group is socially defined on the basis of *physical* characteristics, such as skin colour, hair texture, etc. But equally important in the definition of race is the claim that observable cultural and moral differences or differences in abilities among different races derive directly from the physical characteristics. We shall describe as racism beliefs about race and social

actions based on such beliefs.[7] We insist therefore that racism
exists only if three conditions are simultaneously present, namely,
(1) the physical criteria; (2) beliefs about the inevitable correspondence between the physical and cultural, moral, or intellectual
differences among racial groups; and (3) social actions based on
those beliefs. Of course, racism can exist in a *potential* form—that
would be pretty harmless—and in appropriate circumstances can
be translated into social action, and when that happens we can
properly talk of racism.

RACISM AS AN IDEOLOGY

The belief system, folklores and mythologies, on which racism is
based can be spoken of as an ideology which, on the one hand,
justifies the realities of power relations between racial groups and,
on the other hand, postulates an 'ideal' or 'correct' relationship
which ought to exist between them. The ideology of racism derives
from many sources. We have already indicated that racism as it is
known today is of European origin. As an ideology racism found
support especially in the nineteenth century not only among the
European masses but also justifiers among philosophers, scientists, clergymen, popular writers and propagandists, and statesmen.[8]

The ideology of racism is elaborate. Only its broad outlines can
be indicated here. Its basic ingredient is the dogmatic claim of the
existence of genetically innate and unchanging inequality among
the races. In the broadest sense racism is a system of stratification
by which the 'human race' and their civilisations and cultures are
hierarchically arranged, each race occupying a fixed position from
the bottom to the apex of the pyramid, so to speak. In this system
of stratification some races are supposed to be innately and permanently superior, others are similarly inferior. In terms of the
physical criteria some races are aesthetically beautiful while others
are ugly, and their superior civilisations derive from their physical
attributes. The quotation which follows is typical of such claims
of superiority:

The Caucasian, to which we ourselves belong, is chiefly distinguished by the beautiful form of the head, which approximates
to a perfect oval. It is also remarkable for the variations in the

shade of the complexion, and colour of the hair. From this variety sprung the most civilised nations, and such as have most generally exercised dominion over the rest of mankind.

The Mongolian variety is recognised by prominent cheekbones, flat visage, narrow and oblique eyes, hair straight and black, scanty beard, and olive complexion. This race has formed mighty empires in China and Japan, and occasionally extended its conquests on this side of the Great Desert, but its civilisation has long appeared stationary.

The Negro race is confined to the south of Mount Atlas. Its characters are, black complexion, woolly hair, compressed cranium, and flattish nose. In the prominence of the lower part of the face, in the thickness of the lips, it manifestly approaches to the monkey tribe. The hordes of which this variety is composed have always remained in a state of complete barbarism.[9]

In the above scheme of stratification the black race occupies the bottom of the hierarchy while the whites are at the apex. Differences based on physical characteristics are thus used to explain differences in every other sphere of human activities. Thus, compared with those of other races European institutions, cultures, morals, ethics and aesthetic standards, their religion (Christianity) are claimed to be superior. A further consequence of the belief in the fundamental inequality of the races is the claim that the 'purity' of each race should be preserved, lest the inferior races contaminate the superior ones. On this account inter-racial marriages or sexual relations are taboo. Each race should 'stay in its place' as nature or, in some cases, as God Almighty has ordained. From such beliefs are derived the practical consequences of racial discrimination and segregation: economic exploitation and political oppression, for example.

Complete racial segregation in all spheres of life are the 'ideals' of racist societies: segregation from the cradle to the grave, in marriage and sexual relations, in private and public accommodations, in church and factory and employment opportunities generally, in education, in legal and political status, and at death in the segregated graveyards. In such societies, social privileges are normally determined by the factor of race alone. The ideology of racism incorporates also not only the idea of the proper relationship which should subsist between different racial groups, but each race has a separate destiny in the world. Some races are created to lord over others, while others are simply hewers of wood and drawers of water. This 'division of labour' also derives from the inherent and unalterable differences of quality, intellect and moral stamina of the different races.

In the present century, and not so long ago, the ideology of racism was further elaborated by Adolf Hitler.[10] It was politically acted out first, in the attempt of the German Nazis to annihilate the Jews and second, in the bid to conquer the 'inferior' races of the world. Although the grotesque forms of racism are gradually declining, 'true believers' are still to be found among supporters of 'apartheid' in Southern Africa, and segregationists in the United States of America, and Britain. In South Africa racial separation, officially known as *apartheid*, is deeply entrenched in law as well as in social conventions; and it is absolutely enforced. There white supremacy over the Africans, who form the majority of the population, and the Asians and coloureds reign politically, militarily, economically and socially. But, as Oliver Tambo, one of the leaders of the African National Congress, has observed, *apartheid* is made viable and powerful by great economic interests in South Africa; and the Africans are struggling against a most powerful adversary, '. . . a highly industrialised system, well-armed state manned by a fanatical group of white men determined to defend their privilege and their prejudice, and aided by the complicity of American, British, West German, and Japanese investment in the most profitable system of oppression on the continent.'[11] It is no wonder therefore that those nations which have great economic interests in South Africa ritualistically condemn *apartheid* but invariably develop cold feet on the question of economic sanctions against her. In a sense racism becomes a rationalisation of the *de facto* power relations between a dominant and a subordinated racial group. The ideology of racism seeks to justify and perpetuate the superordinate and subordinate relationship.

Thus far, we have tried to sketch the essential ingredients of racism and have emphasised the necessary conditions which permit us to speak of its presence or absence in a given situation. However, the ideology of racism, excepting in a few countries, has lost much of its earlier glamour since the end of the Second World War. The validity of its claims about the inherent inequalities of non-physical human qualities such as culture, morality, and capabilities between the races have been seriously questioned or denied by many world leading scientists.[12] Furthermore, political and social actions based on purported racial differences have been severely denounced by most civilised nations of the world.

We turn now to the phenomenon of 'tribalism'. However, it seems appropriate at this point that we raise certain questions suggested by the title of this essay. Is 'tribalism' racism or are they separate and distinct social phenomena? If the former is the case, can both be subsumed under a general sociological category? And, if this is plausible, how far can 'tribalism' be compared to, say, 'communalism' in parts of Asia? We shall attempt to answer these questions later, but for the time being we need to define and describe the basic characteristics of 'tribalism'.

TRIBALISM*

The term 'tribe' has been used to categorise human conglomerations in non-European societies, especially in Asia, Africa and America (the Indians, for example). Seldom, if at all, is the term 'tribe' used to categorise human conglomerations in contemporary European societies. 'Tribalism', a derivative from the root word 'tribe', is normally used to describe the social relations, institutions and belief systems of a 'tribe'. In recent years however, the term 'tribalism' has been used to describe patterns of social relations and attitudes of Africans living both in the rural and urban areas.[13]

For the last two decades or so these terms have received such prominence in the mass media that they are almost automatically associated with developments in Black Africa. However, to a great many people—European and non-European alike—the words 'tribe' and 'tribalism' evoke different images, attitudes and emotions. Thus, mention of these words often conjures up an image of something exotic, primitive, backward, unprogressive, etc. Because of these unfavourable associations, Western-educated Africans often feel uncomfortable when these words are used in reference to their societies. Indeed, among the educated Africans themselves 'tribe' and 'tribalism' have become abusive words. Some Africans, for example, use such words as 'tribesman'—which they resent when used by non-Africans—as a term of abuse when reference is

* I acknowledge most gratefully the research assistance on this topic rendered to me by Mr F. E. C. Onyeoziri, a postgraduate student in Political Science.

made to a group other than the one to which they themselves belong.

But above and beyond the emotion and resentment aroused in the educated African, the word 'tribalism' has a pejorative connotation because it is generally believed that it impedes the development of cohesive modern states particularly in Black Africa. However, it is a term freely used by competing leadership groups or individuals purportedly for describing or explaining the behaviour and actions of their opponents. The following quotation is a typical example of an African politician's explanation of 'tribalism':

Tribalism is to make a fetish of one's own tribe and to support members of that tribe at all times whether they are right or wrong. It follows that the tribalist is the fellow who sees nothing but good in his tribe's people, who supports, defends and encourages his tribesman even if he is palpably wrong, who joins in a fight for no reason than that someone is fighting a member of his tribe, who as a Minister, Board Chairman or Manager, awards jobs, contracts or scholarships on the basis of tribal origin and not on merit, efficiency or entitlement. Such a one is a tribalist. To him the highest slogan is: my tribe right or wrong.[14]

For a variety of reasons including those suggested above several scholars have questioned the use of the words 'tribe' and 'tribalism' as analytical concepts. It is worthy of note that when about 1944–46 the International African Institute planned its series of volumes *Ethnographic Survey of Africa*, it decided, for example, to speak of 'The Yoruba speaking people of . . .' and to avoid the use of 'tribe' for large groups of this kind. The word 'tribe' is said to be ambiguous and it is often used to describe both the larger social aggregate, like the Yorubas in Nigeria, as well as 'very much smaller social units enmeshed in one kinship network and organised for collective action.'[15] The Yorubas are divided into several of such units and both the larger entity and its subdivisions are designated by the same term 'tribe'. Apart from the question of ambiguity Stanislav Andreski, for example, has asked why a group numbering 13 million should be called 'tribe' whereas the much less numerous Latvians constitute a nation? The same is also true of, say, the Ibos and Hausas of Nigeria or the Ashantis in Ghana. Is this because 'the former are Africans and latter Europeans?' he asks. He wonders why the word 'nation' except in a purely legal sense, is applied to the heterogeneous populations of Uganda or Tanzania but not to the Yorubas or the Ashantis. Judged by such criteria of nationhood as numbers, cultural distinctiveness, language, territory and political tradition, Andreski argues that the Yorubas seem to satisfy them. However, he qualifies this by suggesting that if they are judged by the will to sovereignty and political unification beyond their borders as the decisive criteria, 'then the Yorubas appear as not quite a nation—or at least not so much as, say, the Germans—but they are certainly nearer to being a nation than a tribe'.[16]

What then shall these human aggregates be called? Andreski suggests the term 'ethny' or 'ethnies' which he defines as 'a social aggregate exhibiting a certain uniformity of culture but not organised for collective action, where the feeling of collective solidarity is rudimentary, and where there is no will for political unification and independence (or preservation thereof)'.[17] He considers the term 'ethnic groups' as unsatisfactory because 'we add to the confusion if we call groups entities whose components are relatively isolated from each other; particularly as what they have in common are cultural traits rather than organs permitting collective action.'[18] In a slightly different way, E. K. Francis suggests the word 'ethnie' or 'ethnos' for describing the same social aggregates defined above by Andreski, but uses 'tribe' to refer to much smaller groups based on descent, whose social structure consists of families, clans and other kinship groups.[19] However, in his analysis of the Nuer, E. E. Evans-Pritchard provides good illustration of the use of the word 'tribe' in the sense used by Francis.[20] Many British social anthropologists have followed the usage by Evans-Pritchard. Lucy Mair, for example, has observed that 'any one who wants to use it (tribe) as a technical term, and not a term of abuse, should be clear that it simply means an independent political division of a population with a common culture.'[21]

Others, however, seem to show a preference for the term 'ethnic groups' for the larger social aggregates defined by Andreski. For example, Paul Mercier seems to use the words 'nation' interchangeably with ethnic groups or 'tribes'. He is inclined to speak, for example, of the Fanti nation, the Ewe nation, the Yoruba nation, etc.[22] The terminological confusion could have been manageable had scholars agreed to use the terms nation, ethnic group and tribe interchangeably, but this is not the case. Immanuel Wallerstein, for example, writing about West Africa reserves the word 'tribe' for 'the group in the rural areas, and ethnic group for the one in the towns'.[23] Gluckman distinguishes between the group in the rural areas, whose membership of a tribe 'involves participation in a working political system, and sharing domestic life with kinsfolk; and that this continued participation is based on present economic and social needs, and not merely on conservatism.' On the other hand, African townsmen constitute a distinct category and their membership of a tribe, which Gluckman calls 'tribalism', is an entirely different phenomenon: 'It is primarily a means of classifying the multitudes of Africans of heterogeneous origin who live together in the towns, and this classification is the basis on which a number of new African groupings, such as burial and mutual help societies, are formed to meet the needs of urban life.'[24] Epstein also maintains this distinction and suggests that the concept of 'tribalism', meaning also membership of a tribe and all that that entails, has two distinct points of reference. First, it is 'intra-tribal' and refers to 'the persistence of, or continued attachment to, tribal custom'. Second, it refers to 'the persistence of loyalties and values, which stem from a particular form of social organisation, and which operate today within a social system much wider than that of the tribe.'[25] However, against these different usages in relation to East Africa Gulliver prefers, and argues for, the retention of the 'older term (tribe): partly because it is still the term used by East Africans themselves, but also because it may be valuable to eschew the somewhat spurious scientific certitude carried by the term "ethnic".' He applies the term 'tribe' to '*any group of people which is distinguished, by its members and by others, on the basis of cultural-regional criteria*'.[26] In other words the term applies to groups of people who are distinguished from each other both territorially and culturally, excepting the special case of Africans living in the towns. But Gulliver warns that the term tribe,

. . . is and must be an essentially dynamic concept to meet the fluidity of contextual conditions within which such groups emerge and operate. This variable character gives no reason at all for dismissing it as an inadequate concept. In fact it is this very character which gives it analytical value . . . It is necessary to get away from the notion that somehow tribes are real and absolute groups of people, whether in an historical or contemporary context. The cultural-regional criteria on which tribe is based, and the underlying realities of the actual world, are both too diffuse and too variable for that.[27]

From the preceding discussion the word tribe is applied to quite different categories: (1) the much smaller social aggregates like the clan based on descent (Evans-Pritchard, Francis); (2) the larger social aggregates—ethny or ethnie (Andreski), ethnie or ethnos (Francis), nation, ethnic group and tribe used interchangeably (Mercier); (3) any group of people distinguishable on the basis of cultural-regional criteria (Gulliver); (4) the social aggregates which participate in and are involved in a complex set of social relations in the rural social structure—tribe (Waller-stein), rural tribalism (Gluckman), intra-tribal (Epstein); (5) a way of classifying multitudes of Africans of heterogeneous origin who live in towns—among whom tribalism (Gluckman, Epstein) or 'ethnicity' (Wallerstein) is manifested. For the purpose of this essay, this writer does not find the first, third, fourth and fifth usages helpful. The first usage refers only to the subdivisions of what we normally regard as a tribe. The third is so permissive that it can lead to a 'Babel' of cultural-territorial groups which are only spuriously distinguishable. Examples of this type of 'tribe' inspired by colonialists and anthropologists abound in Africa. A case in point is the classification of the Ibibio language and ethnic group into Anangs, Efiks and Ibibios in the south-eastern state of Nigeria. The fourth and fifth introduce a fundamental dichotomy between membership of the 'politically organised tribe of history.'[28] ('rural tribalism') and of the ethnic categories of the towns ('town/ urban tribalism'). What therefore goes by the name of 'tribalism' supposedly refers to both but, at the same time, it is insisted that each is a distinct phenomenon. This insistence, of course, derives from the assumption that there exists radical discontinuities between membership of the tribe of history and of the ethnic categories of the towns. Whether or not this dichotomy is justified depends on what one regards as the essence of 'tribalism'. However, for our present purpose the word tribe is to be understood in terms of the second usage (Andreski, Francis, Mercier).

What then is 'tribalism'? Like the root word tribe, the term 'tribalism' connotes different things to different people. Some regard it as a form of nationalism. Connor, for example, recently wrote: 'Surely tribal nationalism is a more momentous fact of the politics within Africa than is African harmony.[29] Although there are certain similarities between, say, European nationalism and tribalism in Africa most writers on this subject are disinclined to equate them.[30] One fairly good reason for not pushing this analogy too far is the striking fact that in recent African experience, especially since the establishment of colonial rule, there have been few, if any, instances when a single ethnic group has demonstrated the will for a separate existence as an independent sovereign state outside the territorial framework demarcated by the colonial powers. This was demonstrated in the two most celebrated recent cases of attempted secession by Biafra and Katanga. In both cases the secession was declared not in the name of one ethnic group but several. The case of the withdrawal of the Southern Cameroons from Nigeria on the basis of a United Nations plebiscite also involved several ethnic groups. Perhaps, the movement among Somalis in Kenya and eastern Ethiopia for unification with the Republic of Somalia is closer to a manifestation of nationalism in the European sense. But this absence of the will to political sovereignty in most African 'tribalism' was rightly noted by Mercier:

Tribalistic movements or 'tribal nationalisms' often express less a rejection of the political framework constituted by the territory (the latter tends to impose itself as a given) than a search for equilibrium within a system progressively accepted by all. They represent a refusal to accept *der facto* domination or monopoly by a given ethnic group, and a claim to universal equality, regardless of origin. Generally, only their language is conservative; their views are modern. Tribalism is rarely a theory which attributes an absolute value to the ethnic as opposed to the national framework. Most often, tribalism is a series of defensive reactions . . .[31]

'Tribalism' is also thought of as involving a complex set of social relations which, in the case of 'rural tribalism', 'centre on the social personalities of chief, hereditary councillors, village headmen and elders, and so forth.[32] But 'town/urban tribalism' involves loyalty to the tribal community (as distinct from loyalty to 'tribal government') within the wider framework of the modern African state.[33] The most significant feature of rural tribalism is that it involves the political loyalties of members of an ethnic group to 'tribal government'. Although such political loyalties ante-dated the establishment of colonial rule, it is known that in many instances the colonial authorities for their political and administrative convenience helped to strengthen them. Many Africans therefore believe that loyalty to the tribal chief was exploited by the colonial authorities 'to combat the growth of national liberation movements'.[34]

It is obviously not possible in this brief essay to exhaust the various conceptions of tribalism or the complexity of issues which it raises. However, we regard tribalism essentially as the sentiments of allegiance generally felt by Africans, especially in Black Africa, towards an ethnic group to which they belong and, in contemporary terms, generally to a 'way of life' or to a culture and heritage common to them. 'This common way of life', Gulliver has remarked, 'includes institutional modes of behaviour (subjectively held to be "right conduct"), accepted values and ideas, artifacts and language; such a way of life, together with the corpus of myth and tradition which informs and supports it, is considered by the people to be their heritage.'[35]

Our idea of tribalism does not rest on allegiance, to 'tribal government'. But the notion of loyalty to 'tribal government' is historically of limited validity because only a few African ethnic groups had centrally organised polities—for example, the Ashantis and the Binis. In the vast majority of cases political allegiance was to chiefs and councillors of subdivisions of the ethnic group, especially to chiefs of clans, villages or other descent groups. Historically, therefore, tribalism was more important in the majority of cases as the feeling of allegiance to a way of life or the general culture of the ethnic group. Among those ethnic groups without centralised political organisation, tribalism assumed political importance only on occasions when the whole tribe was threatened by an external enemy. At the same time, it must be noted that historically there are many instances in Africa when the feeling of political allegiance transcended the ethnic group. Ghana, Mali, Songhay, the Fulani and Benin empires are obvious examples in medieval and pre-colonial Africa. There is evidence that ethnic groups formed large units at one time and broke up into smaller units at another time. They were not static entities. In any case, political allegiance to a central political authority did not preclude members of an ethnic group from identifying with a particular way of life or with its general culture and heritage. Tribalism as a feeling of attachment to a commonly shared culture and heritage is not confined to Africans; in varying degrees it is easily discernible among the French Canadians, the Scots and

Welsh in England, the Irish, Italians, Jews and others in the United States.

We do not distinguish between the tribalism of rural and urban areas because we believe that in both cases tribalism involves the question of individual and group identity and, consequently, it has much to do with how individuals or groups relate to their common culture and heritage. In Africa, the problem of identity involves not only how individuals and groups relate themselves to their common culture and heritage but also to the interaction of the different groups to their cultures and heritage within modern political, economic and social organisations. The problems and tensions posed for individuals and groups in their attempt to forge a new sense of identity—a common set of intelligible institutions, shared values and a way of life—from these related sets of circumstances are particularly acute. The attempt to distinguish between rural and urban tribalism grossly obscures this crisis of identity, which to a great extent similarly confronts both the rural and urban Africans.

The problem of identity in Africa was probably first set in motion among the populations of the coastal towns and villages which came into early contact with European slavers, merchants and Christian missionaries, who each brought to the Africans a variety of 'merchandise' and novel ideas. However, with the establishment of colonial rule, the identity crisis was gradually intensified by subordination of the political authority of the African peoples to European rule, interference with their land tenure systems (land alienation in particular), the introduction of the cash nexus, which linked together the economies of different regions within each colonial territory and ultimately with the world economy, the improvement in communications and transportation, the growth of urban centres, the growth of a middle class and a wage-earning class, the introduction and expansion of Western-type education, the proselytisation of Christianity and other ideas. The problem of identity resulting from this situation was complicated because the colonial political structures brought together several ethnic groups into a new set of ill-defined relationships. In these circumstances the tribes could no longer remain in their relative state of 'spendid isolationism'.

In this situation of new associations of peoples, bound together in a national and international network of communications and by common political and socio-economic institutions, the vast majority of Africans are caught up within a crisis of identity. Today, the vast majority of Africans are neither 'tribesmen' nor 'townsmen'.[36] Or, put differently, they are 'tribesmen' and 'townsmen'; they are 'tribesmen' and nationals of the new states; some are 'tribesmen' and nationals of their particular states and pan-Africanists; some are 'tribesmen' and trade-unionists, 'tribesmen' and Rotarians, and some are 'tribesmen' and professionals; they belong to different social classes and different political persuasions; they are traditionalists and modernists, etc. Consequently, for individuals neither a sense of ethnic nor national identity is coherently articulated.

Tribalism in contemporary Africa should be seen against the background of this identity crisis. It arises primarily from the absence of a coherent 'national society', and the diversity of values and norms which inform the leadership groups and institutions of the African states. The crisis of identity also helps to account for the divided (or at least fragile) loyalty of the citizens to the African states and governments, and for the diversity of standards in the patterns of social and political relations among individuals and groups. Of course, the crisis of identity is compounded by the economic undevelopment of the African states, the limited opportunities for economic gain and prestige, and the struggle for political power. In the absence of commonly shared values there are uncertainties about the norms which should govern conduct in public matters. Consequently in the struggle for scarce resources opportunism becomes the common norm which in large measure governs the African's conduct in the public sphere. In this regard tribalism easily becomes an opportunistic weapon employed by contestants for political power, public offices and economic gain.

The attachment generally felt by Africans to the culture and heritage of their ethnic groups is nothing exceptional. However, there are diverse views about the significance of tribalism for nation-building in Africa. At one extreme, African 'tribal systems' are romanticised and the view that tribalism is a major force working against national unity is dismissed. 'Tribalism', Turnbull writes, 'is nationalism, but, faced with a real need for unity, it is broad-minded, expansive, adaptable nationalism that could well be the basis of a much wider nationalism. If tribalism is destroyed, so, in those areas, is all morality, and in its place can only come, for a time that might be an eternity, the morality of expediency. Far from being incompatible with any modern process of social evolution, tribalism, properly understood, could help it on and, at the same time, bring to it all the richness of the past.'[37] However, most scholars who have written on this subject recognise the disruptive influences of tribalism for national unity in African states and its partial contribution to corruption and nepotism in public life. They seem also to agree that it is to an extent functional. It is said to serve the individual's need for identity, especially in this period of rapid social change; that it has enabled ethnic groups to concert effort for economic, educational and other social goals. It is also argued that tribalism has served to keep class structures fluid and thus prevent the emergence of castes in Africa.[38] Sklar, though aware that he could not 'restore tribalism to grace in Africa', nevertheless argued that tribalism made a crucial contribution to Nigerian nationalism.[39]

At the other extreme is the view which regards tribalism as absolutely inimical to the development of modern national states in Africa. Thus, Ohonbamu has argued that 'for the peace and unity of Nigeria tribalism must be crushed.'[40] As a result of this sort of assessment of the political significance of tribalism, a few African states have legislated against organisations based on tribal affiliations. In Ghana, for example, in 1957, 'The Avoidance of Discrimination Act' was passed with the object of preventing the formation of political parties based on common tribal, racial, religious or regional connections.[41] In Nigeria, on 24 May 1966, the Federal Military Government by decree dissolved along with political parties, tribal unions and cultural associations, and banned the formation of new ones having identical or similar objectives to those dissolved.[42]

Tribalism has gained notoriety in Africa because of the uses to which it has been put by contestants in the struggle for political power, public offices and economic gains. Apart from giving to individuals some sense of identity and security, it contributes also to the crisis of identity and insecurity for individuals within the wider political framework of the modern state. Thus, the feeling of allegiance to the general culture and heritage of an ethnic group and the sense of personal insecurity which it engenders in the national context, both create a situation easily exploited by individuals or groups of individuals. While we share Mercier's view that ethnically inspired political action is an effort to establish an 'equilibrium within a system progressively accepted by all . . . and a claim to universal equality, regardless of origin', evidence abounds that more often than not Africans have perverted such rational considerations for narrow personal or class interests. A political leader who feels insecure about his future invariably appeals to the natural emotions of members of his ethnic group for his political goals. He condemns such tactics when they are employed by his opponents. There are hardly any competitive situations in public life in which those who feel insecure about the outcome of the contest will not resort to an appeal to the ethnic factor. The result is that in such situations personal failures are easily explained away by appeal to the bogey of tribalism. The effort to explain away personal and group failures in ethnic terms has a great deal of appeal for individuals in all social strata; this is because of the simplicity of the logic. For example, one hears quite often: 'I was not given the job or contract because "they" gave it to their own people'. Surely, the question of merit or other personal qualities are not raised, partly because evidence can be adduced to show that on at least one occasion it appeared obvious to all that merit was discarded in favour of the ethnic factor.

However, it is becoming increasingly obvious, at least in West Africa, that tribalism is being exploited principally, though not exclusively, by the elite groups in the society in their struggle for political power and economic gains. This is to be expected because it is at that level that the plums of office are highest and scarcest. Furthermore, experience in West Africa has shown that with the acquisition of political power one's prestige and material wealth seem to rise in geometric proportion. Himmelstrand has aptly summed up how economic conflicts involving different ethnic groups can be infested with 'tribalism':

In contemporary African societies conflicts of an economic nature involving different ethnic groups become infested with tribalism as a result of the competitive strain of modern political and economic structures. . . . Tribalism in the contemporary sense of the word thus is not simply an extension of traditional ethnic loyalties, that is a manifestation of cultural lag. Tribalism is the result of the exploitation of traditional loyalties by contemporary educated elites involved in the political competition required by modern schemes of democratic party politics. Africans less educated and 'westernised' are on the average less ruthlessly tribalistic.[43]

SOME THEORETICAL PROBLEMS

With this sketchy attempt to analyse a problem as complex in its variable and contextual manifestations as tribalism in Africa, the question now arises whether or not tribalism is racism, or are they distinct social phenomena. If the former is the case, can both be subsumed in a general social science theory? How far can tribalism be compared with communalism in parts of Asia? Obviously we cannot pretend to deal exhaustively with these questions. The methodological and conceptual problems involved in a comparative analysis of tribalism, racism and, say, casteism, are immense. Of recent, however, there has emerged an impressive group of social scientists[44] who argue that all situations of intergroup relations can be subsumed in one or other social science theory. Racism, tribalism or ethnicity, communalism, casteism, regionalism, etc. are thus perceived as forms of a general sociological category and can be explained for example, in terms of social stratification and social structures or class domination, conflict and revolution, or in terms of pluralism. However, this writer is sceptical of the value of applying these grand theories for analytical comparisons of tribalism and racism. In fact, some of those who advance these theories often go to such great lengths to prove that racism is a 'special' or 'extreme' case of status differentiation or stratification that one is left wondering whether the game is worth the candle. However, we agree with Gulliver's suggestion that tribalism can be treated as one form of 'particularism', which he regards as 'a component of any sovereign state—and of other larger human groups also—taking different forms, clothed with different details and externalities, according to circumstances'. Furthermore, he maintains that tribalism can be fruitfully compared with other kinds of particularism such as 'regionalism, sectionalism, communalism, casteism, etc'.[45] However, he cautions quite rightly that this kind of analytical comparison should not be pushed too far or its usefulness will be lost. We are not sure that racism is to be included among Gulliver's particularism, but it seems safe to assume that it was not intended since racism is not mentioned or discussed anywhere in the book. Be that as it may, we maintain that although tribalism bears a close resemblance to other kinds of particularism it is not racism or casteism of the Indian type. In fact, we believe that tribalism should be carefully distinguished from some forms of communalism in parts of Asia which are based on a consciously shared religious heritage and generally expressed through a specific language with its own unique script. In the south Asian experience this type of communalism has led to conscious demands for a state, a nation which would incorporate the unique qualities of the religious group.[46] A comparison between tribalism, on the one hand, and casteism and racism, on the other hand, is likely to be most superficial. We are indeed convinced that any comparison between them can only succeed in obscuring the fundamentally different origins of tribalism, casteism and racism, their claims, and the practices based on them.

We have shown already that racism as it is known today is of European origin, deeply rooted in the history, institutions, belief system, and in the folkways of the European peoples. The modern idea of racism was universalised and, through European colonial expansion, it was spread to all parts of the world. The spread of European racism was made possible because of the superior technology and consequent political power acquired by the European peoples at a particular historical period, and by the peculiarities of capitalist development. Its spread was further aided by the fanatical proselytising enterprise of European Christian missionaries in Africa, Asia and America. Racism is a system of stratification based on physical characteristics, which are assumed to explain differences of civilisations, cultures, moral inclinations and intellectual abilities of the different races of man. At one time or other, these ideas have been sanctioned by the Christian Church, scientists, statesmen, etc., and enforced by law, physical coercion, and social conventions.

On the other hand, tribalism as we know it in Africa is essentially an ethno-cultural phenomenon. It is scarcely, if anywhere, based simply on the difference in physical characteristics of groups. Certainly, differences in physical characteristics are nowhere in Africa assumed to explain non-physical attributes of other human groups. However, tribalism shares in common with all ethno-cultural groups the normal sense of pride in the culture and heritage of the group concerned. To that extent, ethnic groups in Africa normally value their general way of life in preference to those of others. Unlike racism and casteism, tribalism in Africa is not a system of social stratification either within or between ethnic groups. Although in recent years such attitudes have been encountered among some groups of Africans, they owe much to the ideas of past anthropologists and colonial administrators, who discovered African 'kingdoms' (which were politically centrally organised) and the segmented societies (those without central political authority) and assigned superior and inferior status respectively to them. The kingdom, thought to possess complex organisations, occupied a higher position in the hierarchy of ethnic groups, and those with segmented political organisations occupied lower positions. The consequence is that some Western-educated Africans began to feel that within this new scale of a colonialist-conceived stratification system their ethnic groups might be superior to other groups. But such attitudes are not skin deep, especially because of the crushing poverty which at present is the great leveller of the vast majority of Africans of all ethnic groups.

Tribalism in Africa differs in other ways from the Hindu caste system and racism. Unlike racism in such countries as the Union of South Africa, Rhodesia and, for a long time in the southern United States, tribalism has no dogmas or absolute prohibitions about social intercourse, for any purposes whatsoever, among members of different ethnic groups. Though there may be certain inhibitions in the social interactions of members of different ethnic groups, more often than not, these result from differences in language and customs, class or social position. It is true that in the past the rate of inter-ethnic marriages, for example, was low, but such inhibitions are increasingly breaking down with urbanisation and modernisation generally. Discrimination based solely on ethnic affiliation in any type of public accommodation, education, housing or private recreational facilities are practically unknown in the non-white controlled African states. It is most significant that, unlike racism in some countries, tribalism receives no legal support anywhere among the states controlled by Africans. It is worthy of note that unlike certain forms of communalism in Asia, tribalism in Africa is not anywhere deeply rooted, if at all, in any indigenous religions or languages which have their unique scripts. If fact, nearly all African ethnic groups these days are distinguished by their borrowed scripts and foreign religions.

We have observed already that in contemporary Africa tribalism is significant, first, because of the identity crisis engendered by on-going socio-cultural change and, second, because of the political usages to which it is put in the struggle for power, public offices, and economic gains. The feeling of allegiance to the general culture and heritage of the ethnic groups are exploited, and ethnic values, symbols and myths are often manipulated in this struggle for power. When tribalism is exploited on issues which might adversely affect the concrete interest of the groups involved, deep passions are aroused and violent conflicts may ensue. When this happens the existence of the state may be endangered. But opportunities for violent outbursts between ethnic groups are likely to differ between different types of political and economic settings. Such opportunities are ample in a neo-colonial, capitalist state. However, it seems to us highly plausible that the political significance of tribalism in Africa will diminish in proportion to the rapidity with which African states are able to establish stable political orders, modernise their economies, expand economic opportunities, and achieve a high sense of national identity. To that extent, while ethnic groups may always remain, tribalism will cease to be an explosive political issue. Forms of communalism rooted in consciously shared religious beliefs and backed by language with a unique script of its own, perhaps in spite of modernisation, may 'wither away' far more gradually than tribalism in Africa. We cannot, with the same degree of confidence, say as much for the 'withering away' of racism in such countries as the Union of South Africa or Zimbabwe (Rhodesia) without violent confrontation between the races.

References

1. W. E. B. Du Bois, *The Souls of Black Folk* (Greenwich, Conn.: Fawcett Publications, Inc., 1961), p. 23.

2. W. E. B. Du Bois, *Dusk of Dawn: An Essay Toward An Autobiography of a Race Concept* (New York: Harcourt, Brace and Company, Inc., 1940), p. 117.

3. W. E. B. Du Bois, *The Souls of Black Folk*, op. cit., p. xiii.

4. International Institute of Differing Civilisations, *Ethnic and Cultural Pluralism in intertropical communities* (Brussels, 1957), p. 498. Quoted by Leo Kuper 'Sociology—Some Aspects of Urban Plural Societies' in Robert L. Lystad (ed.), *The African World: A Survey of Social Research* (New York: Frederick A. Praeger, Publishers, 1965), pp. 122–3.

5. Michael Banton, *Race Relations* (London: Tavistock Publications, 1967). See especially Chapters 2 and 3.

6. Pierre L. van den Berghe, *Race and Racism* (New York: John Wiley and Sons, Inc., 1967), p. 9. *Cf.* 'The Unesco statement by experts on race problems' issued on 18 July, 1950 in Ashley Montagu, *Statement on Race* (New York: Henry Schuman, Inc., 1951), pp. 11–18.

7. Cf. van den Berghe, who defines racism as 'any set of beliefs that organic, genetically transmitted differences (whether real or imagined) between human groups are intrinsically associated with the presence or the absence of certain socially relevant abilities or characteristics, hence that such differences are a legitimate basis of invidious distinctions between groups socially defined as races.' Ibid., p. 11.

8. For a good discussion of these sources, see Banton, op. cit., also, Philip D. Curtin, *The Image of Africa* (London: Macmillan, 1965). Of course, it should be noted also that European scholars, writers and clergymen have also been the foremost demolishers of racists' claims.

9. Georges Cuvier, *The Animal Kingdom* (London, 1827–1835). Vol. 1, p. 97; quoted in Curtin, op. cit., p. 231.

10. Adolf Hitler, *Mein Kampf*, trans. by Ralph Manheim (Boston: Houghton Mifflin Company, 1943), especially Chapters XII and XIII.

11. Oliver Tambo, 'Introduction' to Nelson Mandela, *No Easy Walk to Freedom* (London: Heinemann Educational, 1965), pp. xi–xii.

12. An example of this is the composition of the group of scientists who drafted the 'Unesco Statement on Race'. See Montagu, op. cit., pp. 18–19.

13. For a good account of the variety of meanings historically attached to the term 'tribe' and its derivatives, see P. H. Gulliver (ed.), *Tradition and Transition in East Africa: Studies of the Tribal Element in the Modern Era* (London: Routledge & Kegan Paul, 1969), 'Introduction', pp. 7–10.

14. Chief H. O. Davis, quoted in O. Ohonbamu, *The Psychology of the Nigerian Revolution* (Ilfracombe, Devon: Arthur H. Stockwell, 1969), p. 114.

15. S. L. Andreski, *The African Predicament: A Study in the Pathology of Modernisation* (London: Michael Joseph, 1968), p. 58.

16. Ibid., pp. 58–9.

17. Ibid., p. 59.

18. Ibid., p. 59.

19. E. K. Francis, 'The ethnic factor in nation-building', *Social Forces*, Vol. 46, No. 3 (March 1968), p. 341.

20. E. E. Evans-Pritchard, *The Nuer: A Description of the Modes of Livelihood and Political Instititions of a Nilotic People* (Oxford: The Clarendon Press, 1940), pp. 5–6.

21. Lucy Mair, *Primitive Government* (Harmondsworth: Penguin, 1967), p. 15.

22. Paul Mercier, 'On the Meaning of "Tribalism" in Black Africa', Translated by Pierre L. van den Berghe from an article in *Cahiers*

Internationaux de Sociologie (31, 61–80; 1961). Reprinted in translation in Pierre L. van den Berghe (ed.), *Africa: Social Problems of Change and Conflict* (San Francisco, California: Chandler Publishing Company, 1965), p. 484.

23. Immanuel Wallerstein, 'Ethnicity and National Integration in West Africa' in Pierre L. van den Berghe (ed.), *Africa: Social Problems of Change and Conflicts*, pp. 473–4.

24. M. Gluckman, 'Tribalism in modern British Central Africa' in Immanuel Wallerstein (ed.), *Social Change: The Colonial Situation* (New York: John Wiley & Sons, Inc., 1966), p. 251. This article is a reprint from *Cahiers d'Études Africaines*, Vol. 1 (1960), pp. 55–70. See also Gluckman's 'Anthropological problems arising from the African industrial revolution' in Aidan Southall (ed.), *Social Change in Modern Africa* (London: Oxford University Press, published for the International African Institute, 1961), pp. 66–82.

25. A. L. Epstein, *Politics in an Urban African Community* (Manchester: Manchester University Press, for the Rhodes-Livingstone Institute, Northern Rhodesia, 1958), p. 231.

26. Gulliver (ed.), *Tradition and Transition in Africa* (London: Routledge & Kegan Paul, 1969), p. 24.

27. Ibid., p. 24.

28. Francis, 'The ethnic factor in nation-building', op. cit., p. 344.

29. Walker F. Connor, 'Myths of hemispheric, continental, regional, and state unity', *Political Quarterly*, Vol. 84, No. 4 (December 1969), p. 52.

30. Cf. Gulliver (ed.), *Tradition and Transition in East Africa*, pp. 25–31, Andreski, op. cit., pp. 58–60.

31. Mercier, 'The meaning of "tribalism" in black Africa', in van den Berghe (ed.), *Africa: Social Problems of Change and Conflict*, op. cit., p. 495.

32. Epstein, op. cit., p. 231.

33. Wallerstein, 'Ethnicity and national integration in West Africa' in van den Berghe (ed.), *Africa: Social Problems of Change and Conflict*, p. 477.

34. Kwame Nkrumah, *Class Struggle in Africa* (London: Panaf Books, 1970), p. 59.

35. P. H. Gulliver, 'Anthropology' in Robert A. Lystad (ed.), *The African World: A Survey of Research*, p. 65.

36. Of course, there are opposing view-points on this subject. Compare, for example, those expressed by the various contributions to Peter C. W. Gutkind (ed.), *The Passing of Tribal Man in Africa* (Leiden: E. J. Brill, 1970). The articles in this book are reprinted from *Journal of Asian and African Studies*, Vol. 5. No. 1–2 (1970).

37. C. M. Turnbull, 'Tribalism and social evolution in Africa', *The Annals of the American Academy of Political and Social Science*, Vol. 354 (July 1964), pp. 29–30.

38. The functional and dysfunctional aspects of tribalism are discussed by the following authors: Wallersetin, 'Ethnicity and national integration in West Africa' in P. L. van den Berghe (ed.), *Africa: Social Problems of Change and Conflict*, pp. 477–82. Mercier, 'On the meaning of "tribalism" in Africa', in van den Berghe, op. cit., pp. 483–501; William R. Bascom, 'Tribalism, Nationalism, and Pan-Africanism' in van den Berghe, op. cit., pp. 461–71.

39. R. L. Sklar, 'The contribution of tribalism to nationalism in Western Nigeria' in Wallerstein (ed.) *Social Change: The Colonial Situation*, pp. 290–300. Cf. Francis, 'The ethnic factor in nation-building', op. cit., p. 344.

40. Ohonbamu, op. cit., p. 115.

41. F. A. R. Bennion, *The Constitutional Law of Ghana* (London: Butterworth, 1962), p. 235.

42. 'The public order decree, No. 33, 1966', *Federal Republic of Nigeria Official Gazette—Extraordinary* (Lagos: Federal Ministry of Information, 1966).

43. Ulf Himmselstrand, 'The problem of cultural translation and of reporting different social realities', Paper presented at a Seminar on Reporting Africa held at Mattby (outside Helsinki), October 11–13, 1970 (Mimeograph), pp. 8–9. *Cf.* Nkrumah who writes: 'In the era of neo-colonialism, tribalism is exploited by the bourgeois ruling classes as an instrument of power politics, and as a useful outlet for the discontent of the masses . . .', op. cit., p. 59; also at a different level Abner Cohen in an excellent study based on a detailed analysis of the processes which have been involved in the formation and functioning of a network of socially exclusive and politically autonomous Hausa communities in Yoruba towns of Western Nigeria shows how they have gained control over long-distance trade in certain commodities between the savanna and the forest belt of Nigeria. The study shows how the Hausas manipulate traditional values, myths, symbols and ceremonials to develop informal political organisations, i.e. informal interest groups, which they use as a weapon in the struggle for power and privilege in the contemporary political situation. He notes also the paradox produced by socio-cultural change in Africa, the contradictory phenomena of the process of 'detribalisation' and 'retribalisation' which are occurring at the same time in African states. See his *Custom and Politics in Urban Africa: A Study of Hausa Migrants in Yoruba Towns* (London: Routledge and Kegan Paul, 1969).

44. Compare, among others: Michael Banton, *Race Relations* (1967); van den Berghe, *Race and Racism* (1967); John Rex and Robert Moore, *Race, Community and Conflict: A Study of Sparkbrook* (London: Oxford University Press, 1967); the contributions by Michael Banton, 'The concept of racism', John Rex, 'The concept of race in sociological theory', David Lockwood, 'Race, conflict and plural society', and Sami

Zubaida's 'Introduction' in Sami Zubaida (ed.), *Race and Racialism* (London: Tavistock Publications, 1970), pp. 1–98; Oliver Cromwell Cox, *Caste, Class and Race: A Study in Social Dynamics* (New York: Doubleday, 1948).
45. Gulliver, *Tradition and Transition in East Africa*, p. 30.
46. Kenneth W. Jones, 'Communalism in the Punjab': (The Arya Samaj Contribution), *Journal of Asian Studies*, Vol. 28, No. 1 (November 1968), pp. 39–54. *Cf.* Rajni Kothari, *Politics in India* (Boston: Little, Brown and Company, 1970), Chapter 2; J. H. Hutton, *Caste in India: Its Nature, Functions and Origins* (London: Cambridge University Press, 1946); J. S. Furnivall, *Colonial Policy and Practice* (Cambridge: Cambridge University Press, 1948).

Bibliography

Andreski, Stanislav, *The African Predicament: A study in the Pathology of Modernization* (London: Michael Joseph, 1969).
Banton, Michael, *Race Relations* (London: Tavistock Publications, 1967).
Banton, Michael, *West African City: A Study of Tribal life in Freetown* (London: Oxford University Press for the International African Institute, 1957).
Banton, Michael, 'The concept of racism' in Sami Zubaida (ed.), *Race and Racialism* (London: Tavistock Publications, 1970), pp. 17–34.
Barzun, Jacques, *Race: A Study in Superstition* (New York: Harper, 1965).
Bascom, William R., 'Tribalism, nationalism, and pan-Africanism' in Pierre van den Berghe (ed.), *Africa: Social Problems of Change and Conflict* (San Francisco: Chandler Publishing Company, 1965), pp. 461–71.
Benedict, Ruth, *Race and Racism* (London: Routledge, 1940).
Bunting, Brian, *The Rise of the South African Reich* (Harmondsworth: Penguin Books, 1964).
Cohen, Abner, *Custom and Politics in Urban Africa: A Study of Hausa Migrants in Yoruba Towns* (London: Routledge and Kegan Paul, 1969).
Connor, Walker F., 'Myths of hemispheric, continental, regional, and state unity', *Political Science Quarterly*, Vol. 84, No. 4 (December 1969).
Cox, Oliver C., *Caste, Class and Race: A Study in Social Dynamics* (New York: Doubleday, 1948).

Curtin, Philip D., *The Image of Africa: British Ideas and Action, 1780–1850* (London: Macmillan, 1965).

de Gobineau, Count Arthur, *Essai sur l'inégalité des races humaines*, 2 vols (2nd ed.) (Paris, 1884). Published earlier in the United States as *The Moral and Intellectual Diversity of Races* (Philadelphia, 1856).

Du Bois, W. E. B., *Dusk of Dawn: An Essay Toward An Autobiography of A Race Concept* (New York: Harcourt, Brace and Company, 1940).

Du Bois, W. E. B., *The Souls of Black Folk* (Greenwich, Conn.: Fawcett Publications, Inc., Premier Americana, 1961).

Epstein, A. L., *Politics in an Urban African Community* (Manchester: Manchester University Press, The Rhodes-Livingstone Institute Northern Rhodesia, 1958).

Evans-Pritchard, E. E. *The Nuer: A Description of the Modes of Livelihood and The Political Institutions of a Nilotic People* (Oxford: The Clarendon Press, 1940).

Francis, E. K., 'The ethnic factor in nation-building', *Social Forces*, Vol. 46, No. 3 (March 1968), pp. 338–46.

Freedman, M., 'The growth of a plural society in Malaya (1960)' in Immanuel Wallerstein (ed.), *Social Change: The Colonial Situation* (New York: John Wiley & Sons, Inc., 1966, pp. 278–83).

Fried, Morton H., 'On the concept of "tribe" and "tribal society"', *Transactions of the New York Academy of Sciences* (Ser. II), Vol. 28, No. 41 (1966), pp. 527–40.

Furnivall, J. S., *Colonial Policy and Practice: A Comparative Study of Burma and Netherlands India* (Cambridge: Cambridge University Press, 1948).

Glazer, Nathan and Moynihan, Daniel P., *Beyond the Melting Pot: The Negroes, Puerto Ricans, Jews, Italians and Irish of New York City* (Cambridge, Mass: The MIT Press and Harvard University Press, 1963).

Gluckman, M., 'Tribalism in modern British Central Africa' in Pierre L. van den Berghe (ed.), *Africa: Social Problems of Change and Conflict* (San Francisco: Chandler Publishing Company, 1965, pp. 346–60).

Gluckman, M., 'Anthropological problems arising from the African industrial revolution' in Aidan Sauthall (ed.), *Social Change in Modern Africa* (London: Oxford University Press, for the International African Institute, 1961), pp. 67–82.

Gossett, Thomas F., *Race: The History of An Idea in America* (Dallas: Southern Methodist University Press, 1963.)

Gulliver, P. H. (ed.), *Tradition and Transition in East Africa: Studies of the Tribal Element in the Modern Era* (London: Routledge and Kegan Paul, 1969).

Gulliver, P. H., 'Anthropology' in Robert A. Lystad (ed.), *The African*

World: A Survey of Research (New York: Frederick A. Praeger, 1965), pp. 65–106.

Gutkind, Peter C. W. (ed.), *The Passing of Tribal Man in Africa* (Leiden: E. J. Brill, 1970).

Harow, V. 'Tribalism in Africa', *Journal of African Administration*. Vol. 7 (1955).

Helm, June (ed.), *Essays on the Problem of Tribe, Proceedings of the 1967 Annual Spring Meeting of the American Ethnological Society* (Seatle: The University of Washington Press, 1968).

Himmelstrand, Ulf., 'The problem of cultural translation and of reporting different social realities', Paper presented at a Seminar on Reporting Africa (Mattby (outside Helsinki) 11–13 October, 1970), Mimeograph.

Himmelstrand, Ulf., 'Ethnicity, political power and mobilisation: some determinants of political perception and behavior in a multi-ethnic federal system—the case of Nigeria'. Paper for 7th World Congress of Sociology (Varna, Bulgaria, 14–19 September, 1970), Mimeograph.

Hitler, Adolf, *Mein Kampf*, trans. by Ralph Manheim (Boston: Houghton Mifflin Company, 1943).

Hugget, Frank E., 'Communal problems in Belgium', *World Today*, No. 22 (January–December, 1966), pp. 446–52.

Hutton, J. H., *Caste in India: Its Nature, Functions and Origins* (London: Cambridge University Press, 1946).

Kothari, Rajni, *Politics in India* (Boston: Little, Brown and Company, 1970).

Kuper, Hilda, *The Uniform of Colour: A Study of White-Black Relationships in Swaziland* (Johannesburg: Witwaterstrand University Press, 1947).

Kuper, Leo, 'Sociology—some aspects of urban plural societies' in Robert A. Lystad (ed.), *The African World: A Survey of Research* (New York: Frederick A. Praeger, 1965), pp. 107–30.

Kyle, Keith, 'The Southern Sudan problem', *World Today*, No. 22 (January–December, 1966), pp. 512–20.

Lawrence, John, *The Seeds of Disaster* (London: Victor Gollancz, 1968).

Lévi-Strauss, Claude, *Race and History*, The Race Question in Modern Science Series (Paris: Unesco, 1952).

Lewin, Julius, *The Struggle for Racial Equality* (London: Longmans, Green, 1967).

Lind, Andrew W. (ed.), *Race Relations in World Perspective* (Honolulu: University of Hawaii Press, 1955).

Little, Kenneth, *Race and Society*, The Race Question in Modern Science Series (Paris: Unesco, 1952).

Little, Kenneth, *West African Urbanisation: A Study of Voluntary Associations in Social Change* (London: Cambridge University Press, 1965).

Lockwood, David, 'Race conflict, and plural society' in Sami Zubaida (ed.), *Race and Racialism* (London: Tavistock Publications, 1970), pp. 57–72.

Lovejoy, A. O., *The Great Chain of Being* (New York: Harper Torchbooks, 1960).

Mair, Lucy, *Primitive Government* (Harmondsworth: Penguin Books, 1964, 1967).

Matthews, Z. K., 'The tribal spirit among educated South Africans', *Man*, Vol. 35 (1935).

Mayer, Philip, *Townsmen or Tribesmen: Conservatism and the Process of Urbanisation in a South African City* (Cape Town: Oxford University Press, for Institute of Social and Economic Research, Rhodes University, 1961).

Mercier, Paul, 'On the meaning of "tribalism" in Black Africa' in Pierre L. van den Berghe (ed.), *Africa: Social Problems of Change and Conflict* (San Francisco: Chandler Publishing Company, 1965), pp. 485–501.

Mitchell, Clyde J., *The Kalela Dance* (Manchester: Manchester University Press, Rhodes-Livingstone Paper No. 27, 1956).

Mitchell, J. C., *Tribalism and the Plural Society* (London: Oxford University Press, 1960).

Montagu, Ashley, *Statement on Race* (New York: Henry Schuman, 1951).

Nkrumah, Kwame, *Class Struggle in Africa* (London: Panaf Books Ltd, 1970).

Ohonbamu, O., *The Psychology of the Nigerian Revolution* (London: Ilfracombe, Devon: Arthur H. Stockwell, Ltd, 1969).

Plotnicov, Leonard, *Strangers to the City: Urban Man in Jos, Nigeria* (Pittsburgh: University of Pittsburgh Press, 1967).

Rex, John and Moore, Robert, *Race, Community and Conflict: A Study of Sparkbrook* (London: Oxford University Press, 1967).

Rex, John, 'The concept of race in sociological theory' in Sami Zubaida (ed.), *Race and Racialism* (London: Tavistock Publications, 1970), pp. 35–55.

Sklar, R. L., 'The contribution of tribalism to nationalism in Western Nigeria' in Immanuel Wallerstein (ed.), *Social Change: The Colonial Situation* (New York: John Wiley & Sons, 1966), pp. 290–300.

Tambo, Oliver, 'Introduction' to Nelson Mandela, *No Easy Walk to Freedom* (London: Heinemann Educational Books, 1965).

Turnbull, Colin M., 'Tribalism and social evolution in Africa', *The Annals of the American Academy of Political and Social Science*, Vol. 354 (July, 1964), pp. 22–32.

van den Berghe, Pierre L., *Race and Racism* (New York: John Wiley & Sons, 1967).

van Velsen, J., 'Labour migration as a positive factor in the continuity of Tonga tribal society' in Aidan Southall (ed.), *Social Change in Modern Africa* (London: Oxford University Press, for the International African Institute, 1961), pp. 230–41.

Vatcher, W. H., *White Laager* (London: Pall Mall Press, 1965).

Wallerstein, Immanuel, 'Ethnicity and national integration in West Africa' in Pierre L. van den Berghe (ed.), *Africa: Social Problems of Change and Conflict* (San Francisco: Chandler Publishing Company, 1965), pp. 472–82.

Zubaida, Sami (ed.), *Race and Racialism* (London: Tavistock Publications, 1970).

Racialism and the Urban Crisis

by JOHN REX
Professor of Social Theory and Institutions in the University of Warwick

Racial discrimination and racial prejudice are phenomena of colonialism. It was as a result of the conquest of poor and relatively underdeveloped countries by the technologically advanced nations during the nineteenth century that new kinds of economy, and new forms of social relations of production involving both conqueror and conquered, were brought into being. The inequalities between men of different skin colours which resulted were often justified in terms of biological racist theories or some functional equivalent.

The political scene in these underdeveloped countries today is marked by a revolt of the newly independent nations or by the underprivileged within those nations against their former colonial masters and those who, in neo-colonial or post-colonial society, continue to represent them. The colonial revolt has many names and indeed it has many varieties, but as often as not, this revolt of the poor peasant, or the man who queues at the labour exchange in colonial capitals, or of the descendant of a slave family still living in something like plantation conditions, comes to be understood by the revolutionary himself as a revolt of the black or the yellow man against the white. The main theme of the history of our times is the revolution of these who see themselves as oppressed races in some kind of race war against those who oppress them.

The conflict which has occurred in this post-colonial epoch has been evident primarily in the former colonial countries themselves. Sometimes it has taken the direct form of a war of independence; sometimes there has been a continuing conflict after independence against the newly established native ruling class. Sometimes the colonial revolt has become caught up in the conflict between the great powers and has become another theatre for the cold war.

Sometimes workers have struck or farmers have refused to deliver crops, in order to redefine the terms of the economic relationship between native and colonialist or native and settler.

But the conflict between colonial people and the colonising powers is by no means confined to the colonial territories themselves. For as the age of colonialism has passed and the plantations, the peasant production, the mining operations of the former colonial territories have ceased to be profitable, colonial people have left their own countries to seek work in the rich urban industrial societies of the metropolitan countries themselves. Thus there is a confrontation between workers from colonial economic contexts and the free and organised working class of the metropolitan countries. The confrontation takes place in marginal areas of employment where jobs must be filled, yet cannot be filled from the metropolitan working-class population. It nearly always takes place in *urban* conditions so that the descendants of the colonial people find themselves disadvantaged in their search for housing, and compelled to live in de facto conditions of segregation from the normal urban community and society.

Along with the crisis of post-colonial society therefore a central feature of modern societies in North-West Europe and America is the crisis of race relations in the advanced metropolitan countries themselves. It is a crisis which manifests itself in some countries as a crisis of urban deterioration and of racial discrimination. In others it takes the form of a violent revolt of the underprivileged in these cities. Thus in North America, black populations have burnt down whole blocks of cities. By so doing they have spotlighted the crisis of these cities, which is a crisis of the poor and the underprivileged but, above all, a crisis of race relations.

COLONIAL AND METROPOLITAN FACTORS AFFECTING RACE RELATIONS

The encounter of black and non-white immigrants with the white populations of metropolitan cities is compounded of several elements which, in the main, may be reduced to two. On the one hand there is the fact that those who now meet as fellow-workers, as fellow-citizens, as employers and employees, as politicians and voters, meet within the institutional framework of advanced industrial social systems, whereas some of them had previously met in the context of colonial society, a fact which places an initial strain on the relationships which develop in metropolitan cities and places of employment. But, on the other hand, the structure of the metropolitan society itself is such that to live within it is to live within a complex system of social conflict. Thus a relationship, which in any case has the potential for conflict within it, is further strained by the context within which it occurs.

The Economic and Political Institutions of Colonialism

The peoples of Europe have long been accustomed to the fact that colonial societies involve roles which could not exist in their own societies. This is particularly true of the colonising powers (Britain, France, Portugal, Spain, Belgium and Holland). But an awareness of these roles and of the contrast between them and the acceptable roles of European society is shared with other countries as well. Thus, whereas the industrial worker in European countries would be unlikely to tolerate for long a situation in which his own position was not protected by a right to trade union bargaining and to a minimum of welfare, he will be aware that in the colonial territories, workers and peasants rarely have anything like the same kind of security and freedom. He knows that there is a difference between the position of a free worker like himself and the unfree colonial worker.

The central reference point here is that of the institution of slavery and the plantation system of production. For what trade unionism means, and what welfare benefits as of right mean, is that the worker is a free worker. He can dispose of his labour freely and is not his employer's property. The slave, on the other hand, is someone else's property, and is unfree, and those who are slaves are suspect, both because the existence of slave status makes the free worker's status less secure, and because the free worker may have learned to accept the racialist justification of slavery, i.e. that a man is a slave because he is in some respect an inferior being.

The question here is not simply a psychological question of attitudes but involves the sociology of knowledge. The conception of being a worker or being an employee in the sense in which the terms are used in advanced industrial societies is popular and sociological, and has meaning only in terms of work situations of participants in that society. Thus to know what the term free worker means is to know what its polar opposite—slavery—means.

Between these two types are, of course, many intermediate stages. Thus, for example, many agricultural, mining and industrial activities in colonial contexts have been staffed by labour indentured for a term of years. In the mining industries of Africa workers have been required to live in compounds cut off from their families for a term of nine months or more. And in many places at many times varying degrees of political and military power have been used to recruit a labour force. All these types of labour help to define what free labour is not.

Another dimension to the negation of free labour also exists. The free wage worker usually enters the labour market directly in order to sell his labour and thereby finance his own household and family, but he may form part of his employer's or master's household, e.g. the domestic servant, who stands at one remove from the calculation of market opportunity which is the essence of modern society. It is the domestic servant's master who calculates market opportunity. The fortunes of the servant depend as do those of his children on the fortunes of the *'pater familias'*.

Just as there are degrees of unfreedom culminating in slavery, however, so there are degrees of exclusion from participation in the labour market, degrees to which the individual participates in the budgetary system of his master's household. Where labour and land are abundant, farmers may incorporate the domestic budgets of their farm servants in their own, providing them with what are called in England 'tied cottages' (i.e. cottages whose tenancy depends upon continued employment), providing them with part of their income in kind, demanding that all purchases be made at the farm store, or providing educational and other facilities for the children.

Peasants, similarly, may or may not have direct access to the market, although in their case the market is one through which crops or produce rather than labour are sold. The situation in which he sells his product directly to an ultimate consumer, haggling with his buyer and threatening to sell to another, are rare. In most colonial situations he is dependent upon some kind of marketing agency, which may simply 'charge for its services', but will be more likely exploit the advantages of its situation to the degree that that situation is marked by a power differential.

An alternative restriction of the workers' access to the market occurs in share-cropping, a system under which the tenant is able to dispose directly of a part only of his crop, the remainder being disposed of by his master. Here direct access to the market is combined with participation in the internal economy of the master's household.

A further possibility confronts the peasant, i.e. he may stay out, opt out, or be left out, of the social system based upon market relations. This alternative may, it is true, be freely chosen, and there is evidence that the colonial authorities have at times had to devote much energy to persuading peasants to leave the subsistence sector and join the market sector of the economy. Nonetheless, land shortage, and relative deprivation as modernisation increases, do make existence outside the market economy increasingly irksome to many, and younger and better educated men in peasant societies may well seek to move both from subsistence agriculture and from agriculture itself to wage-earning industrial employment. There will therefore be a continual movement out of the area of what, in British colonial territories, was called 'indirect rule', to colonial towns and indeed to the metropolitan industrial countries themselves. Of some sociological interest here is the colonial town, which may act as a kind of filter through which young men of peasant origin get the taste of urban industrial society. Thus, although many colonial towns are not towns in the same sense as those to be found in urban industrial society, they do nonetheless have some sociological relation to them, as well as to the peasant world from which they recruit their population.

All the economic roles to which we have so far referred—slave, indentured worker, migrant worker in the compound, domestic or farm servant, peasant or share-cropper on a semi feudal estate, peasant living by subsistence—presuppose the existence of a political situation in which there is inequality of power as between the colonialist and the colonised. The history of the countries therefore will be one in which, quite frequently, there is a memory of military conquest or of military action against a rebellion. Failing this, there is always a disparity of technological levels as between the colonising and colonised peoples which renders the latter dependent on the former. It is thus implicit in all that has been said about coloured economic roles that the colonial nation is seen as defeated and educationally and technologically backward. Such a view tends to be stabilised by the development of racist theories in the metropolitan countries and amongst settlers in the colonial country. Paternalistic versions of such theories may indeed be developed, and it may be argued that the colonising power has a mission to raise the standards of the colonial nation and to work for its benefit, but this does not alter the basic position of inequality.

Many of the race relations problems which exist in the world today are in fact colonial problems.

The Structure of Urban Industrial Society

Our purpose here is not to review the full range of situations arising from colonial economies which take on a 'racial' character; our concern is with the problems that arise when people from colonial economies, and more generally black people, find their way to cities in metropolitan countries, and seek to become industrial workers and citizens.

The typical case is found in Britain, France, Holland, Belgium and Portugal. Perhaps similar problems arise in the United States when the descendants of Negro slaves from southern plantations settle in the urban north. Again, in settler societies, local metropolitan-type cities become targets for immigration. Thus, sociologically speaking, Johannesburg is quite different from Freetown. Johannesburg is a metropolitan industrial city in its own right, Freetown is a filter between colonial and metropolitan society of a kind discussed above. Accordingly, a frame of reference for the study of inter-racial contacts in an urban industrial context could take in Chicago and Johannesburg equally with London, Birmingham or Paris. But we must now examine the complex interplay the social structures of the metropolitan societies themselves.

The first point to be noted about the metropolitan countries is the relative stability of their political institutions; despite war and economic crisis, they have succeeded in avoiding a cataclysmic class conflict that might have overthrown their political institutions. Lipset maintains that the Western capitalist democracies have solved their major political problems through the 'incorporation' of the working class into society on the basis of a welfare and trade union bargain,[1] while Bell and others have spoken of the end of ideology, i.e. the end of political conflict about the aims and basic shape of society.[2]

Both, however, largely ignore the existence in the advanced capitalist countries of a new problem of poverty and under-privilege. True, those who suffer this poverty and under-privilege may lack the numbers and the organisation to form the truly revolutionary kind of organisation which Lipset and Bell have in mind as constituting a real threat to the social order. But they are nonetheless a permanent part of the new social order, and any attempt to understand the dynamics of race relations in the countries concerned must take their existences into account.

The new poor and under-privileged are in part the product of uneven economic and social development in the advanced countries. They include the elderly, those employed in less affluent sectors of the economy, the sick and the unemployed. In some cases they may still be in a state of absolute poverty, but most students of the subject would admit that the problem is one of relative deprivation. By the standards of the inter-war period many of those concerned might be held to be relatively well-off. But in relation to the acceptable standards which have resulted from trade union bargaining, they are clearly under-privileged, and politically unrepresented.

Countries are affected differently by whether or not there is a high level of unemployment. In the United States, the unemployed and the underemployed loom large amongst the poor and under-privileged. In Britain in the 1960s and 70s with a relatively high level of employment, the problem has been different.

One important variable is the degree of automation. In Britain, many jobs are unacceptable to most people, not because of the wages offered, but because the conditions or hours are considered intolerable, and consequently those who accept them are considered underprivileged.

Again, even in advanced industry, if the level of production is variable, there are marginal jobs which pay well but are exceptionally vulnerable to economic fluctuations; the workers concerned constantly risk redundancy, and can also be counted as underprivileged.

Clearly, such jobs are likely to be filled (if at all) by those who either lack marketable skills or are discriminated against.

The disappearance of marginal types of employment, and failure to achieve the level of education and skill required for any job at all can leave large numbers permanently unemployed. But even without such differences between the employable and the employed, the number of jobs might be too small, and the people most vulnerable to discrimination will remain permanently unemployed. Even if inferior or menial jobs are available, they may be spurned by the local working class; if these lack the skills or education necessary for other work, they become the equivalent of 'poor whites' in South Africa and the southern United States.

Even without unemployment, however, underprivilege can exist. Indeed, since many rights in the modern welfare state are no longer related to employment and income, two men may find themselves to all intents and purposes in different class situations because of their differential access to welfare or other rights, e.g. housing. Housing in modern society no longer depends solely on ability to pay. Some groups enjoy advantages because of a political situation; other groups are discriminated against, regardless of income and ability to pay for housing. Hence the city, as a social and ecological system is not solely and simply the product of market competition, as Park and Burgess seemed in part of their writings to suggest[3]: differential housing opportunities are not related to economic factors only, but depend also on political criteria.

Thus, certain forms of poverty and underprivilege are built into the structures of urban industrial society. Despite affluence, there may be insufficient jobs to go round. Because of automation and the consequent need for higher skills, some people may be too inadequately skilled to obtain employment at all. In industrially backward areas, or types of industry vulnerable to unemployment, some jobs have built-in disadvantages. There is, moreover, a question of relative access to welfare benefits and to housing. Pensioners are not well enough organised to be able to maintain the level of their pensions. Sick benefits fail to match earnings. And housing allocations may be so politically organised as to aggravate underprivilege in employment.

Finally and crucially, we should note the role of education. Educational disadvantage not only reinforces the disadvantages already mentioned, but transmits them from one generation to another. Schooling is linked to housing. If the underprivileged live together in the same segregated neighbourhood, their children will go to the same schools—and they will be slum schools for the underprivileged. Proposals for the dispersal of school children from their home neighbourhoods only makes the situation worse. For to declare that a child has to be moved to another school indicates either that he is a problem or that his neighbourhood is a problem—both ways of emphasising his inferior status.

THE COLOURED COLONIAL WORKER IN METROPOLITAN
SOCIETY

Underprivileged situations and roles are thus built into the social
structure. They do not depend on the presence of coloured or
colonial people. We have now to see how they are incorporated
into this structure, how the conditions of being colonial, coloured
and poor reinforce and exacerbate one another. The coloured
immigrant or his children are cut off from privately or publicly
controlled gateways to privilege, and then find that their disadvantages as colonials are further increased because their position as 'new poor' serves to confirm suspicions of their inadequacy
(cf. Myrdal on the cumulative cycle of racial discrimination and
prejudice[4]).

The uncontrolled admission of immigrant labour will usually be
resisted by organised labour in metropolitan countries, because of
memories, or the actual experience of prolonged unemployment,
and the inferior bargaining position of the colonial. Even if there
are guarantees that immigrant labour will not be used to undermine conditions of work and that immigrant labour will bear the
brunt if redundancy occurs, there will still be fears that the immigrant worker may be more docile and compliant. Welfare and
trade union advantages may also seem threatened. Even if immigration is offset by emigration, inevitable limitations on housing,
education and health services may seem to indicate that competition for them by immigrants will lessen access to them by metropolitan workers, who will accordingly wish to limit any such
immigration. This of course can in no sense be taken to justify
racial discrimination. The point is structural: it is in the nature of
free unionised labour to seek to strengthen, or at least to avoid
weakening, its market position, and this inevitably produces an
anti-immigrant attitude.

However, its actual behaviour is rarely determined solely by
such purely rational calculation. Many other factors are involved.
Some are a simple carry-over of received beliefs and attitudes, some
derive from a concern with status (as distinct from social class),
some are questions of personality.

Status is particularly important. He may not agree with it, but
every metropolitan worker knows the status which attaches to
different occupations, and will do what he can to enhance that of

his own by associating it with favourable stereotypes. Unfortunately, the stereotype of the coloured colonial implies the lowest status of all, being associated with ignorance, incapacity, evil, and in its more extreme forms, the sub-human. Association with such an image is obviously to be avoided at all costs.

As has already been pointed out, this image of the coloured colonial is a reflection of the role history accorded him. Is it subject to change? How is it originally acquired? The following are some of the agencies or experiences involved: the talk of relations or friends; spoken or written reports by people who have visited the territories concerned; statements by politicians and other influential people; the mass media.

Family contact with colonial peoples is a most important source, and it does not hark back to a remote past. All the major colonial powers and the United States have been militarily involved in the Third World since 1945, and various non-colonial powers have done policing duties on behalf of the United Nations. Hence, events in the Third World are very often interpreted via the experiences of a family member so involved—hardly a favourable source, as soldiers were usually trained to regard the colonial as in some sense an enemy.

Missionaries were another main source of information. During the great era of Christian missions, the African or Asian was usually represented as a heathen living in benighted darkness, and evangelisation was often thought of as converting him into a kind of white man. An apparently more liberal attitude which allowed for the existence of differences between men often did so by automatically assuming the inferiority of the black man; and a European monarch or politician who condescended to be entertained by 'heathen' tribal dancing helped to reinforce derogatory attitudes, even while seeming more liberal in regard to native customs than the missionary.

The mass media also inculcate stereotypes. They provide information, but also sort, classify, stabilise and define. Great influence can be exerted by their owners, and on behalf of their owners' interests. It is extremely difficult to establish a stereotype of the colonial worker as equal, however, and Myrdal's point that even the most liberal newspapers in the United States start by making assumptions which are unfair to the Negro is still largely true.[5]

The suggestion is often made that strangeness of religions,

customs or language creates suspicion of itself, and that there is some sort of natural repugnance to racial miscegenation. This could very easily be argued the other way round: why should strangeness not be exciting and stimulating, and encourage exploration and discovery rather than repugnance? Moreover, the so-called fear of miscegenation is found predominantly in ruling groups, and then miscegenation is discouraged only in certain contexts (e.g. in legal marriage as opposed to concubinage).

To question these prejudices, however, is by no means to deny their influence. A bar on intermarriages at first operates crudely; children of the second generation will believe that intermarriage is a primary evil, and a whole pattern of taboos regarding contacts and relations between races is created.

These problems are partly psychological, to be tackled by re-education; we must also understand the ideas and prejudices held in common in the metropolitan society in which experiences are interpreted in terms of a shared language and a shared set of meanings.[6]

As suggested earlier, one concept common to North-West Europeans and North Americans is free labour, as opposed to what is conveyed by such concepts as slave, servant and serf, as used in association with men with black skins and natives of colonial countries. Thus learning to accept, say, a Negro or Indian migrant worker is, in effect, learning a new social language, or learning to read the social world in a new way.

The easiest way of dealing with the prejudices involved is to suggest that they do not exist and that there is no reason why the social structure should change, i.e. the coloured man must accept the (inferior) social place which popular belief assigns him. This will be justified not only on the grounds of assertions as to what the black man is like, but by theories allegedly showing how the world is, and why it is as it is.

With the stereotype of the ignorant evil heathen enemy went the theory of the supreme justice of the colonial system. The colonial powers encouraged their imperial subjects to recite the equivalent of 'civis romanus sum' and to believe they had a claim to recognition in metropolitan society. This was evidently bound to be brought up when racist affirmations were adduced to justify a policy of discrimination.

Liberal democracy and socialist labour movements are univer-salist, but were fashioned to meet internal European needs: the ideals of Liberty, Equality and Fraternity adopted in 1789 were never intended to cover the case of colonial natives.[7] Nonetheless discrimination can be halted or made less systematic because these ideals are recognised and exist.

DISCRIMINATION AGAINST THE COLOURED COLONIAL WORKER

We can now assess the likely consequences of the arrival of colonial native immigrants in metropolitan society. Colonialism has its history, and these metropolitan societies have their history. Together their two histories and the economic sociology which they imply provide a starting point for the study of race relations in modern cities.

First, there is considerable variation in degree of immigration control. Thus Australia has for many years pursued a 'White Australia' policy which excludes coloured colonials from seeking employment in Australia or taking up permanent residence in its cities. Britain, having reached a total coloured population of about 800,000 by 1969, reduced further immigration from the Commonwealth to a mere trickle.[8] France continued to give the same unrestricted access to French citizens, including natives of Guadeloupe and Martinque, as previously to natives of Algeria.

South Africa dealt with internal migration to the cities by still more severe pass-laws and controls, making entry for a native African as difficult as entry into a foreign country. The United States never attempted to prevent the steady migration of blacks to the cities.

Arriving coloured immigrants tend to be classified and assigned to roles in the host society, or channelled by their ability to pass through various 'gates'. Although some get through the gates, the majority find themselves part of the new poor of metropolitan society, accepted into the inferior and marginal industrial roles mentioned earlier. When there have not been enough jobs, the coloured worker has taken more than his fair share of unemployment, and he lives in whatever form of accommodation and whatever part of the city that is considered least attractive.

However, conditions vary between different countries. In some, coloured men have inferior jobs and inferior incomes, but there is no social barrier to the enjoyment of anything for which they can pay. In others, even the few who earn enough are prevented from using affluence to buy social position. Even if the general level of employment is high, coloured workers do menial work only and are discriminated against in their search for housing. If the employment level is low, they will be largely unemployed. Urban societies differ vastly in the degree to which the economy, and land and building use, are planned; and they differ in the extent to which the immigrants and their descendents can constitute a viable political force.

No single essay can at this stage sum up the implications of this urban race relations crisis in all societies; this could only be achieved after prolonged comparative work. This paper confines itself to the history of race relations in one country, Great Britain, notes what has actually occurred and what factors are now entering, and then, by considering what is unique about the British situation, makes suggestions as to what may happen in other circumstances.

THE COLOURED IMMIGRANT IN BRITAIN 1945–69

The Control of Immigration

Throughout the period of its industrial growth, Great Britain has been a country of both immigration and emigration. As citizens went overseas to find employment in the White Commonwealth countries of Canada, Australia and New Zealand, settler societies such as South Africa, Rhodesia and Kenya and, less permanently, in other colonial territories, they were replaced by immigrants arriving primarily from Europe and from Ireland.

Immigration from foreign countries was restricted in 1904, and has since been the subject of continuous control. However, immigration into Britain and the colonies by citizens from Commonwealth countries was not restricted before 1962. An unknown number of commonwealth citizens entered before 1962, and considerable numbers of Asian Commonwealth citizens exercised their right to settle in British colonial territories in Africa and elsewhere. Ireland, although an independent country, has no form of immigration or emigration control system covering travel to and from the United Kingdom, and no certain estimates of the numbers of Irish entering the United Kingdom is therefore possible.

The immigration of aliens undoubtedly presented problems.[9] The arrival of large numbers of Eastern European Jews at the end of the nineteenth century, in fact, produced a reaction from the British population not unlike that shown in the face of coloured immigration. It was this agitation which led to the control of alien immigration. By and large, however, it could be said that the absorption of limited numbers of white aliens presented no great difficulty, despite the fact that in the first generation they spoke little English.

What did appear to the British people, their journalists, their politicians and finally their Government to create real problems was the immigration, between 1950 and 1962, of considerable numbers of non-white immigrants, first from the Caribbean, and then from India and Pakistan. No statistics were kept until 1962, but the following table summarises the estimates made by the Home Office of net inward immigration, 1955–62, from the 'Tropical Commonwealth' (including Cyprus).

Table 1. *Immigration from the Tropical Commonwealth 1955–62*[10]

	1955	1956	1957	1958	1959	1960	1961	1962 (first 6 months
West Indies	27,550	29,800	23,020	15,020	16,390	49,670	66,290	31,800
India	5,800	5,600	6,620	6,200	2,920	23,750	23,750	19,050
Paki-stan	1,850	2,050	5,170	4,690	860	2,500	25,080	25,090
Totals	42,700	46,850	42,400	29,900	21,600	57,700	136,400	94,890

These figures show that, throughout the period, the West Indians remained the largest single group; that there was an astonishing increase in the numbers coming in from all countries between 1959 and 1962; and that, in 1961, the number of Indians increased sharply and the numbers of Pakistanis increased tenfold.

According to those who argue for immigration control, these figures show that an immigration of unpredictable proportions was beginning in 1961, while those who oppose controls argue that it was precisely fear that controls might be introduced which led to a panic among people who would otherwise have postponed their immigration for a number of years. The Leader of the Opposition, Mr Hugh Gaitskell, argued in opposing control that West Indian immigration was already self-controlled, and cited the relationship between the rate of immigration and the level of employment in Britain.[11]

There can be little doubt, however, that the arrival of coloured immigrants in such large numbers appeared as a threat to some sections of the British population. Riots in Notting Hill and Nottingham in the late fifties were followed by sustained complaints in the correspondence columns particularly of local newspapers alleging that immigrants were making the housing shortage worse, were persistently unemployed and living off public assistance, and that they were turning the houses in which they lived into slums. Such allegations were usually demonstrably false but this alone could not prevent the weight of protest from having some effect.

The facts of the immigrant situation were that they did suffer a higher rate of unemployment than native-born whites, that they did settle in areas where the housing shortage was acute and that, particularly because of the multiple-occupation of houses by coloured households, they did cause these houses to deteriorate. But it was also the case that coloured people suffered discrimination in employment, and housing, that the areas where they settled were areas which were losing population and needed immigrants to man industries, and that housing deterioration occurred because normal housing opportunities were denied to coloured people.

In 1962 the Conservative Government introduced controls on immigration from the Commonwealth. In the following two and a half years, net immigration figures were as follows

Table 2. Commonwealth Immigration 1963–65[12]

	1963	1964	Jan.–June 1965
Canada, Australia and New Zealand	8,951	13,382	15,714
Other Commonwealth countries and dependent territories	59,049	62,117	33,383

Under the new arrangements, all workers coming to settle had to obtain work-vouchers. The number of vouchers issued for the white Commonwealth countries in 1964 was 817; for other

Commonwealth countries, 13,888. Figures for dependants arriving to settle in 1964 were:
White Commonwealth 2,243
Other Commonwealth 38,952

This degree of immigration control was, however, still considered inadequate. The Labour Government's White Paper on Immigration in 1965 argued:

'it must be recognised that the presence in this country of nearly one million immigrants from the Commonwealth with different social and cultural backgrounds raises a number of problems and creates various social tensions in those areas where they have concentrated.'[13]

It was therefore decided to restrict the issue of vouchers to those with special skills and those who had jobs to come to, and to restrict the total number to 8,000, of whom 1,000 would have to be Maltese. Since special skills were defined in terms of higher or further education, the total number of working-class immigrants from the Colonial Commonwealth was likely to be at most about 3,000–4,000. In fact it was substantially less. Since the number to be permitted entry from any one country, moreover, was to be not more than 15% of the total, the total number of Indian, Pakistan, or Jamaican workers who could enter the country legally could not now rise above a few hundred per year.

Subsequent to the passing of the 1965 Act which followed the White Paper, the figures for voucher holders and dependants entering Britain were:

Table 3. Immigration of voucher-holders and dependants from the Commonwealth 1965–67[14]

		1965	1966	1967
White Commonwealth	Voucher holders	755	320	262
	Dependants	1,986	2,896	2,730
Other Commonwealth	Voucher holders	12,125	5,141	4,716
	Dependants	39,228	42,026	50,083

Thus, despite immigration control, the yearly inflow of dependants from the coloured Commonwealth was increasing. This, together with the problem of illegal entry, and the problem of other categories of immigrants who fell outside the scope of the Act altogether, now became a main political issue for those who still saw coloured immigration as a threat.

Illegal entry led to intense police activity on the southern and eastern English coasts to detect secret landings, while immigration officers kept a close watch for forgeries that fraudulently allowed new immigrants to be classified as dependants. The right of entry to British citizens of Asian origin living in East Africa remained, but the number who were allowed to enter in any one year after 1968 was to be restricted under the Commonwealth Immigration Act of 1968. East African residents who could establish that they had a long connection with the United Kingdom were exempted from this control and the Home Secretary was accused of introducing a distinction, based upon colour between two classes of citizen.

Those who regarded any coloured immigration as undesirable now concentrated on two points—the possibility of voluntary repatriation of those immigrants already in the country and the cessation of immigration for dependants. These policies, originally advocated by an alliance of extreme right-wing political organisations called the National Front, were given a new importance in March 1968 when they were advocated by the Conservative Party politician, Mr Enoch Powell.

In fact on both these points, those who opposed immigration by coloured immigrants exaggerated the degree of growth of the coloured British population. The striking feature of immigration from the Coloured Commonwealth to Britain compared with other immigrations was the degree to which it was accompanied by an outflow of returning migrants, and a careful analysis of the dependants problem, based upon the most cautious assumptions, was that the total number of available dependants for those immigrants who had arrived by December 1967 was 236,000 and the total coloured population together with all dependants legally entitled and likely to enter Britain in the next few years after 1969 was 1,406,000.[15]

The important point is that, despite the smallness of scale of the problem, the possibility of continuing coloured immigration was seen as endangering British society, either because of the likely behaviour of the immigrants themselves, or because it was believed that the presence of too many of them might give rise to racial strife. Another possible, more sociological explanation is that the social system was threatened by the merging of the metropolitan and colonial labour systems; immigration control was a means of keeping them apart, and thus maintaining the relative integrity of the metropolitan system. Clearly, a limited number of colonial workers could be accommodated in marginal roles in industry; mass immigration, however, would raise fundamental problems.

The Employment of Coloured Immigrants

The striking fact about the employment of coloured Commonwealth immigrants is not that there was discrimination against them, although this, as we shall see below, there certainly was. What is really surprising is the extent to which they were accepted as workers in certain kinds of employment, without any alarm being raised. The nature of this acceptance has been very well analysed by Peach in his study of the distribution of West Indian immigrants in British industry.[16]

Peach's conclusion was that immigrants were attracted to those regions which were growing rapidly, or which were static provided that there was no rapid inward migration of white immigrants from other regions. That is to say that coloured settlement occurred in London where there was a high degree of economic growth but a net loss of population through migration; in the Midlands, where there was a moderate degree of economic growth coupled with only moderate inward migration; and in the East and West Ridings of Yorkshire, where there was moderate economic growth coupled with outward migration.

Peach considers two hypotheses: that these figures show that coloured immigrants are acting as replacement labour; and that their arrival is the cause of white departures. He concludes that the sociological evidence and the evidence of the Industry Tables of the 1961 census support the former hypothesis. Thus it appears that, although the ratio of West Indian workers in expanding industries was almost the same as in the total working population, they were strongly over-represented in the declining industries. This thesis is further supported by the fact that West Indians have settled in larger and declining towns rather than in small but growing towns.

This would seem to indicate that the roles suggested earlier as being assigned to colonial workers have in fact been assigned to

West Indians. To a surprising degree, they are filling jobs unwanted by white men; they are also playing a part in growth industries where they can well be the marginal employees most
vulnerable to unemployment.

Davison[17] has pointed out an important difference in the
occupational structures of West Indian and Asian immigrants.
According to the 1961 census, the relative percentages for various
immigrant groups and for English workers in the top occupations
(i.e. professional; employers and managers; foremen; skilled
manual; working on own account or non-manual) were as follows:

English	71
Jamaican	44
Other Caribbean	45
Indian	76
Pakistani	54
Polish	71
Irish	48
Cypriot	53

Two points may be noted. First, there is a considerable migration of Asian professional men, especially doctors, and the Asian
migration also services itself to a higher degree than the West
Indian. Second, the major influx of Indian and Pakistani workers
occurred after the 1961 census. Hence we may now expect to find
considerable numbers of Asian workers in replacement manual
employment, and fair numbers in the professional groups either
servicing their own people or filling gaps which have arisen in
middle-class occupations (e.g. the rather lowly paid and not much
sought-after position of junior hospital doctor).

If the replacement labour theory is correct, it may seem a little
superfluous for the research team employed by Political and
Economic Planning[18] to have investigated the level of discrimination at all levels of employment. Many areas of employment, in
relation to which they applied job-testing techniques or interviewed
'those in a position to discriminate', were not areas which coloured
workers ever sought to enter. Not surprisingly they found that
coloured workers tended to under-report discrimination. The study
is nonetheless extremely important; some areas of employment
may be open to replacement labour, but this does not mean that
coloured workers do not seek to enter other areas, or that there is
no discrimination within those which are relatively open. The
social frontier of colour discrimination (i.e. the barrier which the

ex-colonial worker must cross in order to win equality) is a shifting one. Its location is disputed. The study shows where it lay in late 1967. It is the only systematic quantative study of its kind made in Britain.

It produced three basic sorts of evidence: (1) a survey of the experience of coloured people in seeking employment as that experience appeared to them; (2) the evidence of 'job-testers' of varying cultural backgrounds and colour, derived from their experience of applying for work; (3) the response to questioning of 'those in a position to discriminate', including employers and trade unions at national and local levels, labour exchanges of the Department of Labour, and private employment bureaux.

The sample questioned included West Indians, Pakistanis, Indians and Cypriots.

Table 4. Percentage of group claiming they experienced employment discrimination[19]

	West Indian	Paki- stani	Indian	Cypriot	Total
Personal experience claimed, evidence provided	45	34	35	6	36
No exposure through applying where immigrant known to be employed, or applying for only few jobs	17	12	19	7	15
Avoided discrimination through personal or racial characteristics or 'luck'	16	6	9	18	11
Belief in discrimination through knowledge of experience of others. No reason given for self having avoided it.	9	6	10	7	10
Uncertain about existence of discrimination	8	24	12	34	16
No belief in discrimination	5	18	15	28	12
	100	100	100	100	100

Two points stand out. First, it is clear that the Cypriots, who are commonly thought of as white and who come from one of Britain's former strategic colonies, have far less experience of or belief in the existence of discrimination than the West Indians, Pakistanis and Indians. Second, there seems to be a stronger belief in the existence of discrimination among West Indians than among the two groups of Asian immigrants. This might be because Asian labour in fact suffered less discrimination, but regional variations show that it was where Asian labour was acceptable in a replacement role (e.g. in the West Riding of Yorkshire) that less experience of discrimination is reported.[20]

What we are dealing with here is perceived experience, not necessarily the actual extent of discrimination. The figures might accordingly be too low, simply because those who were interviewed had insufficient information. Note, for example that discrimination was most often alleged among immigrants who spoke English. On the other hand it is difficult to assess the variable represented by immigrant education or lack of it; immigrants with English trade qualifications allege discrimination in the same way as those having indigenous trade qualifications or degrees. The first probably does denote discrimination, the second could be due to the lack of comparability, or lack of means of assessing these qualifications by employers.

Applications by English, Hungarian, West Indian and Indian and Pakistani job-testers were made to forty firms cited as discriminatory by immigrants. In only one case was a job offered to a coloured immigrant, while the English and Hungarian testers had fifteen and ten offers respectively. This seems to suggest that discrimination was at least as widespread as was claimed by coloured immigrants. The report, in fact, goes even further and concludes that discrimination was under-reported by immigrants.

The survey of 'those in a position to discriminate' serves to confirm this, revealing attitudes to the possible employment of coloured workers in jobs for which they would not normally apply. It would appear from these results that any serious attempt to press their claims further by coloured immigrants would be met by determined resistance.

Certain important points can be noted: (1) employers generally see no difficulty in employing coloured workers for manual work, but do not consider them suitable for executive positions, while local employers do see difficulties even in regard to manual work and, in particular, objections from local white workers; (2) employers make a complete distinction between executive jobs requiring personal qualities coloured immigrants are not supposed to possess, and technical jobs demanding qualifications and skills which they might possess; (3) 37 out of 150 local companies admitted that they did not employ coloured workers either as a matter of principle (in 4 cases) or because they would only do so as a last resort; (4) the firms that most frequently refused to employ, or avoided employing coloured labour were in the retail and service sectors; (5) although the attitudes of local workers were often cited by employers as a reason for not employing coloured labour, the trade unions, nationally and locally, denied discriminatory practice, though complaining that coloured immigrants were slow to appreciate the benefits of trades unions.

From this evidence it would appear that local employers are the most important 'gatekeepers'. National employers control entry into executive and technical positions, but the crucial decisions as to which manual jobs should be open are left to the local branches and their managers, who do in fact discriminate, even in regard to unskilled manual work. The main reasons given for this discrimination are: (i) problems of language, qualifications and lack of mobility by immigrant workers; (ii) customer resistance to the employment of immigrants; (iii) resistance by other workers.

These reasons were given to some extent by employers, trade unionists, labour exchanges and employment bureaux. It would seem from the evidence, however, that unionists and employment agencies do not ultimately control the situation. The trade unionist may decide to fight or not to fight an individual case, and government-run labour exchanges may bring pressure to bear upon discriminating firms, but employment policy is settled by the firms themselves.

The decision, therefore, as to how far the coloured immigrant could become a full member of the metropolitan society rested with local managers, their personnel managers and foremen. What was the upshot of their decisions? From the study and from other sources we may conclude: (1) that in some industries, labour was so scarce that employers were glad to have coloured and non-English speaking workers; (2) that sometimes a high percentage of the local labour force being coloured was seen as a problem and a formal or informal quota was fixed; (3) immigrants were not commonly promoted to supervisory posts (only 11 such promotions are recorded for the 150 firms); (4) there was considerable resistance to the employment of coloured workers in white-collar jobs and in executive positions; (5) although all those interviewed believed that the principle last-in-first-out should be applied to redundancies, there was pressure at unofficial shop-floor level against the retention of coloured workers in preference to whites.

All of this is quite consistent with the picture drawn earlier of the role assigned to coloured workers in metropolitan society. They are accepted, but in certain jobs only, and only in certain conditions, e.g. a high general level of employment. Employers and white workers may on occasion seek to extend restrictions and coloured workers to break them down, but the inevitable result remains a frontier between two kinds of worker.

The years between 1951 and 1969 did not in fact produce major industrial conflicts over the employment of coloured labour, although there have been small-scale local conflicts over the promotion of individual coloured workers to supervisory posts, and over redundancy, and on one or two occasions unofficial organisations of black workers have drawn the attention of both trades unions and management to their grievances.

Immigrant Labour and Workers' Rights in British Politics

Two factors would bring about a change in attitudes: large-scale unemployment or declining living standards among workers in Britain; and application, on a large scale, for jobs by English-speaking, English-educated children of coloured immigrants.

The fear that immigrant workers would become an unfair charge on the social services and would add to the difficulties of British workers was clearly stated by a leading trade unionist—Sir William (later Lord) Carron—in his valedictory address to his union. Dealing with the economic crisis facing the Labour Government and the trade unions, he discussed first the problem of

'the non-productive sections of our population who are generally found to be enjoying much higher incomes than those of us who are doomed to produce the basic commodities that make the continued existence of these people possible . . .'

and then went on:

'Quite as a separate problem it would be interesting to obtain detailed statistics applying to the grand total that is consumed by educational grants, National Health expenses and subsistence payments that become immediately obtainable by the ever-growing number of individuals who were not born in the country and who in no way contributed towards setting up a fund into which they so willingly dip their fingers. As they so succinctly put it "they know their rights". It would be very acceptable to the rest of us if some small measure of appreciation and thanks were in visible evidence.'[21]

Such figures as were available showed that Carron's statement was misleading. The National Institute for Social and Economic Research[22] produced the following account of the actual and projected social cost of immigrants as compared to the rest of the population:

Table 5. Social cost of immigrants as compared to rest of population[23]

	1961 Total population	1961 Immig. population	1966 Total population	1966 Immig. population	1981 Total population	1981 Immig. population
Health and Welfare	£18·5	£18·4	£18·6	£17·4	£19·0	£16·8
Education and Child Welfare	£12·4	£13·3	£12·1	£13·9	£15·3	£22·9
National Insurance and Assistance	£31·2	£19·2	£31·7	£17·4	£33·5	£18·1
Total	£62·1	£50·9	£62·4	£48·7	£67·8	£57·8

Some evidence was also available on immigrant fertility. An article in the *Eugenics Review* of April 1964[24] had shown that, though coloured fertility is higher than English, it is not as high as fertility in Irish immigrants; other surveys indicated that the normal English family had two or three children, the normal coloured family had three or four. Such differences (which were in any case likely to decline as immigrants became more urbanised) did not seem to confirm the picture of an ever-rising demand on the social services.

Economists have constructed models to estimate the effect of immigration on the British economy. E. J. Mishan and L. Needleman,[25] for example, developed a generalised model for assessing the cost of immigration and then applied it to what is known of the demographic and economic characteristics of Jamaicans.

Their conclusion was that:

'Large-scale inflow of immigrants into Britain over the next few years would lead to an increase in excess of domestic demand and a worsening of the balance of payments situation . . .'

However, although the authors claim that they have preferred to be cautious (i.e. to underestimate the cost of immigration), they ignore the fact that immigrants have substantially less than an an equal share of the available social capital.

Another economist, R. G. Opie, writing in the *New Statesman* and *Nation*,[26] concludes more moderately than Mishan and Needleman that:

'It seems likely that, in the short run, immigration worsens the balance of payments and is at best neutral in its net impact on demand. In the long run it should accelerate the rise in standards of living, reduce cost pressures and strengthen the balance of payments.'

We are less concerned, however, with the accuracy or otherwise of these assessments than with the social effects. What does the man in the street believe will be the effect on his own economic situation of coloured immigrant participation in the economy, and how will he accordingly react? And how will the political decision-makers react to what they suppose public opinion on this matter to be?

As indicated earlier, the social frontiers within which coloured immigrant labour is acceptable may shift, and British workers may not actually resist their employment in certain jobs, but equally certainly, do not welcome them.

Assessing the popular view of the general effect of the presence of coloured workers on the economy is complicated by attitudes to housing competition and to urban dilapidation.

There is evidence that the response of those who had to work and live with coloured workers was not one of unrelieved hostility. However, the relationship was a new one, and ambivalent. The effect of the prolonged debate about the rights and wrongs of immigration was to heighten the idea of the presence of coloured labour in general as a threat.

Between 1962 and 1968 the immigration question became a

central issue in British politics. Previously, the equality of British citizenship was generally accepted. In the early sixties organisations demanding immigration control were set up and, by 1963, at least one local Conservative association had made opposition to coloured immigration the central plank of its platform. In the 1964 General Election its candidate in Smethwick substantially defeated a Labour Minister, despite a massive swing to Labour in the country.

The issue was kept continually alive after 1964 by certain sections of the press and in late 1967 the National Front stated its immediate aim:

'To preserve our British native stock in the United Kingdom, to prevent increased strife, such as seen in the United States and to eradicate race hatred by terminating non-white immigration with human and orderly repatriation of non-white immigrants.'[27]

In April 1968 a programme very much like this was advocated by the Conservative front-bench politician Mr Enoch Powell. Mr Powell argued that it was the duty of politicians to reflect the feeling of their constituents on issues like this, and proceeded to do so by retailing stories which he claimed came from sources he had verified about the misbehaviour of coloured immigrants, of their overwhelming presence in schools and of the increasing hostility of the white population to them. Summing up the situation as he saw it Mr Powell said that Englishmen:

'Found their wives unable to obtain hospital beds in childbirth, their children unable to obtain school places, their homes and neighbourhoods changed beyond recognition, their plans and prospects for the future defeated. At work they found that employers hesitated to apply the same standards of discipline and competence required of the native born worker.'[28]

Mr Powell's speech also contained what his critics claimed were highly emotional words like 'gunpowder' and 'rivers of blood' and, when marches were spontaneously organised by dockers and others in his support, argument broke out about whether or not a speech such as this was racist in character. Whether it was or not, the very least that could be said was that it offered the public a new definition of their relationship with colonial coloured workers. Most of these immigrants, Mr Powell stated in a later speech, could not be assimilated into the British way of life; not to have stopped the immigration at the earliest possible point was a tragic mistake; and, though he called for equal treatment for those with a legal right to be in Britain, he argued that the inflow should be completely stopped.

Whether in the long run Mr Powell's definition of the situation will become that of all political decision-makers or of the man in the street remains to be seen. If it does, the coloured man, though entitled to the rights of citizenship, will seem to be in the society at all only as a result of a major policy error. Thus coloured workers are marked as a distinct group, and this is entirely compatible with what was said above about the coloured colonial's role as the new poor and underprivileged in an advanced society.

Response to Discrimination

The study referred to above makes it clear that coloured workers did not altogether accept their positions as inferior replacement workers in unwanted jobs. But this did not immediately produce a politically militant movement of people fighting for their rights. First generation immigrants were inclined, however reluctantly, to accept their position—the more so if they expected eventually to return home.

This situation is changing. Change was reflected first among those claiming to be immigrant leaders. Most West Indian, Indian and Pakistani leaders were accommodating until 1964. But by then appeals were being made to the rank and file in terms of slogans and ideas drawn from the United States, from the Third World and from China. In 1964, Michael de Freitas formed the Racial Adjustment Association, called himself Michael X and implicitly used the slogan 'Black Power' in his appeal to fellow West Indians. At the same time, Maoist elements struggled for ascendancy in the Indian Workers' Association and in Pakistani organisations. These militant elements were probably not representative of the rank and file in 1964; indeed, immigrant leaders and organisations often rather foreshadow developments than reflect the feelings of the man in the street. But as time went on and white hostility became more vocal, militant views gained wider acceptance in the coloured community.

In 1967-1968, the views of at least four parties to the situation could be distinguished: the Government, acting through the (advisory) National Committee for Commonwealth Immigrants

(NCC), which included selected immigrants and respected leaders who were not identified with political parties; the Campaign Against Racial Discrimination (CARD) which included immigrants and liberals; various Black Power and Maoist groups; and unpolitical immigrants (probably the majority of all the immigrants concerned).

When the balance of power shifted within CARD under the impetus of more militant immigrant groups, this was seen by the white liberal members of the former CARD Executive and some immigrants as a takeover by Black Power and the extreme left. They resigned in protest.

The white liberal members then devoted their attention to lobbying for the extension of race relations legislation to cover employment and housing. They were partially successful in this. But effective campaigning against racial discrimination stopped.

It seemed at first plausible to assume that this was due to the devotion of liberal energies to the examination of the content of the new Race Relations Bill. In fact there was a growing polarisation of white and black views on the immigrant situation. This made a multi-racial anti-racist front difficult to achieve.

The growth of white support for the views of Mr Enoch Powell further aggravated the situation. To many immigrants, and even more so to their British-born children, moderate and integrationist views began to seem increasingly irrelevant. Michael X, imprisoned for racial incitement, and other Black Power leaders, came into prominence, and Stokely Carmichael was deported.

The British-born and British-educated children of coloured immigrants have mostly not yet got to the stage of seeking employment. What is certain, however, is that they will not accept being restricted to the only employment opportunities open to their parents. If they do encounter the same discrimination, their frustration and, presumably their militancy, will increase. They will be determined to achieve equality and integration, and increasingly militant and anti-white as a result of their experience of discrimination.

Housing

The immigrant identifies and is identified much less with the place in which he works than with the place where he lives. White resentment often is with people, who, in Mr Powell's words, have changed 'homes and neighbourhood beyond recognition'.

Peach[29] has shown that immigrants tended to settle predominantly in towns with a population of about 200,000, but decreasing, and much less frequently in smaller towns which were growing. This would suggest that, far from overstraining housing resources at the worst possible points, they were in fact replacement residents as they were replacement workers.

The study quoted earlier documents discrimination in housing. This information has been supplemented by Elizabeth Burney[30] and by Rex and Moore.[31] Table 5 gives data on alleged discrimination in housing (as Table 4 above did for employment).

Table 6. Immigrant experience of discrimination in privately rented housing[32]

	West Indian	Paki-stani	Indian	Cypriot	Total
Personal experience of discrimination claimed and evidence provided	39	15	19	8	26
No exposure through having applied only to places where known to be acceptable	40	72	71	25	53
Belief in existence of discrimination through knowledge of experience of others—avoided discrimination personally through personal or racial characteristics or luck	5	1	3	16	5
Belief in existence among others—no reason given for personal avoidance	12	4	3	25	9
Others	4	8	4	26	7
	100	100	100	100	100

As compared with Table 4, there is a striking increase in the 'no experience' group, particularly among the Indians and Pakistani. Whether this is due to voluntary segregation, or because, when discrimination is taken for granted, contact is avoided, will be discussed below.

Test applications, and interviews with 'those in a position to discriminate' confirm potential discrimination was far greater than Table 6 seems to indicate. This was also true of rented local government housing and houses for private sale, the main obstacles being placed by estate agents, building societies which provide mortgages, and the housing departments of city councils.

Rex has suggested a model of the city, based partly on the notion of housing classes and partly on the concept of the immigrant colony, which can be followed here to show how the immigrant ghetto is formed.[33]

There are differential rights, in the city, in regard to the use of domestic and community buildings. The ideal (a person who owns a whole house for the sole use of his family) is rarely attained. The next best is a mortgaged house if the mortgagee enjoys all the normal benefits of ownership. The decisions to bar or admit particular families to this status will lie mainly with the estate agents and the building societies. According to the study quoted earlier, however, only 47% of the population of England and Wales were house-owners. The remaining 53% were in rented accommodation. The fact that 26% of the total population were in council houses suggests that council housing may be an alternative ideal to ownership. But only 1% of immigrants as compared with 26% of the population at large were in council houses, so that this particular ideal was either not open to, or was not sought by, immigrants. It will be necessary to return to this question later.

Whole houses can of course be rented (as an alternative to ownership), but slum-clearance is continually decreasing the total number of houses available for rent, and rent control prevents the growth of the kind of demand that would produce enough new houses.

What other possibilities are available in the city?

Finance can be obtained through short-term loans, or by paying more interest. Many immigrants found this the simplest way of housing themselves fairly rapidly. The immigrant who purchases a house on these terms can often rely on friends and kinsmen to help him.

In some cases, small houses for which there is not much demand are bought collectively by a group of immigrants who live together in overcrowded conditions. If the cost of the houses is disproportionate to the income of the immigrants, taking in more lodgers offers the only way of meeting repayment obligations.

Landlords who are immigrants themselves may give fellow countrymen or relatives special terms, and charge everyone else as much as they can get; or simply charge everyone as much as they can get. For example, Rex and Moore found that Pakistanis in Birmingham charged their Pakistani tenants 'charitable' or nominal rents only but very high rents indeed to other tenants, including other immigrants. Protestant West Indians tended to charge what they regarded as a fair rent to everyone, regardless of relationships.

The final result, in any case, is the overcrowded lodging house. Once the areas that contain them, the 'twilight zones', as they were called in Birmingham, are seen as a problem, an escalation of racist argument and racialist practice in the white community is likely to occur.

Much could be done to ease this situation by those 'who have power to discriminate'. Even without any increase in the number of houses for purchase or rent, a policy of deliberately excluding racial discrimination would mean a fairer sharing of burdens: many white families are certainly better equipped to cope. But, in any case, the number of houses is in fact continually increasing.

The United States does not much favour public low-cost housing, fearing that low-cost projects may simply become new ghettoes. Council houses are so popular among working-class people in Britain, however, that it might well provide local government authorities with the means of preventing ghettoes from forming.

Rex and Moore identify the following points at which *de facto* discrimination prevents immigrants from benefiting from local authority schemes: (1) the allocation systems, and particularly the waiting period, for local authority housing discriminate against all newcomers; (2) immigrants who nonetheless qualify may be given inferior accommodation (e.g. slums awaiting demolition) on grounds of allegedly inadequate housekeeping standards; (3) redevelopment schemes implying a right to rehousing usually skirt the areas of immigrant settlement.

Immigrants, it may be noted, are not the only occupants of the lodging-house areas. Others are only too glad to find a landlord willing to provide them with a roof over their heads, even at an exorbitant price, e.g. social deviants and down-and-outs of all sorts. Thus the immigrant finds himself segregated, compelled to live with, and be identified with, the city's problem people.

On the other hand, the area also becomes a centre of immigrant social life and cultures. Shops, public-houses, churches, mosques, temples, social and sports clubs provide opportunities for social life and contacts with friends whom the immigrant can trust. His presence there in the first place may in large part be due to discrimination, but it does offer this kind of advantage and, for this reason, segregation may to some degree be self-chosen.

The greater the cultural differences between an immigrant group and the host society, the more likely will such voluntary segregation be. The grocer's shop, for example, has a vital cultural and social role for the Indian immigrant in England.[34] On the other hand, families which have been settled for a number of years are often less dependent upon the colony, and eager to move out.

There were no ghettoes in England in the 1960s in the sense of something approaching a hundred per cent concentration of a particular group. But most immigrant households were segregated and underprivileged as much in their housing as in their jobs.

The Twilight Zones as a Political Issue

As already noted, urban deterioration was at least as much an issue as employment in the case made for immigration control. This particularly concerned public health and housing departments.

Traditional housing policy was not geared to cope with specific problems which arose. Much twentieth-century legislation has been concerned with the abolition of slums. But 'slum' is a technical term. It refers to houses designated as slums by local authorities, who have used physical criteria primarily in so classifying houses; they were slow to recognise that living conditions can be worse in houses which are structurally sound but overcrowded than in slums as officially defined.

The regulatory powers of local authorities proved quite inadequate in the 1960s. The public health authorities could prosecute the landlord if a house was badly managed, overcrowded, or lacking in certain amenities; under the 1964 Act, they could actually take over the management of the house for a period. But as there was no compulsory registration of lodging-houses, the public health departments did not know where the houses were and, in any case, the prosecution of offending landlords could achieve little if there was no real alternative to the service they provided.

Nevertheless, it was pressure by the public health departments that hastened legislative change. First Birmingham, and then other cities, were empowered to require the registration of lodging houses and, in certain defined circumstances, to refuse applications to register.

In the absence of an adequate policy for providing alternative housing, this only meant that local authorities could now prevent the social evil of multiple-occupation from spreading, and confine it to certain areas; this in turn meant effectively segregating the twilight zones from the rest of the city.

This segregation already existed in the early sixties in the main centres of immigrant settlement: the legislation merely formalised it.

The twilight zones inevitably had attendant problems, such as prostitution and violence, that were bound to concern the police. Rooms were available at a price without questions being asked, and living conditions which precluded normal marital relations provided a clientele for the prostitute. Violence was the inevitable concomitant of the absence of family life and the fact that public-houses were the principal social centres.

People used to the respectable areas are almost inevitably shocked by what they see. The police and the social workers become used to it. A question of police policy now arises. To what extent can prostitution and violence be tolerated?

At any time, these are areas in which, despite legislation, prostitution flourishes. Girls solicit on the streets and there are streets of well-recognised brothels. When the public-houses close, the police expect a far higher degree of violence than would be tolerated elsewhere. But, precisely because of their tolerance, they can increase the pressure against the local population at any time. Police often regard themselves as upholders of the morality of the common man; their reaction to hostility on the part of the immigrant may well be to increase the pressure.

Much has been written in the United States about ghetto schools and the handicaps which they impose on the children who attend them. In Britain the most vocal concern has been about white children who have to attend schools in which many pupils are the children of coloured immigrants. In both cases, the most frequently proposed solution is 'integration by bussing'. Aggrieved white parents in Britain are less concerned with integration, however, than with thinning out: no one suggests importing children from all-white schools into a coloured neighbourhood.

Because of language difficulties, attendance of coloured children at white schools is sometimes alleged to slow down the rate of advance in all pupils. If this can be argued in the case of Pakistani children, it seems difficult to justify in the case of West Indian children, who are of course English-speaking.

The segregated problem areas are not clear-cut. Their frontiers are continually shifting. It is possible, however, to outline the kind of pattern that develops.

The coloured immigrants obtain replacement employment, and take the only housing available to them in the 'twilight zone'. They have little hope of escape—no prospect of obtaining a mortgage, a Council house, or rehousing under a development scheme. Their way of life is inextricably associated with bad housing, urban deterioration, vice, violence, police investigations, and with deficient and overcrowded schools. The prosecution of immigrant landlords, and the use of buses to take the children to school elsewhere, seem to demonstrate dramatically that it is the coloured immigrant who is responsible. In the quasi-ghetto, he is institutionally attached to but never integrated into metropolitan society.

Such a population provides a scapegoat to which nearly all social evils can be attributed, and the immigrants 'who have destroyed our towns or changed them beyond recognition' become an issue that looms disproportionately large in urban and national politics.

Things have not gone quite as far as this in Britain. Steps have been taken in the opposite direction. Legal and administrative measures adopted include the machinery set under the Race Relations Act to prevent discrimination in housing and employment, and the Community Relations Commission which employs local liaison officers to assist integration.

Without attempting to assess the work of these agencies,[35] it is doubtful if even those in charge of them would claim to have produced more than an educational effect, an effect that has to be offset against the campaign against coloured immigration and the integration of immigrants already in the country. There is no co-ordinated machinery at city or district level to facilitate the dispersal of coloured people from their twilight areas; and it is in these areas that the pattern of urban race relations is being determined.

THE BRITISH EXPERIENCE AND THE URBAN CRISIS

How relevant is the British experience to that of other countries and especially the United States? Do black-white relations always produce an 'urban crisis', or is the experiences of each country fashioned by its history?

We may begin by pointing to the contrast between British and American conditions. In Britain, what is being debated is how white society will act towards coloured immigrants; in America, there is a black revolt against conditions which were formerly accepted. The coloured population in Britain are largely first generation immigrants who number less than 1 in 60 of the total population. New immigrants will bear much in order to gain acceptance in the host society and, if their numbers are relatively small, they have little prospect of exercising real political influence. The black citizens of the United States, on the other hand, form 1 in 10 of the population, can exercise the same kind of political influence as any other minority group, and see themselves and are seen as being entitled to equal rights.

So far as white racism is concerned the two countries have a similar problem. The United States had the moral legacy of slavery, but fought a civil war on the issue of ending it. There is still conflict amongst those who are committed to racial integration and those like Governor Wallace who oppose it. But the issues have shifted. Segregationists have been concentrating on the issue of 'law and order' because of the black revolt; they are also forced to fight defensively against new rights for blacks, rather than aggressively to deprive them of those they have won.

In Britain, the conflict is between those who accept the notion of equality between Commonwealth citizens and those who want to distinguish between the real British and the rest. The initial assumption was that the coloured British citizen had equal rights. But in fact he was accorded less than equal rights, and when he did not resist he became the target of racist hostility.

It might be argued that, in the two countries, the direction of change was different and opposite. In America the movement was either towards equality or towards racial conflict with blacks who had become stronger than they had ever been before. Britain started from formal equality and moved towards increasing discrimination and the justification of discrimination in terms of increasingly racist avowals.

But none of the factors mentioned so far explains the relative militancy of the urban black American and the relative quiescence of the coloured immigrant in Britain. Two other factors have to be considered: (1) the level of employment; and (2) relations with the police. Even allowing for their relatively greater incidence of unemployment, the level of employment among coloured immigrants in Britain was high, whereas black quarters in American cities contained large numbers of under-educated teenagers who had never worked and had little chance of ever working. They were frequently involved in crime and appeared to have nothing to lose by fighting back against the police.

The question of relations with the police is absolutely crucial. The American Report on the National Advisory Commission on Civil Disorders in 1967[36] showed that police practices were the most common source of grievance amongst blacks in riot areas, and action by the police was nearly always a factor in precipitating a riot. Although coloured immigrants in Britain did complain about unjust treatment by the police, discrimination in employment and housing would almost certainly rank as far worse grievances. However, some factors do suggest movement towards the American model. The children of immigrants will not see themselves as marginal members of society but as people in very much the same position as the black American. As automation and technological unemployment increase, coloured children from slum schools might find themselves ill-equipped and badly placed in the struggle for jobs. And, finally, it is possible that, pressed as they are by racist propaganda, the police might become tougher in immigrant areas.

In such circumstances, the 'colony'—the places of worship, clubs, pubs and shops which, pending integration, allow the new immigrant to continue a social life of his own—could become the retreat in which he detaches himself permanently from society, an insulated world which he can call his own. It could also become the breeding ground of racial revolution.

There can be no doubt that something of this kind has already occurred. Its extent is difficult to measure. It may be in part imitation of and identification with the American model; if so, the change is an important one.

No sociological observer could objectively conclude that, unless there is a black or a coloured immigrant revolt, there will be no urban crisis problem in Britain. It may simply take a different direction.

Continuous scapegoating and existing policy proposals for dealing with Britain's coloured problem constitute a first stage. Repatriation or forcible segregation might be the next. It does not seem wholly inconceivable for someone to decide that, since coloured immigrants are not full members of society, they should be confined to camps or special areas. This could provoke the same kind of urban crisis as the black revolt has caused in the United States.

There seem to be three possibilities: (1) urban society accepts and promotes interracial equality and integration; (2) coloured militants, dissatisfied, as in the United States, with existing programmes for achieving equality, themselves advocate separatism; (3) segregation of the coloured population is complete and they are effectively deprived of the possibility of political protest (cf. South Africa).

CONCLUSION

The incorporation into urban metropolitan society of coloured workers who came or whose ancestors came from colonies or former colonies has been considered, mainly in the light of British experience. As that experience is relatively limited, findings must remain inconclusive. However, there has certainly been considerable discrimination in employment and housing, and a large measure of segregation in cities. The white population might agree to the immigration of a limited number of coloured workers who would not be fully admitted to society but form a deprived enclave within it. This situation would not remain stable. The next stage might be a revolt (probably inspired by ideologies originating in the Third World), increasingly hostile action against the enclave, and perhaps its total elimination. The result in either case would be a continuing sense of urban crisis for many generations to come. Measures so far taken to implement an alternative policy of integration do not appear to have definitively decided development in one sense or the other.

References

1. Seymour M. Lipset, *Political Man; the Social Basis of Politics* (London: Heineman, 1960).
2. Daniel Bell, *The End of Ideology; on the Exhaustion of Political Ideas in the Fifties* (New York: Free Press, 1960).
3. Robert E. Park, et al., *The City* (Chicago: University of Chicago Press, 1967).
4. Gunnar Myrdal (with the participation of Sterner, Richard and Rose, Arnold), *An American Dilemma; the Negro Problem and Modern Democracy* (New York: Harper, 1944).
5. Myrdal, ibid.
6. See Peter L. Berger, and Thomas Luckmann, *The Social Construction of Reality: A Treatise in the Sociology of Knowledge* (New York: Doubleday, 1966).
7. George H. Mead, *Mind, Self and Society* (Chicago: University of Chicago Press, 1934).
8. See Cornelis W. (de) Kiewet, *History of South Africa* (Oxford: Oxford University Press, 1941). *Chapter II, Social and Economic.*
9. HMSO, *Immigration from the Commonwealth* (CMND 2739) (August 1965).
10. See Paul Foot, *Immigration and Race in British Politics* (Baltimore: Penguin Books, 1965).
11. Reproduced from Robert B. Davison, *Black British: Immigrants to England* (London, for Institute of Race Relations by Oxford University Press, 1966).
12. See *Hansard*, House of Commons, 5 Dec., 1961, cols. 1172–3.
13. *Immigration from the Commonwealth*, op. cit., note 9.
14. Ibid.
15. HMSO, *Commonwealth Immigrants Act 1962, Control of Immigration Statistics* (CMND 3258 and 6594), 1966 and 1967.
16. See David E. C. Eversley and F. Sudkeo, *Dependants of the Coloured Commonwealth Population of England and Wales* (London: Institute of Race Relations, 1970), p. 56.
17. Ceri Peach, *West Indian Migration to Britain* (Oxford: Oxford University Press, 1968).
18. Davison, op. cit.
19. William W. Daniel, *Racial Discrimination in England: Based on the P.E.P. Report* (Harmondsworth: Penguin, 1968).

20. An abbreviated version of the table on p. 20 (a) in: *Racial discrimination in England: based on the P.E.P. report*, op. cit.

21. See also Eric Butterworth, *Immigrants in West Yorkshire*; contribution of the authors, John Goodall and Brian Hartley (London: Institute of Race Relations, 1968).

Sheila Patterson, *Immigrants in Industry* (London: Oxford University Press, 1968).

Peter L. Wright, *The Coloured Worker in British Industry, with Special Reference to the Midlands and North of England* (London: for the Institute of Race Relations by the Oxford University Press, 1968).

22. Amalgamated Engineering Union, Annual Conference Proceedings, 1967.

23. National Institute of Economic Research, August 1967.

24. See *Eugenics Review*, Edinburgh (published by Eugenic Society), April 1964, K. Waterhouse, and E. Brabban.

25. E. J. Mishan, and L. Needleman, 'Immigration: some economic effects' in *Lloyds Bank Review* (London, July 1966), p. 33.

26. *New Statesman* and *Nation*, 15 March, 1968.

27. *The Times*, 24 April, 1968.

28. *The Times*, 22 April, 1968.

29. Peach, op. cit., pp. 80–2.

30. Elizabeth Burney, *Housing on Trial* (London: Oxford University Press, 1967).

31. John Rex and Robert Moore, *Race, Community and Conflict: a Study of Sparkbrook* (with the collaboration of Alan Shuttleworth, and Jennifer Williams) (London, New York: for the Institute of Race Relations by Oxford University Press, 1967).

32. An abbreviated version of the table on p. 73(a) in: *Racial Discrimination in England: based on the P.E.P. report*, op. cit.

33. Rex and Moore, op. cit. See also John Rex (ed.), *The Sociology of the zone of transition in Pahl, Reading in Urban Sociology* (London: Pergamon, 1968).

34. Rashim Desai, *Indian Immigrants in Britain* (London: Oxford University Press, 1963).

35. For a more personal comment, see John Rex, 'The race relation catastrophe' in *Matters of Principle: Labour's Last Chance* (by Burgess, Tyrell and others) (Harmondsworth: Penguin, 1967).

36. United States National Advisory Commission on Civil Disorders (New York: Bantam Books, 1968).

The Changing Trade Position of the Chinese in South-East Asia*

by GO GIEN TJWAN

Senior Lecturer, Centre for Modern Asian History, University of Amsterdam

THE CONCEPT OF THE 'THIRD CHINA'

Chinese minorities long before colonial times, have settled in the Nanyang, the area of the Southern Seas, from China's border states (Vietnam, Laos and Burma) to New Guinea and the remote Tanimbar Islands of Indonesia. Twelve or thirteen million ethnic Chinese[1]—but all sharing a common way of life distinct from the indigenous cultures of the host nations—form a not inconsiderable proportion of the total population of the region of roughly 230 million, in proportions varying from country to country. They also share another common trait: in each country they exercise an important economic role. For this reason, it may be surmised, they have suffered from persecution, ranging from legal discrimination to outright *pogroms*, committed by either the former colonial administrations or the new independent governments and indigenous populations.

There is a danger underlying the concept of a Chinese minority that can be conceived of as that of an unassimilated, alien middle-class group within a backward society. Such a view could easily lead to emphasising the persistence of Chinese cultural traits through the ages and overlooking the changes which have taken place (and are still taking place) within the minority group itself as well as in the host society. The purpose of this article is to make a few tentative comments on current sociological and socio-historical findings relative to the Chinese minority position in South-East Asia.

* First published in the *International Social Science Journal*, Vol. 23, No. 4 (1971).

Victor Purcell (whose standard work[2] is still indispensable for any student of the sociology and history of the Nanyang Chinese) at a meeting of the Chung Hua Hui (the Chinese Association in the Netherlands) at Leiden in 1946, attended by a hundred or so Indonesian Chinese, was struck by the dark complexion so common among them in marked contrast to the Chinese in Malaya, except for some in Penang and Malacca. If, as Purcell observed, there is a difference in physical appearance between the Malayan and the Indonesian Chinese the same holds true among the Indonesian Chinese themselves. A peasant girl in the Tanggerang area near Djakarta, who claims Chinese ancestry even though she has evolved a high degree of assimilation to Indonesian culture, is both physically and culturally quite a different person[3] from the sophisticated, rich merchant's daughter of Chinese origin studying in a Roman-Catholic school run by the sisters of Sancta Ursula in cosmopolitan Djakarta. Differences of this sort are equally evident within the Chinese community of Malaysia. On the other hand, if one surveys all the Chinese communities settled in South-East Asia, it is just as correct to perceive in all these ethnic Chinese a common cultural trait distinct from the host cultures.

If we now turn to a description of the economic position of Nanyang Chinese, it is possible to discern an analogous situation with regard to their way of life. In a recent study, Lea E. Williams has analysed the stereotype of the Chinese trader of the Nanyang.[4] He admits that a huge share of trade goes through Chinese hands, but goes on to say:

'Nevertheless, it is false to believe that the overseas Chinese are exclusively or even usually great merchants. For every overseas Chinese commercial giant, there are thousands of petty traders, and for every small shopkeeper or itinerant peddler, there are scores of labourers. Furthermore, there are overseas Chinese in almost every occupation, skilled or unskilled, manual or intellectual, lucrative or subsistent. Chinese work as servants, stevedores, sailors, and surgeons, as rubber tappers, radio announcers, race-track touts, and real-estate brokers. There is probably not an occupation without Chinese representation, although in Southeast Asia as a whole relatively few Chinese pursue political, bureaucratic, or military careers.'[5]

A socio-historical analysis might lead to a better understanding of the current position of the Nanyang Chinese, which to judge by

THE
goe to e
goe to h
measure
primaril
mighty
usually
advanta

Wert
such ra
competi
evolved
the old
pletely (
with its
aiming
more cc
than caɪ
is much
in a hig

Fron
the Sho
two Mc
imperia
the nor
highly a
Tomé P
this to s

'At the
many ɪ
Bengale
Moors
grow ɪ
These lc
but they
these m
and sta

Data
there w
Indones
Huan a

the brief description presented above obviously calls for a scho-larly reappraisal.

The current position of the Nanyang Chinese—the Thai Chinese being the only exception—has evolved through three historical phases: a pre-colonial period, a colonial period, and the present era of the new nations. First of all, I would like to comment on the widely held stereotype among scholars, journalists, and politicians that the Nanyang Chinese have taken to trade and commerce by preference. In an earlier study[6] I tried to put forward the hypothesis that, prior to the colonial period, Chinese immi-grants had settled as agriculturists and introduced the cultivation of pepper and sugar-cane in the virtually unpopulated and un-cultivated region of Banten, to the west of Djakarta. Basing him-self on archaeological research in West Banten and southern Sumatra, Van Orsoy de Flines inferred that these Chinese settle-ments most probably dated back to the beginning of the Christian era,[7] upon which von Heine Geldern commented that this in-ference was undoubtedly correct and that Chinese colonists or traders must have lived in Indonesia as early as the Han period.[8] From an entry in Edmund Scot's *Discourse of Java* there is an indication supporting my hypothesis: 'The Javans are generally exceeding proud, although extreame poore, by reason that no one amongst an hundred of them will worke . . . The Chinois, doe both plant, dresse and gather the Pepper, and also sowe their Rice, living as Slaves under them, but they sucke away all the wealth of the Land, by reason that the Javans are idle.'[9]

However, the main socio-economic function of the Chinese in the Nanyang prior to the colonial period was in the sphere of trading, handicraft, and small-scale manufacturing (e.g. sugar mills combined with arrack distilleries and potteries as found in early Djakarta). We are indebted to Van Leur[10] and M. A. P. Meilink-Roelofsz[11] for their analyses of Asian trade, in which, prior to European hegemony, Chinese preponderance is manifest. I can therefore restrict myself to a few remarks on the changing trade position of the Chinese.

CHINESE TRADERS IN PRE-COLONIAL TIMES

Before the appearance of the Europeans on the South-East Asian scene Chinese traders were mainly engaged in import and export

that there was a *masdjid Patjinan* (Chinese mosque) in early Banten, warrants the conclusion that they were not so completely assimilated as to have lost their identity. It is interesting to note that in never-colonised Thailand, occupying an otherwise comparable situation, Sino-Thai relations resulted in the complete assimilation of the Chinese.[20] Whatever socio-cultural pattern evolved, one of complete or one of partial assimilation, the fact remains that there were ethnic Chinese who identified themselves with their country of residence. Wang Gungwu mentions two instances of official missions to the Chinese emperor from, respectively, Siam and Java in which a Siamese and a Javanese of Chinese origin acted as envoys, the latter even as chief envoy. The Siamese, by the name of Tseng Shou-hsien, was sent twice (in 1405 and in 1411); the Javanese envoy was an ethnic Chinese called Ch'en Wei-ta.[21]

Three points emerge regarding the position of Chinese traders in pre-colonial times. The first is that within the socio-economic pattern of that time, characterised by lack of modern capitalist competition, the trade position of an alien was no impediment to assimilation. The relationship between the Javanese and the alien traders in the staple ports might be compared with that between the *Co-hong* merchants of Canton and the Western traders in the early nineteenth century: 'They shared a spirit of camaraderie with the foreign traders, each helping the other out of difficulty and insolvency'.[22] It was the relationship of comprador and foreign trader: they needed each other, since they performed complementary functions.

The second point concerns those Chinese who, when the South-East Asian economy shifted from self-sufficiency to interdependence with world markets, began to penetrate the interior of the country. Here also there was no competition with indigenous counterparts. The Chinese ventured into densely populated areas —the Tonkin delta and the river basins of the Mekong, Mae Nam Chao Phraya, and Irrawaddy on the continent, the delta of the Brantas and Solo rivers on Java—where rice cultivation was the main means of subsistence,[23] assuring the livelihood of a large section of the population and a harvest surplus to be offered as tribute to the god-king. In these civilisations the occupation of trader was not held in high esteem, neither by the peasants—for whom there was no reason to abandon the traditional socio-economic pattern—nor by the nobility. According to traditional law, outsiders were prevented from becoming members of the closed village community. Excluded from the occupation of farming and from acquiring land, the Chinese came to fill a social gap and fulfil the function of traders or to practise a handicraft unknown among the host people.[24] The absence of inter-ethnic competition was conducive to friendly relationships. The few Chinese traders in the old Khmer capital, Angkor Thom, in the interior, however, seem to have enjoyed high prestige, since the indigenous population reportedly venerated them to the extent of prostrating themselves before them.[25]

The third point is that the Chinese did not come to the Nanyang with a religious background like that of other foreign traders (Islam or Hinduism from India, Christianity from the West) giving rise to a contemptuous attitude towards those they considered as pagans. The traditional Chinese religion—a syncretic blend of confucianism, Buddhism, and Taoism, more a way of life than a religion in any theistic sense, and above all basically rational—created no inhibitions towards embracing another creed, whether Buddhism in Siam, Khmer, or Burma or Islam in Indonesia. It must moreover be borne in mind that traders tend to be spiritually more flexible than peasants. As a matter of fact even today the Chinese peasants in western Java, though culturally almost entirely assimilated, are not Islamised.[26] They have remained *peranakans*, a section of the Indonesian population that has retained a distinctly Chinese identity. Neither have the *babas* of Malacca and Penang become Moslems. In these two places Chinese settlements are comparatively large, enabling them to retain a more Chinese character.

RACIAL TENSIONS AND ECONOMIC COMPETITION IN THE TWENTIETH CENTURY

Unlike the pre-colonial socio-economic structure which afforded the Chinese trader every opportunity to become integrated to the indigenous society, the Western colonial structure gradually imposed upon the old civilisations of South-East Asia had a negative effect on opportunities for integration. Ousted from international trade by powerful and politically protected European interests which also destroyed nascent indigenous commerce (in South-East Asia the Indonesian maritime traders were the most advanced) the Chinese were gradually accorded the role of middlemen, distributing the goods imported by Europeans and collecting agricultural products to be exported by Europeans. Such a sandwich position is precarious, for the Chinese trader could easily be held responsible for the misfortune and misery resulting from a drop in the world market prices of agricultural products or from increased prices of imported goods. Nevertheless it is remarkable that during the Great Depression of the early 1930s, in Java, where the Chinese form the most typical minority group in South-East Asia, except for a serious outburst of anti-Chinese feelings in Pekalongan in 1931, no racial riot of importance has been reported. It is interesting to note that the 1931 riot was neither a result of the world economic crisis which affected Indonesia severely, nor a spontaneous outbreak of latent anti-Chinese resentment. Rather it was a repetition of the violent anti-Chinese outbursts in 1912 and 1918 sparked off by contending indigenous merchants and manufacturers of *batik* textiles and *kretek* cigarettes, and organised by the militant *Sarekat Islam* party.

It would seem that, despite the colonial colour-caste barriers a specific patron-client relationship had developed which lessened the danger of latent anti-Chinese feelings flaring up violently. This patronage institution is a complementary economic function, characterised by a more personal relationship between the *bah-buyut* (something like 'great-grandfather', even though the Chinese trader may be younger than the Javanese peasant) or the *pauk paw* ('next-of-kin') in Burma and the indigenous population. This subject calls for further investigation in connection with recent sociological findings on dependency relationship patterns in the developing countries.[27] Patronage is mentioned here merely as a novel element in the arguments against Furnivall's concept of colonial plural society, which is 'a society, comprising two or more elements of social orders which live side by side, yet without mingling.'[28]

The suggestion that there is a specific relationship between the Chinese trader in the hinterland and the indigenous peasant population has also been elaborated by William Willmott for Chinese-Khmer relations: 'Despite the fact that plural society may lack a "social will", as Furnivall put it, the nature of the economic ties between Chinese trader and indigenous peasant are such that mutual advantage demands their continuation and elaboration. Without the trader, the peasant has no source of the various manufactured goods he has come to need; without the peasant, the trader has neither customer for his goods nor supplier for the grain he sells in the city. Furthermore, credit arrangements that neither wishes to break, necessarily based on mutual trust, tie the two inseparably. In other words, the economic relations between functionally specific categories generate shared interests that bind the plural society together, whether or not the external pressures of colonial power enforce peace.'[29]

The impression of quite smooth relations between Chinese traders and indigenous peasants, as reported by qualified observers like Purcell,[30] Donald Willmott[31] and William Willmott must, I believe, be credited to patronage institutions in the rural areas of Burma, Java and Cambodia.

But this description and analysis of the position of the Chinese trader as retailer is only part of the picture. An ideal-type in the Weberian sense, it serves well to illuminate the intermediary position of the Chinese minority between the Europeans at the top of the colonial hierarchy and the indigenous population at the bottom. It also fits in with Furnivall's concept that in such a society the distribution of economic functions coincides largely with racial differences.[32] The assertion, however, that 'every Chinese is a trader' is not borne out by close scrutiny of social reality. An examination of the position of the ethnic Chinese on Java, probably the most typical minority group of the Nanyang Chinese, is quite revealing on this point.

From the 1930 census reports, it appears that 57·66% of the Chinese exercising a profession were engaged in trading, 20·81% in industry, 2·83% in communications, 9·11% in the production of raw materials (native agriculture, growing fruit and vegetables, cattle breeding, fishing, hunting, forestry etc.), and 9·59% in other professions (medicine, law, journalism, education, civil service, domestic services, and other insufficiently described occupations). Those engaged in trade can be broken down into the following percentages: shopkeepers and hawkers (27·02), trade in victuals, tobacco etc. (12·88), trade in textiles (9·23), wholesale trade and commission (0·43), credit institutions (2·93), and others (5·17).[33] Even if we bear in mind that these percentages comprise both employers and employees and therefore do not reveal class differences within the Chinese group, it is clear that retail trade was not the main profession of the Chinese in Java in 1930.

Statistical data on the economic position of the Chinese in other

South-East Asian countries should be evaluated in the same way. If the Chinese in the Federation of Malaya—prior to the foundation of Malaysia—produced over 70% of the national income and owned 72% of road transport, 40% of tin mining and 35% of the rubber plantations,[34] we should never forget that the numerous Chinese coolies working in the tin mines and on the plantations, building roads and loading ships earned only a small part of what the Chinese rubber giants were able to collect.

Economic dynamics were not the only force to function explosively in the caste-like colonial society by providing a route for sons to move up from their fathers' and grandfathers' occupations. Education played the same role,[35] operating independently of conscious or unconscious colonial intentions to change the commercial orientation of the Chinese. In the case of Indonesia, until early in this century no more could be expected than that all Chinese would follow the trader's path in keeping with the precolonial and colonial tradition. In 1900 a Chinese school system was started by Indonesian-born Chinese, and eight years later educational opportunities for Chinese children were expanded with the foundation of government-sponsored Dutch-Chinese schools. It is remarkable that in places where there was no opportunity to enter either of these two Chinese-type schools, Chinese children attended the Dutch government schools intended for Indonesian children. In 1929/30, as many as 8,000 Chinese children were attending the latter type of school.[36] Moreover, children of wealthy Chinese parents were admitted to European schools.

The conclusion to be drawn from these data is that it was unlikely that all children of a small trader could earn a living from their father's business. Perhaps one or two could do so, but the modern education they had received gave them the opportunity to opt for new professions. Moreover, in a colour-caste society to know a European language and to have adopted a Western way of life leads one to look down on the profession of small shopkeeper. Hard economic pressure as a consequence of the world economic crisis in the 1930s provided no alternative for the Western-educated young Chinese but to become clerks for a European concern or to enter the colonial civil service in a position open to Chinese. It is imperative to stress the importance of education as a factor of change in the traditional Chinese trading position. According to Chinese norms, the learned are at the top of the social hierarchy. It is undeniable that even the richest Nanyang

Chinese preferred his children to get as much education as possible. No one can expect a physician to run a retail shop or even to manage a tin mine.

Caste-like societies such as those of colonial South-East Asia, are not conducive to the assimilation of ethnic minorities. The integrating factors mentioned above mitigated the rigidity of the divisive forces inherent to the colonial structure. The very existence of communities of local-born Chinese in every South-East Asian country in pre-colonial times which were wont to adopt elements of the host culture, is living proof that cultural differences, even though emphasised within the colonial setting, do not prevent ethinic groups from developing rather smooth interrelationships. The racial tensions that exist in South-East Asia cannot be ascribed solely to colonial vestiges. Ethnocentrism, fostered by colonisalism, can certainly lead to racism. But there must be other factors to explain why it was only after 1900 that anti-Chinese disturbances on a relatively large scale were time and again indulged in by indigenous populations. It was even in an independent country, Siam, that anti-Sinicism was first formulated in 1914, in the pamphlet entitled *The Jews of the East*, by no less an author than King Rama VI (who, incidentally, was part-Chinese himself).

Wertheim has been the first to advance the theory that racial tensions between Chinese minorities in South-East Asia and the host nations originated from economic competition based on racial differences.[37] The beginning of this century witnessed the emergence of a native trading class in South-East Asia. The complementary economic relationship between equally powerful indigenous compradors and foreign Chinese traders no longer dominates the historical scene of twentieth-century South-East Asia. It has been replaced by fierce competition between capitalist groups with a similar orientation. Wickberg asserts that this competition began even earlier in the Philippines: 'After 1850 the growth in size, distribution and economic power of the Chinese brought a competitive situation with the mestizo and Philippino enterprises developing during the century 1750–1850. In the anti-Chinese arguments of the 1880s and 1890s cultural biases were implicit. But economic factors were decisive.'[38] The same situation arose in Indonesia and elsewhere somewhat later. In Malaysia the first large-scale outburst occurred as late as 13 May 1969. The Indonesian experience probably best reveals the general pattern of Chinese South-East Asian group conflict as it developed since the beginning of this century, after South-East Asian nationalism had gradually become an important factor (and since the achievement of independence by all South-East Asian nations the dominant factor) in inter-ethnic relations.

The *Sarekat Dagang Islam*, an association of Javanese traders founded in 1911, attracted a large following both as a result of and as a reaction to the increasingly strong economic position of the Chinese. By 1916, the *Sarekat Islam*, as it was renamed in 1912, had become a militant political organisation. By appealing to the religious sentiments of the masses, the traders leading the *Sarekat Islam* were able to launch a series of campaigns of violence against their Chinese competitors. It was essentially a feeling of religious solidarity and not a national or class consciousness that induced Indonesian peasants and labourers to respond to the call of their equally capitalist leaders to attack 'the evil capitalists', the Chinese. Ever since, and everywhere in South-East Asia, economic nationalism combined with a powerful political nationalism has been a threat to the position of the Chinese minority. But there is at least one South-East Asian country where, throughout the centuries, no race conflicts between the indigenous population and the Chinese minority are on record: that is Cambodia, and that in spite of discriminatory measures barring the Chinese from political activities and from eighteen occupations. Endorsing Wertheim's theory that existing antagonisms are mainly due to economic rivalry within the context of ethnic differentiation, William Willmott has explained that no Khmer-Chinese group conflict has ever developed because of the absence of a Khmer middle class of any sort.[39]

To digress upon Chinese reactions to encroachment on their position falls outside the scope of this article. Yet I may be allowed to quote one reaction, bitter though scholarly, for it may be symptomatic for the Chinese view of present-day conditions in most of the South-East Asian countries. After pointing out that the great majority of Thai Chinese remain labourers or petty traders to the end of their lives Joseph P. L. Jiang concludes:

'Appointing powerful politicians to the boards of directors, or reorganising their business firms into Sino-Thai ventures, with Thai officials supplying protection, official privileges and government contracts, many individual business leaders not only do not suffer from restrictive measures but actually prosper under them. Thus a sort of "antagonistic symbiosis" is established between the political elite and the pariah entrepreneurs in a typical transitional setting. The pariah entrepreneur cannot be liquidated because his activities finance the new elite's growing leisure and luxury. Neither can he be assimilated, for such a step not only means the destruction of a useful scapegoat in a transitional process but also considerable financial loss for the elite as well. Militant economic nationalism has resulted, not in the defeat of the enemy, but in a precarious co-operation between the antagonists.'[40]

Wang Gungwu has recently analysed the process of transformation of the Malaysian Chinese to Malaysian politicians.[41] In another paper I myself have concluded that pending a solution of the economic aspects of the total problem, the *peranakans* of Indonesia are still aliens in the land of their birth, despite their positive response to the post-war realities in Indonesia and South-East Asia.[42] Traditional ethnic specialisation in the economic sphere was already breaking down in colonial times, and the caste-like social structure of South-East Asia is more and more giving way to a class structure. A process of cultural and political integration drawing the Chinese communities completely within the domestic orbits of the various South-East Asian countries is perceptible to every competent observer. It remains to be seen, however, whether South-East Asian leaders and policy-makers will respond to this process by making use of the managerial skills and capital of the Chinese traders, the knowledge of so many Chinese scholars and the zest for work of numerous Chinese labourers, peasants and artisans. Economic competition based on ethnic difference can and must be eliminated. The task of the South-East Asian leaders it to open up broad opportunities for all citizens irrespective of ethnic or religious background. Writing about the problem of modernisation in politics and government, Howard Wriggins has stated that: 'Economic growth and diversification provide another way in which opportunity can rapidly expand. A growing mesh of business activities or government responsibilities, transcending traditional communal and regional differences, will lead men away from local loyalties and make them citizens of the whole nation.'[43] He is not the only scholar to believe that opening new opportunities is the only solution for the racial problems in the developing countries. In concluding the exposition of his theory of economic rivalry based on ethnic differences, Wertheim quotes Raymond Smith to the effect that: 'It would be ideal if the rapidity of economic development opened up so many opportunities that the jealousies and fears based on race assumed an insignificant role.'[44] I should be only too happy if this became true.

References

1. Lea E. Williams, *The Future of the Overseas Chinese in Southeast Asia* (New York: McGraw-Hill, 1966), p. 11.

2. Victor Purcell, *The Chinese in Southeast Asia* (2nd ed.) (London: Oxford University Press, 1966), p. 6, note 5.

3. Go Gien Tjwan, *Eenheid in Verscheidenheid in een Indonesisch Dorp* [Unity in Diversity in an Indonesian Village] (Amsterdam: Sociologisch Historisch Seminarium voor Zuid-Oost Azië, Universiteit van Amsterdam, 1966), p. 267.

4. Williams, op. cit., p. 17ff.

5. Ibid., p. 20.

6. Go Gien Tjwan, op. cit.

7. Quoted in Go Gien Tjwan, op. cit., p. 29.

8. Quoted in Go Gien Tjwan, op. cit., pp. 29–30.

9. Edmund Scot, 'A discourse of Java, and of the first English factorie there, with divers Indian, English and Dutch occurents', in Samuel Purchas, *Hakluytus Posthumus or Purchas His Pilgrimes* (Glasgow: James MacLehose and Sons, 1905), Vol. II, Chap. IV, pp. 440–1.

10. J. C. Van Leur, *Indonesian Trade and Society* (The Hague: Van Hoeve, 1955), p. 465.

11. M. A. P. Meilink-Roelofsz, *Asian Trade and European Influence* (The Hague: Nijhoff, 1962), p. 471.

12. Tomé Pires, *The Suma Oriental: An Account of the East, from the Red Sea to Japan, Written in Malacca and India in 1512–1515*, Vol. I (London: Hakluyt Society, 1944), pp. 192–3.

13. W. P. Groeneveldt, *Historical Notes on Indonesia and Malaya, Compiled from Chinese Sources* (Djakarta: Bhratara, 1944), p. 47.

14. Willem Lodewijcksz, *De Eerste Schipvaart der Nederlanders naar Oost-Indië onder Cornelis de Houtman 1595–1597* [The First Voyage of the Dutch to the East Indies under Cornelis de Houtman, 1595–1597] (The Hague: Nijhoff, 1915), p. 122.

15. William E. Willmott, *The Chinese in Cambodia* (Vancouver: University of British Columbia, 1967), p. 5.

16. W. F. Wertheim, 'Trading minorities in Southeast Asia', *East-West Parallels* (The Hague: Van Hoeve, 1964), p. 53.

17. B. Schrieke, *Indonesian Sociological Studies: Selected Writings* (The Hague: Van Hoeve, 1955), Vol. I, p. 21. Schrieke provides a general description of the eastern Javanese area of trade in its heyday. My conclusion about the barter-trade character of early Asian trade is drawn from this description.

18. Groeneveldt, op. cit., p. 49.

19. Pires, op. cit., p. 182.

20. G. W. Skinner, *Chinese Society in Thailand: An Analytical History* (Ithaca, N.Y.: Cornell University Press, 1957), pp. 128–34.

21. Wang Gungwu, 'China and South-East Asia 1402–1424' in: J. Ch'en and Nicholas Tarling (eds.), *Studies in the Social History of China and South-East Asia* (London: Cambridge University Press, 1970), pp. 396, 398.

22. Immanuel C. Y. Hsü, *The Rise of Modern China* (New York: Oxford University Press, 1970), p. 196.

23. H. J. H. Alers, *Dilemma in Zuid-Oost Azië* [Dilemma in South-East Asia] (Leiden: Brill, 1955), p. 102.

24. Go Gien Tjwan, op. cit., pp. 208–10.

25. William E. Willmott, op. cit. pp. 4–5; see also his article 'History and sociology of the Chinese in Cambodia prior to the French Protectorate', in *Journal of Southeast Asian History*, Vol. 7 (1966), pp. 20–2.

26. Go Gien Tjwan, op. cit., pp. 163–204.

27. W. F. Wertheim, 'Patronage, vertical organisation and populism', paper read at the VIIIth International Congress of Anthropological and Ethnological Sciences in Tokyo, 1968.

28. J. S. Furnivall, *Netherlands India: A Study of Plural Economy* (2nd ed.) (London: Cambridge University Press, 1944), p. 446.

29. William E. Willmott, op. cit., p. 96.

30. Purcell, op. cit., pp. 69–70.

31. Donald E. Willmott, *The National Status of the Chinese in Indonesia 1900–1958* (rev. ed.) (Ithaca, N.Y.: Cornell University Press, 1961), p. 12.

32. Furnivall, op. cit., p. 451.

33. *Volkstelling 1930* [Census of 1930 in the Netherlands Indies]. Vol. VII: *Chineezen en andere Vreemde Oosterlingen in Nederlandsch-Indië* [Chinese and other Non-Indigenous Orientals in the Netherlands Indies] (Batavia: Departement van Economische Zaken, 1935), see subsidiary table No. 26, p. 136.

34. Alice Tay Erh Soon, 'The Chinese in South-East Asia', *Race: Journal of the Institute of Race Relations*, Vol. 4, No. 1 (November 1962), p. 35.

35. Raymond Kennedy, 'The colonial crisis and the future', in Ralph Linton (ed.), *The Science of Man in the World Crisis* (New York: Columbia University Press, 1945), p. 311.

36 *Volkstelling 1930*, Vol. 7, op. cit., p. 108.

37. Wertheim, *East-West Parallels*, op, cit., p. 76ff.

38. E. B. Wickberg, 'Early Chinese economic influence in the Philippines, 1850–1898', *Pacific Affairs*, Vol. 35, No. 3 (Autumn 1962), p. 285.

39. William E. Willmott, op. cit., pp. 96–7.

40. Joseph P. L. Jiang, 'The Chinese in Thailand', *Journal of Southeast Asian History*, Vol. 7, No. 1 (1966), pp. 64–5.

41. Wang Gungwu, 'Chinese politics in Malaya', *The China Quarterly* (London), No. 43 (July-September 1970), pp. 1–31.

42. Go Gien Tjwan, 'The role of the overseas Chinese in the South-East Asian revolutions and their adjustment to new states', in Michael Leifer (ed.), *Nationalism, Revolution and Evolution in South-East Asia* (Hull: Centre for South-East Asian Studies, 1970), p. 59ff.

43. Howard Wriggins, 'National Integration', in Myron Weiner (ed.), *Modernization: The Dynamics of Growth* (New York and London: Basic Books, 1966), p. 191.

44. Raymond T. Smith, *British Guiana* (London: Oxford University Press, 1962), p. 143 (as quoted in Wertheim, *East-West Parallels*, op. cit., p. 82).

Part III

CHANGING PERSPECTIVES

New Dimensions of Change, Conflict and Settlement*

by MAX GLUCKMAN

Professor, Department of Social Anthropology, University of Manchester

SCIENTIFIC THEORIES ABOUT THE NATURE OF HUMAN BEINGS AND THEIR SOCIETIES

When I was a student, I was taught to distinguish between *Homo sapiens*—modern man—and *Homo fossilis neanderthalensis*. The latter wherever he appeared, in Europe or Asia or Africa, was considered to be far less intelligent than modern man, a cul-de-sac in the physical development of human kind. Last Christmas I watched a BBC television programme for youngsters, in which Dr John Napier taught them that *Neanderthalensis* Man has been renamed *Homo sapiens neanderthalensis*; and Napier insisted that that gentleman was not so very different in his physical attributes and his mental faculties from our own progenitors, now doubly distinguished for wisdom as *Homo sapiens sapiens*.

I find something strikingly symbolical in this assertion that Neanderthal Man was of the same species as modern man. Viewed in the light of the vision we now have of early tool-using hominids developing from our relatively undifferentiated primate ancestor perhaps more than a million years ago, physical anthropologists have eliminated a sharp racial discrimination which seemed to be firmly set in our zoological history: the forward-leaning, beetle-browed, smaller-brained *Homo* of Neanderthal, Broken Hill, and elsewhere, is now classified as someone whom

* First published in the *International Social Science Journal* Vol. 23, No. 4 (1971) (written as a lecture, delivered at Unesco in Paris, in March 1971).

Homo sapiens could regard as a brother or sister, or a potential spouse. He walked upright, striding manfully, and was intelligent, making tools by complicated and transmitted techniques. If his tools were cruder and less differentiated than those of later times, they were more sophisticated than the tools of earlier times, made indeed by *Homo sapiens sapiens*. The making of tools bred improvement in tools. Men taught other men: what happened in the very early history of mankind, has continued into the present.

Yet at the same time men were at war; and though we do not know why *Homo sapiens neanderthalensis* became extinct, since we know that he lived at the same time as *Homo sapiens sapiens*, one cannot help fearing that *Homo sapiens sapiens* helped his Neanderthal brother to disappear off the face of the earth.

If, then, the previously alleged differences between these two ancient types of men are now said to have been considerably less than they were previously thought to be, it gives strong support to those long-established and well-validated findings, by most objective biologists, psychologists, social scientists and historians, that the biogenetic differences between groups of *Homo sapiens sapiens*, if any exist other than superficial ones, are negligible when compared with the effects of historical contacts, of health and nutrition, of economic situation, of culture and education, and so forth. Others have dealt in technical terms with these problems, and with continually resurging attempts to demonstrate that there may be a biogenetic cause for the varying performance of groups of mankind in producing technology, in answering intelligence tests, and the like. I take it for granted that the differences we find in the achievements and actions of groups are the product of their history, and of existing medical, social and cultural factors. As a social anthropologist working in my native Africa among fellow Africans of different racial stock and culture from myself, and granted by them the privilege of being allowed to enter into their way of life and thought, I certainly found no barriers of intelligence or emotion to my understanding of them—nor, I hope, were there any to their understanding of me.

Thus in terms of organic endowment there is no reason why we should not recognise our common humankindness—what in the Bantu languages I know is called *Ubuntu* and *Butu*, the quality of being human. And one strong stream in the humanistic tradition of our own, and many other wrongly called primitive civilisations, moves us to similar conclusions. In those terms we can accept the introductory clauses of the United Nations International Convention on the Elimination of All Forms of Racial Discrimination, proclaiming human dignity in freedom and equality, morally and legally, and rejecting 'any doctrine of superiority based on racial differentiation . . . (as) scientifically false, morally condemnable, socially unjust and dangerous'. But despite all demonstrations of this potential equality of humankind, existing differences between groups and categories of mankind continually breed new forms of scientific, or pseudo-scientific, interpretations that ascribe them largely to biogenetic factors, and deny that they are the product of the conditions in which men are reared. One of the constant dimensions of change is the recurrent production in new forms of old theories of inherent differences. Thus there is in the United States of America a new school which argues that part of the variations in results of performance in intelligence tests of different ethnic groups may have to be ascribed to genetic factors, and hence in justice different forms of schooling would be appropriate to these different groups. This school of thought has already produced strong responses from scientists of all types in the United States as well as from national official opinion. The difficulty is that the very cultural differences which make mankind so interesting lead so obviously to this kind of theory.

I consider thus that the weight of scientific evidence states that there are no inherent biogenetic differences between groups of mankind: but I would still argue that those who believe there are such differences—and they could only be marginal—dare not base discrimination on such beliefs. All our values demand that we do not discriminate between groups, any more than we should discriminate against individuals who are in any way handicapped. Indeed, in modern civilisation such persons are more and more protected.

The Articles of the Convention themselves expose the resulting persisting dilemma with which we are confronted because of what is most characteristically human: culture and cultural differences. Recognition of human equality implies the recognition of the right of all human beings to aspire to all those freedoms set out in the Convention, particularly in Article 5. Among them is 'the right to equal participation in cultural activities', which I take to mean that any person is entitled to adopt any form of culture he pleases so long as this does not involve an attack on others. That is, the Convention, as set out in the Preamble, rejects all 'policies of apartheid, segregation or separation'. This does not, of course, assert that anyone shall be compelled to be integrated into a single culture—he may, if he chooses, be so integrated, or on the other hand remain apart, with again the saving qualification, that he do nothing which attacks others' rights. The difficult dilemma, in moral and political terms, as shown clearly in the debates on the Convention,[1] is how the freedom to be different is to be achieved while the right to become similar is granted. This means that we must expect continually in the future to be confronted with new dimensions of change, conflict and settlement, in the fields of relationships between groups of different culture and to some extent between groups of different racial or ethnic stock.

As I have already stated, this is liable to lead to new forms of theorising to explain the basis of group differences as inherent. Ethnology is now a fruitful—and very fashionable—line of research, at least in Western Europe and in North America. It is fruitful in the understanding it is giving us of the behaviour of animals and birds in their relationships with their own fellows, and with other species, in an ecological environment. It is fashionable also to use those findings not only as analogies, but also as modes of interpreting the social behaviour of human beings. And here I judge it to be dangerous. Clearly we have to accept human biogenetic constitution as one of the parameters of socio-cultural life. But it is something quite different to attempt to argue that forms of socio-cultural organisation in groups of mankind can be traced by parallels among other primates to the forms of organisation among our primordial hominid ancestors, and to argue that those forms of organisation are transmitted genetically, i.e. that forms of human behaviour can be explained directly by reference to physical constitution. Such attempts distract attention from the social and cultural factors which to a far, far greater extent account for the hostilities shown by members of one group against another, or the subordination of one group by another. Inevitably therefore such arguments also distract attention from the way in which forms of social organisation can be changed and thereby forms of hostility can be ameliorated. As a striking example of this kind of reasoning I take L. Tiger's *Men in Groups*—though this is not an example of racial discrimination unless we accept the contention of some members of Women's Liberation movements that women are the most-discriminated-against race of all. Tiger postulates a theory that in the hominid era those co-operative groups of all-male hunters which did not handicap themselves by taking females along with them would be more successful, since females run less fast and throw less far and less accurately than do males. Hence such males would be more likely to survive and breed. Correspondingly, females who insisted on accompanying the males would be more likely to miscarry or to die. Therefore the tendency would be to breed males who cohered with males, and females who associated less with males outside of mating relationships. Tiger postulates that these predispositions in successfully surviving males and females might be carried in the genes, and continue to affect our society after many millennia. The argument jumps backwards and forwards over the millions of years involved in evolution: his case for the greater fertility of home-loving females is supported by statements that modern 'career women' are more often barren or have fewer children than do other women. I know no better example of a sophisticated argument, supported by numerous citations (as it happens, somewhat selected), going so far wrong. Even if the jumping over of eras is overlooked, Tiger pays no attention to such crucial facts as that barren women or women with few children would have a greater chance, in present conditions, of making a career; that the age of marriage of women pursuing professional careers may be later than for other women: that such educated women have greater access to contraceptive devices and use them more skilfully in more suitable home conditions; and so forth.

Similar types of arguments could be, and have been, induced to account for hostility between racial and ethnic groups. To refer such hostility to the behaviour of birds and animals in defending their territories, and the like, so that it seems to be 'natural', is to evade examination of the complex of historical and cultural factors that account for the hostility more simply—and unfortunately, to evade, even if unintentionally, the well-proven fact that if sociocultural organisation be changed, the behaviour of people involved in that organisation can be changed. All of us who have lived in African territories when they were dominated by white colonial powers, and after they gained independence, know how quickly the attitudes of, and the relationships between, both whites and Africans altered. And here I refer not to the liberal whites, who always contended for equality of races and tried to act by that maxim, but to many whites who regarded Africans as inferior. The same observation applies to many Africans who struggled rightfully and bitterly against their subordination: their attitudes to whites have undergone substantial changes as they have gained independence and social equality—or even social superiority.

When we are dealing, therefore, with cultural differences and with social attitudes which to any extent coincide in their distribution with the distribution of social and economic privileges, we clearly may expect that a whole series of new theories will be produced to warrant their inequality. This is obvious enough; but what is obvious nevertheless needs to be stated again. For we need to appreciate that justification of such inequality on grounds that it is inherent may appear in very subtle forms. It is for this reason that I have cited Tiger's argument that the tendency of men to form groups for political, economic and social purposes, as it has been observed in almost all societies, is transmitted in mankind's genes and has had—perhaps may yet have—advantages for survival. I am sure that the argument is not intended to lead to the conclusion that the segregation of men and women is natural and inevitable: but it does so lead. Similarly, when theories relating identification of members of groups of animals with their groups or with territory or modes of display or pecking orders, are applied to human forms of social organisation, they are liable to lead to assumptions that present social arrangements, including subordination and segregation, are natural, part of our biological endowment.

The theories themselves, in my opinion, prove any such assumption to be unwarranted. They show a peculiarly human characteristic. This arises from the ability of men to use words, those most flexible of symbols, to formulate arguments explaining the internal and external worlds. Since the words are so flexible, arguments can be pushed to seemingly logical conclusions. Or to put it another way, a behavioural or social scientist may sometimes follow the seeming logic of his analysis beyond what it itself proves, and use it to interpret other phenomena than those investigated. Freud created a new climate of opinion about the internal working of the human psyche: when he applied his theory to explain forms of human social organisation and the outcome of political struggles, without taking account of historical socio-economic forces, he went sadly astray. Periodically, in new forms we are confronted with scientific theories that give a new dimension to existing forms of discrimination and/or hostility between groups of varying ethnic stock, or between the sexes, and that justify anew existing forms of segregation. Recent studies of the social life of animals are such a dimension: and though—I repeat—most of their proponents are doubtless liberal and humane, I affirm as strongly as I can that the drawing of any analogy from animal to human social behaviour is not, as we say in English, on all fours. The analogy is false: and any lesson learnt from studying animals must be applied with extreme care to human society.

It is now well validated that scientific theories about the nature of human beings and their societies are liable to be very strongly influenced by the political, economic or social position of the proponents of such theories. I do not myself consider that the influence is one hundred per cent determined. Some men are able to escape that influence and to follow where the logical analysis of facts, in so far as facts can be established, leads them. The danger then is, as I hope I have shown, that that logic of itself may carry them too far.

If this danger threatens from the logic of scientific analysis itself, *a fortiori* it threatens even more strongly from the logic of other forms of intellectual effort. As a South African anthropologist, I have always been impressed by the fact that in some ways the most sympathetic and even laudatory analyses of indigenous African cultures in South Africa come from the studies of scholars who believed in the policy of ethnic segregation. They described the culture of each African people in an idealistic form—and therein was contained the implication that those cultures were good for the peoples concerned, an essential part of their being, something to which they were entitled and which they should be helped to maintain. As Leo Kuper has pointed out, there are Afrikaner, nationalist, segregationist intellectuals who consider that the Afrikaner people have struggled to establish their own language and culture against the great pressure of the language and culture of Britain and its English-speaking offshoots and of America. Hence they argue, it is similarly right that all small populations should be supported in such struggles. From there it was a small step to the argument that people should—in their own best interests—be virtually compelled to abide in their own cultures, to which many of them were, of course, attached. On the other hand, South African anthropologists who politically were actively opposed to segregation, have in describing the same or similar African cultures indicated their weaknesses and even cruelties. And the politically neutral, have on the whole written neutrally.

MODERN TECHNOLOGY AND SOCIAL CONFLICT

In the continuing development and change involved in relationships between ethnic groups, intellectual discourse will play its part and there will be contention in terms of adverse scientific theories. I start from, and stress, this aspect because the premise on which Unesco is founded is that intellectual discourse must eventually lead men to see, in the words of the United Nations Convention, which I repeat, that 'any doctrine of superiority based on racial differentiation is scientifically false'. To some extent, that is an article of faith. It is also, I believe, a statement of the conclusion supported by the best research. Unfortunately, it is very difficult to prove an absolute negative; and since there are obviously considerable differences in the technologies and cultures which pertain to groups of differing ethnic stock, it is always possible to argue plausibly that those differences are related to variations in genetic endowment. Nor are contentions of that kind restricted to persons who in the arrangement of social advantages and disadvantages are privileged. The underprivileged may come to attach value and virtue to that which separates them. What is peculiarly theirs may come to be highly esteemed. Many years ago I was doing field research as an anthropologist among the Zulu of South Africa, who were not only subjected to the political domination of whites but were also restricted by the colour bar from acquiring much of the culture of the whites: I found then that some of the best-educated Zulu had reacted to those restrictions by forming a Zulu Cultural Society to maintain the practice of Zulu culture. Some at least of them argued that Zulu culture was all good. (It was not surprising that the movement was supported by the South African Government.) We would, I suppose, all be in favour of any organisation that seeks to maintain pride in a group's culture: what shocked me was to hear one member, at a meeting of thousands of Zulu, argue that in order to solve a certain social problem they should reinstitute a Zulu magical practice which was clearly, by modern medical standards, most dangerous to the health of their children. I was equally disturbed when I attended a dinner in London to raise funds for the establishment of a cultural home for Nigerians in Britain, when that very valid endeavour was based on the idea, then popular among black Africans, of the unique African personality. It seemed to me that the speakers were arguing precisely what South African segregationists argue: that there are deep inborn differences in the personalities of groups of different ethnic stock to which they should adhere. I told the chairman, a close friend of mine who later became a minister in an African state when it acquired independence, what my fears were; and he remained unconvinced. Similar movements are occurring in other parts of the world; and all such movements, springing from the variable distribution of culture as well as of economic and social privileges, among underprivileged as well as privileged, will produce new streams of struggle and obstruct efforts at settlement.

The legitimate desire of people to preserve their own culture hence in many ways can obstruct realistic efforts at settlement in terms of civic and cultural equality. I speak of cultural 'equality' here, and not of cultural 'identity'. It has become increasingly manifest that if anyone ever thought that with the spread of industrial technology cultural differences between the various groups of mankind would disappear, such ideas were mistaken. Nor is this likely to happen in the immediately foreseeable future. This does not deny that many forms of culture, previously restricted in their provenance, have not become more and better known through many regions of the world. But there remain considerable local variations in the realm of cosmology, in the ordering of domestic life, and in linguistic and artistic differentiation. What then is part of the common world culture, and what persists of the more localised cultures of various ethnic groups?

It is the technology of industrial civilisation that has spread most rapidly and been accepted most readily; and the skill with which peoples to whom that technology was until recently new use it shows how false are theories which hold that biogenetic differences between races account for differences in technical efficiency. As the stone tools of *Homo sapiens sapiens* were produced by developing the tools made by the skill of *Homo sapiens neanderthalensis*, so indeed have some of the peoples who took over Western European technology developed at least some parts of that technology. If we allow for the effects on people of poor nutrition, endemic diseases, inadequate basic education in the first years of learning, and the like, there is no doubt that recent history shows that any group of mankind can, given the chance, take over the technology of any other group, and potentially improve upon it.

This fact is to some extent concealed because when the technical achievements and output of newly industrialised peoples are measured, they are too often assessed against false models. I have myself specialised in the study of African society, but I have also been involved in the study of 'committees' in factories and villages in Britain, in India and in Israel. What has always struck me is how frequently, for example, the performance of African managers and workers in mines or factories is measured against the idea that in Britain, or the United States, or some other Western state, the personnel of these enterprises work perfectly. Performance in newly industrialised states is measured against an ideal operating in a never-never-land. For studies in these latter cases have demonstrated only too frequently that in these there are also many obstructions and difficulties. Hence any contention on this basis that there is an inherent incapacity in any people to work an industrial system effectively and efficiently is based on invalid comparison, even though there are undoubtedly degrees of effectiveness and efficiency in the operation of industrial plants. But if we make a valid comparison, of actual plant with actual plant, we can more accurately refer variations not only to the machinery, but also to specific social and cultural conditions, including such factors as differences in standard of living and expectations based on that standard, on traditional practices, on size of markets, etc. I consider that it is furthermore well validated that any idea that it takes generations of training in technology, for those groups whose productivity is low, to attain the standard of groups whose productivity is high, is also incorrect. Given the tools and a system of organisation which allows skill to develop, and good health of workers, those who lag at present can rapidly catch up on those who are at present ahead.

There is a second type of false comparison which vitiates the assessment of variations between ethnic groups, and which therefore continually breeds new conflicts. It arises from the failure adequately to take into account the extent to which the behaviour of people varies from situation to situation. Many African cultures contained beliefs in witchcraft and sorcery, as did those of other cultures, including, in their fairly recent past, those of European peoples. These beliefs were held to explain why a particular individual at a particular time suffered a particular misfortune. The beliefs could thus explain why some individuals were lucky and productive and others were not. These types of beliefs and the reasoning implicit in them are still compared with the modes of reasoning of Western scientists or technologists in their laboratories, to give a picture of people whose thinking was vitiated by magical and other occult ideas as against people whose thinking was scientific. The fallacy of this mode of comparison has long been demonstrated; yet it persists. There can be no simple step from cultural beliefs and ideas to the processes of thought of individuals. The fair comparison is of agriculturist with agriculturist, pastoralist with pastoralist, fisherman with fisherman, religious believer with religious believer. As we all know, a scientist or technologist may be a religious devotee, a believer in magic, or an atheist or agnostic. The sets of premises vary: the models of logical reasoning within them may be similar. Hence when we assess the capacity of persons of a particular ethnic stock to alter their premises of thought and their behaviour, we do not have to argue that they have to change all premises and all actions. It would be sufficient in theory if they adopted modern scientific patterns only in those situations where these were appropriate. I must note, however, that there are certain incompatibilities: for example, considerable research has demonstrated that beliefs in magic and witchcraft are a way of thinking about and hence of handling certain social tensions in societies at a relatively low stage of technical development; and technical development itself will lead to their obsolescence. Similar social tensions remain: they are handled in different terms.[2]

Meanwhile, what I have said about the ability of human beings to employ different social modes of thought in different situations emphasises that when we consider how human beings are to be re-educated or re-trained, we can to some extent cease to think of the problem of completely altering a whole personality. Alter the situation and we alter modes of thought. Provide the opportunity, and anyone can adopt appropriate forms of action and understanding, even if he continues in other situations to use quite other patterns of ideas.

The course of my argument here is to stress that the horse has to be harnessed in front of the cart. The horse is technological development: it can be harnessed in front of many makes of cart, each cart being, in my simile, a particular group, racial or ethnic or other, which holds perhaps specific beliefs and ideas and practises particular modes of behaviour. The technology determines at least in part the type of the cart—but I must abandon my simile. If all groups are given access to modern technology and science, they must, in the situations appropriate to those activities, act and think in appropriate terms. In other situations—in domestic life, in philosophy or ritual, in leisure—the members of each group may continue to adhere to their own culture, if they so wish.

The objection to policies of apartheid is that insofar as they are held and argued intellectually, they deny to other races the right, and sometimes the ability, to adopt modern technology and science, and to acquire the education necessary to acquire these. They deny to those races also any chance of equality within the system of social relationships based on the material parts of the technology.

I used the simile of the horse and the cart to emphasise what indeed we all know—that technological development for the so-called underprivileged nations and the underprivileged sections within nations is essential if those people are to be able to step into such brotherhood as modern mankind shares. That is the only way of achieving any hope that we can end many of the bases of racial or other group differentiation which produce, ever anew, theories of group superiority, in intelligence or civic virtue. And it is in opposition to such theories of group superiority, and not against group differences as such, that this symposium is directed.

No one, of course, is so naïve as to believe that were all the peoples of the world equipped equally with modern science and technology this would eliminate sources of group conflict, including perhaps racial conflict, by leading to a settlement of all such conflicts. What seems certain is that so long as some people are denied, or in fact, do not have, a modern technology, racial differentiation and conflict will continue, both between, and within, nations. The cure for old-style conflicts is patent, even if the cure for new-style conflicts has yet to be found.

TECHNOLOGICAL DEVELOPMENT AND POLITICAL
INSTABILITY

Many studies have demonstrated that through the longest part of human history political units have been beset by civil wars based on vertical divisions. In the earliest periods of history—and till recently still to be observed in what I hesitatingly call the tribal cultures of the world—tools and weapons and goods for consumption were relatively simple. Since consumer goods were simple and there were few luxuries, powerful men used their wealth to support and to attach personal followers directly to them. With simple tools, each man could produce little beyond his own needs to support the more powerful. Such luxuries as there were, were therefore mainly symbolic. Since weapons were simple, each follower had its own arms and added directly to the strength of his leader, who thereby had a small private army to support his aspirations to power. Leader and followers were thus not separated by widely diverse standards of living and hence were closely identified. Trade from each political unit was restricted in range and in the goods exchanged, because means of transport were simple. Basic foods were difficult to transport, but some specialised tools and luxuries could be moved thus; and from one political unit to another they might be exchanged slowly and eventually move great distances. The trade was often ceremonial, linking partners in standardised exchanges. Because of a high infantile mortality rate, as well as high death rates at later ages, the population increased slowly, though in total it might be subject to considerable fluctuations. Yet even in such situations, modern anthropological research has shown that political units were elaborately divided and cross-divided in a whole series of customary linkages based on descent, on age, on sex, on ritual beliefs, special association, etc. Thus social organisation was far from simple: it was indeed elaborately complicated. And here studies of groups of other primates, which begin to show such complications, may indeed enable us to speculate on the situation out of which human societies developed their own further complications, aggravated immensely with the high development of principles stated in words and with other symbolic valuations. This cross-cutting of linkages, through multiple divisions, produced a situation where societies were riven with conflicts, but held together nevertheless through attachment to common symbols and through the fact that those who were a man's enemies in one situation might be his allies in another. These cross-linkages thus produced some persons who had an interest in redressing quarrels, and could exert social pressure to do so or a series of relationships may concentrate on one person, who thus develops influence—and even power—that he may use to bring about peace. There were thus unifying forces which were based on multiple social allegiances and which acted to hold units together in the absence of a unifying, differentiated economic system. Despite this, smaller local units developed strong internal loyalties, and men competed both for goods and for power in recurrent civil wars. These wars were fought within the framework of the existing political system and only periodically were there substantial changes in organisation.

From this situation of rebellious egalitarianism, in some places the development of techniques of production, of building, of cloth-weaving, of metal-working and of transport led both to higher outputs and to the emergence of varying standards of living, allowing a social segregation of leaders from their subordinates. The range of conquests was extended. Classes began to emerge. Weapons became more costly, and instead of civilian armies there were also mercenaries. Yet civil war continued between territorial sections. Those with followers, who commanded troops, continued to try to seize power, either for themselves, or for some superior to whom they gave allegiance and their armed support.

One of the intellectual curiosities of modern times is the extent to which much educated public opinion in the industrialised world considers that military coups, such as have occurred in recent times in many of the countries of the so-called Third World, to be exceptional deviations, marks of political instability. I say this is curious because if we even barely scrutinise the course of human history, it becomes at once apparent that the seizure of power by those who command troops is more common than is the opposite situation—one in which men who command troops are content, or at least agree, to continue to subordinate themselves to the civil power. This latter situation has in fact existed only in a limited number of countries for a limited period of time. It has existed only in those countries which have undergone considerable technological development since the Industrial Revolution. It seems reasonable to conclude that the Industrial Revolution itself, by leading to a high degree of mutual interdependence between the vertically divided sections of states, through utilitarian economic exchange, inhibits civil war in open battle. Furthermore, the complications of the economy make it more difficult for power to be seized by a swift military coup when a few key places can be occupied to give control of the whole state. These states may be said to be held together, in Durkheim's terms, in an organic, utilitarian interdependence. Seemingly this could for a long period hold together large populations in some kind of internal peace, despite severe conflicts, which were handled in established ways by relatively peaceable means. Moreover, the establishment of organic interdependence allowed considerable variation in the cultures of incapsulated groups and categories within the state, and even the existence of a considerable degree of dissent. Values, religious beliefs, types of domestic life, and artistic cultures of a very different kind could be fitted into the interstices of the embracing political and economic systems. Groups of people could live domestically in relative isolation from one another, provided that they could participate fully in the developed economic system and were not prevented from moving freely to seek to attain new positions both in the economic system and in its multiple cultural associations, through education, through marriage, through leisure activities, etc. It is this free movement that policies of segregation, separation and apartheid prevent; and hence policies of segregation of that kind run contrary to recent developments in human history.

Seen in this light, the degree of political instability, in the form of military coups, etc., which occurs in many countries of the Third World, has to be explained as the result, and not the cause, of lack of full technological development. Recent years have been marked by many examples of armed dispute between some ethnic sections of the new states of the world, particularly where the territories of such states have been demarcated by the accidents of colonial subjection and have not developed as the gradual outgrowth of a long process of history which might have given rise to some sense of solidarity, and particularly where it might have led to the establishment of economic interdependence between the constituent units of the state. Some such process of interdependence, based on a wide interconnection through a developed technology, alone has enabled states comprised of diverse local units, and of several ethnic sections, to hold together in a political system which is not marked by endemic civil wars. Hence the policy of the United Nations, in trying to foster the technological development of the underdeveloped nations, is justified by more than moral arguments. Those moral arguments, taking account of the elimination of poverty, disease and ignorance, are in themselves cogent. Beyond them, as often stated, it is necessary that the gap between the poor and the rich nations—a gap which to a large extent coincides with large ethnic divisions—be reduced considerably for obvious reasons, since it produces continual sources of conflict. But in addition the economic development of the poor nations should lead to their member local and ethnic sections becoming bound together in mutual utilitarian dependence on one another so as to give support to emerging sentiments of national unity, which will overcome to some extent hostilities between such sections. If the past is in any way a model for the future, it will also allow each such section, where it has a distinctive culture, to practise that culture in domestic life, in religion and in leisure, if it so chooses, while its members move freely and collaborate in association with persons of other cultures in specialised economic and political activities.

Furthermore, as the economic system which binds people together becomes more complex and more differentiated, the social system as a whole comes to be organised in more sets of relationships so that power tends to be more dispersed. There are also more crucial centres of organisation which have to be seized to take control of the state: an armed coup becomes difficult. In a less-developed state, with the complexity of modern armaments, which no longer allow every citizen to be a fighting man possessing his own weapons, commanders of the armed forces can seize and hold a few centres of power and take over the government. In a highly differentiated politico-economic system this is far more difficult.

In many countries, in the past as in feudal Europe, and in some in the present, such military coups were carried out by leaders drawn from a wealthier stratum. These coups involved struggles between sections of the wealthier stratum for control of the state in their own interests. Such coups in most of the underdeveloped states today have a different basis. The fight for independence from the colonial power, and for the establishment of national identity often where there was none in the past, involved also a demand for many things which had been seen to be the fruits of modern technology: an end to poverty, greater material facilities, better health and education. The difficulties involved in solving such problems are most intractable, save where a country is blessed with rich mineral deposits. That is, in many places the material problems are intractable, leaving aside the difficulties of social readjustment. Hence the high enthusiasm which accompanies a revolution is disappointed: and there is undoubtedly a tendency for a small section of the population to emerge who benefit largely from the small sector of the developed economy, while the mass of the population remains poor. Some of the military élite react against the seeming inefficiency and sometimes corruption from which only a small number of people are benefiting and seize power to put an end to this situation and to try to solve the pressing problems of poverty. But these problems are deeply rooted in material intractabilities and in the pressing demands on resources of a rapidly increasing population as a result of better medical facilities. Hence the new-style military revolts are in part expressions of a kind of populist discontent, and their leaders are animated by desires to help the people at large and not always entirely by desires to entrench their own privileges. It is therefore essential in trying to comprehend what is happening to distinguish between political movements which superficially seem similar. In addition, since the nations concerned are still nations in which sentiments of unity are only recently developed, the personnel who occupy positions of authority are often identified with particular ethnic sections. And competition for advantages proceeds still between ethnic sections. The actions of key persons are therefore interpreted in terms of their ethnic affiliations; and hence struggles which emerge from the underdevelopment and the inadequacy of the economy and the polity are seen in terms of ethnic discrimination and are complicated by ethnic loyalties. Hence here too economic development must precede the development of a national unity which will override ethnic divisions, and lead to an ending of ethnic differences as a source of recurrent armed struggles.

These processes are sometimes aggravated by the fact that owing to historical accidents in the distribution of education in modern knowledge, some ethnic sections of a new state may be better educated than others. Members of the better-educated ethnic sections may, naturally enough, tend to favour their fellows, and a few their relatives: but even without such a tendency, it will appear to the less well-educated ethnic groups that a particular other group is entrenched in its privileges and acting to maintain them.

In some countries part of the answer to this particular problem has been sought in what has been termed 'favourable discrimination', i.e. the provision of facilities and privileges to enable the economically and socially 'backward' (in terms of modern education and skilled positions) ethnic sections to catch up on the rest of the population. Measures of this kind seem just and humanitarian, and without them some sections may be quite unable to make up their leeway. Unfortunately there may then develop a situation in which not only may individuals in the better-educated sections be penalised against their own abilities, but also there develops a vested interest in being underprivileged. More and more groups will strive thus to be declared backward. They will even combine politically to achieve this end. Again, there are aggravating factors here: for one of the trends which has been documented in detail through recent research is that where formerly persons interacted in terms of their ethnic, tribal, caste or religious affiliations, within relatively localised areas, now these smaller groups combine in much larger categories which begin to operate politically. The characteristic phenomenon of this kind is what M. N. Srinivas has called the emergence of the 'dominant caste', which aims to protect its interests regionally. This provokes reactions of other castes in turn. The same phenomenon has been reported and analysed in Africa, in terms of tribal affiliations within larger ethnic stocks. Hence struggles may emerge between ethnic units both to protect privilege and to maintain into the present a past identity of underprivilegement.

ALTERNATIVE LINES OF DEVELOPMENT

I have argued so far by analysing social systems where technological and economic development has been accompanied by a reduction in the overt use of force and the emergence of unity through political and economic association, despite ethnic and cultural differences. I have tried to assess what is happening in new states against this background. But there are, of course, alternative lines of development. One is the suppression by force of that equality of citizens and their free movement which is demanded by the developed economy, if it is to function properly. This is the situation in South Africa. South Africa has a very highly developed technology and economy, in a large part of its area: it is rich in minerals and relatively highly industrialised. Had I the time, I could demonstrate at length that the complexity of the economy gives a very large number of the subordinated races (Africans, coloured and Indians) a vested interest in the system, in that they make a fair if inferior living out of it, provided they are involved in the mining-industrial sector of the cities. But large numbers are very impoverished, and this applies particularly to whole sections of the Africans in what are called in South Africa the 'native reserves'. From these reserves for over a century in some cases men have been migrating periodically to work in the white mines, industries and farms, and then returning to their rural homelands, also periodically. But over half the population is permanently urbanised. Here developments in South Africa parallel developments throughout the world, which has seen a general reduction in agricultural population. By controlling the movement of labour out of the rural homelands and by ruthlessly repatriating those who are out of work in the urban areas, the South African Government has tried to prevent the emergence of a troublesome out-of-work section of the urban population. This would leave an African urban population dependent on the working of the industrial economy. But without a corresponding agricultural revolution, it leaves an impoverished peasantry, within which we can already detect signs of peasant revolts. In most highly industrialised countries the fertility rate of the more skilled sections of the population, and particularly of professional and technical grades, tends to drop, and these grades do not produce enough children to fill the new skilled positions which are continually created by the expansion of the system. Hence there have developed educational systems through which the more able and ambitious children of the more fertile members of the population, occupying positions of less skill, can move into higher occupations. A high social mobility characterises such systems, save where ethnic or racial discrimination, or even severe underprivilegement in physical and educational conditions, inhibit mobility. In South Africa (and also in Rhodesia) such mobility is prevented by law. There neither the birth rate nor the immigration of whites is sufficient to staff the expanding economy. Occasionally, therefore, the restrictive bans of the colour bar are lifted to admit the darker ethnic sections to slightly more skilled occupations: I do not believe that this indicates any radical change in the colour bar itself. Even though many of the superordinate ethnic strata, for many reasons, react against the system, there is no evidence that a change is likely to occur in measurable time, short of international efforts. Reciprocal economic interests involving some members of all ethnic sections help keep the system working, but in the end it depends on increasing application of force to smother dissent.

The last few years have shown that the connections which

maintain the working of complex social systems based on highly developed technologies are now so complicated that, like the mechanisms of clocks, they become to some extent highly vulnerable to small-scale attacks, which can cause considerable dislocation, even if they do not overturn the system as a whole. Given this danger, it may well be that highly complex states of this kind may cease to tolerate dissenting sections of opinion to the same extent that they have done in the past. Wherever dissent of this kind arises from the inability of ethnic sections to acquire economic and political equality in practice, even where it is guaranteed by law, the world-wide demand for an end to racial discrimination is aggravating deeply the sense of grievance and giving rise to further efforts at dislocating. One fears that this may lead in the future to even those states that ruled through consent resorting to increasing force and suppression to keep the system working, and thus becoming less tolerant of dissent. Wherever dissent coincides with ethnic and cultural divisions the resulting struggles are likely to be increasingly embittered, and less capable of settlement even after material problems have been solved.

For as has been frequently stated, human beings come to attach high value to their ideologies, their cultures, their beliefs, and so forth; and this adds to the bitterness with which they quarrel and fight. In addition, as has been also validated, in some ways the closer they come together, the more significant do small differences of culture and dogma become and the more intense the quarrels. It seems inevitable that as different sections of the world are based on similar technologies they must to a large extent have similar systems of social relationships arising from that technology. The differences between the social systems of industrialised countries are likely to reside in the subsidiary organisation of relationships of domestic life, friendship, ideological association, authority and patronage, historical association, and the like. These may become indices of cultural and ethnic differentiation, and lead to attempts to maintain separate identities. Countering these processes are two major developments. The first is the possibility of an increasing economic interdependence between different countries, though this may produce its own disputes. The second is the spread of a new form of universal culture. In past centuries, over certain regions the educated strata of different countries have learnt one *lingua franca*, and shared an interest in literature, art and so forth. At other times common religions have not so much united large regions as given members of different areas a common faith. In more recent times there has been the spread of militant political faiths.

Some indeed argue for the isolated preservation of each individual culture. I do not accept that this is the main path to cultural richness. For example, European art, music, textiles and furnishings have been richly stimulated by Africa, Asia, native America, Australasia, Melanesia and Polynesia, as was vividly shown in the exhibition of *World Cultures and Modern Art* staged at Munich in connection with the 1972 Olympic Games.[3] That exhibition showed too a reverse enrichment to, for example, Chinese and Japanese art and music. One must look forward to a similar process occurring among peoples who were not aware previously of the culture of other regions of the world; and one has only to think of the fine novels and plays written by men and women whose traditional culture had no writing, to appreciate how new art forms may release creative energies.

Most recently, the 'pop' culture has become universal for at least the younger generations of very many widely spread countries. The effect of this situation was aptly put by the great American jazz trumpeter, the late Louis 'Satchmo' Armstrong, when he visited Ghana and said that he could take his trumpet anywhere in the world and speak to everyone. I myself felt it dramatically when in what Australians would call the 'outback' of Uganda, I danced European-style dances in an old-style African wattle-and-daub hut to gramophone records of pop music played by Zulu bands singing in Zulu—the Zulu whom I had studied in South Africa, thousands of miles away, thirty years earlier, under the colour bar. This culture, with forms of art and literature, with music and dances, unfortunately with cannabis smoking, is associated with a strong sense of mutual identification, and hence a strong resentment against all forms of racial and ethnic discrimination, as well as all forms of social deprivation. Some of its aspects may disturb, even frighten, what its proponents call 'the establishment': in its universalistic sentiments it struggles against one great plague of the present-day world, ethnic differentiation and racial discrimination.

References

1. Nathan Lerner, *The U.N. Convention on the Elimination of All Forms of Racial Discrimination: A Commentary* (Leyden: A. W. Sijthoff, 1970).

2. See essays in M. Gluckman (ed.), *The Allocational Responsibility* (Manchester: Manchester University Press, 1972).

3. See *World Cultures and Modern Art* (Munich: Bruckmann Publisers, 1972) (in German, English and French).

Appendix

FOUR STATEMENTS ON
THE RACE QUESTION

1 Statement on Race

Paris, July 1950

1. Scientists have reached general agreement in recognising that mankind is one: that all men belong to the same species, *Homo sapiens*. It is further generally agreed among scientists that all men are probably derived from the same common stock; and that such differences as exist between different groups of mankind are due to the operation of evolutionary factors of differentiation such as isolation, the drift and random fixation of the material particles which control heredity (the genes), changes in the structure of these particles, hybridisation, and natural selection. In these ways groups have arisen of varying stability and degree of differentiation which have been classified in different ways for different purposes.

2. From the biological standpoint, the species *Homo sapiens* is made up of a number of populations, each one of which differs from the others in the frequency of one or more genes. Such genes, responsible for the hereditary differences between men, are always few when compared to the whole genetic constitution of man and to the vast number of genes common to all human beings regardless of the population to which they belong. This means that the likenesses among men are far greater than their differences.

3. A race, from the biological standpoint, may therefore be defined as one of the group of populations constituting the species *Homo sapiens*. These populations are capable of inter-breeding with one another but, by virtue of the isolating barriers which in the past kept them more or less separated, exhibit certain physical differences as a result of their somewhat different biological histories. These represent variations, as it were, on a common theme.

4. In short, the term 'race' designates a group or population characterised by some concentrations, relative as to frequency and distribution, of hereditary particles (genes) or physical characters, which appear, fluctuate, and often disappear in the course of time by reason of geographic and/or cultural isolation. The varying manifestations of these traits in different populations are perceived in different ways by each group. What is perceived is largely preconceived, so that each group arbitrarily tends to misinterpret the variability which occurs as a fundamental difference which separates that group from all others.

5. These are the scientific facts. Unfortunately, however, when most people use the term 'race' they do not do so in the sense above defined.

To most people, a race is any group of people whom they choose to describe as a race. Thus, many national, religious, geographic, linguistic or cultural groups have, in such loose usage, been called 'race', when obviously Americans are not a race, nor are Englishmen, nor French- men, nor any other national group. Catholics, Protestants, Moslems, and Jews are not races, nor are groups who speak English or any other language thereby definable as a race; people who live in Iceland or England or India are not races; nor are people who are culturally Turkish or Chinese or the like thereby describable as races.

6. National, religious, geographic, linguistic and cultural groups do not necessarily coincide with racial groups: and the cultural traits of such groups have no demonstrated genetic connection with racial traits. Because serious errors of this kind are habitually committed when the term 'race' is used in popular parlance, it would be better when speaking of human races to drop the term 'race' altogether and speak of ethnic groups.

7. Now what has the scientist to say about the groups of mankind which may be recognised at the present time? Human races can be and have been differently classified by different anthropologists, but at the present time most anthropologists agree on classifying the greater part of the present-day mankind into three major divisions as follows: (a) the Mongoloid division; (b) the Negroid division; and (c) the Caucasoid division. The biological processes which the classifier has here embalmed, as it were, are dynamic, not static. These divisions were not the same in the past as they are at present, and there is every reason to believe that they will change in the future.

8. Many sub-groups or ethnic groups within these divisions have been described. There is no general agreement upon their number, and in any event most ethnic groups have not yet been either studied or de- scribed by the physical anthropologists.

9. Whatever classification the anthropologist makes of man, he never includes mental characteristics as part of those classifications. It is now generally recognised that intelligence tests do not in themeslves enable us to differentiate safely between what is due to innate capacity and what is the result of environmental influences, training and education. Wherever it has been possible to make allowances for differences in environmental opportunities, the tests have shown essential similarity in mental characters among all human groups. In short, given similar degrees of cultural opportunity to realise their potentialities, the average achievement of the members of each ethnic group is about the same. The scientific investigations of recent years fully support the dictum of Con- fucious (551–478 B.C.): 'Men's natures are alike; it is their habits that carry them far apart.'

10. The scientific material available to us at present does not justify the conclusion that inherited genetic differences are a major factor in

producing the differences between the cultures and cultural achievements of different peoples or groups. It does indicate, however, that the history of the cultural experience which each group has undergone is the major factor in explaining such differences. The one trait which above all others has been at a premium in the evolution of men's mental characters has been educability, plasticity. This is a trait which all human beings possess. It is indeed, a species character of *Homo sapiens*.

11. So far as temperament is concerned, there is no definite evidence that there exist inborn differences between human groups. There is evidence that whatever group differences of the kind there might be are greatly overridden by the individual differences, and by the differences springing from environmental factors.

12. As for personality and character, these may be considered raceless. In every human group a rich variety of personality and character types will be found, and there is no reason for believing that any human group is richer than any other in these respects.

13. With respect to race mixture, the evidence points unequivocally to the fact that this has been going on from the earliest times. Indeed, one of the chief processes of race formation and race extinction or absorption is by means of hybridisation between races or ethnic groups. Furthermore, no convincing evidence has been adduced that race mixture of itself produces biologically bad effects. Statements that human hybrids frequently show undesirable traits, both physically and mentally, physical disharmonies and mental degeneracies, are not supported by the facts. There is, therefore, no biological justification for prohibiting intermarriage between persons of different ethnic groups.

14. The biological fact of race and the myth of 'race' should be distinguished. For all practical social purposes 'race' is not so much a biological phenomenon as a social myth. The myth of 'race' has created an enormous amount of human and social damage. In recent years it has taken a heavy toll in human lives and caused untold suffering. It still prevents the normal development of millions of human beings and deprives civilisation of the effective co-operation of productive minds. The biological differences between ethnic groups should be disregarded from the standpoint of social acceptance and social action. The unity of mankind from both the biological and social viewpoints is the main thing. To recognise this and to act accordingly is the first requirement of modern man. It is but to recognise what a great biologist wrote in 1875: 'As man advances in civilisation, and small tribes are united into larger communities, the simplest reason would tell each individual that he ought to extend his social instincts and sympathies to all the members of the same nation, though personally unknown to him. This point being once reached, there is only an artificial barrier to prevent his sympathies extending to the men of all nations and races.' These are the words of Charles Darwin in *The Descent of Man* (2nd edn, 1875, pp. 187–8). And,

indeed, the whole of human history shows that a co-operative spirit is not only natural to men, but more deeply rooted than any self-seeking tendencies. If this were not so we should not see the growth of integration and organisation of his communities which the centuries and the millenniums plainly exhibit.

15. We now have to consider the bearing of these statements on the problem of human equality. It must be asserted with the utmost emphasis that equality as an ethical principle in no way depends upon the assertion that human beings are in fact equal in endowment. Obviously individuals in all ethnic groups vary greatly among themselves in endowment. Nevertheless, the characteristics in which human groups differ from one another are often exaggerated and used as a basis for questioning the validity of equality in the ethical sense. For this purpose we have thought it worth while to set out in a formal manner what is at present scientifically established concerning individual and group differences.

(a) In matters of race, the only characteristics which anthropologists can effectively use as a basis for classifications are physical and physiological.

(b) According to present knowledge there is no proof that the groups of mankind differ in their innate mental characteristics, whether in respect of intelligence or temperament. The scientific evidence indicates that the range of mental capacities in all ethnic groups is much the same.

(c) Historical and sociological studies support the view that genetic differences are not of importance in determining the social and cultural differences between different groups of *Homo sapiens*, and that the social and cultural changes in different groups have, in the main, been independent of changes in inborn constitution. Vast social changes have occurred which were not in any way connected with changes in racial type.

(d) There is no evidence that race mixture as such produces bad results from the biological point of view. The social results of race mixture whether for good or ill are to be traced to social factors.

(e) All normal human beings are capable of learning to share in a common life, to understand the nature of mutual service and reciprocity, and to respect social obligations and contracts. Such biological differences as exist between members of different ethnic groups have no relevance to problems of social and political organisation, moral life and communication between human beings.

Lastly, biological studies lend support to the ethic of universal brotherhood; for man is born with drives toward co-operation, and unless these drives are satisfied, men and nations alike fall ill. Man is born a social being who can reach his fullest development only through interaction with his fellows. The denial at any point of this social bond between men and man brings with it disintegration. In this sense, every man is his brother's keeper. For every man is a piece of the continent, a part of the main, because he is involved in mankind.

Original statement drafted at Unesco House, Paris, by the following experts:

Professor Ernest Beaglehole (New Zealand);
Professor Juan Comas (Mexico);
Professor L. A. Costa Pinto (Brazil);
Professor Franklin Frazier (United States of America);
Professor Morris Ginsberg (United Kingdom);
Dr Humayun Kabir (India);
Professor Claude Lévi-Strauss (France);
Professor Ashley Montagu (United States of America) *(rapporteur).*

Text revised by Professor Ashley Montagu, after criticism submitted by Professors Hadley Cantril, E. G. Conklin, Gunnar Dahlberg, Theodosius Dobzhansky, L. C. Dunn, Donald Hager, Julian S. Huxley, Otto Klineberg, Wilbert Moore, H. J. Muller, Gunnar Myrdal, Joseph Needham, Curt Stern.

2 Statement on the Nature of Race and Race Differences

Paris, June 1951

The reasons for convening a second meeting of experts to discuss the concept of race were chiefly these:

Race is a question of interest to many different kinds of people, not only to the public at large, but to sociologists, anthropologists and biologists, especially those dealing with problems of genetics. At the first discussion on the problem of race, it was chiefly sociologists who gave their opinions and framed the 'Statement on race'. That statement had a good effect, but it did not carry the authority of just those groups within whose special province fall the biological problems of race, namely the physical anthropologists and geneticists. Secondly, the first statement did not, in all its details, carry conviction of these groups and, because of this, it was not supported by many authorities in these two fields.

In general, the chief conclusions of the first statement were sustained, but with differences in emphasis and with some important deletions.

There was no delay or hesitation or lack of unanimity in reaching the primary conclusion that there were no scientific grounds whatever for the racialist position regarding purity of race and the hierarchy of inferior and superior races to which this leads.

We agreed that all races were mixed and that intraracial variability in most biological characters was as great as, if not greater than, interracial variability.

We agreed that races had reached their present states by the operation of evolutionary factors by which different proportions of similar hereditary elements (genes) had become characteristic of different, partially separated groups. The source of these elements seemed to all of us to be the variability which arises by random mutation, and the isolating factors bringing about racial differentiation by preventing intermingling of groups with different mutations, chiefly geographical for the main groups such as African, European and Asiatic.

Man, we recognised, is distinguished as much by his culture as by his biology, and it was clear to all of us that many of the factors leading to the formation of minor races of men have been cultural. Anything that tends to prevent free exchange of genes amongst groups is a potential race-making factor and these partial barriers may be religious, social and linguistic, as well as geographical.

We were careful to avoid dogmatic definitions of race, since, as a product of evolutionary factors, it is a dynamic rather than a static concept. We were equally careful to avoid saying that, because races were all variable and many of them graded into each other, therefore races did not exist. The physical anthropologists and the man in the street both know that races exist; the former, from the scientifically recognisable and measurable congeries of traits which he uses in classifying the varieties of man; the latter from the immediate evidence of his senses when he sees an African, a European, an Asiatic and an American Indian together.

We had no difficulty in agreeing that no evidence of differences in innate mental ability between different racial groups has been adduced, but that here too intraracial variability is at least as great as interracial variability. We agreed that psychological traits could not be used in classifying races, nor could they serve as parts of racial descriptions.

We were fortunate in having as members of our conference several scientists who had made special studies of the results of intermarriage between members of different races. This meant that our conclusion that race mixture in general did not lead to disadvantageous results was based on actual experience as well as upon study of the literature. Many of our members thought it quite likely that hydridisation of different races could lead to biologically advantageous results, although there was insufficient evidence to support any conclusion.

Since race, as a word, has become coloured by its misuse in connection with national, linguistic and religious differences, and by its deliberate abuse by racialists, we tried to find a new word to express the same meaning of a biologically differentiated group. On this we did not succeed, but agreed to reserve race as the word to be used for anthropological classification of groups showing definite combinations of physical (including physiological) traits in characteristic proportions.

We also tried hard, but again we failed, to reach some general statement about the inborn nature of man with respect to his behaviour toward his fellows. It is obvious that members of a group show co-operative or associative behaviour towards each other, while members of different groups may show aggressive behaviour towards each other and both of these attitudes may occur within the same individual. We recognised that the understanding of the psychological origin of race prejudice was an important problem which called for further study.

Nevertheless, having regard to the limitations of our present knowledge, all of us believed that the biological differences found amongst human racial groups can in no case justify the views of racial inequality which have been based on ignorance and prejudice, and that all of the differences which we know can well be disregarded for all ethical human purposes.

L. C. Dunn (rapporteur), June 1951

1.

Scientists are generally agreed that all men living today belong to a single species, *Homo sapiens*, and are derived from a common stock, even though there is some dispute as to when and how different human groups diverged from this common stock.

The concept of race is unanimously regarded by anthropologists as a classificatory device providing a zoological frame within which the various groups of mankind may be arranged and by means of which studies of evolutionary processes can be facilitated. In its anthropological sense, the word 'race' should be reserved for groups of mankind possessing well-developed and primarily heritable physical differences from other groups. Many populations can be so classified but, because of the complexity of human history, there are also many populations which cannot easily be fitted into a racial classification.

2.

Some of the physical differences between human groups are due to differences in hereditary constitution and some to differences in the environments in which they have been brought up. In most cases, both influences have been at work. The science of genetics suggests that the hereditary differences among populations of a single species are the results of the action of two sets of processes. On the one hand, the genetic composition of isolated populations is constantly but gradually being altered by natural selection and by occasional changes (mutations) in the material particles (genes) which control heredity. Populations are also affected by fortuitous changes in gene frequency and by marriage customs. On the other hand, crossing is constantly breaking down the differentiations so set up. The new mixed populations, in so far as they, in turn, become isolated, are subject to the same processes, and these may lead to further changes. Existing races are merely the result, considered at a particular moment in time, of the total effect of such processes on the human species. The hereditary characters to be used in the classification of human groups, the limits of their variation within these groups, and thus the extent of the classificatory sub-divisions adopted may legitimately differ according to the scientific purpose in view.

3.

National, religious, geographical, linguistic and cultural groups do not necessarily coincide with racial groups; and the cultural traits of such groups have no demonstrated connection with racial traits. Americans are not a race, nor are Frenchmen, nor Germans; nor *ipso facto* is any other national group. Moslems and Jews are no more races than are Roman Catholics and Protestants; nor are people who live in Iceland or Britain or India, or who speak English or any other language, or who are culturally Turkish or Chinese and the like, thereby describable as races. The use of the term 'race' in speaking of such groups may be a serious error, but it is one which is habitually committed.

4.

Human races can be, and have been, classified in different ways by different anthropologists. Most of them agree in classifying the greater part of existing mankind into at least three large units, which may be called major groups (in French *grand-races*, in German *Hauptrassen*). Such a classification does not depend on any single physical character, nor does for example, skin colour by itself necessarily distinguish one major group from another. Furthermore, so far as it has been possible to analyse them, the differences in physical structure which distinguish one major group from another give no support to popular notions of any general 'superiority' or 'inferiority' which are sometimes implied in referring to these groups.

Broadly speaking, individuals belonging to different major groups of mankind are distinguishable by virtue of their physical characters, but individual members, or small groups belonging to different races within the same major group are usually not so distinguishable. Even the major groups grade into each other, and the physical traits by which they and the races within them are characterised overlap considerably. With respect to most, if not all, measurable characters, the differences among individuals belonging to the same race are greater than the differences that occur between the observed averages for two or more races within the same major group.

5.

Most anthropologists do not include mental characteristics in their classification of human races. Studies within a single race have shown that both innate capacity and environmental opportunity determine the results of tests of intelligence and temperament, though their relative importance is disputed.

When intelligence tests, even non-verbal, are made on a group of non-literate people, their scores are usually lower than those of more civilised people. It has been recorded that different groups of the same race occupying similarly high levels of civilisation may yield considerable differences in intelligence tests. When, however, the two groups have been brought up from childhood in similar environments, the differences are usually very slight. Moreover, there is good evidence that, given similar opportunities, the average performance (that is to say, the performance of the individual who is representative because he is surpassed by as many as he surpasses), and the variation round it, do not differ appreciably from one race to another.

Even those psychologists who claim to have found the greatest differences in intelligence between groups of different racial origin and have contended that they are hereditary, always report that some members of the group of inferior performance surpass not merely the lowest ranking member of the superior group but also the average of its members. In any case, it has never been possible to separate members of two groups on the basis of mental capacity, as they can often be separated on a basis of religion, skin colour, hair form or language. It is possible, though not proved, that some types of innate capacity for intellectual and emotional responses are commoner in one human group than in another, but it is certain that, within a single group, innate capacities vary as much as, if not more than, they do between different groups.

The study of the heredity of psychological characteristics is beset with difficulties. We know that certain mental diseases and defects are transmitted from one generation to the next, but we are less familiar with the part played by heredity in the mental life of normal individuals. The normal individual, irrespective of race, is essentially educable. It follows that his intellectual and moral life is largely conditioned by his training and by his physical and social environment.

It often happens that a national group may appear to be characterised by particular psychological attributes. The superficial view would be that this is due to race. Scientifically, however, we realise that any common psychological attribute is more likely to be due to a common historical and social background, and that such attributes may obscure the fact that, within different populations consisting of many human types, one will find approximately the same range of temperament and intelligence.

6.

The scientific material available to us at present does not justify the conclusion that inherited genetic differences are a major factor in producing the differences between the cultures and cultural achievements of different peoples or groups. It does indicate, on the contrary, that a major factor in explaining such differences is the cultural experience which each group has undergone.

7.

There is no evidence for the existence of so-called 'pure' races. Skeletal remains provide the basis of our limited knowledge about earlier races. In regard to race mixture, the evidence points to the fact that human hybridisation has been going on for an indefinite but considerable time. Indeed, one of the processes of race formation and race extinction or absorption is by means of hybridisation between races. As there is no reliable evidence that disadvantageous effects are produced thereby, no biological justification exists for prohibiting inter-marriage between persons of different races.

8.

We now have to consider the bearing of these statements on the problem of human equality. We wish to emphasise that equality of opportunity and equality in law in no way depend, as ethical principles, upon the assertion that human beings are in fact equal in endowment.

9.

We have thought it worth while to set out in a formal manner what is at present scientifically established concerning individual and group differences:

(a) In matters of race, the only characteristics which anthropologists have so far been able to use effectively as a basis for classification are physical (anatomical and physiological).
(b) Available scientific knowledge provides no basis for believing that the groups of mankind differ in their innate capacity for intellectual and emotional development.
(c) Some biological differences between human beings within a single race may be as great as, or greater than, the same biological differences between races.
(d) Vast social changes have occurred that have not been connected in any way with changes in racial type. Historical and sociological studies thus support the view that genetic differences are of little significance in determining the social and cultural differences between different groups of men.
(e) There is no evidence that race mixture produces disadvantageous results from a biological point of view. The social results of race mixture, whether for good or ill, can generally be traced to social factors.

Text drafted at Unesco House, Paris, on 8 June 1951, by:

Professor R. A. M. Borgman, Royal Tropical Institute, Amsterdam;
Professor Gunnar Dahlberg, Director, State Institute for Human Genetics and Race Biology, University of Uppsala;
Professor L. C. Dunn, Department of Zoology, Columbia University, New York;
Professor J. B. S. Haldane, Head, Department of Biometry, University College, London;
Professor M. F. Ashley Montagu, Chairman, Department of Anthropology, Rutgers University, New Brunswick, N.J.;
Dr A. E. Mourant, Director, Blood Group Reference Laboratory, Lister Institute, London;
Professor Hans Nachtscheim, Director, Institut ür Genetik, Freie Universität, Berlin;

Dr Eugène Schreider, Directeur adjoint du Laboratoire d'Anthropologie Physique de l'Ecole des Hautes Etudes, Paris;

Professor Harry L. Shapiro, Chairman, Department of Anthropology, American Museum of Natural History, New York;

Dr J. C. Trevor, Faculty of Archaeology and Anthropology, University of Cambridge;

Dr Henri V. Vallois, Professeur au Museum d'Histoire Naturelle, Directeur du Musée de l'Homme, Paris;

Professor S. Zuckerman, Head, Department of Anatomy, Medical School, University of Birmingham;

Professor Th. Dobzhansky, Department of Zoology, Columbia University, New York;

Dr Julian Huxley contributed to the final wording.

3 Proposals on the Biological Aspects of Race

Moscow, August 1964

The undersigned, assembled by Unesco in order to give their views on the biological aspects of the race question and in particular to formulate the biological part for a statement foreseen for 1966 and intended to bring up to date and to complete the declaration on the nature of race and racial differences signed in 1951, have unanimously agreed on the following:

1. All men living today belong to a single species, *Homo sapiens*, and are derived from a common stock. There are differences of opinion regarding how and when different human groups diverged from this common stock.

2. Biological differences between human beings are due to differences in hereditary constitution and to the influence of the environment on this genetic potential. In most cases, those differences are due to the interaction of these two sets of factors.

3. There is great genetic diversity within all human populations. Pure races—in the sense of genetically homogeneous populations—do not exist in the human species.

4. There are obvious physical differences between populations living in different geographical areas of the world, in their average appearance. Many of these differences have a genetic component.

Most often the latter consist in differences in the frequency of the same hereditary characters.

5. Different classifications of mankind into major stocks, and of those into more restricted categories (races, which are groups of populations, or single populations) have been proposed on the basis of hereditary physical traits. Nearly all classifications recognise at least three major stocks.

Since the pattern of geographic variation of the characteristics used in racial classification is a complex one, and since this pattern does not present any major discontinuity, these classifications, whatever they are, cannot claim to classify mankind into clearcut categories; moreover, on account of the complexities of human history, it is difficult to determine the place of certain groups within these racial classifications, in particular that of certain intermediate populations.

Many anthropologists, while stressing the importance of human variation, believe that the scientific interest of these classifications is limited, and even that they carry the risk of inviting abusive generalisations.

Differences between individuals within a race or within a population are often greater than the average differences between races or populations.

Some of the variable distinctive traits which are generally chosen as criteria to characterise a race are either independently inherited or show only varying degrees of association between them within each population. Therefore, the combination of these traits in most individuals does not correspond to the typological racial characterisation.

6. In man as well as in animals, the genetic composition of each population is subject to the modifying influence of diverse factors: natural selection, tending towards adaptation to the environment, fortuitous mutations which lead to modifications of the molecules of deoxyribonucleic acid which determine heredity, or random modifications in the frequency of qualitative hereditary characters, to an extent dependent on the patterns of mating and the size of populations.

Certain physical characters have a universal biological value for the survival of the human species, irrespective of the environment. The differences on which racial classifications are based do not affect these characters, and therefore, it is not possible from the biological point of view to speak in any way whatsoever of a general inferiority or superiority of this or that race.

7. Human evolution presents attributes of capital importance which are specific to the species.

The human species which is now spread over the whole world, has a past rich in migrations, in territorial expansions and contractions.

As a consequence, general adaptability to the most diverse environments is in man more pronounced that his adaptation to specific environments.

For long millenniums progress made by man, in any field, seems to have been increasingly, if not exclusively, based on culture and the transmission of cultural achievements and not on the transmission of genetic endowment. This implies a modification in the role of natural selection in man today.

On account of the mobility of human populations and of social factors, mating between members of different human groups which tend to mitigate the differentiations acquired, has played a much more important role in human history than in that of animals. The history of any human population or of any human race, is rich in instances of hybridisation and those tend to become more and more numerous.

For man, the obstacles to interbreeding are geographical as well as social and cultural.

8. At all times, the hereditary characteristics of the human popula-

tions are in dynamic equilibrium as a result of this interbreeding and of the differentiation mechanisms which were mentioned before. As entities defined by sets of distinctive traits, human races are at any time in a process of emergence and dissolution.

Human races in general present a far less clearcut characterisation than many animal races and they cannot be compared at all to races of domestic animals, these being the result of heightened selection for special purposes.

9. It has never been proved that interbreeding has biological disadvantages for mankind as a whole.

On the contrary, it contributes to the maintenance of biological ties between human groups and thus to the unity of the species in its diversity.

The biological consequences of a marriage depend only on the individual genetic make-up of the couple and not on their race.

Therefore, no biological justification exists for prohibiting intermarriage between persons of different races, or for advising against it on racial grounds.

10. Man since his origin has at his disposal ever more efficient cultural means of nongenetic adaptation.

11. Those cultural factors which break social and geographic barriers, enlarge the size of the breeding populations and so act upon their genetic structure by diminishing the random fluctuations (genetic drift).

12. As a rule, the major stocks extend over vast territories encompassing many diverse populations which differ in language, economy, culture, etc.

There is no national, religious, geographic, linguistic or cultural group which constitutes a race *ipso facto*; the concept of race is purely biological.

However, human beings who speak the same language and share the same culture have a tendency to intermarry, and often there is as a result a certain degree of coincidence between physical traits on the one hand, and linguistic and cultural traits on the other. But there is no known causal nexus between these and therefore it is not justifiable to attribute cultural characteristics to the influence of the genetic inheritance.

13. Most racial classifications of mankind do not include mental traits or attributes as a taxonomic criterion.

Heredity may have an influence in the variability shown by individuals within a given population in their responses to the psychological tests currently applied.

However, no difference has ever been detected convincingly in the hereditary endowments of human groups in regard to what is measured by these tests. On the other hand, ample evidence attests to the influence of physical, cultural and social environment on differences in response to these tests.

The study of this question is hampered by the very great difficulty of determining what part heredity plays in the average differences observed in so-called tests of over-all intelligence between populations of different cultures.

The genetic capacity for intellectual development, like certain major anatomical traits peculiar to the species, is one of the biological traits essential for its survival in any natural or social environment.

The peoples of the world today appear to possess equal biological potentialities for attaining any civilisational level. Differences in the achievements of different peoples must be attributed solely to their cultural history.

Certain psychological traits are at times attributed to particular peoples. Whether or not such assertions are valid, we do not find any basis for ascribing such traits to hereditary factors, until proof to the contrary is given.

Neither in the field of hereditary potentialities concerning the over-all intelligence and the capacity for cultural development, nor in that of physical traits, is there any justification for the concept of 'inferior' and 'superior' races.

The biological data given above stand in open contradiction to the tenets of racism. Racist theories can in no way pretend to have any scientific foundation and the anthropologists should endeavour to prevent the results of their researches from being used in such a biased way that they would serve non-scientific ends.

Moscow, 18 August 1964

Professor Nigel Barnicot, Department of Anthropology, University College, London;

Professor Jean Benoist, Director, Department of Anthropology, University of Montreal, Montreal;

Professor Tadeusz Bielicki, Institute of Anthropology, Polish Academy of Sciences, Wroclaw;

Dr A. E. Boyo, Head, Federal Malaria Research Institute, Department of Pathology and Haematology, Lagos University Medical School, Lagos;

Professor V. V. Bunak, Institute of Ethnography, Moscow;

Professor Carleton S. Coon, Curator, The University Museum, University of Pennsylvania, Philadelphia, Pa (United States);

Professor G. F. Debetz, Institute of Ethnography, Moscow;

Mrs Adelaide G. de Diaz Ungria, Curator, Museum of Natural Sciences, Caracas;

Professor Santiago Genoves, Institute of Historical Research, Faculty of Sciences, University of Mexico, Mexico;

Professor Robert Gessain, Director, Centre of Anthropological Research, Musée de l'Homme, Paris;

Professor Jean Hiernaux, (Scientific Director of the meeting), Laboratory of Anthropology, Faculty of Sciences, University of Paris, Institute of Sociology, Free University of Brussels;

Dr Yaya Kane, Director, Senegal National Centre of Blood Transfusion, Dakar;

Professor Ramakhrishna Mukherjee, Head, Sociological Research Unit, Indian Statistical Institute, Calcutta;

Professor Bernard Rensch, Zoological Institute, Westfälische Wilhelms-Universität, Münster (Federal Republic of Germany);

Professor Y. Y. Roguinski, Institute of Ethnography, Moscow;

Professor Francisco M. Salzano, Institute of Natural Sciences, Pôrto Alegre, Rio Grande do Sul (Brazil);

Professor Alf Sommerfelt, Rector, Oslo University, Oslo;

Professor James N. Spuhler, Department of Anthropology, University of Michigan, Ann Arbor, Mich. (United States);

Professor Hisashi Suzuki, Department of Anthropology, Faculty of Science, University of Tokyo, Tokyo;

Professor J. A. Valsik, Department of Anthropology and Genetics, J. A. Komensky University, Bratislava (Czechoslovakia);

Dr Joseph S. Weiner, London School of Hygiene and Tropical Medicine, University of London, London;

Professor V. P. Yakimov, Moscow State University, Institute of Anthropology, Moscow.

4 Statement on Race and Racial Prejudice

Paris, September 1967

1. 'All men are born free and equal both in dignity and in rights.' This universally proclaimed democratic principle stands in jeopardy wherever political, economic, social and cultural inequalities affect human group relations. A particularly striking obstacle to the recognition of equal dignity for all is racism. Racism continues to haunt the world. As a major social phenomenon it requires the attention of all students of the sciences of man.

2. Racism stultifies the development of those who suffer from it, perverts those who apply it, divides nations within themselves, aggravates international conflict and threatens world peace.

3. Conference of experts meeting in Paris in September 1967, agreed that racist doctrines lack any scientific basis whatsoever. It reaffirmed the propositions adopted by the international meeting held in Moscow in 1964 which was called to re-examine the biological aspects of the statements on race and racial differences issued in 1950 and 1951. In particular, it draws attention to the following points:

(a) All men living today belong to the same species and descend from the same stock.

(b) The division of the human species into 'races' is partly conventional and partly arbitrary and does not imply any hierarchy whatsoever. Many anthropologists stress the importance of human variation, but believe that 'racial' divisions have limited scientific interest and may even carry the risk of inviting abusive generalisation.

(c) Current biological knowledge does not permit us to impute cultural achievements to differences in genetic potential. Differences in the achievements of different peoples should be attributed solely to their cultural history. The peoples of the world today appear to possess equal biological potentialities for attaining any level of civilisation.

Racism grossly falsifies the knowledge of human biology.

4. The human problems arising from so-called 'race' relations are social in origin rather than biological. A basic problem is racism, namely, antisocial beliefs and acts which are based on the fallacy that discriminatory intergroup relations are justifiable on biological grounds.

5. Groups commonly evaluate their characteristics in comparison

with others. Racism falsely claims that there is a scientific basis for arranging groups hierarchically in terms of psychological and cultural characteristics that are immutable and innate. In this way it seeks to make existing differences appear inviolable as a means of permanently maintaining current relations between groups.

6. Faced with the exposure of the falsity of its biological doctrines, racism finds ever new stratagems for justifying the inequality of groups. It points to the fact that groups do not intermarry, a fact which follows, in part, from the divisions created by racism. It uses this fact to argue the thesis that this absence of intermarriage derives from differences of a biological order. Whenever it fails in its attempts to prove that the source of group differences lies in the biological field, it falls back upon justifications in terms of divine purpose, cultural differences, disparity of educational standards or some other doctrine which would serve to mask its continued racist beliefs. Thus, many of the problems which racism presents in the world today do not arise merely from its open manifestations, but from the activities of those who discriminate on racial grounds but are unwilling to acknowledge it.

7. Racism has historical roots. It has not been a universal phenomenon. Many contemporary societies and cultures show little trace of it. It was not evident for long periods in world history. Many forms of racism have arisen out of the conditions of conquest, out of the justification of Negro slavery and its aftermath of racial inequality in the West, and out of the colonial relationship. Among other examples is that of antisemitism, which has played a particular role in history, with Jews being the chosen scapegoat to take the blame for problems and crises met by many societies.

8. The anti-colonial revolution of the twentieth century has opened up new possibilities for eliminating the scourge of racism. In some formerly dependent countries, people formerly classified as inferior have for the first time obtained full political rights. Moreover, the participation of formerly dependent nations in international organisations in terms of equality has done much to undermine racism.

9. There are, however, some instances in certain societies in which groups, victims of racialistic practices, have themselves applied doctrines with racist implications in their struggle for freedom. Such an attitude is a secondary phenomenon, a reaction stemming from men's search for an identity which prior racist theory and racialistic practices denied them. Nonetheless, the new forms of racist ideology, resulting from this prior exploitation, have no justification in biology. They are a product of a political struggle and have no scientific foundation.

10. In order to undermine racism it is not sufficient that biologists should expose its fallacies. It is also necessary that psychologists and sociologists should demonstrate its causes. The social structure is always an important factor. However, within the same social structure, there

may be great individual variation in racialistic behaviour, associated with the personality of the individuals and their personal circumstances.

11. The committee of experts agreed on the following conclusions about the social causes of race prejudice:

(a) Social and economic causes of racial prejudice are particularly observed in settler societies wherein are found conditions of great disparity of power and property, in certain urban areas where there have emerged ghettoes in which individuals are deprived of equal access to employment, housing, political participation, education, and the administration of justice, and in many societies where social and economic tasks which are deemed to be contrary to the ethics or beneath the dignity of its members are assigned to a group of different origins who are derided, blamed, and punished for taking on these tasks.

(b) Individuals with certain personality troubles may be particularly inclined to adopt and manifest racial prejudices. Small groups, associations, and social movements of a certain kind sometimes preserve and transmit racial prejudices. The foundations of the prejudices lie, however, in the economic and social system of a society.

(c) Racism tends to be cumulative. Discrimination deprives a group of equal treatment and presents that group as a problem. The group then tends to be blamed for its own condition, leading to further elaboration of racist theory.

12. The major techniques for coping with racism involve changing those social situations which give rise to prejudice, preventing the prejudiced from acting in accordance with their beliefs, and combating the false beliefs themselves.

13. It is recognised that the basically important changes in the social structure that may lead to the elimination of racial prejudice may require decisions of a political nature. It is also recognised, however, that certain agencies of enlightenment, such as education and other means of social and economic advancement, mass media, and law can be immediately and effectively mobilised for the elimination of racial prejudice.

14. The school and other instruments for social and economic progress can be one of the most effective agents for the achievement of broadened understanding and the fulfilment of the potentialities of man. They can equally much be used for the perpetuation of discrimination and inequality. It is therefore essential that the resources for education and for social and economic action of all nations be employed in two ways:

(a) The schools should ensure that their curricula contain scientific understandings about race and human unity, and that invidious distinctions about peoples are not made in texts and classrooms.

(b) (i) Because the skills to be gained in formal and vocational education become increasingly important with the processes of technological development, the resources of the schools and other
resources should be fully available to all parts of the population
with neither restriction nor discrimination;

(ii) Furthermore, in cases where, for historical reasons, certain
groups have a lower average education and economic standing,
it is the responsibility of the society to take corrective measures.
These measures should ensure, so far as possible, that the limitations of poor environments are not passed on to the children.

In view of the importance of teachers in any educational programme,
special attention should be given to their training. Teachers should be
made conscious of the degree to which they reflect the prejudices which
may be current in their society. They should be encouraged to avoid
these prejudices.

15. Governmental units and other organisations concerned should
give special attention to improving the housing situations and work
opportunities available to victims of racism. This will not only counteract
the effects of racism, but in itself can be a positive way of modifying
racist attitudes and behaviour.

16. The media of mass communication are increasingly important in
promoting knowledge and understanding, but their exact potentiality
is not fully known. Continuing research into the social utilisation of the
media is needed in order to assess their influence in relation to formation
of attitudes and behavioural patterns in the field of race prejudice and
race discrimination. Because the mass media reach vast numbers of
people at different educational and social levels, their role in encourag-
ing or combating race prejudice can be crucial. Those who work in these
media should maintain a positive approach to the promotion of understanding between groups and populations. Representation of peoples in
stereotypes and holding them up to ridicule should be avoided. Attachment to news reports of racial designations which are not germane to the
accounts should also be avoided.

17. Law is among the most important means of ensuring equality
between individuals and one of the most effective means of fighting
racism.

The Universal Declaration of Human Rights of 10 December 1948
and the related international agreements and conventions which have
taken effect subsequently can contribute effectively, on both the national
and international level, to the fight against any injustice of racist origin.

National legislation is a means of effectively outlawing racist propaganda and acts based upon racial discrimination. Moreover, the policy
expressed in such legislation must bind not only the courts and judges
charged with its enforcement, but also all agencies of government of
whatever level or whatever character.

It is not claimed that legislation can immediately eliminate prejudice. Nevertheless, by being a means of protecting the victims of acts based upon prejudice, and by setting a moral example backed by the dignity of the courts, it can, in the long run, even change attitudes.

18. Ethnic groups which represent the object of some form of discrimination are sometimes accepted and tolerated by dominating groups at the cost of their having to abandon completely their cultural identity. It should be stressed that the effort of these ethnic groups to preserve their cultural values should be encouraged. They will thus be better able to contribute to the enrichment of the total culture of humanity.

19. Racial prejudice and discrimination in the world today arise from historical and social phenomena and falsely claim the sanction of science. It is, therefore, the responsbility of all biological and social scientists, philosophers, and others working in related disciplines, to ensure that the results of their research are not misused by those who wish to propagate racial prejudice and encourage discrimination.

This statement was prepared by a committee of experts on race and racial prejudice which met at Unesco House, Paris, from 18 to 26 September 1967. The following experts took part in the committee's work:

Professor Muddathir Abdel Rahim, University of Khartoum (Sudan);
Professor Georges Balandier, Université de Paris (France);
Professor Celio de Oliveira Borja, University of Guanabara (Brazil);
Professor Lloyd Braithwaite, University of the West Indies (Jamaica);
Professor Leonard Broom, University of Texas (United States);
Professor G. F. Debetz, Institute of Ethnography, Moscow (USSR);
Professor J. Djordjevic, University of Belgrade (Yugoslavia);
Dean Clarence Clyde Ferguson, Howard University (United States);
Dr Dharam P. Ghai, University College (Kenya);
Professor Louis Guttman, Hebrew University (Israel);
Professor Jean Hiernaux, Université Libre de Bruxelles (Belgium);
Professor A. Kloskowska, University of Lodz (Poland);
Judge Kéba M'Baye, President of the Supreme Court (Senegal);
Professor John Rex, University of Durham (United Kingdom);
Professor Mariano R. Solveira, University of Havana (Cuba);
Professor Hisashi Suzuki, University of Tokyo (Japan);
Dr Romila Thapar, University of Delhi (India);
Professor C. H. Waddington, University of Edinburgh (United Kingdom).

Index